LAW ENFORCEMENT:
A Selected Bibliography

Second Edition

by

George T. Felkenes

and

Harold K. Becker

The Scarecrow Press, Inc.
Metuchen, N.J. 1977

Library of Congress Cataloging in Publication Data

Felkenes, George T
Law enforcement.

In the 1st ed. Harold K. Becker's name appeared first on t.p.
Includes index.
1. Criminal procedure--United States--Bibliography.
2. Criminal law--United States--Bibliography. 3. Law enforcement--Bibliography. 4. Police--Bibliography.
I. Becker, Harold K., joint author. II. Title.
KF9201.F44 016.364'973 76-50010
ISBN 0-8108-0995-8

Manufactured in the United States of America

FOREWORD

Since publication in 1968 of the first edition of Law Enforcement: A Selected Bibliography, numerous changes have occurred. The federal, state, and local governments have poured billions of dollars into the law enforcement services. Hundreds of thousands of police officers have been seeking a college education. And finally, the public constantly has placed new and more professional demands on the profession of law enforcement. The state of law enforcement is one of transition. The law enforcement officer cannot be just a good patrolman. He needs a knowledge of public administration, law, criminology, comparative police practice and the social sciences in general. This bibliography will provide a good reference for research as well as general reading in the total scheme of law enforcement and the general administration of justice. We hope that the diversity of subjects and opinions contained in the citations herein will open the door to the broad interdisciplinary nature of the field of the administration of criminal justice.

The authors would like to thank the following persons for their assistance and contributions to this book: Ms. Sherri Vacarella, Mr. William Pelfrey, Mr. Rickie D. Lovell, Mrs. Patricia Riley, Mrs. Barbara Smith, Mr. John Pendergrass, Mr. Burt Butler, and fellow faculty members who offered assistance and advice in reviewing and compiling suitable articles.

George T. Felkenes
Harold K. Becker

CONTENTS

I. POLICE PERSONNEL ADMINISTRATION (1000)

A. RECRUITMENT AND SELECTION

Balch, Robert. "The Police Personality: Fact or Fiction?" Journal of Criminal Law, Criminology and Police Science, 63:106-119, March 1972. There is remarkable agreement on the characteristics believed to make up the police mentality. They are supposed to be very suspicious and always on the lookout for the unusual. They suspect evil wherever they go and supposedly have no faith in their fellow man. They are realistic, respect authority, and know how to take orders. They like to give orders and demand respect from juveniles, criminals, and minorities 1000

Bouza, Anthony V. "The Policeman's Character Investigation: Lower Standards or Changing Times?" Journal of Criminal Law, Criminology and Police Science, 63:120-24, March 1972. The author compares New York City police character investigation processes prior to 1966 and now. In 1966 a candidate review board was established composed of four policemen and three civilian police employees. The candidate is now granted two personal interviews before the board and never is a candidate rejected without stated reasons. This has resulted in fewer rejections of Negro and Puerto Rican applicants. 1001

Brandstatter, A. F. "A Career Concept for Police." Journal of Criminal Law, Criminology and Police Science, 61:438-445, Sept. 1970. The future of police agencies depends on the character of their leaders and the strength and quality of their ideas. Police departments compete in the labor market and to obtain the best qualified personnel must have something to offer. Requirements of higher education will bring in better people receptive to training programs. Agencies must provide adequate pay and departmental classifications. 1002

Cohen, Bernard. "Minority Retention in the New York City Police Department: A Police Study." Criminology: An Interdisciplinary Journal, 11:287-306, Nov. 1973. Extremely informative on how an individual goes about joining the New York City Police Department. Various tests and forms that must be completed are mentioned. Of considerable importance is information on why blacks and Puerto Ricans are in the minority as police officers. One reason for the dropout rate is that many withdraw their applications before they are investigated. 1003

Flynn, J. T., and Peterson, M. "The Use of Regression Analysis in Police Patrolman Selection." Journal of Criminal Law, Criminology and Police Science, 63:564-569, Dec. 1972. Originally, a police officer was considered appropriately selected and adequately trained if he possessed the necessary skills to fire a weapon and interpret the penal code. Changes have been made to reevaluate these standards for selection and training. 1004

Grady, Bernard E. "I.Q. Tests: The New Castle County Experience." Police Chief, 40:66, Feb. 1973. In recent years this Delaware county department has made particular efforts to recruit and hire minority group members as patrolmen. Minority applicants were being disqualified by the written testing process required by the Merit System Ordinances. The use of an I.Q. measure was recommended by the IACP in 1967. The county had used the Otis Quick Scoring Mental Ability Test, Gamma Form, on which applicants failing to achieve an I.Q. of 100 were excluded from further consideration. Most minority group applicants were failing. The Otis Test relied heavily on verbal skills in which minority group applicants were prone to difficulty. The Revised Beta Examination, an almost totally nonverbal test, yielded good results: the number of minority group applicants failing decreased 65 per cent. 1005

Hooke, James F., and Krauss, Herbert H. "Personality Characteristics of Successful Police Sergeant Candidates." Journal of Criminal Law, Criminology and Police Science, 62:104-105, March 1971. The relationship of personality characteristics, determined by three tests, to success as sergeant. Successful sergeant candidates tend to depend more upon themselves, appear more self-confident, and more sensitive in interpersonal relationships, and be more outgoing and genial than the patrolmen. Several conclusions were reached: (1) successful candidates are psychologically normal; (2) those candidates rated as good sergeants were also rated as good patrolmen; and (3) the psychological test did not differentiate between candidates rated as good sergeant material and those rated as poorer candidates. 1006

Kreins, Edward S. "The Behavioral Scientist in Law Enforcement." Police Chief, 41:46-48, Feb. 1974. Behavioral scientists could help in selection of personnel and development of training programs. Psychiatric evaluation could help weed out undesirables and continued use of psychiatrists in formal training sessions would be desirable. Additional social scientists could also be used in training to help round out an otherwise entirely technical program. 1007

Teske, Raymond and Nelson, Bardin. "Selected Requirements for Law Enforcement Personnel." Police, 16:32-35, July 1972. Although requirements may be regulated by state law, civil service boards, county officers, police chiefs, or state governors, there are some standards that seem to hold for all states:

(1) vision--most agencies require both a minimum for uncorrected and a minimum for corrected vision; (2) residential--most states require residence upon application; (3) height and weight--several different requirements--some require that height and weight be proportionate; others impose arbitrary height and weight limits; (4) age--varies from state to state, but one must normally have a high school diploma. 1008

B. TRAINING AND EDUCATION

Adams, Gerald B. "Law Enforcement Interdepartment Educational Exchange Program." Police Chief, 40:22-23, April 1973. This article discusses one such program. Numerous police management exchange programs are in existence today. However, the one described in this article, involving only the line officer, is the first known to be employed in the Pacific Northwest. 1009

Ashburn, Franklin G., and Ward, Payton. "Education and Training: The Moment of Truth." Police Chief, 40:40-41, July 1973. 1010

Asper, Ellis I. "A Training Technique: Motivated Involvement." Police Chief, 40:28-32, Oct. 1973. A platoon training program in the Riverside, Calif., P.D. It describes how a man in a platoon was used to teach a subject in which he was proficient and explores baton technique, street orientation, manhandling, and the building check. A short evaluation report of the program's effects on the department is given. 1011

Badalamente, Richard V.; George, Clay E.; Halterlein, Paul J.; Jackson, Thomas T.; Moore, Shirley A.; and Rio, Paul. "Training Police for Their Social Role." Journal of Police Science and Administration, 1:440-453, Dec. 1973. The popular conception is that most police activity involves chasing criminals and fighting crime. Several studies indicate that it is taken up with other matters. This article deals with a job analysis, and traits, knowledges and skills required in social role of police. It also looks at the characteristics of police applicants. Some training methods and performance evaluation are touched on. 1012

Barocas, Harvey, and Katz, Myron L. "Dayton's Pilot Training Program: Crisis Intervention." Police Chief, 38:20-26, July 1971. 1013

Bell, John H. "The Development of a Code of Police Ethical Practice: Some Perspectives and Problems." Police Chief, 40:20-21, Jan. 1974. 1014

Boer, Byron L., and McIver, Bruce C. "Human Relations Training: Laboratories and Team Policing." *Journal of Police Science and Administration,* 1:162-167, June 1973. Human relations training, though slow in reaching P.D.'s, often has tended to be of the "sound and fury" variety. Part of the problem is that there is rarely anything to which to relate. They tend to be pointless "pseudo-labs." This article discusses the use of a real training laboratory in this field. 1015

Bohardt, Paul A., and Rasmussen, Howard M. "The Selection and Training of Organized Crime Investigations." *Police Chief,* 38: 34-45, Sept. 1971. 1016

Bonamarte, Michael F., Jr., and Principe, Andrew H. "Training a Task Force of Evidence Technicians." *Police Chief,* 37:48-53, June 1970. There is a paucity of highly trained evidence technicians throughout the U.S., particularly at the smaller department level where they are usually in significant demand. A course of instruction is outlined that would effectively train this kind of professional technician. The use of the trained technician and aspects of on-going training are also described in depth.
1017

Brownlee, E. Gardner. "A Judge's Views on Law Enforcement and Training." *F.B.I. Law Enforcement Bulletin,* 42:8-11, Sept. 1973. Brownlee's views in favor of training law enforcement officers to be better witnesses in court; he says officers today make better witnesses than those of past years. 1018

Buck, Walter E. "'Hands-On' Training." *Police Chief,* 40:48-50. June 1973. As a part of overall training, "hands-on" training has helped develop better prepared policemen. Missouri requires 600 hours of training for all police officers in counties of the first class. This article describes on-location training.
1019

Buren, R. Michael. "A Police Management Training Program: Efficient Use of Man and Money." *Journal of Police Science and Administration,* 1:294-302, Sept. 1973. 1020

Carter, Robert M., and Nelson, E. K. "The Law Enforcement Education Program--One University's Experience." *Journal of Police Science and Administration,* 1:491-494, Dec. 1973. A discussion of LEEP, designed to provide financial aid to law enforcement, courts, and correction personnel and to students preparing for careers in the criminal justice system. Most of the article is a breakdown of personnel who attended U.S.C. under LEEP. 1021

Cauthen, William R. "Police Cadet Corps." *F.B.I. Law Enforcement Bulletin,* 43:22-25, Feb. 1974. 1022

Constantine, Thomas A. "Higher Education for Police: Some Operational Difficulties." Police Chief, 39:18-20, June 1972. Some of the problems caused by so many officers' seeking higher education. The writer lists some of them as intra-agency relationships, role conflicts, loyalty, and manpower. 1023

Cromwell, P. F., Jr. "Training--Education--Understanding Bridge the Gap." Police Chief, 39:54-56, March 1972. Creating community understanding between police and citizen is an adjunct duty of police officials they often are unprepared for. Various efforts by P.D.'s to cope with community problems are described; one program is presented based on police cadets. 1024

Cusach, William E. "Law Enforcement Education in New Jersey." Police Chief, 37:56-58, Aug. 1970. Elucidation of the N.J. Council of Educational Institutions for Law Enforcement; not so much a compendium of what schools consist of in N.J. as an attempt to clarify the efforts being made by the schools to coordinate educational programs. Difficulties of starting the program stressed to illustrate its present success and promising future. 1025

Donelan, Charles A. "The Imperative of Police Legal Training." F.B.I. Law Enforcement Bulletin, 42:23-28, July 1973. Training an officer to understand the rights of citizens and their property. An officer must know when it is lawful to enter onto private property; he also must learn he cannot violate another's rights without proper authorization. If an officer acts on his own, contrary to proper procedure, important evidence may be thrown out of court; and a known criminal may be set free. 1026

Eastman, George, and McCain, James. "Police Managers and Their Perceptions of Higher Education." Journal of Criminal Justice, 1:113-124, summer 1973. 1027

Feeny, Floyd. "Teaching Law to the Police Officer." Police, 16: 25-36, Jan. 1972. Not limited to the teaching of merely elementary aspects of law to police. Nation-wide surveys find out who exactly is teaching law to police and how they are doing it. The author refers to institutional programs that have been successful and the reasons why, and discusses topics that should be stressed. 1028

Flammang, Chris J. "A Summary of the Spelling Competence of Students in Four Basic Police Training Classes." Police, 16: 25-30, July 1972. A limited research project conducted by the author to dispel the belief that police officers are worse than others when it comes to spelling, writing, and general expression. 1029

Folley, Vern L. "College Based Police Training." Law and Order, 22:32-40, March 1974. Advantages of having a police academy and a community college on the same campus--as at the Harrisburg (Pa.) Area Community College, also the police academy for eight surrounding counties. The learning atmosphere is very beneficial and the cadets' association with regular students helps the cadets to adapt to their new role. It also shows the students that "cops" are people. The cadets are taught through situational, classroom, and videotape instruction; and after 400 hours of training, receive a semester's credit. 1030

Giddings, G. E. "Criminal Justice Curriculum; A New Approach to Criminal Justice Education." Police Chief, 37:44-46, Feb. 1970. The need to create a new criminal justice curriculum for all non-professional criminal justice personnel, insuring that each person now enrolled in one aspect of the criminal justice system would receive additional training. The new man coming in would be totally educated in steps, i.e., two-year degree, four-year degree, and M.A., each step a prerequisite for a position in the system. Advantages and disadvantages of such a program are listed and debated. 1031

Gourley, G. Douglas. "Higher Education for Police Personnel." Law and Order, 20:34-36, Feb. 1972. 1032

Gregory, G. Howard. "A Practical Guide to Human Relations for the Individual Police Officer." Law and Order, 21:30-33, Nov. 1973. Upon receiving word, an officer should go to the scene of an accident as quickly and safely as possible; high speed is not necessary. The officer's immediate concern is to (1) give first aid to the injured; (2) protect the victim's property, and (3) restore the orderly flow of traffic. For criminal violations and in regard to human relations, the officer should act in these terms: (1) be courteous but firm, (2) maintain strict impartiality, (3) avoid the use of insulting terms or names, (4) not reply to verbal abuse, (5) maintain a calm but determined attitude, (6) not debate the issues with the crowd, (7) when action is required, be vigorous and decisive, (8) always act together as a unit, and (9) use only that amount of force necessary to maintain order. 1033

Gross, Solomon. "Higher Education and Police: Is There a Need for a Closer Look?" Journal of Police Science and Administration, 1:477-483, Dec. 1973. Riots of the 1960's influenced the President's Commission of Law Enforcement and Administration of Justice in 1967 to emphasize the need for college education of police: some of the pro's and con's are presented. Survey interviews are needed--the article suggests a formulation for such interviews. 1034

Haley, Keith N. "Responsibilities of the University Law Enforcement Teacher." Police, 16:48-52, May 1972. A discussion only of the problems usually associated with teaching police officers at the university level. 1035

Hamilton, Lander C., and Bimstein, Donald. "Attracting College

Graduates to Police Departments." Police Chief, 39:40-42, Aug. 1972. 1036

Hancock, Donald. "The Police Administrator's Role in Correlating Academic Resources." Police Chief, 39:53-55, April 1972. With continued availability of LEEP funds and the increasing availability of police training-oriented college courses, effective use of the various educational resources becomes a matter of increased concern to the police administrator. 1037

Hartenstein. "A Cooperative Approach to Police Management Training." Journal of Police Science and Administration, 1:433-439, Dec. 1973. 1038

Heaphy, John. "Field Training." Police Chief, 37:41-43, Feb. 1970. Does field training work? As head of the New Haven P.D. Training Div. the author seems to think positively about field training and argues his point of view clearly. 1039

Hoover, Larry T. "Michigan's Extension Course in Police Supervision." Law and Order, 20:36-39, Feb. 1972. 1040

Huseman, Richard C. "Interpersonal Communication Training for Police: An Evaluation." Journal of Police Science and Administration, 1:355-361, Sept. 1973. Three major communication training methods: videotape, role playing, and communication in conflict, with group exercises and communication in conflict film-based case study. The article then presents the results and their evaluation by 23 officers from five southeastern states who participated in a pilot training program. 1041

Isom, James E. "Law Enforcement Education in Public Schools." Police Chief, 41:74-78, March 1974. 1042

Jagiello, Robert J. "College Education for the Patrolman: Necessary or Irrelevant." Journal of Criminal Law, Criminology and Police Science, 62:114-121, March 1971. 1043

Jameson, Samuel Haig. "Controversial Areas in 20th Century Policing: Quest for Quality Training in Police Work." American Society of Criminology, 123-33, 1964. 1044

Katz, Myron. "Family Crisis Training: Upgrading the Police While Building a Bridge to the Minority Community." Journal of Police Science and Administration, 1:30-35, March 1973. "Community relations" is often perceived as "public relations" and as a con game by the community, whose members cannot see the relationship between the activities of the community relations specialist and those of the patrolmen on the street. A discussion of the problem of community relations at the family crisis intervention level, including programs and training of officers in such intervention. 1045

Kelly, Clarence M. "The College Coordinator: A New Police Post." Police Chief, 37:48-50, April 1970. 1046

Kirwen, William E. "Interdepartmental Traffic Science Training Program." Police Chief, 38:34-35, March 1971. Setting up a traffic training program in the New York Police Academy, the academic subjects of which are given credit by the College of General Studies of the State University of New York. 1047

Knowles, Lyle. "Evaluating Training and Educational Programs in Criminal Justice." Journal of Police Science and Administration, 1:333-344, Sept. 1973. 1048

________. "The Policeman in the Ivory Tower: A Challenge for the Professional Educator." Police, 16:35-43, March 1972. 1049

________. "Teaching Cops." Police Chief, 38:22-24, Feb. 1971. The author opens: "It's tough to teach cops," and tries to explain exactly why such a statement may be made, particularly by persons who have not had policemen in their classes. 1050

Lankes, George. "How Should We Educate the Police?" Journal of Criminal Law, Criminology and Police Science, 61:587-592, Dec. 1970. 1051

________. "A Profile of the Police Science Student." Police Chief, 38:60-64, April 1971. Police curricula and how they compare to business administration curricula. People entering a police science program are average or above average students and most are sincere, completing their education whether it was in a two- or four-year curriculum. 1052

McGowan, James F. "Criminal Justice Unit, Broward County Community College at Fort Lauderdale, Florida." Police Chief, 41:46, Jan. 1974. A new concept of universalizing police training throughout the state. The institutes, goals, functions, and assets are listed. 1053

McNamara, Joseph D. "Profile: Harvard Law School's Center for the Advancement of Criminal Justice." Police Chief, 39:24-26, Jan. 1972. 1054

Manella, Frank L. "Humanism in Police Training." Police Chief, 38:26-28, Feb. 1971. A survey of what the American people think about the quality of police service they receive. Also the varying activities of the police are discussed. Increasing attention is being given to a study of attitudes, values, beliefs, and perceptions in training courses. This article evaluates the advantage of having an officer well trained in the philosophy of human behavior. 1055

Meyer, Schuyler, III, and Topham, Charles S. "Sensitivity Training/Rap Sessions for Police and Pupils." Police Chief, 38:63-

65, Sept. 1971. The effectiveness of face-to-face confrontations with the police in rap sessions; a "mock" arrest of a local school teacher. In various training sessions, youth as well as police could get rid of preconceived ideas about the other. 1056

Michael, Geraldine. "Social Science Education for Police Officers." Police Chief, 38:56-61, June 1971. 1057

Morgan, J. P. "Considerations on Law Enforcement Education." Police Chief, 37:36-40, Aug. 1970. 1058

Moyer, Clifford A. "Developing a Criminal Justice Training Program." F.B.I. Law Enforcement Bulletin, 40:24-26, Nov. 1971. 1059

Moynahan, James McCauslin. "Training the Police Officer in a Liberal Arts College." Police Chief, 40:58-60, Nov. 1973. Several years ago, V. A. Leonard observed that educational requirements in American P.D.'s varied from ability to read and write to high school graduation with a trend developing toward a college degree in the police major. He further noted that the "accidental infiltration" of men with college training into the police services escaped the attention of most observers. Moynahan suggests that policemen need to be college trained and discusses this. 1060

Odell, Brian Neal. "America's New Anti-Police Sentiment." Journal of Human Relations, 19:347-355, 3rd qtr. 1971. Anti-police sentiment has intensified since the early 60's. The policeman became a threat and target of resentment to the lower class, a reason for suspicion to the middle class, and an insult to the upper class. Increased recruitment of minority group members and an emphasis on the college-trained police officer have been suggested. Odell feels that officers should be recruited from all possible social classes to make the department more representative of the American people. Officers would be assigned to "beats" according to social class rather than race or education. 1061

Oldham, Charles Carlton. "Kentucky Law Enforcement Council," F.B.I. Law Enforcement Bulletin, 42:8-12, July 1973. 1062

O'Neill, Michael E., and Benaderet, Frank R. "Training: Conceptual Model for Organizational Development." Police Chief, 40: 66-68, Feb. 1973. Brief comments on police organizations' ability to identify the environment they are working in, to assess their needs, to see where they have been, and where they are, and then to develop training programs accordingly. 1063

________; Stoval, William; and Lloyd, C. N. "Police vs. College Students: Attitudes Toward Education." Police, 16:19-21, Jan. 1972. The differences of opinion of college sociology students and enrolled police officers. The article is largely of statistical tables but is comprehensive and clear. Essentially, the attitudes of the students depend upon their level in school and their confrontations with the police. Police attitudes differed in the same respect. 1064

O'Reilly, James T. "Bridging the Gap: Law Enforcement and Legal Education." Police Chief, 40:54-57, Nov. 1973. 1065

Pantalioni, C. A. "Law Enforcement Academia: Crossroads for Concern." Police Chief, 37:42-46, Aug. 1970. 1066

Partotage, Frank M. "Sensitivity Training." Police Chief, 39:60, Oct. 1972. Police-community relations in metropolitan centers across the nation. The college, according to the author, will serve as a catalyst for change using sensitivity training in its curriculum to improve police-community relations. The article generally deals with negative police-community perceptions and how community colleges deal with this dilemma. 1067

Phelps, Lourn G.; Schwartz, Jeffrey A.; and Liebman, Donald A. "Training an Entire Patrol Division in Domestic Crisis Intervention." Police Chief, 38:18-19, July 1971. Training specialists versus generalists in coping with the family crisis. Training only a few specialists is expensive and time consuming. 1068

Prout, Robert S. "A Methodology to Developing an Educational-Training Curriculum in Law Enforcement Education." Police, 16:32-35, March 1972. The dilemma of education and training. Are both necessary? Is one preferable? Time-honored arguments and counter-arguments are presented; a combination of the two is discussed as an effective form of curriculum. 1069

Raymond, Thomas T. "Realistic Emergency Medical Training for the Police Professional." Police Chief, 40:26-27, April 1973. Today we hear such terms as "paramedical" and "emergency medical technician" with greater frequency and there is a widening interest by the public in just how good emergency care is. This short article discusses realistic emergency medical training using a male mannequin developed by the Alderson Research Lab. 1070

Reese, Charles D. "Police Academy Training and Its Effects on Racial Prejudice." Journal of Police Science and Administration, 1:257-268, Sept. 1973. 1071

Schultz, Arthur A. "Regional Training for Professional Proficiency." Police Chief, 38:50-51, March 1971. Setting up a regional training program--for police and other personnel involved in the criminal justice system--concerned with not only training but academia as well. 1072

Schwarz, Ted. "Suburban Police Training in Ohio." Law and Order, 20:46-48, Feb. 1972. 1073

Sharkitt, Robert L. "Training and Investigative Uses of Audiovisual Equipment." Police Chief, 40:63-64, Nov. 1973. 1074

Siemon, Joyce M., and Black, Charles C. "A New Approach to In-Service Training." F.B.I. Law Enforcement Bulletin, 42:11-15, Nov. 1973. 1075

Skillen, Charles R. "Versatile Instruction." F.B.I. Law Enforcement Bulletin, 41:21-24, Dec. 1972. A brief discussion of the Montana Academy for Law Enforcement. 1076

Teasley, C. E., III, and Wright, Leonard. "The Effects of Training on Police Recruit Attitudes." Journal of Police Science and Administration, 1:241-248, June 1973. 1077

Tielsch, George P. "Community Field Training for Police Recruits." Police Chief, 39:30-31, Nov. 1972. Groups of recruits are assigned to different situations in society. At meetings, each group discussed their findings with other groups. 1078

Tracy, Charles A. "Survey of Criminal Justice Subject Matter Baccalaureate Programs." Journal of Criminal Law, Criminology and Police Science, 61:576-579, Dec. 1970. Some of the college and university programs offered across the U.S. in criminal justice; qualifications of instructors are dealt with. 1079

Turner, Ralph F. "Comparative Criminal Justice Education; A Report on an Overseas Experiment." Journal of Criminal Law, Criminology and Police Science, 63:129-133, March 1972. 1080

Wachtel, Julius. "The Need for Change in Police Science Curricula." Police Chief, 39:64-66, Nov. 1972. A police science student's view on college courses offered to today's law enforcement officers: liberal arts should be taken by all such students. 1081

Wall, Charles R., and Culloo, Leo A. "State Standards for Law Enforcement Selection and Training." Journal of Police Science and Administration, 1:425-432, Dec. 1973. Statistical research comparing the training of police in the various states. Recommendations are made as to what standards should be adhered to. 1082

Wasby, Stephen L. "Police Training and Criminal Procedure." Police Chief, 39:24-31, Oct. 1972. 1083

Webb, Donald G., and Westergren, Gene F. "The Detraining Syndrome." Police Chief, 40:36-38, Nov. 1973. One significant cause of police officer attrition is examined with recommendation for change: premature loss of the idealistic and highly motivated young officer who becomes disillusioned with the profession to the extent that he resigns. 1084

Webb, Horace S. "The Police Professional: Consistent Training Plus Standardization." *Police Chief,* 39:76-77, April 1972. 1085

Wicker, Irving B. "Training Law Enforcement Officers to Rate." *Police,* 16:46-52, June 1972. The problems inherent in the rating system within the police field. Most supervisors are inadequately trained to rate their subordinates fairly and comprehensively. Rating can be taught; effective training programs should be instituted. 1086

Younger, Evelle J. "A Legal Training Program Over Closed-Circuit TV." *F.B.I. Law Enforcement Bulletin,* 40:2-4, April 1971. 1087

C. PROFESSIONALIZATION

Balch, Robert. "The Police Personality: Fact or Fiction?" *Journal of Criminal Law, Criminology, and Police Science,* 63: 106-119, March 1972. 1088

Ball, John H. "The Development to a Code of Ethical Practice: Some Perspectives and Problems." *Police Chief,* 41:20-23, Jan. 1974. 1089

Bopp, William J. *Police Personnel Administration.* Boston: Holbrook Press, 1974. 425pp. 1090

Davis, Edward M. "Professional Police Principles." *Federal Probation* (Washington, D.C.), 35:29-34, March 1971. Every business has general principles and philosophies essential to its success. Law enforcement is no exception. Police exist to prevent crime and disorder as an alternative to the repression of crime and disorder by military force and severity of legal punishment. 1091

Dunne, J. A. "Counseling Alcoholic Employees in a Municipal Police Department." *Quarterly Journal of Studies on Alcohol,* 34(2):423-34, 1973. 1092

Fink, Joseph. "Police in a Community: Improving a Deteriorated Image." *Journal of Criminal Law, Criminology and Police Science,* 59:624-631, Dec. 1968. The necessity of understanding and applying techniques of good human relations and good public relations. The curriculum in social studies for students at the police academy is constantly revised and strengthened. The importance of higher education for all ranks is stressed. However, the solutions are not all in the hands of the police. The word "relations" indicates a partnership between the community and the police. 1093

Flynn, J. T., and Peterson, M. "The Use of Regression Analysis in Police Patrolman Analysis." *Journal of Criminal Law, Criminology and Police Science,* 63(4):564-569, 1972. 1094

Furstenberg, Frank, Jr., and Wellford, Charles. "Calling the Police: The Evaluation of Police Service." *Law and Society Review,* 7:393-406, spring 1973. The way in which citizens evaluate the work of the police. Conclusions drawn from interviews conducted with both police and private citizens were that most people believe that police service is good; blacks are more critical than whites; and blacks generally have a lower opinion of police. Private interviewers also were found to be able to get a truer representative attitude than police interviewers. 1095

Goldstein, H. "Guidelines for Effective Use of Police Manpower." *Public Management,* 45:218-22, Oct. 1963. 1096

Gould, Marvin. "Does a Policeman Need to Have a College Degree to Be a Professional?" *Law and Order,* 21:68-69, Feb. 1973. Some of the advantages and disadvantages of an officer's having a college degree are described. A survey of two groups shows the difference in pay for those having a degree and those not having a degree. Frustration regarding education affects the outlook of the average policeman. 1097

Hahn, Harlan. "A Profile of Urban Police." *Law and Contemporary Problems,* 36:449-466, autumn 1971. Characteristics of and attitudes in the typical urban police department. The majority of the force is white and comes from lower middle-class backgrounds. Joining the police force is usually an opportunity for upward social movement. Only a small minority have higher than a high school diploma. Job security is a major attraction as is in many cases a desire for a position of power. Very little time is spent in courses dealing with human relations. Policemen show a high degree of cohesion and fraternal loyalty and tend to socialize together during off-hours. Constant exposure to danger creates feeling of ambivalence and tension toward the public and caution. Suspicion can develop into low expectations of human behavior. 1098

Hood, Roger, and Sparks, Richard F. *Key Issues in Criminology.* New York: McGraw-Hill, 1970. 256pp. 1099

Kelley, Clarence. "Professional Status." *Law and Order,* 22:10-13, March 1974. The answer to creating more professional law enforcement agencies is training. While executive decision is important as preparation for changes in our society, training teaches both "traditional functioning and a receptiveness to change" and "this is the route by which true professional status in law enforcement can be achieved." Kelley reviews the new F.B.I. academy curriculum. Requirements include criminal law, principles of management, behavioral sciences, forensic sciences, and education-communication arts. 1100

Kronholm, William C. "Blue Power: The Threat of the Militant Policeman." Journal of Criminal Law, Criminology, and Police Science, 63:294-299, June 1972. A small but dangerous minority of militant policemen has arisen. Two types are noted: those that work to fill political or ideological causes and those who see lawful restraints on police as hindrances which can be ignored in order to "do his job." If carried to an extreme, this would lead to a police state. The rise can be attributed to alienation of police from the society it serves. The article points out the effects of decreased respect for police which leads to decreased effectiveness of policemen, which leads to decreased respect--a vicious circle. 1101

McMahon, Daniel F. "Capital Punishment." F.B.I. Law Enforcement Bulletin, 42:20-21, Feb. 1973. 1102

Niederhoffer, Arthur. The Ambivalent Force--Perspectives on the Police. Waltham, Mass.: Ginn and Co., 1970. 360pp. 1103

O'Brien, Daniel. "Half-Century Mark for Illinois State Police." Police Chief, 39:62-72, June 1972. 1104

Pettit, M. L., and Holmberg, B. K. "Let's Put It All Together: An Integrated Approach to Criminal Law and Justice." Journal of Police Science and Administration, (1):113-119, 1973. 1105

Press, S. James. Some Effects of an Increase in Police Manpower in the 20th Precinct of New York City. Santa Monica, Calif.: Rand Institute, 1971. 158pp. 1106

Rubenstein, Jonathan. City Police. New York: Farrar, Straus and Giroux, 1973. 1107

Schiller, S. A. "More Light on a Low Visibility Function: The Selective Enforcement of Laws. III. The Law Does Not Appear to Support the Development of Selective and Discriminatory Policies." Police Law Quarterly, 2:17-20, 1973. 1108

Singer, S. "October 1971 Term of the United States Supreme Court: Decisions of Importance to Police Personnel." Police Law Quarterly, 2(3):6-13, 1973. 1109

Smith, William H. T. "Deceit in Uniform." Police Chief, 40:20-21, 1973. 1110

Sterling, James W. Changes in Role Concepts of Police Officers. Gaithersburg, Md.: International Assoc. of Chiefs of Police, 1972. 329pp. 1111

Stoddard, Elluyn. "The Informal Code of Police Deviancy: A Group Approach to Blue-Coat Crime." Journal of Criminal Law, Criminology, and Police Science, 59:201-213, June 1968. The traditional stereotype of a policeman engaged in unlawful activity is usually that of an isolated deviation by a morally weak and personally corrupt individual. The author explores the process of recruit socialization into unlawful practices, preservation of group code secrecy and group acceptance for practitioners. Difficulty in breaking the "code" without destroying police professionalism is one of the major problems in the deterrence of blue-coat crime. 1112

Struggle for Justice--A Report on Crime and Punishment in America. American Friends Service Committee. New York: Hill and Wang, 1971. 179pp. 1113

Sundeen, Richard A. "Police Professionalism and Community Attachments and Diversion of Juveniles." Criminology, 11:570-578, Feb. 1974. The relationship of the number of juvenile offenders sent to court and the type of police agency handling the matter: whether or not a highly professional police force sends more juveniles to court than a force whose members are closely tied in with the community. 1114

Webster, John A. Realities of Police Work. Iowa: Kendall/Hunt, 1973. 104pp. 1115

Wilson, J. V. "Alternatives to Military Rank Titles in Law Enforcement." Police Chief, (4), 1974. 1116

Wilson, James Q. Varieties of Police Behavior, The Management of Law and Communities. Cambridge, Mass.: Harvard University Press, 1968. 309pp. 1117

D. POLICE UNIONS

Bolinger, H. E. "Police Officers' Views on Collective Bargaining and Use of Sanctions." Police Chief, 41(2):39-42, 1974. 1118

Bopp, W. J. "The Boston Police Strike of 1919." Police, 16(11): 54-58, 1972. 1119

Burpo, J. H. "Improving Police Agency and Employee Performance Through Collective Bargaining." Police Chief, 41(4):30, 32, 34, 36, 1974. 1120

______. The Police Labor Movement: Problems and Perspectives. Springfield, Ill.: Charles C. Thomas, 1972. 203pp. 1121

"Cops and Unions, Jackson, Mississippi." Newsweek, 24:34, July 3, 1944. Discusses the problem of police unionization. 1122

Gammage, A. Z., and Sachs, S. L. Police Unions. Springfield, Ill.: Charles C. Thomas, 1972. 194pp. 1123

Gifford, J. P. "Professionalizing Police Labor Relations: The New York City Police Department's Response to Unionization." *Journal of Police Science Administration,* 2(1):94-106, 1974. 1124

Halpern, S. C. "Do Police Unions Have any Effect on Police Department Operations?" *Police Chief,* 41(2):35, 1974. 1125

Olmos, R. A. "A New Approach to Collective Bargaining for Police Unions." *Police Chief,* 41(2):28-30, 1974. 1126

________. "Some Effects of Police Unionism on Discipline." *Police Chief,* 41(4):24-26, 28, 1974. 1127

Vessey, S. C. "Understanding Workers on Strike." *Police Journal,* 46(4):321-337, 1973. 1128

II. POLICE FUNCTIONS AND PRACTICES (2000)

A. CRIMINAL INFORMATION AND IDENTIFICATION

Abrams, S., and Weinstein, E. "The Validity of the Polygraph with Retardates." Journal of Police Science Administration, 2(1):11-14, 1974. 2000

Alexander, H. L. V. Classifying Palmprints, A Complete System of Coding, Filing and Searching Palmprints. Springfield, Ill.: Charles C. Thomas, 1973. 120pp. 2001

"An Analysis of Standards in Fingerprint Identification." F.B.I. Law Enforcement Bulletin, 41(6):7-11, 29-30, 1972. 2002

Becker, Harold K. "A Phenomenological Inquiry into the Etiology of Female Homosexuality." Journal of Human Relations, 17(4): 570-580, 1969. 2003

______. "Pupillometrics and Criminal Justice." The Police Journal (British), 44(2):117-123, April-June 1971. 2004

Cohen, A. A. 'Number of Features, and Alternatives Per Feature, in Reconstructing Faces with the Identi-Kit." Journal of Police Science and Administration, 1(3):349-354, 1973. 2005

Cressey, Donald Ray. Crime and Criminal Justice. New York: Quadrangle Books, 1971. 289pp. 2006

Curran, William J. Law, Medicine, and Forensic Science, 2nd ed. Boston: Little, Brown, 1970. 1,046pp. 2007

Curry, Alan S. Advances in Forensic and Clinical Toxicology. Cleveland: Chemical Rubber Co., 1972. 280pp. 2008

"An Electrostatic Method for Lifting Footprints." International Criminal Police Review, 28(272):287-292, 1973. 2009

"The Emergence of the Polygraph at Trial." Columbia Law Review, 73(5):1120-1144, 1973. 2010

Ferguson, R. J., Jr., and Miller, A. L. The Polygraph in Court. Springfield, Ill.: Charles C. Thomas, 1973. 346pp. 2011

Flaugher, P. R. "The Cincinnati/Hamilton County Regional Crime Information Center. Operations, Security, Ethics." Police Chief, 40(10):24-27, 1973. 2012

Gavin, J. "'Operation Identification' Goes Nationwide." Law and Order, 21(5):66-69, 1973. 2013

Guenther, Anthony L. Criminal Behavior and Social Systems, Contributions of American Sociology. Chicago: Rand McNally, 1970. 561pp. 2014

Harrell, J. R. "Recovering the Bloody Fingerprint." Criminologist, 8(28):49-58, 1973. 2015

Hunter, G. L., and Ash, P. "The Accuracy and Consistency of Polygraph Examiners' Diagnoses." Journal of Police Science and Administration, 1(3):370-375, 1973. 2016

Lance, J. E. "The Long Beach Automated Field Interview System." Police Chief, 40(10):56-58, 1973. 2017

Lee, E. L. "Operation Identification: A Step in the Right Direction." Police Chief, 39(8):50-52, 1972. 2018

Lesk, J. J. "Development of Latent Fingerprints by the Ninhydrin Method." Fingerprint and Identification Magazine, 54(1):13-15, 1972. 2019

Lipton, Dean. The Faces of Crime and Genius; The Historical Impact of the Genius-Criminal. South Brunswick, N.J.: A. S. Barnes & Co., 1970. 252pp. 2020

Lopez-Rey y Arrojo, Manuel. Crime--An Analytical Appraisal. New York: Praeger, 1970. 227pp. 2021

McWilliam, S. T. "A County Police Information System." F.B.I. Law Enforcement Bulletin, 42(8):27-31, 1973. 2022

Meyer, J. C., Jr. "The Reactive and Proactive Models of Information Search and Utilization by Police: Search for an Alternative." Journal of Police Science and Administration, 1(3):311-318, 1973. 2023

"The National Crime Information Center. A Special Report." F.B.I. Law Enforcement Bulletin, 43(1):8-10, 1974. 2024

Nimmer, Raymond T. Two Million Unnecessary Arrests, Removing a Social Service Concern from the Criminal Justice System. Chicago: American Bar Foundation, 1971. 202pp. 2025

O'Brien, Kevin P. Criminalistics, Theory and Practice. Boston: Holbrook Press, 1972. 283pp. 2026

O'Hara, Charles E. Fundamentals of Criminal Investigation. 2nd ed. Springfield, Ill.: Charles C. Thomas, 1970. 2027

________. An Introduction to Criminalistics. Bloomington: Indiana University Press, 1972. 705pp. 2028

________, and Osterburg, James W. An Introduction to Criminalistics. New York: Macmillan, 1949. 695pp. Modern scientific instruments and methods of analysis in criminal investigation. 2029

Quinney, Richard. Crime and Justice in Society. Boston: Little, Brown, 1969. 535pp. 2030

________. The Problem of Crime. New York: Dodd, Mead, 1970. 227pp. 2031

________. The Social Reality of Crime. Boston: Little, Brown, 1970. 339pp. 2032

Rifas, Richard A. "Legal Aspects of Video Tape and Motion Pictures in Law Enforcement." Evanston, Ill.: Northwestern University Traffic Institute, 1972. 19pp. 2033

Romig, C. H. A. "State Legislation Concerning the Polygraph in June 1973." Polygraph, 2(2):81-88, 1973. 2034

Sansone, Sam J. Modern Photography for Police and Firemen. Cincinnati: W. H. Anderson Pub. Co., 1971. 478pp. 2035

Schur, Edwin M. Our Criminal Society, The Social and Legal Sources of Crime in America. Englewood Cliffs, N.J.: Prentice-Hall, 1969. 244pp. 2036

Sevilla, C. M. "The Polygraph Examiner as a Witness in Court." Polygraph, 2(2):122-142, 1973. 2037

Short, James F. Modern Criminals. Chicago: Aldine, 1970. 192pp. 2038

Sykes, Gresham M. Law and The Lawless, A Reader in Criminology. New York: Random House, 1969. 437pp. 2039

Tosi, Oscar. "An Experiment on Voice Identification." Excerpts from a report, Michigan State University, 1971. 2040

Walrod, T. H. "Suicide Attempts--Who and Why." National Sheriff, 25(2), 26 & 30-31, 1973. 2041

Walters, L. M. "Progress of Automation and Other Phases of Fingerprint Identification." F.B.I. Law Enforcement Bulletin, 41(10):15 & 30, 1972. 2042

Willmer, M. A. P. Crime and Information Theory. Edinburgh: Edinburgh University Press, 1970. 124pp. 2043

Zavala, Albert. Personal Appearance Identification. Springfield, Ill. Charles C. Thomas, 1972. 331pp. 2044

Zimmermann, E. "XYZ: Open File. Assisting the Police and Television Viewers." International Crime and Police Review, 28(272):280-283, 1973. 2045

B. COMMUNITY RELATIONS

Abrahamsen, David. Our Violent Society. New York: Funk & Wagnalls, 1970. 298pp. 2046

Ahern, James F. Police in Trouble. New York: Hawthorn Books, 1972. 260pp. 2047

Becker, Harold K. "Is It Too Late for Police Community Relations?" Police, 15(6):13-15, July-Aug. 1971. 2048

Brannan, R. G. "Freedom of the Press v Pretrial News Release: A View from the Arena." Police Chief, 40(12):68-72, 1973. 2049

Bridge, P. A. "Communication Barriers Within the Criminal Justice System." Police Chief, 39(4):30-33, 1972. 2050

Cahn, Edgar S., and Passett, Barry A. Citizen Participation--Effecting Community Change. New York: Praeger, 1971. 294pp. 2051

Carte, Gene E. "Changes in Public Attitudes toward the Police: A Comparison of 1938 and 1971 Surveys." Journal of Political Science and Administration, 182-200, June 1972. 2052

Chinn, H. J. "Law and Justice Awareness Program." F.B.I. Law Enforcement Bulletin, 43(2):26-30, 1972. 2053

Crawford, T. J. "Police Overperception of Ghetto Hostility." Journal of Police Science and Administration, 1(2):168-174, 1973. 2054

Earle, Howard H. Student Instructor Guide on Police Community Relations, Crisis in Our Time, 2nd ed. Springfield, Ill.: Charles C. Thomas, 1970. 216pp. 2055

Erikson, J. M. "Community Service Officer. New York's Model Cities Effect on Law Enforcement." Police Chief, 40(6):40-44, 46, 1973. 2056

Foley, C. P. "Columbus, Ohio Police/Community Program Uses 'Talking Slides'." *Police Chief,* 39(3):44-46, 1972. 2057

Fortier, K. N. "The Police Culture--Its Effect on Sound Police-Community Relations." *The Police Chief,* 39(2):33-35, 1972. 2058

Goodin, C. V. "Crime Reduction: A Community Approach." *F.B.I. Law Enforcement Bulletin,* 42(11):20-22, 31, 1973. 2059

Gray, B. M. "Police Reports to the Community." *Police Chief,* 41(3):54-56, 1974. 2060

Hartjen, C. A. D. "Police-Citizen Encounters. Social Order in Interpersonal Interaction." *Criminology,* 10(1):61-84, 1972. 2061

Hewitt, William H. *Police-Community Relations, An Anthology and Bibliography.* Mineola, N.Y.: Foundation Press, 1970. 360pp. 2062

Hofstadter, Richard, and Wallace, Michael. *American Violence; A Documentary History.* New York: Knopf, 1970. 478pp. 2063

Kelly, J. A., and O'Rourke, T. W. "An Appraisal of the Attitudes of Police Officers Toward the Concept of Police-Community Relations." *Journal of Police Science and Administration,* 1(2):224-231, 1973. 2064

Klyman, F. I. "The Police-Community Relations Survey: A Quantitative Inventory of Services and Work Units." *Journal of Police Science Administration,* 2(1):77-81, 1974. 2065

________. "A Survey of Police-Community Relations." *Police Law Quarterly,* 3(1):13-27, 1973. 2066

McArdle, E. C., and Betjemann, W. N. "A Return to Neighborhood Police." *F.B.I. Law Enforcement Bulletin,* 41(7):8-11 & 28, 1972. 2067

Moody, L. A. "Landlords and Tenants. Oakland's Landlord/Tenant Intervention Unit." *Police Chief,* 39(3):32-34, 1972. 2068

National Advisory Commission on Criminal Justice Standards and Goals. *Community Crime Prevention.* Washington, D.C.: U.S. Gov. Printing Office, 1973. 364pp. 2069

Newman, C. L. "Police and Families: Factors Affecting Police Intervention." *Police Chief,* 39(3):24-26, 28, 30, 1972. 2070

Radelet, L. A. "Police-Community Relations: At This Point in Time...." *Police Chief,* 41(3):24-25, 28-32, 1974. 2071

Rafky, David M., et al. "Are Cops Prejudiced?" *Police Chief,*

40:60-62, March 1973. 2072

Reasons, Charles E., and Kuykendal, Jack L. Race, Crime and Justice. Pacific Palisades, Calif.: Goodyear Pub. Co., 1971. 416pp. 2073

Roberts, M. A. "A Community Relations Program for a Small Department." Police Chief, 41(3):49-50, 1974. 2074

Roger, L. C. "Crime Prevention Through Community Relations. A Different Approach." F.B.I. Law Enforcement Bulletin, 42 (5):14-17, 1973. 2075

Rossi, S. S. "A Community Involvement Program for Police Students." Police, 16(11):59-64, 1972. 2076

Shaw, M., and Williamson, W. "Public Attitudes to the Police." Criminologist, 7(26):18-33, 1972. 2077

Smith, P. E., and Hawkins, R. O. "Victimization, Types of Citizen-Police Contacts, and Attitudes Toward the Police." Law and Society Review, 8(1):135-152, 1973. 2078

State-Local Relations in the Criminal Justice System. Washington, D.C.: U.S. Gov. Printing Office, 1971. 2079

Steadman, R. F., ed. The Police and the Community. Baltimore: Johns Hopkins University Press, 1972. 103pp. 2080

Strecher, Victor G. The Environment of Law Enforcement, A Community Relations Guide. Englewood Cliffs, N.J.: Prentice-Hall, 1971. 107pp. 2081

Trabucco, E. A., and Skiff, D. A. "Police-Community Relations As a Function of Credibility." Police Chief, 41(3):44, 46, 48, 85, 1974. 2082

Trojanowicz, Robert C. "Police-Community Relations. Problems and Process." Criminology, 9(4):401-423, 1973. 2083

________, and Dixon, Samuel L. Criminal Justice and the Community. Englewood Cliffs, N.J.: Prentice-Hall, 1974. 464pp. 2084

Wasserman, Robert, et al. Improving Police-Community Relations. Washington, D.C.: National Criminal Justice Reference Service, Law Enforcement Assistance Admin., U.S. Dept. of Justice, 1973. 2085

Wynne, R. D. "Community Action to Regulate the Illicit Drug Market." Drug Forum, 3(1):79-90, 1973. 2086

C. POLICE PROCEDURES

Adams, Thomas F. Police Patrol: Tactics and Techniques. Englewood Cliffs, N.J.: Prentice-Hall, 1971. 250pp. 2087

Allen, W. A. "The Police Agent." F.B.I. Law Enforcement Bulletin, 42(10):2-6, 1973. 2088

Andersen, R. R. "Strike Force Against Street Crime." F.B.I. Law Enforcement Bulletin, 41(5):3-5 & 30, 1972. 2089

Aubry, Arthur S., Jr. "Inspection in the Internal Revenue Service." Police, 15:5-12, July-Aug. 1971. 2090

Auten, J. "The Domestic Disturbance: A Policemen's Dilemma." Police Chief, 39(10): 16-17, 20 & 22, 1972. 2091

Ayoob, M. F. "Explosives Training Course for Police." Law and Order, 21(2):73-74, 1973. 2092

Bannon, James D. "Foot Patrol--The Litany of Law Enforcement." Police Chief, 39(4):44-45, April 1972. 2093

Bard, Morton. "Alternatives to Traditional Law Enforcement." Police, 14:20-23, Nov.-Dec. 1970. 2094

Barrett, D. "The Police Baton." Law and Order, 20(10):44-45 & 58, 1972. 2095

Becker, Harold K. "Do Police Helicopters Justify Their Cost?" The American City, 70-71, Nov. 1969. 2096

Beechen, P. D. "Oral Search Warrants: A New Standard on Warrant Availability." U.C.L.A. Law Review, 21(2):691-718, 1973. 2097

Bennett, W. "Contacting and Paying Informants." Law and Order, 21(4):28-31, 1973. 2098

Bernstein, P. "Prosecution and the Polygraph." Polygraph, 2(2): 108-115, 1973. 2099

Bloch, Peter B. Neighborhood Team Policing. Washington, D.C.: National Criminal Justice Reference Service, Law Enforcement Assistance Admin., U.S. Dept. of Justice, 1974. 2100

________, and Ulberg, C. "The Beat Commander Concept." Police Chief, 39(9):55-63, 1972. 2101

Blum, Richard H. Deceivers and Deceived, Observations on Confidence Men Informants and Their Quarry. Springfield, Ill.: Charles C. Thomas, 1972. 328pp. 2102

Brown, P. "Cycle Scheduling for Eight and Ten Hour Days." Law and Order, 21(5):28-33, 1973. 2103

Caldwell, Harry. Basic Law Enforcement. Pacific Palisades, Calif.: Goodyear Pub. Co., 1972. 160pp. 2104

Callahan, John J. "Viability of the Small Police Force." Police Chief, 40:56-59, March 1973. 2105

Carlin, J. L., and Moodie, C. L. "A Comparison of Some Patrol Methods." Police, 16(12):27-31, 1972. 2106

Casper, Jonathan D. American Criminal Justice: The Defendant's Perspective. Englewood Cliffs, N. J.: Prentice-Hall, 1972. 192pp. 2107

Cawley, D. F. "Homicide Investigation." Police Chief, 41(4):67, 1974. 2108

Chambliss, William J. Crime and Legal Process. New York: McGraw-Hill, 1969. 447pp. 2109

______. Sociology of the Law--A Research Bibliography. Berkeley, Calif.: Glendessary Press, 1970. 113pp. 2110

Chamelin, Neil C. Criminal Law for Policemen. Englewood Cliffs, N. J.: Prentice-Hall, 1971. 228pp. 2111

Clark, J. "The Police Officer As a Witness." F. B. I. Law Enforcement Bulletin, 42(3):16-17, 1973. 2112

Clawson, C. "A Theoretical Approach to the Allocation of Police Preventive Patrol." Police Chief, 40(7):53-59, 1973. 2113

Clinard, Marshall B. "Some Implications of 'The New Criminology'." International Journal of Criminology and Penology, 85-91, Feb. 1974. 2114

Coakley, Leo J. Jersey Troopers. New Brunswick, N. J.: Rutgers University Press, 1971. 289pp. 2115

Collella, L. J. "Harassment: A Statute in Turmoil." Albany Law Review, 38(2):301-316, 1974. 2116

Congressional Quarterly. Crime and the Law. Washington, D. C., 1971. 91pp. 2117

Coningsby, F. "Unsolved Crimes." Criminologist, 8(29):33-39, 1973. 2118

Conklin, John E. Robbery and the Criminal Justice System. Philadelphia: Lippincott, 1972. 208pp. 2119

_______, and Bittner, E. "Burglary in a Suburb." Criminology, 11(2):206-232, 1973. 2120/1

Connor, G. J., and Harvie, R. A. "The Role of the Police in Environmental Protection." Police, 16(10):20-23, 1972. 2122

Cook, Le Roy. "Missouri Highway Patrol Evaluates New Aircraft." Law and Order, 20:86, May 1972. 2123

Cordrey, J., and Pence, G. K. "An Analysis of Team Policing in Dayton, Ohio." Police Chief, 39(8):44-49, 1972. 2124

Cullinane, M. J. "The Police Patrol Officer: The Backbone of the Law Enforcement Effort." Police Chief, 40(9):37-39, 1973. 2125

Damos, J. P.; Richman, P.; and Miller, E. "PREWARNS. A Police Response Early Warning System." Police Chief, 40(8): 24-25, & 27, 1973. 2126

Daniels, Hiram, and Hilton, K. R. "Crime Prevention: Ideas and Techniques." Military Police Journal, 22:4-6, Feb. 1973. 2127

Degarmo, J. W., Jr. "The Future of Non-Lethal Weapons in Law Enforcement." Police, 16(12):50-51, 1972. 2128

Doob, A. N., and Kirshenbaum, H. M. "Bias in Police Lineups--Partial Remembering." Journal of Police Science and Administration, 1(3):287-293, 1973. 2129

Douglas, Jack D. Crime and Justice in American Society. Indianapolis: Bobbs-Merrill, 1971. 297pp. 2130

Downie, Leonard, Jr. Justice Denied--The Case for Reform of the Courts. New York: Praeger, 1971. 224pp. 2131

Elliott, James Franklin. Interception Patrol--An Examination of the Theory of Random Patrol as a Municipal Police Tactic. Springfield, Ill.: Charles C. Thomas, 1973. 87pp. 2132

_______, and Sardino, Thomas J. Crime Control Team; An Experiment in Municipal Police Department Management and Operation. Springfield, Ill.: Charles C. Thomas, 1971. 121pp. 2133

Federal Aviation Admin. "Rules for Escorting Prisoners via Air Transportation." Law Officer, 6(4):49-50, 1973. 2134

Fernez, F. "Evidence Technicians: Innovations in Training, Photographic and Field Operation Techniques." Law and Order, 21 (7):66-71, 1973. 2135

Flaherty, David H. "Law and the Enforcement of Morals in Early

America." *Perspectives in American History*, 5:203-53, 1971.
2136

Flynn, John Joseph. *History of the Chicago Police: From the Settlement of the Community to the Present Time.* Chicago: Police Book Fund, 1887; reprinted, 1971. 2137

Folley, V. L. *Police Patrol Techniques and Tactics.* Springfield, Ill.: Charles C. Thomas, 1973. 210pp. 2138

Fox, Richard H., and Cunningham, Carl L. *Crime Scene Search and Physical Evidence Handbook.* Washington, D.C.: National Criminal Justice Reference Service, Law Enforcement Assistance Admin., U.S. Dept. of Justice, 1973. 2139

Franey, W. H. "An Academy for Police and Public Safety Aviation." *Police Chief,* 38:16-18, June 1971. 2140

Frank, John P. *American Law; The Case for Radical Reform.* New York: Macmillan, 1969. 216pp. 2141

Fraser, Gordon. *Modern Transportation and International Crime.* Springfield, Ill.: Charles C. Thomas, 1970. 108pp. 2142

Gallati, R. J. "The Role of the Courts in a State-wide Criminal Justice Information System." *Police,* 16(9):18-23, 1972. 2143

Glaser, Daniel. *Adult Crime and Social Policy.* Englewood Cliffs, N.J.: Prentice-Hall, 1972. 128pp. 2144

_______. *Crime in the City.* New York: Harper, 1970. 308pp.
2145

Goebel, Julius, Jr., and Naughton, T. Raymond. *Law Enforcement in Colonial New York.* Montclair, N.J.: Patterson Smith Pub. Corp., 1944; reprinted, 1970. 2146

Gwynne, J. L. "The Specific Concern Test for the Detection of Deception." *Journal of Police Science Administration,* 2(1):38-39, 1974. 2147

Hair, Robert A., and Samm, Sinclair. *How to Protect Yourself Today.* New York: Stein and Day, 1970. 301pp. 2148

Halleck, Seymour L. *Psychiatry and the Dilemmas of Crime.* Berkeley: University of California Press, 1971. 382pp. 2149

Hansom, C. B. 'Modern Interrogation Techniques." *Outpost,* 11-14, Sept. 1972. 2150

Herren, Riidiger. "Psychograph of the International Swindler." *International Criminal Police Review,* 210-215, Oct. 1972.
2151

Hicks, R. D. Undercover Operations and Persuasion. Springfield, Ill.: Charles C. Thomas, 1973. 91pp. 2152

Horan, Michael J.; Baines, John M.; and Hajjar, Sami G. "The Sheriff's Role in Law Enforcement." Police, 15, Sept. 1971. 2153

Hubbard, D. G. "The Skyjacker and Security--A Disconcerting Profile. Paper Presented at the International Security Conference in Chicago, Illinois, May, 1973." Security World Magazine, 10(7):16-28, 1973. 2154

"The Illinois Bureau of Investigation--An Innovation in Law Enforcement." Police, 14:71-72, Nov.-Dec. 1970. 2155

Inbau, Fred E. Criminal Law for the Police. Philadelphia: Chilton Book Co., 1969. 164pp. 2156

________; Moenssens, A. A.; and Vitullo, L. R. Scientific Police Investigation. Philadelphia: Chilton Book Co., 1972. 204pp. 2157

Interpol. Powers and Duties of the Police: Search of Persons and Premises and the Seizure of Property. XLIIth General Assembly Session, Vienna, 2nd-9th October, 1973. Paris, Interpol, 1973. 223pp. 2158

Irwin, John. The Felon. Englewood Cliffs, N.J.: Prentice-Hall, 1970. 2159

Jacob, Herbert. Urban Justice: Law and Order in American Cities. Englewood Cliffs, N.J.: Prentice-Hall, 1973. 145pp. 2160

Jennings, John B. The Flow of Arrested Adult Defendants Through the Manhattan Criminal Court in 1968 and 1969. New York: N.Y. City Rand Institute, 1971. 131pp. 2161

________. The Flow of Defendants Through the New York City Criminal Court in 1967. New York: N.Y. City Rand Institute, 1970. 29pp. 2162

Kakalik, James S., and Wildhorn, Sorrel. Aid to Decisionmaking in Police Patrol. A Report Prepared for the Department of Housing and Urban Development. Santa Monica, Calif.: Rand Corp., 1971. 115pp. 2163

________, ________. Law and Private Police. Santa Monica, Calif.: Rand Corp.; Washington, D.C.: L.E.A.A. National Institution of Law Enforcement and Criminal Justice, 1972. 85pp. 2164

Kelley, Clarence M. "Major Case Squad for Metropolitan Areas." F.B.I. Law Enforcement Bulletin, 42:22-25, May 1973. 2165

Kelly, David B. "State Police Tactical Patrol: A Very Logical Conclusion." Police Chief, 40:66-69, May 1973. 2166

Klonoski, James Richard, and Mendelsohn, Robert I. The Politics of Local Justice. Boston: Little, Brown, 1970. 2167

Koverman, R. B. "Team Policing: An Alternative to Traditional Law Enforcement Techniques." Journal of Police Science Administration, 2(1):15-19, 1974. 2168

Kuykendall, J. L. "Alternative Models for Determining Community Police Manpower." Journal of California Law Enforcement 7(4): 169-174, 1973. 2169

_______, and Gould, J. V. "Cooperative Police Serves: A Study Design." Police, 16(9):40-47, 1972. 2170

Lamson, P. A. "A Concentrated Robbery Reduction Program." F. B. I. Law Enforcement Bulletin, 40(12):16-20, & 26, 1971. 2171

Larsen, R. C. Urban Police Patrol Analysis. Cambridge, Mass.: MIT Press, 1972. 289pp. 2172

Leonard, Vivian Anderson. Criminal Investigation and Identification. Springfield, Ill.: Charles C. Thomas, 1971. 152pp. 2173

_______. Police Crime Prevention. Springfield, Ill.: Charles C. Thomas, 1972. 195pp. 2174

_______. The Police Detective Function. Springfield, Ill.: Charles C. Thomas, 1970. 111pp. 2175

_______. Police Patrol Organization. Springfield, Ill.: Charles C. Thomas, 1970. 105pp. 2176

_______. The Police, the Judiciary, and the Criminal. Springfield, Ill.: Charles C. Thomas, 1969. 235pp. 2177

Lipsky, Michael. Law and Order, Police Encounters. Chicago: Aldine Pub. Co., 1970. 144pp. 2178

Mann, Floyd H. "A New Image for Campus Police." F. B. I. Law Enforcement Bulletin, 42:13-17, 30, Feb. 1973. 2179

Martin, R. W. "Transparent Bullet-Resisting Glazing Materials Separating Fact from Fiction." Police, 16(10):28-32, 1972. 2180

Merrill, W. Jay, et al. Case Screening and Selected Case Processing in Prosecutors' Offices. Washington, D. C.: National Criminal Justice Reference Service, Law Enforcement Assistance Admin., U. S. Dept. of Justice, 1973. 2181

Messer, R. A. "Anti-Hijacking Program." Law Officer, 6(4):27, 1973. 2182

Mishkin, Barry D. "Police Patrols in New York City." International Criminal Police Review, 28(265):36-44, Feb. 1973. 2183

Mitchell, P. S. "Optimal Selections of Police Patrol Beats." Journal of Criminal Law and Criminology, 63(4):577-584, 1972. 2184

Moolman, Van. Practical Ways to Prevent Burglary and Illegal Entry. Buffalo, N.Y.: Cornerstone Library, 1970. 2185

Mooney, W. R. "The Special Operations Group. Chicago's Answer to Unusual Demands for Police Service." F.B.I. Law Enforcement Bulletin, 41(4):11-14, & 32, 1972. 2186

More, Harry W., Jr. The New Era of Public Safety. Springfield, Ill.: Charles C. Thomas, 1970. 233pp. 2187

Motto, Carmine J. Undercover. Springfield, Ill.: Charles C. Thomas, 1971. 2188

Newman, O. Defensible Space; Crime Prevention Through Urban Design. New York: Macmillan, 1972. 264pp. 2189

Pace, Denny F. Handbook of Vice Control. Englewood Cliffs, N.J.: Prentice-Hall, 1971. 84pp. 2190

________, and Styles, Jimmie C. Handbook of Narcotics Control. Englewood Cliffs, N.J.: Prentice-Hall, 1972. 96pp. 2191

The Patrol Operation. Gaithersburg, Maryland: International Assoc. of Chiefs of Police, 1970. 2192

Pendland, Melvin B., and Gay, Wayne G. "Foot Patrols: The Fort Worth Experience." Police Chief, 39(4):46-48, April 1972. 2193

Reichert, I. "Shoot-out in Kensington High Street: The British Response to a London Bank Robbery." California State Bar Journal, 48(2):144-150, 1973. 2194

Reiser, Martin. The Police Department Psychologist. Springfield, Ill.: Charles C. Thomas, 1972. 119pp. 2195

________; Sokol, R. J.; and Saxe, S. J. "An Early Warning Mental Health Program for Police Sergeants." Police Chief, 39(6):38-39, 1972. 2196

Ringel, William E. Searches and Seizures, Arrests and Confessions. New York: Clark Boardman Co., 1972. 511pp. 2197

Roberts, Duke. <u>An Introduction to Modern Police Firearms.</u> Beverly Hills, Calif.: Glencoe Press, 1969. 170pp. 2198

Robitaille, E. W. "Court Time Costs for Police: They Can Be Reduced!" <u>Police Chief,</u> 39(4):14-15, 1972 2199

Sagall, Elliot L. <u>The Law and Clinical Medicine.</u> Philadelphia: Lippincott, 1970. 224pp. 2200

Schwartz, A. J. "Crisis-communication and the Police Officer." <u>Police,</u> 16(6):11-13, 1972. 2201

Schwartz, Louis B. <u>Law Enforcement Handbook for Police.</u> St. Paul, Minn.: West Pub. Co., 1970. 333pp. 2202

Schwartz, Richard D., and Skolnick, Jerome H. <u>Society and the Legal Order, Cases and Material in the Sociology of Law.</u> New York: Basic Books, 1970. 652pp. 2203

Shaw, W. "The Kodak Technical Library." <u>Law and Order,</u> 20(4): 38-40, 42, 44, 50, 1972. 2204

________. "Should We Develop a Nonlethal Sidearm for Police Use?" <u>Law and Order,</u> 21(6):84-89, 1973. 2205

Shook, H. C. "Revitalized Methods Needed for Investigation of Rape Complaints." <u>Police Chief,</u> 40(12):14-15, 1973. 2206

Sweizer, R. B., and Sanfelice, G. "The Personal Patrol Car Program." <u>F.B.I. Law Enforcement Bulletin,</u> 42(9):16-20, 1973. 2207

Sylvain, Georges. <u>Defense and Control Tactics.</u> Englewood Cliffs, N.J.: Prentice-Hall, 1971. 74pp. 2208

Tobias, M. W. <u>Locks, Safes and Security; A Handbook for Law Enforcement Personnel.</u> Springfield, Ill.: Charles C. Thomas, 1971. 338pp. 2209

Torres, Donald. "The Colorado Bureau of Investigation." <u>Police Chief,</u> 78-81, March 1972. 2210

________. "The Minnesota Bureau of Criminal Apprehension: A State Investigation Agency." <u>Police Chief,</u> 39:42-45, Jan. 1972. 2211

________. "The Oklahoma Bureau of Investigation." <u>Police Chief,</u> 39:80-82, April 1972. 2212

Vandervelde, Marjorie. "Chief of Police on the Last Frontier." <u>Law and Order,</u> 21:53, July 1973. 2213

Weis, Charles W. <u>Diversion of the Public Inebriate from the</u>

Criminal Justice System. Washington, D.C.: National Criminal Justice Reference Service, Law Enforcement Assistance Admin., U.S. Dept. of Justice, 1973. 2214

Westbrook, J. W. "Crimes Without Plaintiffs. The Challenging Concept of 'Victimless Crimes'." Baylor Law Review, 25(1):37-51, 1973. 2215

Weston, Paul B. Criminal Investigation: Basic Perspectives, 2nd ed. Englewood Cliffs, N.J.: Prentice-Hall, 1974. 448pp. 2216

_______. Criminal Justice and Law Enforcement: Cases. Englewood Cliffs, N.J.: Prentice-Hall, 1972. 185pp. 2217

_______, and Wells, Kenneth M. Law Enforcement and Criminal Justice: An Introduction. Pacific Palisades, Calif.: Goodyear Pub. Co., 1972. 320pp. 2218

Wilkie, F. E. "Police Monitoring of Holdup and Burglary Alarms." Police Chief, 41(4):65-66, 1974. 2219

Williams, M. "The M-1 30 Caliber Carbine for Police Work." Law and Order, 20(6):66-67, 70-71, 108, 1972. 2220/1

D. URBAN VIOLENCE

Brown, Richard Maxwell. "The American Vigilante Tradition," in Graham, Hugh Davis, and Gurr, Ted Robert, eds., History of Violence in America (New York: Signet, 1969). 2222

Campbell, James S., and Sahid, Joseph R. Law and Order Reconsidered: U.S. National Commission on Prevention of Violence. Washington, D.C.: U.S. Gov. Printing Office, 1969. 2223

Carson, D. G., and Richardson, M. P. 'Mobile Emergency Command Center." F.B.I. Law Enforcement Bulletin, 42(12):6-21, 1973. 2224

Chaiken, J. M., and Larson, R. C. Methods for Allocating Urban Emergency Units. New York: N.Y. City Rand Institute, 1971. 55pp. 2225

Cohen, Nathan, ed. Los Angeles Riots: A Socio-Psychological Study. New York: Praeger, in cooperation with Institute of Government and Public Affairs, University of California. 1970. 742pp. 2226

Conant, Ralph Wendell. The Prospects for Revolution; A Study of Riots, Civil Disobedience and Insurrection in Contemporary

America. New York: Harper's Magazine Press, 1971. 290pp. 2227

________, and Molly Apple Levin. Problems in Research on Community Violence. New York: Praeger, 1969. 97pp. 2228

Danto, B. L. "A Step Toward Control of Violence by Firearms." Police Law Quarterly, 3(2):44-47, 1974. 2229

Fawcett, Jan. Dynamics of Violence. Chicago: American Medical Assoc., 1971. 198pp. 2230

Feshbach, Seymour. Television and Aggression; An Experimental Field Study. San Francisco: Jossey-Bass, 1971. 186pp. 2231

Fogelson, Robert M. Violence As Protest; A Study of Riots and Ghettos. Garden City, N.Y.: Doubleday, 1971. 265pp. 2232

Fooner, M. "The Vulnerable Society. Crisis in Technology, Terror, and Victimization." Police Chief, 41(2):26-27, 1974. 2233

Graham, Hugh D., and Gurr, Ted Robert. Violence in America--Historical and Comparative Perspectives; U.S. National Commission on Prevention of Violence. Washington, D.C.: U.S. Gov. Printing Office, 1969. 2234

Gupta, O. P. "Short-Notice Bomb-Scare Warning System." Police, 16(2):14-15, 1972. 2235

Gurr, Ted Robert. Why Men Rebel. Princeton, N.J.: Princeton University Press, 1970. 421pp. 2236

Hormachea, C. R. Confrontation, Violence and the Police. Boston: Holbrook Press, 1971. 183pp. 2237

Hortsman, P. L. "Assaults on Police Officers. How Safe Are You?" Police Chief, 40(12):44, 46-48, 53, 1973. 2238

Kirkham, James F. Assassination and Political Violence; A Report to the National Commission on the Causes and Prevention of Violence. New York: Bantam Books, 1970. 752pp. 2239

Kronholm, W. C. "Blue Power: The Threat of the Militant Policeman." Journal of Criminal Law, Criminology and Police Science, 63(2):294-299, 1972. 2240

Lenz, Robert R. "The Bomb Squad." Police, 39-43, Nov. 1971. 2241

Leonard, V. A. Police Pre-Disaster Preparation. Springfield, Ill.: Charles C. Thomas, 1973. 330pp. 2242

Lowi, Theodore J. The Politics of Disorder. New York: Basic Books, 1971. 193pp. 2243

Mark, Vernon H. Violence and the Brain. New York: Harper & Row, 1970. 170pp. 2244

Morgan, J. P., Jr., and Dankel, J. "Community Action Unit Works with Demonstrators to Head Off Violence." Police Chief, 40(3): 36-37, 1973. 2245

Mulvihill, Donald F.; Tumin, Melvin, M.; and Curtis, Lynn A. Crimes of Violence. Washington, D.C.: U.S. Gov. Printing Office, 1969. 2246

Najmuddin, D. "The Kidnapping of Diplomatic Personnel." Police Chief, 40(2):18-23, 1973. 2247

'National Bomb Data Center." F.B.I. Law Enforcement Bulletin, 42(12):13-15, 1973. 2248

Ochberg, Frank M.; Daniels, David N.; and Gilula, Marchall F. Violence and the Struggle for Existence. Work of the Committee on Violence of the Department of Psychiatry, Stanford University. Boston: Little, Brown, 1970. 451pp. 2249

O'Neill, M. E. and Bloom, C. J. "The Field Officer: Is He Really Fighting Crime?" Police Chief, 39(2):30-32, 1972. 2250

Pickney, Alphonso. The American Way of Violence. New York: Random House, 1972. 235pp. 2251

Quinney, R. 'Who Is the Victim?" Criminology, 10(3):314-323, 1972. 2252

Report on Urban Violence Problems; Transcript of Nimlo Seminar on Urban Violence and Environmental Problems. National Institution of Municipal Law Officers, 1970. 2253

Short, James F., and Wolfgang, Marvin E. Collective Violence. Chicago: Aldine, 1972. 387pp. 2254

Singer, Jerome L. The Control of Aggression and Violence--Cognitive and Physiological Factors. New York: Academic Press, 1971. 171pp. 2255

Steverson, D. L. "The Revolutionary-Arsonist." Fire Arson Investigator, 24(1):27-36, 1973. 2256

Vandalism and Violence-Innovative Strategies Reduce Cost to Schools. National School Public Relations Assoc., 1971. 2257

E. JUVENILES

Becker, Harold K. "Policeman or Teacher?" Police Chief, 39(10): 54-285, Oct. 1972. 2258

_______. "The Student and the Law." Police Chief, 39(3):75-77, March 1972. 2259

Binder, A.; Green, R. P.; and Newkirk, M. "University-Police Cooperative Approach to Juvenile Diversion: Evaluating Its Applicability and Effectiveness." Journal of Criminal Justice, 1(3):255-264, 1973. 2260

Buss, William G. "Legal Aspects of Crime Investigation in the Public Schools." National Organization on Legal Problems of Education, 1971. 2261

Cain, T. J. "Youth Services: A Police Alternate to the Juvenile Justice System." Law and Order, 21(1):2-23, 33, 1973. 2262

Clinton, J. "Working with Youth." Law and Order, 21(12):58-60, 1973. 2263

Cortes, Juan B. Delinquency and Crime, A Biopsychosocial Approach. New York: Seminar Press, 1972. 468pp. 2264

Cressey, Donald R. Delinquency, Crime, and Social Process. New York: Harper & Row, 1969. 1,151p. 2265

Damos, J. P., and Barry, W. "Four Program Models in Delinquency Prevention." F.B.I. Law Enforcement Bulletin, 43(1): 26-30, 1974. 2266

Dill, R. K., and Grahm, R. F. "Police-Youth Relations." Military Police Journal, 22(11):8-9, 1973. 2267

Duxbury, E. "Law Enforcement and Youth Service Bureaus." In: Evaluation of Youth Service Bureaus (Sacramento: State of California Dept. of the Youth Authority, 1973). 2268

Emerson, Robert M. Judging Delinquents, Context and Process in Juvenile Court. Chicago: Aldine, 1969. 283pp. 2269

Farnen, R. F., Jr., and German, D. B. "The Jurisprudence of Youth and Adults. Some Research Findings." Youth and Society, 4(4):443-482, 1973. 2270

Flammang, C. J. The Police and the Underprotected Child. Springfield, Ill.: Charles C. Thomas, 1970. 310pp. 2271

Fox, Sanford J. The Law of Juvenile Courts in a Nutshell. St. Paul, Minn.: West Pub. Co., 1971. 286pp. 2272

Gibbons, Don C. *Delinquent Behavior.* Englewood Cliffs, N. J.: Prentice-Hall, 1970. 288pp. 2273

Hahn, P. H. *The Juvenile Offender and the Law.* Cincinnati: W. H. Anderson Co., 1971. 416pp. 2274

Harris, T. O. "Alternatives Available in Solving the Juvenile Problems." *Police Chief,* 40(9):42-43, 1973. 2275

Haskell, Martin R., and Yablonsky, Lewis. *Crime and Delinquency.* Chicago: Rand McNally, 1970. 517pp. 2276

Hauser, Stuart T. *Black and White Identity Formation--Studies in the Psychosocial Development of Lower Socioeconomic Class Adolescent Boys.* New York: Wiley-Interscience, 1971. 160pp. 2277

Healy, William. *The Individual Delinquent--A Text-Book of Diagnosis and Prognosis for All Concerned in Understanding Offenders.* Montclair, N. J.: Patterson Smith, 1969 (orig. pub. 1915). 830pp. 2278

Hicks, H. C. "Juvenile Delinquency and One Vehicle for Its Control." *Police Chief,* 39(10):278-283, 1972. 2279

Isom, J. E. "Law Enforcement in Public Schools: A Case Study." *Journal of California Law Enforcement*, 8(3):140-142, 144-145, 1974. 2280

Kobetz, R. W. *The Police Role and Juvenile Delinquency.* Gaithersburg, Md., International Assoc. of Chiefs of Police, 1971. 264pp. 2281

Kreins, E. S. "A Community Resource Program for Youth; De-emphasizing the Punitive/Accentuating the Positive." *Police Chief,* 39(3):36, 38 and 41, 1972. 2282

Madison, Arnold. *Vandalism; The Not-So-Senseless Crime.* New York: Seabury Press, 1970. 148pp. 2283

Manella, F. L. "The Three Worlds of Youth." *Police Chief,* 39(9): 53-54, 1972. 2284

Miller, Frank W. *The Juvenile Justice Process.* New York: Foundation Press, Inc., 1971. 2285

Polk, Kenneth, and Schafer, Walter E., eds. *Schools and Delinquency.* Englewood Cliffs, N. J.: Prentice-Hall, 1972. 265pp. 2286

Portune, R. G. *Changing Adolescent Attitudes Toward Police; A Practical Sourcebook for Schools and Police Departments.* Cincinnati: W. H. Anderson Co., 1971. 273pp. 2287

Reed, Hohn P., and Baali, Fuad, eds. Faces of Delinquency: A Reader. Englewood Cliffs, N. J.: Prentice-Hall, 1972. 432pp. 2288

Seymour, J. A. "Youth Services Bureaus." Law and Society Review, 7(2):247-272, 1972. 2289

Somerville, James G. "A Study of the Preventive Aspect of Police Work with Juveniles." Criminal Law Review, Aug. 1969, pp. 407-414; Sept. 1969, pp. 472-484. 2290

Thomson, D., and Treger, H. "Police-Social Work Cooperation and the Over-Burden of the Juvenile Court." Police Law Quarterly, 3(1):28-39, 1973. 2291

Tobias, J. J. "Guidelines for Disposition of Juvenile Cases." Police Chief, 39(10):40-43, 1972. 2292

Trojanowicz, Robert C. Juvenile Delinquency: Concepts and Control. Englewood Cliffs, N. J.: Prentice-Hall, 1973. 368pp. 2293

Voss, Harwin L. Ecology, Crime, and Delinquency. New York: Appleton-Century-Crofts, 1971. 328pp. 2294

Walker, R. N. Psychology of the Youthful Offender, 2nd ed. Springfield, Ill.: Charles C. Thomas, 1973. 150pp. 2295

F. DRUGS

Ambrose, Myles J. "How U.S. Customs Fights the Drug Traffic." Police Chief, 38:60-63, Jan. 1971. 2296

Bishop, C. "Metro Narcs: A Collective Effort." Police Chief, 39(10):56-57, 1972. 2297

Bridge, Carl J. Alcoholism and Driving. Springfield, Ill.: Charles C. Thomas, 1972. 84pp. 2298

Eckerman, William C. Drug Usage and Arrest Charges. Washington, D. C.: Bureau of Narcotics and Dangerous Drugs, 1971. 73pp. 2299

Leblanc, A. G., and Brennan, M. E. "The Drinking Driver; Use of Videotape and Personality Testing in Detection and Study." Police Chief, 40(12):58-76, 1973. 2300

Little, J. W. "An Empirical Description of Administration of Justice in Drunk Driving Cases." Law and Society Review, 7(3):473-492, 1973. 2301

Mikkelsen, M. "Drug Law Enforcement; Report Submitted to the Second International Congress on Drug Abuse and Addiction Held in Paris, 11-15, September, 1972." International Criminal Police Review, 28(271):259-271, 1973. 2302

Nash, G. "The Rights and Responsibilities of Drug Abusers and Those Affected by Them." Drug Forum, 3(1):43-50, 1973. 2303

Robertson, L. S.; Rich, R. F.; and Ross, H. L. "Jail Sentences for Driving While Intoxicated in Chicago: A Judicial Policy That Failed." Law and Society Review, 8(1):55-67, 1973. 2304

Schenck, W. J. "The Drinking Driver: Citations Instead of Jail?" Police Chief, 39(7):38-40, 1972. 2305

Solursh, Lionel P. Illusinogenic Drugs-Their Effects on Criminal Responsibility. Toronto: Canadian Mental Health Assoc., 1970. 37pp. 2306

Standards for the Staffing and Organization of Municipal Narcotics and Dangerous Drug Enforcement Units. International Assoc. of Chiefs of Police, 1970. 2307

Travnikoff, Basil. How to Examine a Chemist in Drug Abuse Cases. Carmichael, Calif., 1971. 44pp. 2308

III. CRIMINAL LAW (3000)

Part III lists and annotates articles, periodicals and books relating to the field of criminal law. In the General Works section especially, the writings of well known legal scholars on the theory of criminal law and criminal responsibility are included along with works on the socio-legal aspect of crimes. Articles, books, and cases dealing with criminal law are listed.

Further, the compilers have attempted to include as much of the country as possible by locating and often annotating articles that pertain both to specific geographical sections of the country and to states which have furnished clear guidance on the law involved in the specific subject area.

Homicide is covered in detail as well as some of the more common criminal offenses such as abortion, kidnapping, robbery, burglary and so on. Defenses in general have been presented. The various rules of determining insanity have been covered in detail with many of the citations annotated.

A. GENERAL WORKS

(1) ARTICLES

Amsterdam, A. "Criminal Law Today and Tomorrow." Hawaii Bar Journal, 9:31, summer 1972. 3000

"Anti-Crime Club." Business Week, 1266:126, Dec. 1953. Businessmen in Cleveland formed the Crime Clinic to help police combat crime in their places of business. 3001

Austin, E. C. "Expanding Scope of the Criminal Law." Chicago Bar Record, 55:177, Jan.-Feb. 1974. 3002

"Bill of Obligations: Balance Is Vital to U.S." Vital Speeches of the Day, 29:634, Aug. 1, 1963. 3003

Brakel, S. J., and Sanda, G. R. "Diversion from the Criminal Process in the Rural Community." American Criminal Law Quarterly, 7:122, spring 1969. 3004

Brands, J. V. "Criminal Law in the Seventies." American Bar Association Journal, 56:769, Aug. 1970. Maintains that simple changes in laws and court procedures, state and federal, are necessary to enhance the esteem accorded our criminal law by the public. Calls for the legal profession to scrutinize its procedures in arrest, bail interrogation, trial procedure and sentencing. 3005

_______. "Criminal Law in the Seventies: Some Suggestions." New York State Bar Journal, 42:282, June 1970. 3006

Burke, L. H., and Patton, R. H. "Emergency War Powers of Cities." The American City, 57:107, Feb. 1942. Brief summary of the law and major cases of law relating to suspension of legal rights in times of extreme danger. 3007

Campbell, W. J. "Delays in Criminal Cases." Oklahoma Bar Journal Quarterly, 44:626, June 1973. 3008

_______. "Proposals for Improvements in the Administration of Criminal Justice." Chicago Bar Review, 54:75, Nov. 1972. 3009

"Challenge of Obsolete Criminal Statutes." Journal of Criminal Law and Criminology, 65:315, summer 1974. 3010

Clark, T. C. "Courts, the Police and the Community." Southern California Law Review, 46:1, Dec. 1972. 3011

_______. "Criminal Justice in America." Texas Law Review, 46:742, April 1968. 3012

Cohn, A. W. "Training in the Criminal Justice Nonsystem." Federal Probation, 38:32, June 1974. 3013

"The Constitutionality and Social Effect of 'Stop and Frisk'." Maryland Law Forum, 11:97, spring 1972. 3014

"Crime Does Pay Because We Do Not Back Up Our Police." New York Times Magazine, June 13, 1965, 44pp. Statistics show the rapid crime rate rise in the past several years. Discusses the problems of police dealing with an apathetic public and the public attitude. 3015

"Criminal Law and Criminal Procedure: A Symposium." The Hastings Law Journal, 51:77, summer 1965. Contains the following: "Shortcomings in the Administration of Criminal Law," by A. Holtzoff; "Some Weak Points in the Model Penal Code," by R. M. Perkins; "Police Interrogation and the Right to Counsel, post Escobedo v. Illinois: Application v. Emasculation," by H. B. Rothblatt; "Penal Code Section 654: The Prosecutor's Dilemma," by G. M. Schneider; "Fair Trial and Prejudicial Publicity: A Need for Reform," by J. T. McCarthy. 3016

"Criminal Law: New Common Law Crimes by Judicial Fiat." University of Florida Law Review, 27:266, fall 1974. 3017

"Crisis in Crime Control." America, 113:238, Sept. 4, 1965. 3018

Daniels, C. W. "Impact of the Equal Rights Amendment in the New Mexico Criminal Code." New Mexico Law Review, 3:106, Jan. 1973. 3019

Dash, S. "Means and Methods Employed in Penal Law." Criminal Law Bulletin, 10:57, summer 1974. 3020

Denner, B. "Did a Crime Occur? Should I Inform Anyone? A Study of Deception." Journal of Personality, 36:454, Sept. 1968. 3021

Finney, D. J. "Police Duties at Crime Scenes." Journal of Criminal Law, Criminology and Police Science, 27:231, July 1936. 3022

Gilverber, D. J. "Application of Equal Protection Principles to Selective Enforcement of the Criminal Law." University of Illinois Law Forum, 1973:88, 1973. 3023

Grafton, Samuel. "What Has Happened to Law and Order in the U.S.?" Look, 26:13, July 13, 1962. Rising crime rates in the U.S. and suggestions for citizens that would help lower the rates. 3024

Gramenos, J. N. "Investigation and Discovery in a Criminal Case." Chicago Bar Record, 49:386, June 1968. 3025

Gresman, B. A. "The Discretionary Enforcement of Law." Chitty's Law Journal, 21:46, Feb. 1973. 3026

Hall, J. "Perennial Problems of Criminal Law." Hofstra Law Review, 1:15, Sept. 1973. 3027

Hartt, E. P. "Some Thought on the Criminal Law and the Future." Canadian Bar Review, 51:59, March 1973. 3028

Hooper, A. "Discovery in Criminal Cases." Canadian Bar Review, 50:445, September 1972. 3029

Hug, J. P. "Presumptions and Inferences in Criminal Law." Milwaukee Law Review, 56:81, spring 1972. 3030

Kahn, E. J., Jr. "Annals of Law (A False Arrest); Be Just and Fear Not." New Yorker, 96:76, Feb. 6, 1971. 3031

Liebmann, G. W. "Chartering a National Police Force." American Bar Association Journal, 56:1070, Nov.-Dec. 1970. 3032

Lunden, Walter A. "Pioneers in Criminology: Emile Durkheim." Journal of Criminal Law, Criminology and Police Science, 49:2,

May-June 1958. Durkheim said that crime is due to any imperfection of human nature or society; it is not only normal for society but necessary. Without crime there could be no evolution in law. The kind and the degree of punishment and the rationale behind sanctions have varied according to the organizational structure of a society. 3033

McGee, M. C. "Towards a New Criminal Code for Alabama." Alabama Lawyer, 35:19, Jan. 1974. 3034

McKinnon, Harold R. "Terror in the Streets; Behind the Rise in U.S. Crime." U.S. News and World Report, 53:54, Dec. 24, 1962. Reasons certain crime rates are rising: willingness to violate certain laws on the part of the otherwise law-abiding citizenry because the law is unpopular. 3035

Miller, C. J. "Silence and Confessions--What Are They Worth." Criminal Law Review, 1973:239, June 1973. 3036

"News and the Accused." Prospectus, 3:95, Dec. 1969. 3037

Parker, William H. "The California Crime Rise." The Journal of Criminal Law, Criminology and Police Science, 47:721, May 26, 1956. Various causes for crime rate increase, from the training of police officers to the court decisions. 3038

Penegar, K. L. "Appraising the System of Criminal Law, Its Processes and Administration." North Carolina Law Review, 47:69, Dec. 1968. 3039

Phillips, L., and Votey, H. L., Jr. "Economic Analysis of the Deterrent Effect of Law Enforcement in Criminal Activity." Journal of Criminal Law, 63:330, Sept. 1972. 3040

Powell, M. "Old Problems Resurrected?" New Law Journal, 124:47, Jan. 17, 1974. 3041

"Recent Trends in Criminal Law." Journal of Criminal Law and Criminology, 65:514, Dec. 1974. 3042

"Review of the U.S. Supreme Court's Recent Criminal Law and Procedure Decisions." Pennsylvania Bar Association Quarterly, 45:52, Jan. 1974. 3043

Rezneck, D. A. "Justice Brennan and Discovery in Criminal Cases." Rutgers-Camden Law Journal, 4:85, fall 1972. 3044

"Women and Criminal Law: A Symposium." American Criminal Law Review, 11:291, winter 1973. Introduction: Women and the criminal law, women and the correctional process; The trial of a rape case: An advocate's analysis of corroboration, consent and character; The victim in a forcible rape case: A feminist view; Discretionary sentencing of women offenders: The argument for ERA in a nutshell. 3045

(2) BOOKS

Allen, Francis. *Borderline of Criminal Justice.* Chicago: University of Chicago Press, 1964. 3046

Armitage, Arthur L., and Turner, James W. C. *Cases on Criminal Law,* 3rd ed. Cambridge, England: Cambridge University Press, 1964, 3rd ed. Second revision keyed to Kenny's Outline of Criminal Law. Discipline of criminal evidence as material to be covered in the regular course of evidence. 3047

Asch, Sidney. *Police Authority and the Rights of the Individual,* 2nd ed. New York: Arco Publishers, 1968. 3048

Bassiouni, M. Cheriff. *Criminal Law and Its Processes.* Springfield, Ill.: Charles C. Thomas, 1969. This book markedly separates the general part of substantive criminal law from the specific part, for the first time in any comprehensive work, a unified study of all legal defenses follows the study of "principles and theories of criminal law." These legal defenses cover such questions as chronic alcoholism, drug addiction, AUBI, contrasting insanity and incompetency, and former jeopardy, self-defense and infancy. The section on "status criminality" as a defense is probably the only one of its kind to be found in any textbook. 3049

Becker, Harold K.; Felkenes, George T.; and Whisenand, Paul M. *New Dimensions in Criminal Justice.* Metuchen, N.J.: Scarecrow Press, 1968. 3050

Bishop, Joel Prentice. *Bishop on Criminal Law.* Chicago: T. H. Flood and Co., 1923, 2 vols. 3051

Blumberg, Abraham. *Criminal Justice.* Chicago: Quandrangle Books, 1967. 3052

________. *The Scales of Justice.* Chicago: Aldine Publishers, 1970. 3053

Bopp, William. *Principles of American Law Enforcement and Criminal Justice.* Springfield, Ill.: Charles C. Thomas, 1974. 3054

Burdick, William L. *The Law of Crime.* New York: Matthew Bender and Co., 1946. 3 vols. Basic reference work in criminal law for common law and statutory crimes. 3055

Caldwell, Robert G. *Criminology,* 2nd ed. rev. New York: Ronald Press, 1957. The causation of crime and delinquency, their repression and prevention: the individual and the group, biological factors, environmental influences, crime and the criminal, the limitations and contributions of the scientific method, the responsibility of the private citizen and the professional. 3056

Cohn, Nathan, ed. *Criminal Law Seminar.* Brooklyn, N.Y.: Central Book Co., 1961. 3057

Cole, George F. *Criminal Justice: Law and Politics.* Belmont, Calif.: Duxbury Press, 1972. 3058

Conyers, Robert W. *Law--Its Nature, Functions, and Limits.* Englewood Cliffs, N.J.: Prentice-Hall, 1965. The author has "captured the excitement of living in law." Contains a practical table of cases, quoted materials, and extensive bibliographies. 3059

Day, Frank D. *Criminal Law and Society.* Springfield, Ill.: Charles C. Thomas, 1964. The right of individuals, the protection of individual rights and the individual's responsibility to society. 3060

Deming, Richard. *Man and Society: Criminal Law at Work.* New York: Hawthorne, 1970. 3061

Donnelly, Richard C. *Criminal Law.* New York: Free Press of Glencoe, 1962. Discusses criminal law, problems of promulgation, invocation, and administration. 3062

Douglas, Jack, D., ed. *Crime and Justice in American Society.* New York: Bobbs-Merrill, 1971. 3063

Earle, Howard H. *Police-Community Relations.* Springfield, Ill.: Charles C. Thomas, 1970. 3064

Eldefonso, Edward. *Readings in Criminal Justice.* Beverly Hills, Calif.: Glencoe Press, 1973. 3065

Felkenes, George T. *The Criminal Justice System: Its Function and Personnel.* Englewood Cliffs, N.J.: Prentice-Hall, 1973. 3066

Fisher, Edward C. *Vehicle Traffic Law.* Evanston: Traffic Institute, Northwestern University, 1961. Development of traffic problems and laws, power to regulate, validity, double jeopardy, elements, general issues and defenses, types of violations, such as right-of-way, and prosecution. 3067

Fricke, Charles W. *California Criminal Law,* 8th ed., rev. Los Angeles: Legal Book Store, 1961. Comprehensive reference book. Basic rules of criminal law as declared by the appellate decisions in California and the U.S. Supreme Court. Trends are discussed as necessary. 3068

Goldstein, Abraham S. *The Insanity Defense.* New Haven, Conn.: Yale University Press, 1967. 3069

Hart, H. L. A. *The Concept of Law.* Oxford, England: Clarendon Press, 1961. 257pp. A new analysis of the notions of legal validity, sovereignty, and the foundation of a legal system; a re-examination of natural law and legal positivism; an original discussion of the limits of formalism in the judicial process; and an assessment of the character of international law. 3070

Hartung, Frank E. Crime, Law and Society. Detroit: Wayne State University Press, 1965. Broad candid statement of the causes and nature of crime and of the problems involved in societal (including legal) responses to crime. Contains much illustrative material. 3071

Hill, Jerome. Cases and Materials on Criminal Law and Procedure, 2nd ed. New York: Bobbs-Merrill, 1965. 3072

Housel, Theodore W., and Walser, Guy O. Defending and Prosecuting Federal Criminal Cases. New York: Dennis and Co., 1956. 3073

Hutnick, Melroy B. Criminal Law and Court Procedures. Albany, N.Y.: Delmar Publishers, 1974. 3074

Inbau, Fred. Criminal Law for the Layman. Philadelphia: Chilton, 1970. 3075

Kaplan, John. Criminal Justice: Introductory Cases and Materials. Mineola, N.Y.: Foundation Press, 1973. 3076

Kerper, Hazel B., Jr. Introduction to the Criminal Justice System. St. Paul, Minn.: West Pub. Co., 1972. 3077

Klotter, John. Constitutional Law for Police, 2nd ed. Cincinnati: Anderson, 1971. 3078

La Fave, Wayne. Handbook on Criminal Law. St. Paul, Minn.: West Pub. Co., 1972. 3079

LeGrand, James L. The Basic Processes of Criminal Justice. Beverly Hills, Calif.: Glencoe Press, 1973. 3080

Miller, Justin. Handbook of Criminal Law. St. Paul, Minn.: West Pub. Co., 1934. Early textbook attempts to provide a clear statement of the rules and principles of law wherever possible. The larger aspects of criminal law are discussed and a variety of approaches to the administration of criminal justice offered. 3081

Millspaugh, Arthur C. Local Democracy and Crime Control. Washington, D.C.: Brookings Institute, 1936. 3082

Morris, Terence. The Criminal Area. New York: Humanities Press, 1957. A study in social ecology. 3083

Mueller, Gerhard O. W. Crime, Law and the Scholars. Seattle:

University of Washington Press, 1969. 3084

National Clearinghouse for Mental Health Information. International Bibliography on Crime and Delinquency. Washington, D. C.: U. S. Gov. Printing Office, various vols. 3085

National Commission on Reform of Federal Criminal Laws. A Proposed New Federal Criminal Code. Washington, D. C.: U. S. Gov. Printing Office, 1971. 3086

Niederhoffer, Arthur, and Blumberg, Abraham S. The Ambivalent Force: Perspectives on the Police. Waltham, Mass.: Ginn and Co., 1970. 3087

Pakenham, Fancis Aungier. Causes of Crime. London: Weidenfeld and Nicolson, 1958. 3088

Patrick, Clarence. The Police, Crime, and Society. Springfield, Ill.: Thomas 1972. 3089

Reasons, Charles E., and Kuykendal, Jack L., eds. Race, Crime and Justice. Pacific Palisades, Calif.: Goodyear Pub. Co., Inc., 1972. 3090

Reinhardt, James Melvin. The Psychology of Strange Killers. Springfield, Ill.: Charles C. Thomas, 1962. Individual studies of a small group of "multicides." 3091

Skolnick, Jerome H. Justice Without Trial: Law Enforcement in Democratic Society. New York: John Wiley, 1967. 3092

Smith, Alexander. Crime and Justice in a Mass Society. Waltham, Mass.: Xerox College Printing, 1972. 3093

Toch, Hans, ed. Legal and Criminal Psychology. New York: Holt, Rinehart and Winston, 1961. Anthology "to provide the student, the interested layman, and the specialist with facts about people involved in the process of criminal justice." Its authors--lawyers, social scientists, and practicing criminologists--report, in unusually clear language, some of the basic data on the causation of crime, its treatment, and the psychology of those who practice law. 3094

Trebach, Arnold. The Rationing of Justice. New Brunswick, N. J.: Rutgers University Press, 1964. 3095

Waters, James R., and McGrath, Sheree A. Introduction to Law Enforcement. Columbus, Ohio: Charles E. Merrill Pub. Co., 1974. 3096

Webster, John A. The Realities of Police Work. Dubuque, Iowa: Kendall/Hunt Pub. Co., 1973. 3097

Weston, Paul B., and Wells, Kenneth M. Law Enforcement and Criminal Justice. Pacific Palisades, Calif.: Goodyear Pub. Co., 1972. 3098

Wharton, Francis, and Ruppenthal, J. C. Wharton's Criminal Law. New York: Lawyers' Co-operative Pub. Co., 1932. 3 vols. Complete analysis of criminal law. Discusses the basis of criminal jurisprudence and all of the various crimes against society. 3099

Whisenand, Paul M.; Cune, James L.; and Felkenes, George T. Police-Community Relations: Readings in the Development of Effective Environmental Relations. Pacific Palisades, Calif.: Goodyear Pub. Co., 1974. 3100

Winslow, Robert W., ed. Crime in a Free Society. Endino, Calif.: Dickenson Pub. Co., 1968. 3101

Young, R. Bryce. Criminal Law: Codes and Cases. New York: McGraw-Hill, 1972. 3102

Zarr, Melvyn. The Bill of Rights and the Police. Dobbs Ferry, N.Y.: Oceana Publishers, 1970. 3103

B. THE NATURE OF CRIME

(1) THE LANGUAGE OF PENAL STATUTES

Barwick, G. "Divining the Legislative Intent." Australian Law Journal, 35:97, Aug. 1961. 3104

Bishin, W. R. "Law Fingers: An Essay in Statutory Interpretation." Southern California Law Review, 38:1, 1965. 3105

Brazil, P. "Legislative History and the Sure and True Interpretation of Statutes in General and the Constitution in Particular." University of Queens Law Journal, 4:1, April 1961. 3106

"Challenge of Obsolete Statutes." Journal of Criminal Law and Criminology, 65:315, summer 1974. 3107

"Counsel at the Interrogation Stage." American Criminal Law Quarterly, 8:41, fall 1969. 3108

"Criminal--in General--Courts Have Power as Custodes Morum to Punish Conspiracy to Do Acts Newly Defined as Corruptive of Public Morals." Harvard Law Review, 75:1652, June 1962. 3109

Dickerson, F. R. "Statutory Interpretation: Core Meaning and

Marginal Uncertainty." Montana Law Review, 29:1, winter 1964. 3110

"Judicial Law Making in Relation to Statutes: A Symposium." Indiana Law Journal, 36:411, summer 1961. 3111

MacCallum, G. C., Jr. "Legislative Intent." Yale Law Journal, 75:754, April 1966. 3112

Merrill, M. H. "Judicial Interpretation of Legislation." Oklahoma Bar Association Journal, 32:1347, July 29, 1961. 3113

"Miranda and Minor Offenses." Arizona Law Review, 14:766, 1972. 3114

Packer, Herbert L. "The Case for Revision of the Penal Code." Stanford Law Review, 13:252, March 1961. 3115

"Presence Requirement and the 'Police-Team' Rule in Arrest for Misdemeanors." Washington and Lee Law Review, 26:119, spring 1969. 3116

Rault, G. A., Jr. "On Louisiana's New Homicide Statutes: Purpose, Constitutionality and Problems of Interpretation." Loyola Law Review, 19:563, fall 1973. 3117

Roybal, E. R. "Void for Vagueness: State Statutes Proscribing Conduct Only for a Juvenile." Pepperdine Law Review, 1:1, 1973. 3118

"Statutory Construction--Legislative Intent--Use of Extrinsic Aids in Wisconsin." Wisconsin Law Review, 1964:660, July 1964. 3119

"Unexplained Possession Principal Challenged on Fifth Amendment Grounds." South Carolina Law Review, 20:457, 1968. 3120

Wilson, W. A. "Complexity of Statutes." Modern Law Review, 37:497, summer 1974. 3121

(2) EX POST FACTO LAWS

Bender, P. "Retroactive Effect of an Overruling Constitutional Decision: Mapp. v. Ohio." University of Pennsylvania Law Review, 110:650, March 1962. 3122

"Constitutional Law--Procedural Alterations Applied Retroactively." Mercer Law Review, 24:491, winter 1973. 3123

"Constitutional Rules of Criminal Procedure and the Application of Linkletter (Linkletter v. Walker)." Journal of Public Law, 16:193, 1967. 3124

"Partial Retroactivity: A Question of Equal Protection." Temple Law Quarterly, 43:239, spring 1970. 3125

"Prospectivity and Retroactivity of Supreme Court Constitutional Interpretations." University of Richmond Law Review, 5:129, fall 1970. 3126

"Retroactivity." Memphis State University Law Review, 4:521, spring 1974. 3127

'Retroactivity and Prospectivity of Supreme Court Constitutional Interpretation." New York Law Foundation, 19:289, fall 1973. 3128

"Retroactivity in Criminal Procedure: The Supreme Court Monday Morning Quarterback." University of Miami Law Review, 24:139, fall 1969. 3129

"Retroactivity of Constitutional Decision." Notre Dame Lawyer, 41:206, Dec. 1965. 3130

"Retroactivity of Criminal Procedure Decisions." Iowa Law Review, 55:1309, June 1970. 3131

Rossum, R. A. 'New Rights and Old Wrongs: The Supreme Court and the Problem of Retroactivity." Emory Law Journal, 23:381, spring 1974. 3132

"Tehan v. U. S. 86 Supreme Court 459." North Carolina Law Review, 44:1096, June 1966. 3133

"Today's Law and Yesterday's Crime: Retroactive Application of Ameliorative Criminal Legislation." University of Pennsylvania Law Review, 121:120, Nov. 1972. 3134

Torcia, C. E., and King, D. B. 'Mirage of Retroactivity and Changing Constitutional Concepts." Dickinson Law Review, 66:269, spring 1962. 3135

(3) CONFLICT BETWEEN JURISDICTIONS

"Accord and Conflict Between State and Federal Court Jurisdictions." New York County Bar Bulletin, 27:58, 1969-1970. 3136

Anderson, L. L. "Line Between Federal and State Court Jurisdiction." Michigan Law Review, 63:1203, May 1965. 3137

"Application of Criminal Law to Acts Committed Outside the Jurisdiction." American Criminal Law Quarterly, 6:32 fall 1967. 3138

"Governmental Lawbreaking and Contrived Jurisdiction Under the

Travel Act." Connecticut Law Review, 6:577, spring 1974. 3139

Le Flair, R. A. "Conflict of Laws: Choice of Law in Criminal Cases." Case Western Reserve Law Review, 25:44, fall 1974. 3140

Moore, J. W. "Conflict of Jurisdiction." Louisiana Law Review, 23:29, Dec. 1962. 3141

"Piggyback Jurisdiction in the Proposed Federal Criminal Cases." Yale Law Journal, 81:1209, May 1972. In depth view of the reform measures of the proposed federal criminal code as released to federal jurisdiction and the provision for "piggyback" jurisdiction; concludes with alternatives to the piggyback jurisdiction of the federal criminal code. 3142

"Place of Crime Determines Jurisdiction as Well as Venue." Dickinson Law Review, 77:561, spring 1973. 3143

Schindler, P. M. "Interjurisdictional Conflict and the Right to a Speedy Trial." University of Cincinnati Law Review, 35:279, spring 1966. 3144

Schwab, H. J. "Have Crime, Will Travel: Borderlines and California Jurisdiction." California State Bar Journal, 50:30, Jan.-Feb. 1975. 3145

Vollmann, T. "Criminal Jurisdiction in Indian Country: Tribal Sovereignty and Defendant's Rights in Conflict." Kansas Law Review, 22:387, spring 1974. 3146

(4) DOUBLE JEOPARDY

"Application of the Fifth Amendment--Double Jeopardy Clause to the States Through the Fourteenth Amendment." Villanova Law Review, 15:233, fall 1969. 3147

"Bentin v. Maryland: A Further Extension of the Rights of the Individual in Criminal Proceedings." Kansas Law Review, 18:309, winter 1970. 3148

Carr, J. G. "Effect of the Double Jeopardy Clause in Juvenile Proceedings." University of Toledo Law Review, 6:1, fall 1974. 3149

"Constitutional Law: Double Jeopardy, Equal Protection and Due Process--Harsher Sentences on Retrial." American University Law Review, 19:290, March 1970. 3150

"Criminal Justice: Double Jeopardy--Abolition of the Dual Sovereignty Theory of City-State Prosecutions." Louisiana Law Review, 31:540, April 1971. 3151

"Criminal Law: The Same Offense in Oklahoma--Now You See It, Now You Don't." Oklahoma Law Review, 28:131, winter 1975. 3152

"Double Jeopardy and Government Appeals of Criminal Dismissals." Texas Law Review, 52:303, Jan. 1974. 3153

"Double Jeopardy and Reprosecution After Mistrial: Is the Manifest Necessity Test Manifestly Necessary?" Northwestern University Law Review, 69:887, Jan.-Feb. 1975. 3154

"Double Jeopardy and the Juvenile." Journal of Family Law, 11: 603, 1972. 3155

"Double Jeopardy--Grants of Mistrial for Marginal Improper Conduct of Defense Counsel Is Error and Bars Reprosecution Under Fifth Amendment." Harvard Law Review, 82:1752, June 1969. 3156

"Double Jeopardy, Multiple Prosecution and Multiple Punishment: A Comparative Analysis." California Law Review, 50:853, Dec. 1962. 3157

"Double Jeopardy--The 'Same Evidence Test' Applied." Louisiana Law Review, 33:474, Sept. 1973. 3158

"Double Jeopardy v. Double Punishment--Confusion in California." San Diego Law Review, 2:86, Jan. 1965. 3159

"First Degree Murder Trial After Reversal of Manslaughter Conviction, State v. Thomas, 346 P. 2d 20." Arizona Law Review, 3:287, winter, 1961. 3160

Fisher, W. T. "Double Jeopardy and Federalism." Minnesota Law Review, 50:607, March 1966. 3161

"Interest Balancing: An Alternative Approach to Resolution of Double Jeopardy Claims." Iowa Law Review, 58:1000, April 1973. 3162

Kimmelman, W. M. "Double Jeopardy: A Political Perspective." Cumberland-Samford Law Review, 5:369, winter 1975. 3163

Maddux, David. "Identity of Offenses in Double Jeopardy Problem." Southern California Law Review, 32:51, fall 1958. 3164

"Mistrial and Double Jeopardy." New York University Law Review, 49:937, Nov. 1974. 3165

Sigler, J. A. "Federal Double Jeopardy Policy." Vanderbilt Law Review, 19:375, March 1966. 3166

Thompson, C. A. "Reversals for Insufficient Evidence: The Emerging Doctrine of Appellate Acquittal." Indiana Law Review, 8:497, 1975. 3167

"Towards an Integrated Theory of Interjurisdictional Double Jeopardy: An Alternative to Section 707 of the Proposed Federal Criminal Code." Cornell Law Review, 58:734, April 1973. 3168

C. HOMICIDE

(1) GENERAL WORKS

Arthur, C. "Homicide, Assault, Kidnapping and Related Offenses." Oregon Law Review, 51:459, spring 1972. 3169

Ashwarth, A. J. "Self-Induced Provocation and the Homicide Act." Criminal Law Review, 1973:483, Aug. 1973. 3170

Bailey, W. C. "Murder and the Death Penalty." Journal of Criminal Law and Criminology, 65:416, summer 1974. 3171

Blake, L. W. "Case for Retribution." New Law Journal, 123:862, Sept. 20, 1973. 3172

Boudouris, J. "Classification of Homicides." Criminology, 11:525, fall 1974. 3173

Bromberg, Walter. The Mold of Murder. New York: Grune & Stratton, 1961. A "panoramic view of the psychopathology of violent crime." Describes wanton killers, professional assassins, and mentally retarded persons; categories of "neurotic conditions--defensive act against unconscious homosexual impulses, compulsive sexual acts, reactions against impotence and the like." 3174

"California's Corpus Delicti Rule: The Case for Review and Clarification." UCLA Law Review, 20:1055, June 1973. 3175

Collings, Rex A. "Negligent Murder." California Law Review, 49: 254, May 1961. Circumstances exclusive of intent to kill, injure seriously, intent to commit a felony or resist arrest, and the "reasonable man" doctrine. 3176

"Corpus Delicti in Homicide--Absence of Body [People v. Scott, 176 Cal. Appl 504]." Tulane Law Review, 34:820, June 1960. 3177

Dieckmann, Edward A., Sr. Practical Homicide Investigation. Springfield, Ill.: Charles C. Thomas, 1961. 3178

Snyder, LeMoyne. Homicide Investigation. Springfield, Ill.: Charles C. Thomas, 1956. 3179

Southwestern Law Enforcement Institute. Institute on Homicide Investigation Techniques, Dallas, 1961. Springfield, Ill.: Charles C. Thomas, 1961. Experiences of qualified peace officers, doctors, lawyers and technical experts in solving problems of investigating violent deaths. Some topics are: interrogation of suspects and witnesses, identification of human remains, sexual motivation in killing, the peace officer as a witness, firearms identification. 3180

Tanay, E. "Murder, Psychiatry and the Law." Michigan State Bar Journal, 44:17, May 1965. 3181

Tappan, P. W. "Official Homicide." The Forum, 106:398, Nov. 1946. 3182

A Treatise on the Law of Homicide. Supervised by Thomas Johnson Michie. Charlottesville, Va.: Michie Co., 1914. 2088pp. One of the first and foremost works on homicide; exhaustive treatment of homicide, murder, manslaughter, assault with intent to kill, excusable or justifiable homicide, and the use of evidence to establish guilt. 3183

Willett, T. C. Criminal on the Road: A Study of Serious Motoring Offenses and Those Who Commit Them. London: Tavistock Publications, 1964. English investigation of three basic questions: (1) Is there justification for regarding serious motoring offenses as crimes on a par with other criminal offenses? (2) Is the popular image of the serious motoring offender correct? (3) Are serious motoring offenders and their offenses valid subjects of criminological study? Willett's findings support affirmative answers to questions 1 and 3 and a negative answer to question 2. 3184

Wilson, Robert A., ed. Homicide Investigation Techniques. Springfield, Ill.: Charles C. Thomas, 1961. Papers delivered at 1961 Institute on Homicide Investigation conducted by the Southwestern Law Enforcement Institute, Dallas. Sixteen lectures; six cover non-medical aspects, two relate to law, and eight cover medico-legal problems. 3185

Witkin, B. E. California Crimes. San Francisco: Bender-Moss Co., 1963. 2 vols. Critical text treatment of the entire law of crimes, for law enforcement officials as well as the judge and lawyer. Cases, statutes, and the common law are discussed in great detail. Excellent reference in criminal laws. 3186

Zigler, M. S. "Use of Death Penalty v. Outrage at Murder." Crime and Delinquency, 20:333, Oct. 1974. 3187

(2) MALICE AND THE MENTAL ELEMENT

Burns, P. "Attempted Murder--Specific Intent to Kill--Recklessness--Constructive Malice." University of British Columbia Law Review, 8:364, 1973. 3188

Buxton, R. "Malice Afore Thought." Modern Law Review, 37:6761, Nov. 1974. 3189

Conradson, J. M. "Mens Rea in Relation to Drug Offenses." Otago Law Review, 2:131, Aug. 1970. 3190

"Constitutionality of the Common Law Presumption of Malice in Maine." Boston University Law Review, 54:973, Nov. 1974. 3191

"Criminal Intent." Modern Law Review, 30:431, July 1967. 3192

Cuomo, A. A. "Mens Rea and Status Criminality." Southern California Law Review, 40:463, spring 1967. 3193

Dubin, Gary V. "Mens Rea Reconsidered: A Plea for a Due Process Concept of Criminal Responsibility." Stanford Law Review, 18:322, Jan. 1966. The meaning behind the concept of criminal law excuses, constitutional issues, and the principles of criminal responsibility. Extensive reform in the criminal law of excuses needed. 3194

Elliot, D. W. "Mens Rea of Accessories After the Fact." Criminal Law Review, 1963:159, March 1963. 3195

Ferracuti, F. "Psychology of the Criminal Homicide." Revista Juridica de la Universidad de Puerto Rico, 32:569, 1963. 3196

Gibbens, T. C. N. "Sane and Insane Homicide." Journal of Criminal Law, Criminology and Police Science, 49:110, July-Aug. 1958. 3197

"Graduated Responsibility as an Alternative to Current Tests of Determining Criminal Capacity." Maine Law Review, 25:343, 1973. 3198

Irvine, C. N. "Mens Rea in Statutory Offenses." New Zealand Law Journal, 1963:345, June-July 1963. 3199

Lamming, D. J. "Vicarious Criminal Liability." New Law Journal, 122:740, Aug. 1972. 3200

Lowe, J. T. "Murder and the Reasonable Man." Criminal Law Review, 1958:453, July 1958. 3201

Luby, E. D. "Murder with Malice." Michigan State Bar Journal, 43:39, Aug. 1964. 3202

"Mens Rea and Murder by Torture in California." Stanford Law Review, 10:672, July 1958. Malice and premeditation in first degree murder. Explains murder by torture and the inference of the deed itself as not requiring proof of malice and/or premeditation. 3203

"Mens Rea Evaluated in Terms of the Essential Elements of a Crime, Specific Intent and Drunkenness." Ottawa Law Review, 4:356, winter 1971. 3204

"Mens Rea in Manslaughter." New Law Journal, 117:950, Sept. 1967. 3205

"Mental Ability in Assessing Culpability for Act Committed in Self-Defense." Stanford Law Review, 13:591, May 1961. Whether, as a basic proposition of criminal law, control over criminal behavior can best be achieved by reference to the actor's state of mind rather than the consequences of the act. 3206

"Mental Attitude Requirement in Criminal Law--And Some Exceptions." Journal of Criminal Law, 59:4, March 1968. 3207

Nutter, Ralph N. (Judge). "A Change in Rules of Criminal Responsibility?" Journal of State Bar of California, 39:101, Jan.-Feb. 1964. 3208

Packer, H. L. "Mens Rea and the Supreme Court." Supreme Court Review, 1962:107, 1962. 3209

"Punishment Rationale for Diminished Capacity." UCLA Law Review, 18:561, Feb. 1971. The origin and rationale of the use of diminished capacity as a defense in murder cases; calls for a reemphasis of the legal purposes and functions of the diminished capacity doctrine to include considerations of the goals and reality of punishment. 3210

Seidman, R. B. "Witch Murder and Mens Rea: A Problem of Society under Radical Social Change." Modern Law Review, 28:46, Jan. 1965. 3211

Silving, H. "Mental Incapacity in Criminal Law." Current Law, 2:3, 1961. 3212

Smith, J. M. "Case of Reckless Murder." New Law Journal, 123:792, Aug. 23, 1973. 3213

Stuart, D. "Mens Rea, Negligence and Attempts." Criminal Law Review, 1968:647, Dec. 1968. 3214

Turpin, C. C. "Mens Rea in Manslaughter." Cambridge Law Journal, 1962:200, Nov. 1962. 3215

Yashuda, J. "Mens Rea in Statutory Offenses." New Law Journal

118:330, April 4, 1968. 3216

(3) DEFENSES TO HOMICIDE

"Codification of 'Rights of Self-Defense'." Creighton Law Review, 3:174, fall 1969. 3217

"Criminal Law--Homicide--Self-Defense--The Duty to Retreat." Duquesne Law Review, 9:313, winter 1970. The case of commonwealth v. Johnston, 438 PA 485, 263 A. 2d 376 (1970) viewed as a change from retreat rule to no retreat rule by the Pennsylvania Supreme Court. 3218

"Defensive Physical Force: How Much Is Too Much?" Oregon Law Review, 51:579, spring 1972. 3219

"Diminished Capacity and Non-Statutory Involuntary Manslaughter--Diminished Capacity Due to Mental Defect or Mental Illness Can Reduce Homicide to Involuntary Manslaughter." Santa Clara Lawyer, 15:210, fall 1974. 3220

Frosh, S. B. "Unnecessary Killing by the Over-Zealous Peace Officer." Journal of Criminal Law, Criminology and Police Science, 31:601, Jan. 1941. 3221

"Homicide--Heat of Passion--Self-Defense--Imminence of Danger." Washburn Law Journal, 1:146, winter 1960. 3222

"Homicide in Defense and Under Provocation." Law Quarterly Review, 78:166, April 1962. 3223

"Justification for the Use of Force: Self-Defense." Stanford Law Review, 13:566, May 1961. How much force can be used to protect one's interests; a detailed examination of the necessity and degree of force, and of duty to retreat. 3224

"Justified Use of Deadly Force." Criminal Law Bulletin, 4:3, Jan.-Feb. 1968. 3225

Murray, C. R. "Civil Disturbance, Justifiable Homicide and Military Law." Military Law Review, 54:129, fall 1971. 3226

O'Regan, R. S. "Duress and Murder." Modern Law Review, 35:596, Nov. 1972. 3227

________. "Indirect Provocation and Misdirected Retaliation." Criminal Law Review, 1968:319, June 1968. 3228

Parker, G. E. "Plea of Self-Defense Resulting in Manslaughter." Alberta Law Review, 3:16, 1963. 3229

Robin, G. D. "Justifiable Homicide by Police Officers." Journal of Criminal Law, Criminology and Police Science, 54:244, June 1963. 3230

Samuels, A. "Excusable Loss of Self--Control in Homicide." Modern Law Review, 34:163, March 1971. 3231

"Self-Defense-Duty to Retreat--Retreats from the Porch of One's Own Home Not Required." Seton Hall Law Review, 3:532, spring 1972. 3232

"Strict Vicarious Liability for the Acts of a Victim." Capital University Law Review, 1:232, 1972. 3233

"Use of Deadly Force in the Apprehension of Fugitives from Arrest." McGill Law Journal, 14:293, June 1968. 3234

(4) CAUSATION

"Confessions and Causation." Law Quarterly Review, 75:464, Oct. 1959. 3235

"Effect of Willfulness on the Burden of Proof of Factual Causation." Iowa Law Review, 55:1073, April 1970. 3236

Green, E. "Race, Social Status, and Criminal Arrest." American Sociological Review, 35:476, April 1970. 3237

Haddad, William A. "Proximate Cause: Must an Intervening Force Be Foreseeable." University of Florida Law Review, 17:538, winter 1965. Summary of the causation issues in a homicide. The "foreseeability test", is exemplified by a Florida case decision. 3238

"Judicial Affirmance of the Validity of the Year-and-a-Day Rule in Maryland." University of Baltimore Law Review, 4:186, fall 1974. 3239

Montagu, A. "Chromosomes and Crime." Psychology Today, 2:43, Sept. 1968. 3240

Rosenberg, A. H., and Dunn, L. J., Jr. "Genetics and Criminal Responsibility." Massachusetts Law Quarterly, 56:413, 1971. 3241

Rubin, L. "Premenstrual Syndrome and Criminal Responsibility." UCLA Law Review, 19:209, Dec. 1971. 3242

Williams, J. E. H. "Chromosome Abnormality and Legal Accountability." Criminologist, 5:29, Nov. 1970. 3243

Wood, J. C. "Two Problems in Causation." Modern Law Review, 22:514, Sept. 1959. 3244

(5) CRIMINAL NEGLIGENCE

Desch, S. C. "Negligent Murder." Modern Law Review, 26:660, Nov. 1963. 3245

"Duty to Take Reasonable Care." Law Quarterly Review, 86:454, Oct. 1970. 3246

Evans, J. V. "Willful Misconduct--What Does It Really Mean?" Trial Lawyers Guide, 17:203, summer 1973. 3247

Fletcher, G. P. "Theory of Criminal Negligence: A Comparative Analysis." University of Pennsylvania Law Review, 119:401, Jan. 1971. 3248

"Manslaughter--Culpable Negligence." University of Miami Law Review, 13:384, spring 1959. 3249

"Negligence and the General Problem of Criminal Responsibility." Yale Law Journal, 81:949, April 1972. 3250

"Negligence--Intervening Criminal Act--Jury May Find That Retail Store Which Cooperated with Armed Robbers While Summoning Police by Automatic Silent Alarm Caused the Death of a Customer Killed by a Robber." Fordham Urban Law Journal, 2:661, spring 1974. 3251

"Negligent Homicide--Its Elusive Standard of Gross Negligence." Willamette Law Journal, 1:627, fall 1961. 3252

O'Hearn, P. J. T. "Criminal Negligence: An Analysis in Depth." Criminal Law Quarterly, 7:27, June 1964. 3253

(6) FELONY-MURDER AND MISDEMEANOR-MANSLAUGHTER RULES

Busch, J. P., and Fulgoni, D. J. "Diminished Capacity Applied to the Felony Murder Rule." Los Angeles Bar Bulletin, 47:291, June 1972. 3254

"California Supreme Court Assaults the Felony-Murder Rule." Stanford Law Review, 22:1059, May 1970. Reviews the criticisms of the California Supreme Court from 1965-1970 of the felony-murder rule and shows the rationale the court uses in such cases. 3255/6

"Criminal Law: California's 'Vicarious Murder Theory' Extends Felony-Murder Doctrine." Valparaiso University Law Review, 5:676, spring 1971. 3257

"Criminal Law--Vicarious Liability--Robber Convicted of Murder When Robbery Victim Killed Accomplice." West Virginia Law Review, 74:204, Nov., Jan. 1971-72. 3258

"Criminal Liability of a Participant in Crime for the Death of a Fellow Participant." Syracuse Law Review, 22:1065, 1971. 3259

"Criminal Responsibility for the Death of a Co-Felon: Taylor v. Superior Court of Alameda County (CA) 477 P. 2d 131." California Western Law Review, 7:522, spring 1971. 3260

"Diminished Capacity Defense to Felony-Murder." Stanford Law Review, 23:799, April 1971. 3261

"Felon Not Responsible for Accidental Death of Bystander Shot by Police." Dickinson Law Review, 74:756, summer 1970. 3262

"Felony Murder--An Anomaly in the Intent Element of Robbery [Jones v. People(Cdo) 360 P. 2 686]." Rocky Mountain Law Review, 8:438, spring 1962. 3263

"Felony-Murder--Elimination of the Element of Scrambling Possession for Application of the Felony-Murder Rule to Robbery." Santa Clara Lawyer, 14:188, fall 1973. 3264

"Felony-Murder in Georgia: A Lethal Anachronism." Georgia State Bar Journal, 9:462, May, 1973. 3265

"Felony-Murder in Illinois." University of Illinois Law Forum, 1974:685, 1974. 3266

"Merger and the California Felony-Murder Rule." UCLA Law Review, 20:250, Dec. 1972. 3267

Rickett, Robert R. "California Rewrites Felony Murder Rule." Stanford Law Review, 18:690, Feb. 1966. The history of felony murder rule in California up to 1965, when a significant change in the doctrine was made by the California Supreme Court. Discusses malice per se doctrine in the felony murder rule. 3268

"Taming the Felony-Murder Rule." Santa Clara Lawyer, 14:97, fall 1973. 3269

(7) MURDER

Burns, P. "Attempted Murder--Specific Intent to Kill--Recklessness--Constructive Malice." University of British Columbia Law Review, 8:364, 1973. 3270

"California Rewrites Felony Murder Rule." Stanford Law Review, 18:690, fall 1966. 3271

"Circumstantial Evidence of Corpus Delicti Held Sufficient for Murder Conviction." Maryland Law Review, 20:180, spring 1960. 3272

"Criminal Law--Heat of Passion--Inclusive and Exclusive Nature." Brooklyn Law Review, 27:351, April 1961. 3273

"Criminal Law--Psychiatric Evidence Ruled Admissible in Murder Prosecution to Determine Whether Defendant Acted in Heat of Passion." Dickinson Law Review, 77:435, winter 1973. 3274

Danforth, F. W., Jr. "Model Penal Code and Degrees of Criminal Homicide." American University Law Review, 20:148, spring 1963. 3275

"Deliberation and Premeditation in First Degree Murder [Cummings v. State (165 Atlantic 2d 886)]." Maryland Law Review, 21:349, fall 1961. 3276

O'Regan, R. S. "Duress and Murder." Modern Law Review, 35: 596, Nov. 1972. 3277

Perkins, R. M. "Corpus Delicti of Murder." Virginia Law Review, 48:173, March 1962. 3278

Tanay, E. "Psychiatric Study of Homicide." American Journal of Psychiatry. 125:1252, March 1969. 3279

White, S. "Note on Provocation (Murder)." Criminal Law Review, 1970:446, Aug. 1970. 3280

Williams, J. E. H. "Developments in the Law of Homicide, 1954-1963." Criminal Law Review, 1964:84, fall 1964. 3281

(8) MANSLAUGHTER

"Criminal Law--Involuntary Manslaughter." Iowa Law Review, 47: 168, fall 1961. 3282

"Criminal Law--Involuntary Manslaughter--Proximate Cause." Boston University Law Review, 42:140, winter 1962. 3283

"Fallacy and Fortuity of Motor Vehicle Homicide." Nebraska Law Review, 41:793, June 1962. 3284

"Heroin Deaths: Homicidal Responsibility of the Seller in New York." Albany Law Review, 37:497, 1973. 3285

"Homicide--Defendant's Unlawful or Reckless Conduct Must Be Direct Cause of Death to Constitute Involuntary Manslaughter." Maryland Law Review, 22:78, winter 1962. 3286

"Homicide--Manslaughter--Causal Connection Between Act and Death Under Misdemeanor Rule." Notre Dame Lawyer, 38:127, Jan. 1962. 3287

Leigh, L. H. "Manslaughter and the Limits of Self-Defense." Modern Law Review, 34:685, Nov. 1971. 3288

"Manslaughter and the Adequacy of Provocation: The Reasonableness of the Reasonable Man." University of Pennsylvania Law Review, 106:1021, May 1958. 3289

(9) PUNISHMENT IN GENERAL

Andenaes, J. "General Preventive Effects of Punishment." University of Pennsylvania Law Review, 114:949, May 1966. 3290

Antunes, G., and Hunt, A. L. "Impact of Certainty and Severity of Punishment on Levels of Crime in American States: An Extended Analysis." Journal of Criminal Law, 64:486, Dec. 1973. 3291

Bennett, L. A. "Should We Change the Offender System?" Crime & Delinquency, 19:332, July 1973. 3292

Brooker, F. "Deterrent Effect of Punishment." Criminology, 9:469, Feb. 1972. 3293

Chambliss, W. J. "Deterrent Influence of Punishment." Crime & Delinquency, 12:70, Jan. 1966. 3294

"Criminal Law--Retrospective Application of Statute Reducing Penalty." Wayne Law Review, 18:1157, May-June 1972. 3295

"Double Punishment for Burglarious Offenses." Washington & Lee Law Review, 23:161, spring 1966. 3296

Gerstein, R. S. "Punishment and Self-Incrimination." American Journal of Jurisdiction, 16:84, 1971. 3297

Gilman, D. "Developments in Correctional Law." Crime and Delinquency, 21:163, April 1975. 3298

"Impact of Court Decisions on the Correctional Process." Crime and Delinquency, 20:129, April 1974. 3299

Maurithe, H. E. "Correctional Dilemma: The Societal Deviant." Journal of Beverly Hills Bar Association, 6:69, Sept. 1972. 3300

Morris, N. "Future of Punishment: Toward a Punitive Philosophy." Michigan Law Review, 72:1161, May 1974. 3301

Mueller, G. O. W. "Tasks of Penology: A Symposium of Prisons and Correctional Law." Nebraska Law Review, 45:7, Jan. 1966. 3302

"Murder-Evidence Sufficient to Infer Deliberation and Premediation [People v. Steward 318 P. 2d 806]." Villanova Law Review, 3:565, June 1958. 3303

Pettigrew, R. A. "Corrections: Protecting Society or Recycling Criminals?" Florida Bar Journal, 48:260, April 1974. 3304

"Pre-trial Detention: Constitutional Standards." Arkansas Law Review, 28:129, spring 1974. 3305

"Prisoners and Their Basic Rights." Idaho Law Review, 11:45, fall 1974. 3306

Rubin, S. "Developments in Correctional Law." Crime and Delinquency, 17:213, April 1971. 3307

Scott, J. E. "Use of Discretion in Determining the Severity of Punishment for Incarcerated Offenders." Journal of Criminal Law and Criminology, 65:214, June 1974. 3308

Shover, N. "Experts and Diagnosis in Correctional Agencies." Crime and Delinquency, 20:347, Oct. 1974. 3309

Stubbs, R. S. "On Crime and Punishment." Manitoba Law Journal, 1:283, 1964-65. 3310

Sultan, A. "Recent Judicial Concepts of 'Cruel and Unusual' Punishment." Villanova Law Review, 10:271, winter 1965. 3311

"Trial Judge's Freedom and Responsibility in Administering Probation [U. S. v. Worcester 190 Federal Supplement 548]." Yale Law Journal, 71:551, Jan. 1962. 3312

Warren, M. Q. "Classification of Offenders as an Aid to Efficient Management and Effective Treatment." Journal of Criminal Law, 62:239, June 1971. 3313

"What Constitutes Punishment." Notre Dame Lawyer, 39:594, Aug. 1964. 3314

(10) DEATH PENALTY

Bedan, H. A. "The Death Penalty as a Deterrent: Arraignment and Evidence." Ethics, 80:185, April 1970. 3315

________. "Death Penalty in America." Federal Probation, 35:32, June 1971. 3316

________. "Deterrence and the Death Penalty: A Reconsideration." Journal of Criminal Law, 61:539, Dec. 1970. 3317

________. "Nixon Administration and the Deterrent Effect of the

Death Penalty." University of Pittsburgh Law Review, 34:557, summer 1973. 3318

Browning, J. R. "New Death Penalty Statutes: Perpetuating a Costly Myth." Gonzaga Law Review, 9:651, spring 1974. 3319

"Capital Punishment Statutes After Furman." Ohio State Law Journal, 35:651, 1974. 3320

Carroll, J. M. "Death Penalty Provision of the New Penal Code." Kentucky Bar Journal, 38:15, Oct. 1974. 3321

Caswell, S. "Capital Punishment: Cementing a Fragile Victory." Trial, 10:47, May-June 1974. 3322

Cohen, B. L. "The Need for Capital Punishment." Chitty's Law Journal, 20:86, March 1972. 3323

"Constitutional Law: Capital Punishment for Rape Constitutes Cruel and Unusual Punishment When no Life is Taken or Endangered." Minnesota Law Review, 56:95, Nov. 1971. 3324

"Death Penalty: A Cruel and Unusual Punishment." Southwestern Law Journal, 27:298, May 1973. 3325

"Death Penalty--The Alternatives Left After Furman v. Georgia (92 Sup. Ct. 2726)." Albany Law Review, 37:344, 1973. 3326

"Discretion and the Constitutionality of the New Death Penalty Statutes." Harvard Law Review, 87:1690, June 1974. 3327

"In Defense of Capital Punishment." Kentucky Law Journal, 54:742, summer, 1966. 3328

Jewel, H. H. "Death Penalty." California State Bar Journal, 36: 228, March-April 1961. 3329

Meltsner, M. "Capital Punishment: The Moment of Truth." Juris Doctor, 2:4, Nov. 1971. 3330

"Mental Suffering Under Sentence of Death: A Cruel and Unusual Punishment." Iowa Law Review, 57:814, Feb. 1972. 3331

O'Halloran, A. "Capital Punishment." Federal Probation, 29:33, June 1965. 3332

Polsby, D. D. "Death of Capital Punishment? Furman v. Georgia (92 Sup. Ct. 2727)." Supreme Court Review, 1972:1, 1972. 3333

"Response to Furman (Furman v. GA, 92 Sup. Ct. 2726): Can Legislation Breathe Life Back into Death?" Cleveland State Law Review, 23:172, winter 1974. 3334

"Survival of the Death Penalty." Baylor Law Review, 23:499, summer 1971. 3335

"Trial Courts' Power to Reduce Punishments Fixed by Juries in First Degree Murder Trials." Hastings Law Journal, 13:474, May 1962. 3336

Vidmar, N., and Ellsworth, P. "Public Opinion and the Death Penalty." Stanford Law Review, 26:1245, June 1974. 3337

D. PHYSICAL AND PSYCHICAL INJURY

(1) ASSAULTS

"Assault on 'Assault'." Rutgers Camden Law Journal, 3:98, spring 1971. 3338

"Assault-Related Conduct Under the Proposed California Criminal Code." Hastings Law Journal, 25:657, Feb. 1974. 3339

"Assaulting and Obstructing the Police." Solicitors' Journal, 109: 542, July 9, 1965. 3340

"Battered Child: Logic in Search of Law." San Diego Law Review, 8:364, March 1971. 3341

Byrn, R. M. "Assault, Battery, and Maiming in New York: From Common Law Origins to Enlightened Revision." Fordham Law Review, 34:613, May 1966. 3342

"Defendant Cannot Be Convicted of Conspiracy to Assault Federal Officer Without Knowledge of His Victim's Federal Identity." Fordham Law Review, 43:128, Oct. 1974. 3343

"Evidentiary Problems in Criminal Child Abuse Prosecutions." Georgetown Law Journal, 63:257, Oct. 1974. 3344

"Final Assault on Attempted Assault." Santa Clara Lawyer, 14:83, fall 1973. 3345

Gamble, R. A. "Threats as Criminal Assault." Cleveland State Law Review, 20:75, Jan. 1971. 3346

"Legal Response to Child Abuse." William and Mary Law Review, 11:960, summer 1970. 3347

McKenna, J. J. "Case Study of Child Abuse: A Former Prosecutor's View." American Criminal Law Review, 12:165, summer 1974. 3348

Morse, H. N. "Aggression Syndrome." Georgia State Bar Journal, 9:451, May 1973. Defines aggression and correlates it with assaults, provocation and unexpected or unwarranted response and the holdings of various courts on those issues. 3349

North, P. M. "Civil and Criminal Proceedings for Assault." Modern Law Review, 29:16, Jan. 1966. 3350

Perkins, R. M. "Analysis of Assault and Attempts to Assault." Minnesota Law Review, 47:71, Nov. 1962. 3351

Pittman, D. J., and Handy, W. "Patterns in Criminal Aggravated Assault." Journal of Criminal Law, Criminology and Police Science, 55:462, Dec. 1964. 3352

"Recognition and Protection of the Family's Interests in Child Abuse Proceedings." Journal of Family Law, 13:803, 1973-74. 3353

Shepherd, R. E., Jr. "Abused Child and the Law." Washington and Lee Law Review, 22:182, fall 1965. 3354

(2) RAPE

Aitken, J. "Rape Prosecutions." Women Lawyers Journal, 60:176, fall 1974. 3355

Bornstein, F. P. "Investigation of Rape; Medicolegal Problems." Medical Trial Technique Quarterly, 9:61, March 1963. 3356

Dworkin, Roger B. "The Resistance Standard in Rape Legislation." Stanford Law Review, 18:680, Feb. 1966. Various tests of resistance by the female used by courts; the California law concerning consent discussed in detail. 3357

Findley, B. "Cultural Context of Rape." Women Lawyers Journal, 60:176, fall 1974. 3358

Goldner, N. S. "Rape As a Heinous But Understudied Offense." Journal of Criminal Law, 63:402, Sept. 1972. 3359

"Limitations on the Right to Introduce Evidence Pertaining to the Prior Sexual History of the Complaining Witness in Cases of Forcible Rape: Reflection of Reality or Denial of Due Process." Hofstra Law Review, 3:403, spring 1975. 3360

Landau, S. "Rape: The Victim As Defendant." Trial, 10:19, July-August 1974. 3361

Myers, L. W. "Reasonable Mistake of Age: A Needed Defense to Statutory Rape." Michigan Law Review, 64:105, Nov. 1965. 3362

"Nebraska's Corroboration Rule." Nebraska Law Review, 54:93, 1975. 3363

"People v. Hernandez, 393 P. 2d 673." Harvard Law Review, 78: 1257, April 1965; Hastings Law Journal, 16:270, Nov. 1964; Southern California Law Review, 38:131, 1965; Stanford Law Review, 17:309, Jan. 1965. This case involved a change in California law wherein a defendant in a statutory rape case is not permitted to establish as a defense the reasonableness of his belief that a female is over the statutory age limit. General state laws in the U. S. also discussed. 3364

"Prosecution for Assault with Intent to Rape Is Permissible Even After a Prior Acquittal for Rape and a Present Intent to Rape in the Future Completes the Offense." Texas Law Review, 51:360, Jan. 1973. 3365

"Rape and Rape Laws: Sexism in Society and Law." California Law Review, 61:919, May 1973. Rape laws, carefully based on traditional attitude about the social roles of women, do not deter rape and may even promote inadequate enforcement and judicial treatment. Change in law called for to relate more rationally to the reality of the crime and to the goal of sexual equality. 3366

"Rape Corroboration Requirement: Repeal Not Reform." Yale Law Journal, 81:1365, June 1972. 3367

"Rape in Illinois: A Denial of Equal Protection." John Marshall Journal of Practice and Procedure, 8:457, spring 1975. 3368

"Rape Victim: A Victim of Society and the Law." Willamette Law Journal, 11:36, winter 1974. 3369

"Resistance Standard in Rape Legislation." Stanford Law Review, 64:105, Nov. 1965. 3370

Shaffer, H. B. "Crime of Rape." Editorial Research Reports, 1972:43, 1972. 3371

Smith, C. J. "History of Rape Laws." Women Lawyers Journal, 60:176, fall 1974. 3372

Snelling, H. A. "What Is a Non-Consent (in Rape)." Australian Journal of Forensic Sciences, 2:103, March 1970. 3373

"Victim in a Forcible Rape Case: A Feminist View." American Criminal Law Review, 11:335, winter 1973. 3374

(3) KIDNAPPING

Caplan, Hilard D. "Some Other Faces of Kidnapping." Maryland

Law Forum, 2:109, spring 1972. Presents an analysis of Md.'s kidnapping statute in light of recent decisions in Calif. and Mass. and the distinctions between false imprisonment and kidnapping. 3375

"Criminal Law--Kidnapping--Asportation or Carrying Away is a Necessary Element of the Offense of Kidnapping." St. Mary's Law Journal, 4:119, spring 1972. 3376

"Extraterritorial Jurisdiction and Jurisdiction Following Forcible Abduction: A New Israeli Precedent in International Law." Michigan Law Review, 72:1087, April 1974. 3377

"Kidnapping and the Element of Asportation [Cotton v. Superior Ct. (Cal) 364 P. 2d 241]." Southern California Law Review, 35:212, winter 1962. 3378

"Kidnapping: Transportation as an Element [Cowan v. State (Tenn) 347 Sw 2d 37]." Georgia Bar Journal, 24:264, Nov. 1961. 3379

"People v. Dean (114 Cal Rptr. 555): Another Swipe at Miranda." University of San Fernando Valley Law Review, 4:85, spring 1975. 3380

Prosser, W. L. "Lindbergh Case Revisited: George Waller's 'Kidnap'." Minnesota Law Review, 46:383, Dec. 1961. 3381

"Room-to-Room Movement: A Risk Rationale for Aggravated Kidnapping [People v. Wein (Cal) 326 P. 2d 457]." Stanford Law Review, 11:554, May 1959. 3382

"Slight Movements Within an Enclosure Constitute Kidnapping." [People v. Wein (Cal) 326 P. 2d 457]." Hastings Law Journal, 11:323, Feb. 1959. 3383

"Specific Intent: An Element of 'Simple Kidnapping' [People v. Oliver (Cal) 361 P. 2d 593]." Southern California Law Review, 35:217, winter 1972. 3384

"Specific Intent as an Element of Simple Kidnapping." Hastings Law Journal, 10:323, Feb. 1959. The specific intent element of simple kidnapping is not predicted on the act itself, but may be coupled with many factors. The intent to kidnap does not even have to be present. The act of forcibly detaining a person for one of many criminal reasons may be enough to show specific intent to kidnap. 3385

Sponsler, T. H. "International Kidnapping." The International Lawyer, 5:27, Jan. 1971. 3386

"State v. Dix (N.C. 193 S.E. 2d 897): Common Law Kidnapping Requires a Substantial Asportation and an Increased Risk of Harm." North Carolina Central Law Review, 6:116, fall 1974. 3387

(4) ABORTION

"Abortion: A Legal Cop Out." New England Law Review, 7:311, spring 1972. 3388

"Abortion: Twenty-Four Weeks of Dependency." Baylor Law Review, 27:122, winter 1975. 3389

Bates, J. E. "Presentence Investigation in Abortion Cases." Crime and Delinquency, 9:306, July 1963. 3390

Brody, B. A. "Abortion and the Law." Journal of Philosophy, 68: 357, June 1971. 3391

Byrn, R. M. "Abortion Amendments: Policy in the Light of Precedent." St. Louis University Law Journal, 18:380, spring 1974. 3392

Byrne, R. P. "Critical Look at Legalized Abortion." Los Angeles Bar Bulletin, 41:320, May 1966. 3393

"Case of Abortion." Journal of Urban Law, 52:277, Nov. 1974. 3394

"Criminal Law--Feticide--The Unborn Child as a 'Human Being'." Tulsa Law Review, 45:408, Feb. 1971. 3395

"Father's Rights in the Abortion Decision." Texas Tech Law Review, 6:1075, spring 1975. 3396

"Feticide: Mens Rea with Partial Immunity?" Washburn Law Journal, 10:403, spring 1971. 3397

"Fetus as a Legal Entity--Facing Reality." San Diego Law Review, 8:126, 1971. 3398

Finnis, J. "Abortion and Legal Rationality." Adelaide Law Review, 3:431, Aug. 1970. 3399

Fox, R. W. "Abortion: A Question of Right or Wrong?" American Bar Association Journal, 57:667, July 1971. 3400

Gerber, R. J. "Abortion: Two Opposing Legal Philosophies." American Journal of Juris, 15:1, 1970. 3401

Harrington, P. V. "Human Life and Abortion." Catholic Lawyer, 17:11, winter 1971. 3402

Horan, D. J. "Abortion and the Conscience Clause." Catholic Lawyer, 20:289, autumn 1974. 3403

"In Defense of Liberty: A Look at the Abortion Decisions." Georgia Law Journal, 61:1559, July 1973. 3404

"Is Legalized Abortion the Solution to Criminal Abortion?" University of Colorado Law Review, 37:283, winter 1965. 3405

"Landmark Abortion Decisions: Justifiable Termination or Miscarriage of Justice?--Proposals for Legislative Response." Pacific Law Journal, 4:821, July 1973. 3406

Leavy, Z., and Kummer, J. M. "Criminal Abortion: A Failure of Law." American Bar Association Journal, 50:52, Jan. 1974. 3407

______ and ______. "Criminal Abortion: Human Hardship and Unyielding Laws." Southern California Law Review, 35:123, winter 1962. 3408

"Legislation-Abortion-Michigan's Conscience Act." Wayne Law Review, 21:175, Nov. 1974. 3409

Lessard, Suzannah. "Aborting a Fetus: The Legal Right, the Personal Choice." Washington Monthly, 4:29, Aug. 1972. 3410

Moore, M. M. "Antiquated Abortion Laws." Washington & Lee Law Review, 20:250, fall 1963. 3411

"Oh My God, I'm Pregnant." Ohio Northern Law Review, 1:119, 1973. 3412

Pilpel, H. "The Right of Abortion." Atlantic, 223:69, June 1969. 3413

"Roe and Doe: Substantive Due Process and the Right of Abortion." Hastings Law Journal, 25:867, March 1974. 3414

"Roe v. Wade: Compelling State Interest Test in Substantive Due Process." Washington and Lee Law Review, 30:628, fall 1973. 3415

"Role of the Law of Homicide in Fetal Destruction." Iowa Law Review, 56:658, 1971. 3416

Rubin, E. R. "Abortion Cases: A Study in Law and Social Change." North Carolina Central Law Journal, 5:215, spring 1974. 3417

"Symposium: Abortion and the Law." Western Reserve Law Review, 17:369, Dec. 1965. 3418

Tietle, C., and Lewit, S. "Abortion." Scientific American, 220:21, Jan. 1969. 3419

Tooley, Michael. "Abortion and Infanticide." Philosophy and Public Affairs, 3:37, fall 1972. 3420

Waterson, N. "After the Lane Report." New Law Journal 124:761, Aug. 15, 1974. 3421

(5) SEX OFFENSES

"California Penal Code Section 314 (1): Nudeness or Lewdness?" Hastings Law Journal, 24:1327, May 1973. 3422

Cantor, D. J. "Deviation and the Criminal Law." Journal of Criminal Law, Criminology and Police Science, 55:441, Dec. 1964. 3423

Chappell, D. and Wilson, P. R. "Changing Attitudes Towards Homosexual Law Reform." Australian Law Journal, 46:22, Jan. 1972. 3424

"Consenting Adult Homosexual and the Law: An Empirical Study of Enforcement and Administration in Los Angeles County." UCLA Law Review, 13:643, March 1966. Raises question "whether homosexual behavior between consenting adults in private should remain a criminal offense." Presents facts as a basis for examining past and future studies of sexual morality and the criminal law. 3425

"Constitutional Law--Sodomy Statutes: The Question of Constitutionality." Nebraska Law Review, 50:567, spring 1971. 3426

"Decoy Enforcement of Homosexual Laws." University of Pennsylvania Law Review, 112:259, Dec. 1963. 3427

Derr, A. R. "Criminal Justice: A Crime Against Women." Trial, 9:24, Nov.-Dec. 1974. 3428

Fisher, J. H. "Obtaining and Presenting Evidence in Sex Cases." Criminal Law Quarterly, 4:150, Aug. 1961. 3429

Grey, A. "Civilizing Our Sex Laws." Journal of the Society of Public Teachers of Law, 13:106, July 1974. 3430

Hughes, G. "Consent in Sexual Offenses." Modern Law Review, 25:672, Nov. 1962. 3431

________. "Crime of Incest." Journal of Criminal Law, Criminology and Police Science, 55:322, Sept. 1964. 3432

Jacobs, D. "Psychiatric Examination in the Determination of Sexual Dangerousness in Massachusetts." New England Law Review, 10:85, fall 1974. 3433

Leggett, Stephen. "The Character of Complainants in Sexual Charges." Chitty's Law Journal, 21:132, April 1973. 3434

"Oral Copulation: A Constitutional Curtain Must Be Drawn." San Diego Law Review, 11:523, fall 1974. 3435

"Plight of the Sexual Psychopath: A Legislative Blunder and Judicial

Acquiescence." Notre Dame Lawyer, 41:527, April 1966. 3436

Savitsch, Eugene de. Homosexuality, Transvestism and Change of Sex. London: W. Heinemann Medical Books, 1958. 3437

Schwartz, L. B. "Morals Offenses and the Model Penal Code." Columbia Law Review, 63:669, April 1963. 3438

Scott, G. H. "Sex and the Law." New Law Journal, 123:168, Feb. 22, 1973. 3439

"Sexual Freedom for Consenting Adults--Why Not?" Pacific Law Journal, 2:206, Jan. 1971. 3440

"Sexual Psychopath in the District of Columbia." Howard Law Journal, 16:166, fall 1970. 3441

Slovenko, R., and Phillips, C. "Psychosexuality and the Criminal Law." Vanderbilt Law Review, 15:797, June 1962. 3442

Snow, F. W. "Relations of Police and Health Officers to the Problem of Prostitution and Venereal Disease." The Journal of Social Hygiene, 18:340, July 1932. Reports 1927 Conference on Social Hygiene opinion that the police should control prostitution and let the health department control the disease. Police should act in control of disease only if persons involved refused to obey the orders of the health department. In many instances the male is let go; he should be held and checked. 3443

Tuteur, W. "Child Molesters and Men Who Expose Themselves--An Anthropological Approach." Journal of Forensic Science, 8:515, Oct. 1963. 3444

"Victimless Sex Crimes: 'To the Devil, Not the Dungeon'." University of Florida Law Review, 25:139, fall 1972. 3445

Virkkunen, M. "Incest Offenses and Alcoholism." Medicine, Science and the Law, 14:124, April 1974. 3446

Willemsen, M. "Sex and the School Teacher." Santa Clara Lawyer, 14:839, summer 1974. 3447

Williams, D. G. T. "Sex and Morals in the Criminal Law." Criminal Law Review, 1964:253, April 1964. 3448

(6) ADULTERY

Andrews, J. A. "Evidence of Adultery." Law Quarterly Review, 77:390, July 1961. 3449

Baker, B. "Can Adultery Save Your Marriage? Questions and Answers." Harper's Bazaar, 108:85, June 1975. 3450

Daube, D. "Lex Julia Concerning Adultery." The Irish Jurist, 7: 373, winter 1973. 3451

Moore, M. M. "Diverse Definitions of Criminal Adultery." University of Kansas City Law Review, 30:219, summer 1962. 3452

Murray, D. E. "Ancient Laws on Adultery; A Synopsis." Journal of Family Law, 1:89, spring 1961. 3453

"Prosecution of Adultery and Bigamy in Oklahoma." Oklahoma Law Review, 14:203, May 1961. 3454

(7) NARCOTICS AND OTHER DRUGS

Abruzzi, W. "5,000 Bad Trips." Contemporary Drug Problems, 3:345, fall 1974. 3455

Bazelon, David L. "Drugs That Turn on the Law." Journal of Social Issues, 27:47-53, 1971. 3456

Begal, Bernard L. "New Frontiers in the Defense of Drug Cases." Contemporary Drug Problems, 1:47-67, winter 1971-72. 3457

"Bibliography [On the Legal Aspects of Drugs and Narcotics]." Contemporary Drug Problems, 1:165, winter 1971-72. 3458

"Bibliography." Contemporary Drug Problems, 3:429, fall 1974. 3459

Bowen, O. R. "The Medico-Legal Conflict in Drug Usage." Journal of School Health, 39:165, March 1969. 3460

Brown, Thorvald T. The Enigma of Drug Addictions. Springfield, Ill.: Charles C. Thomas, 1961. 350pp. 3461

Cavers, D. F. "The Legal Control of the Clinical Investigation of Drugs: Some Political, Economic, and Social Questions." Daedalus, 98:427, spring 1969. 3462

Cazalas, M. W. "Addiction in the United States: A Medical-Legal History." Loyola Law Review, 18:1, 1971-72. 3463

Clague, Christopher. "Legal Strategies for Dealing with Heroin Addiction." American Economic Review, 63:263, May 1973. 3464

"Constitution and the Narcotics Addict." Santa Clara Law, 11:140, fall 1970. 3465

Cross, John C., and Harney, Malachi L. The Narcotic Officer's Notebook. Springfield, Ill.: Charles C. Thomas, 1961. 276pp. Main topics: Uses and necessity for informers, How and where to find informers, How to handle informers--development, control and protection, and Informers and the law. 3466

Currie, Arthur J.; Decker, John F.; and Van der Vaart, Johonna. "International Control of Cannabis Sativa--Alternative Approaches." Journal of Drug Issues, 3:240, summer 1973. 3467

Cushman, P. "Relationship Between Narcotic Addiction and Crime." Federal Probation, 38:38, summer 1974. 3468

"Dangerous Drugs and Narcotics: Part III of a Report on Non-Victim Crime in San Francisco." Contemporary Drug Problems, 1:69, winter 1971-72. 3469

Diamond, M. R. "Criminal Responsibility of the Addict: Conviction by Force of Habit." Fordham Urban Law Journal, 1:395, spring 1973. 3470

"Drug Abuse and Criminality: Note Prepared by the Secretary-General for the First Session of the Committee on Crime Prevention and Control." Bulletin of Narcotic, 24:35, Oct.-Dec. 1972. 3471

"Drug Bounty Programs: A Misguided Approach to the Narcotics Problem." Southern California Law Review, 47:1575, Aug. 1974. 3472

"Due Process in Automobile Forfeiture Proceedings." University of Baltimore Law Review, 3:270, spring 1974. 3473

Dunn, R. L. "Agency Defense in Sale of Drug Cases." Air Force Law Review, 16:46, summer 1974. 3474

Ellinwood, E. "Assault and Homicide Associated with Amphetamine Abuse." American Journal of Psychiatry, 127:1170, March 1971. 3475

Ellis, R. D., and Stephens, R. C. "Narcotic Addicts and Crime: Analysis of Recent Trends." Criminology, 12:474, fall 1975. 3476

"Employment Discrimination Against Rehabilitated Drug Addicts." New York University Law Review, 49:67, April 1974. 3477

Feinglass, S. J. "Special Symposium on Drug Abuse; With Introduction." Journal of Secondary Education, 43:196, May 1968. 3478

Fingarette, H. "Addiction and Criminal Responsibility." Yale Law Journal, 84:413, Jan. 1975. 3479

Fort, J. "Drug Use and the Law: A Case for Legalizing Marijuana." Current, 113:4, Dec. 1969 3480

________. "Social Problems of Drug Abuse and Drug Policies." International Journal of the Addictions, 5:321, June 1970. 3481

Geis, G. "Social and Epidemiological Aspects of Marijuana Use." Journal of Psychedelic Drugs, 2:67. 3482

Gross, Nelson G., and Greenwald, G. Jonathan. "The 1972 Narcotics Protocol." Contemporary Drug Problems, 2:119, spring 1973. 3483

Helman, N. T. "Drug Abuse and the Courts." Parts 1-9, New York Law Journal, 164-1+, Dec. 1970. 3484

Hollister, L. E. "Criminal Laws and the Control of Drugs of Abuse, An Historical View of the Law (or, It's the Lawyer's Fault)." Journal of Clinical Pharmacology and the Journal of New Drugs, 9:345, Nov.-Dec. 1969. 3485

Hughes, M. E. "The Role of Law in the Control of Alcohol and Drug Use." Addictions, 16:1, summer 1969. 3486

Kaplan, J. "Primer on Heroin." Stanford Law Review, 27:801, fall 1975. 3487

Keniston, K. "Heads and Seekers: Drugs on Campus, Counter-Cultures and American Society." American Scholar, 38:97, winter 1968-69. 3488

King, Rufus. "Narcotic Drug Laws and Enforcement Policies." Law and Contemporary Problems, 22:113, winter 1957. A report on the need for better legislation and some reasons for the ineffectiveness of enforcement teams. 3489

Kolb, Laurence. Drug Addiction, A Medical Problem. Springfield, Ill.: Charles C. Thomas, 1962. 183pp. 3490

Kozel, Nicholas J.; Dupont, Robert L.; and Brown, Barry S. "Narcotics and Crime: A Study of Narcotics Involvement in an Offender Population." International Journal of the Addictions, 7: 443, 1972. 3491

Krotoszynski, B. K.; Mullaly, J. M.; and Dravnicks, A. "Olfactronic Detection of Narcotic and Other Controlled Drugs." Police, 13:20, Jan.-Feb. 1969. 3492

Kurzman, M. G. "Drug Education: Boom or Bust." Contemporary Drug Problems, 3:61, spring 1974. 3493

"Law and Order and Drugs--One Year Later: A Panel." Contemporary Drug Problems, 3:547, winter 1974. 3494

Lennard, H. L.; Epstein, L. J.; and Rosenthal, M. S. "The Methadone Illusion." Science, 176:881, May 26, 1972. 3495

Lindesmith, Alfred R. The Addict and the Law. Bloomington: Indiana University Press, 1965. 337pp. 3496

Lockman, J. S. "Legal Aspects of the Drug Problem." Nassau Lawyer, 17:311, June 1970. 3497

McGlothlin, W. H. "Toward a Rational View of Hallucinogenic Drugs." California School Health, 4:1, winter 1968. 3498

Mann, Geoffrey Thomas, and Jordan, Thomas D. Personal Injury Problems. Springfield, Ill.: Charles C. Thomas, 1963. 368pp. Problems resulting from trauma, with special reference to automobile accidents. 3499

Maurer, David W., and Vogel, Victor H. Narcotics and Narcotic Addiction. Springfield, Ill.: Charles C. Thomas, 1954. 3500

Merwin, J. D. "Drug Addiction and the Law." Virgin Islands Bar Journal, 4:62, Jan. 1973. 3501

Morgenbesser, M. "Role of a Police Officer in a Drug Treatment Program." Contemporary Drug Problems, 3:213, summer 1974. 3502

Munsey, R. R. "FDA and the Courts." Lex et Scientia, 5:147, Oct.-Dec. 1968. 3503

Musto, D. F. "Dangerous Substance Use: An Uncommon History." Trial, 10:59, Nov., Dec. 1974. 3504

Napley, D. "Drugs and Criminal Responsibility." British Journal of Addiction, 63:83, Sept. 1968. 3505

Narcotic Education. Edited Report of the Proceedings of the First World Conference on Narcotic Education, Philadelphia, 1926. 3506

"Narcotics--Strict Liability for Criminal Possession." Gonzaga Law Review, 7:329, spring 1972. 3507

"Narcotic Rehabilitation Act." Duquesne Law Review, 12:366, winter 1974. 3508

"Nonusable Amounts of Narcotics: The Residual Dilemma." Southwestern University Law Review, 6:224, spring 1974. 3509

O'Neill, C. W. "Legal Aspect of Drug Abuse." Cleveland State Law Review, 19:461, Sept. 1970. 3510

Owen, A. S. "Dangerous Drugs--Possession." The New Law Journal, 122:844, Sept. 28, 1972. 3511

Parry, H. J. "Use of Psychotropic Drugs by U. S. Adults." Public Health Reports, 83:799, Oct. 1968. 3512

Percy, C. H. "Legacy of No-Knock: Drug Enforcement Abuse." Contemporary Drug Problems, 3:3, spring 1974. 3513

"Possession of Dangerous Drugs in a Car--New York's Criminal Presumption Statute." Buffalo Law Review, 21:188, fall 1971. 3514

"A Procuring Agent May Not Be Convicted of Narcotics Sale." Kansas Law Review, 22:272, winter 1974. 3515

Raymond, F. B. "Sociological View of Narcotics Addiction." Crime and Delinquency, 21:11, Jan. 1975. 3516

Reasons, C. E. "Addict As a Criminal: Perpetuation of a Legend." Crime and Delinquency, 21:19, Jan. 1975. 3517

Rosenthal, Michael P. "Legal Controls on Mind-and Mood-Altering Drugs." Journal of Social Issues, 27:53, 1971. 3518

Shoben, E. J., Jr. "Dangerous Drugs: Volstead Exhumed?" Nation, 207:306, Sept. 1968. 3519

Simmons, B. F. "Implications of Court Decisions on Peyote for the Users of LSD." Journal of Church and State, 11:83, winter 1969. 3520

Simrell, E. V. "History of Legal and Medical Roles in Narcotic Abuse in the U. S." Public Health Reports, 83:587, July 1968. 3521

Singer, M. "The Vitality of Mythical Numbers (Property Crimes Committed by Drug Addicts; New York, N. Y.)." Public Interest, 22:3, spring 1971. 3522

Skinner, W. J. "Drug Abuse and the Lawyer." Res Gestae, 13:6, Feb. 1969. 3523

"Special Report on Canada ... Commission of Inquiry into the Non-Medical Use of Drugs." Marijuana Review, 1:8012, Oct.-Dec. 1969. 3524

"Statutory Penalty for Possession of Marijuana Violates Cruel and Unusual Punishments Clause." Mississippi Law Journal, 45: 1297, Nov. 1974. 3525

"Toward an International System of Drug-Control." University of Michigan Journal of Law Reform, 8:103, fall 1974. 3526

Vance, C. S. "Drug Abuse and the Law." Texas Southern University Law Review, 3:1, spring 1973. 3527

Wald, P. M. "Alcohol, Drugs, and Criminal Responsibility." Georgetown Law Journal, 63:69, Oct. 1974. 3528

Weppner, Robert S.; Stephens, Richard D.; and Conrad, Harold T. "Methadone: Some Aspects of Its Legal and Illegal Use." American Journal of Psychiatry, 129:451, Oct. 1972. 3529

Whealy, A. C. "Drugs and the Criminal Law." Criminal Law Quarterly, 12:254, July 1970. 3530

Wilson, P. "Drug Abuse As a Legislative Problem." California School Health, 4:1, spring 1968. 3531

(8) MISCELLANEOUS

"Airport Security Systems and the Fourth Amendment." Louisiana Law Review, 34:860, summer 1974. 3532

Arena, Jay M. Poisoning. Springfield, Ill.: Charles C. Thomas, 1963. 3533

Brodsky, J. A. "Terry and the Pirates: Constitutionality of Airport Searches and Seizures." Kentucky Law Journal, 62:623, 1973-74. 3534

Cooper, Peter. Poisoning by Drugs and Chemicals. Springfield: Charles C. Thomas, 1962. 3535

Cumming, Gordon. The Management of Acute Poisoning. Springfield, Illinois: Charles C. Thomas, 1961. 3536

Curry, Allan S. Poison Detection in Human Organs. Springfield: Charles C. Thomas, 1963. 3537

Evans, A. E. "Aircraft Hijacking: What Is Being Done?" American Journal of International Law, 67:641, Oct. 1973. 3538

Green, L. C. "Piracy of Aircraft and the Law." Alberta Law Review, 10:72, 1972. 3539

Horlick, G. N. "Developing Law of Air Hijacking." Harvard International Law Journal, 12:33, winter 1971. 3540

Lew, J. D. M. "Shot-Down Airliners-Legal Implications." New Law Journal, 123:408, May 3, 1973. 3541

Minor, W. W. "Skyjacking-Crime Control Models." Journal of Criminal Law and Criminology, 66:94, March 1975. 3542

Olivier, A., and Finkelstein, I. "Report on 'Victimless Crimes' in New York State." New York Law Forum, 18:77, summer 1972. 3543

Sonnemann, W. R. "Aerial Piracy." American Bar Association Section of Insurance, Negligence and Compensation Law, 1971: 135, 1971. 3544

Westbrook, J. W. "Crimes Without Plaintiffs." Baylor Law Review, 25:37, winter 1973. 3545

E. CRIMES AGAINST PROPERTY ACCOMPANIED BY DANGER TO PERSON

(1) ARSON

"Arson Investigation and the Fourth Amendment." Washington and Lee Law Review, 30:133, spring 1973. 3546

Battle, B., and Weston P. Arson; A Handbook of Detection and Investigation. New York: Greenberg, 1954. 3547

Bennett, B. D. "Arson Investigator and Technical Aids." Journal of Criminal Law, 49:172, July-Aug. 1958. 3548

Borton, E. C. "Arson in California." Southern California Law Review, 35:375, summer 1962. 3549

Burd, D. Q. "Arson and Fire Investigation: The Function of the Criminalist." Journal of Forensic Science, 7:417, Oct. 1962. 3550

"Criminal Law--Aggravated Arson--Firemen as Endangered Persons." Loyola Law Review, 17:182, 1970-71. 3551

"Diminished Capacity and Arson--Crime of Arson Does Not Require Specific Mental State and Therefore Diminished Capacity Defense May Not Be Asserted." Santa Clara Lawyer, 13:349, winter 1972. 3552

Hurley, W., and Monahan, T. M. "Arson: The Criminal and the Crime." British Journal of Criminology, 9:4, Jan. 1969. 3553

MacDonald, J. M. "Pathological Firesetting." Journal of Forensic Medicine, 6:53, April-June 1959. 3554

Soothill, K. L., and Pope, P. J. "Arson: A Twenty-Year Cohort Study." Medicine, Science and the Law, 13:127, April 1973. 3555

(2) BURGLARY

"Burglary--Entry Defined [State v. Pigques (MO) SW 2d 942]."

Missouri Law Review, 24:371, June 1959. 3556

"Burglary--Inhabited Dwelling House [Thomas v. State (Ala) 100 S. 2d 329]." Alabama Law Review, 10:443, spring 1958. 3557

"Burglary--Its Drain on the Public." F. B. I. Law Enforcement Bulletin, 35:16, Jan. 1966. A major law enforcement problem; techniques, and precautions discussed. 3558

"Burglary: Punishment Without Justification." University of Illinois Law Forum, 1970:391, 1970. 3559

"Cabins, Corncribs, and Fruitstands--What Structures Can Be Burglarized Under the New Penal Code." Baylor Law Review, 26: 589, fall 1974. 3560

Conklin, J. E., and Bittner, E. "Burglary in a Suburb." Criminology, 11:206, Aug. 1973. 3561

"Criminal Law--Burglary--A Summer Home Is an Inhabited Dwelling During the Time When It Is Unoccupied." University of Cincinnati Law Review, 39:421, spring 1970. 3562

"Intent to Break and Enter in Common-Law Burglary." New York University Intramural Law Review, 15:119, Jan. 1960. 3563

Moylan, C. E. "Historical Intertwining of Maryland's Burglary and Larceny Laws: The Singular Adventure of the Misunderstood Indictment Clerk." University of Baltimore Law Review, 4:28, fall 1974. 3564

"Sufficiency of Evidence As to Time of Offense Under Ohio Burglary Statute [State v. Stuttler (Ohio) 175 NE 2d 728]." Ohio State Law Journal, 23:160, 1962. 3565

(3) ROBBERY

Andrews, J. A. "Robbery." Criminal Law Review, 1966:524, Oct. 1966. 3566

"Armed Robbery--Use of a Dangerous Weapon Subsequent to the Taking [People v. Pond (Cal) 337 P. 2d 877]." Iowa Law Review, 46:151, fall 1960. 3567

"Criminal Law--Concurrent Sentencing--Multiple Convictions--Colorado Rev. Stat. Ann. 40-1-508 and DeBose v. People [(Colo.) 488 P. 2d 69]." Denver Law Journal, 48:591, 1972. 3568

"Jury May Find That Retail Store Which Cooperated with Armed Robbers While Summoning Police by Automatic Silent Alarm Caused the Death of a Customer Killed by a Robber." Fordham Urban Law Journal, 2:661, spring 1974. 3569

Ozeene, T. "Economics of Bank Robbery." Journal of Legal Studies, 3:19, Jan. 1974. 3570

"Prior Crime Evidence Admissible Only When Relevant to Crime Charged." Florida State University Law Review, 2:197, winter 1974. 3571

"Robbery--Necessity That Apprehension of Victim Be Actual [Cassidy v. State (Tex) 324 SW. 2d 857]." Mississippi Law Journal, 31: 181, March 1960. 3572

"Unloaded and Unworkable Pistol As a Dangerous Weapon When Used in a Robbery." Louisiana Law Review, 32:158, Dec. 1971. 3573

"Unloaded Pistol As a Dangerous Weapon Within the Robbery Statute [Hayes v. State (MD) 126 A. 2d 576]." Maryland Law Review, 17:257, summer 1957. 3574

"Violent Taking of Property Under a Claim of Right as Robbery." New York University Law Review, 11:302, May 1956. 3575

(4) EXTORTION

Beigel, H. "Investigation and Prosecution of Police Corruption." Journal of Criminal Law and Criminology, 65:135, June 1974. 3576

"Extortion--Collection of Debts by Threat of Criminal Prosecution." Baylor Law Review, 13:383, fall 1961. 3577

"Extortion--Defendant Need Not Initiate the Fear [People v. Dioquardi (NY) 168 NE. 2d 683]." Brooklyn Law Review, 27:346, April 1961. 3578

"Extortion 'Under Color of Official Right': Federal Prosecution for Official Corruption Under the Hobbs Act." Loyola University Law Journal (Chicago), 5:513, summer 1974. 3579

Mackenna, B., and Hogan, B. "Blackmail: A Criticism." Criminal Law Review, 1966:467, 474, Sept. 1966. 3580

"Threats and Extortion [Furlotte v. State (Tenn) 350 SW. 2d 72]." Tennessee Law Review, 29:462, spring 1962. 3581

F. CRIMES AGAINST PROPERTY NOT ACCOMPANIED BY DANGER TO PERSON

(1) THEFT

"Attempted Grand Theft by False Pretenses Where Victim Is Not Deceived [People vs. Camodeca (Cal) 338 P. 2d 903]." Southern California Law Review, 33:227, winter 1960. 3582

"Attempted Theft by False Pretenses: Impossibility in Fact [People v. Camodeca (Cal.) 224 P. 2d 353]." California Law Review, Dec. 1969. 3583

Bentil, J. K. "Taking a Motor Vehicle or Other Conveyance Without Authority." New Law Journal, 124:1133, Dec. 5, 1974. 3584

Cake, George F. "This Store Stops Crime: George F. Cake Company." Coronet, 36:26-9, May 1954. 3585

Cross, R. "Theft Bill." Criminal Law Review, 1966:415, Aug. 1966. 3586

Elliott, D. W. "Dishonesty Under the Theft Act." Criminal Law Review, 1972:625, Oct. 1972. 3587

________. "Ten Years of Larceny and Such--1954-1963." Criminal Law Review, 1964:182, March 1964. 3588

Hearn, A. M. "Larceny by a Custodian--Failure to Account." Judge Advocate General Journal, 16:154, Nov.-Dec. 1962. 3589

Heaton, R. "Taking Advantage." New Law Journal, 124:721, Aug. 1, 1974. 3590

Hooper, A. "Larceny by Intimidation." Criminal Law Review, 1965: 532, Sept.-Oct. 1965. 3591

Howard, C. "Stealing by Fraud." Adelaide Law Review, 2:33, June 1963. 3592

"Insurance--Proof of Mysterious Disappearance Under Theft Policies." Louisiana Law Review, 24:930, June 1964. 3593

"Larceny by Bailee--Criminal Intent [State v. Smith (Mont) 334 P. 2d 1099]." Montana Law Review, 20:246, spring 1959. 3594

Meyers, T. J. "Contribution to the Psychopathology of Shoplifting." Journal of Forensic Science, 15:295, July 1970. 3595

Orchard, G. F. "Borderland of Theft Revisited." New Zealand Law Journal, 1973:110, March 1973. 3596

"Procedural Problem Resulting from Distinction Between Larceny and Embezzlement [Nolan v. State (MD) 131 A. 2d 851]." Maryland Law Review, 18:237, summer 1958. 3597

Robin, G. D. "Patterns of Department Store Shoplifting." Crime and Delinquency, 9:163, April 1963. 3598

________. "White-Collar Crime and Employee Theft." Crime and Delinquency, 20:251, July 1974. 3599

Rose, G. M. G. "Classification of Theft and Malicious Damage." Criminal Law Review, 1971:76, 162, Feb.-March 1971. 3600

"Shoplifting Law: Constitutional Ramifications of Merchant Detention Statutes." Hofstra Law Review, 1:295, spring 1973. 3601

"Shoplifting: Protection for Merchants in Wisconsin." Marquette Law Review, 57:141, 1973. 3602

"Theft in the Texas Penal Code: Old and New." Houston Law Review, 11:440, Jan. 1974. 3603

"Theft of Labor and Services [Chappel v. U.S. 270, P. 2d 274]." Stanford Law Review, 12:663, May 1960. 3604

"Utah's New Penal Code: Theft." Utah Law Review, 1973:718, winter 1973. 3605

White, S. "Theft Act Under Way." Solicitors' Journal, 116:262, 285, 306, April 7-21, 1972. 3606

Williams, C. R. "Crimes (Theft) Act 1973." Law Institute Journal, 48:75, March 1974. 3607

(2) EMBEZZLEMENT

"Commonwealth v. Shafer [PA 202 A. 2d 308]: Liability for Embezzlement of Sales Tax Funds by Vendors as Tax Collectors." Dickinson Law Review, 69:181, winter 1965. 3608

Dworak, R. F. "What Is a Loss of Funds?" JAG Journal, 6:23, July-Aug. 1964. 3609

"Federal Income Taxation--Embezzlement--Taxation of the Corporate Entity." Wayne Law Review, 30:1393, summer 1974. 3610

Newman, Donald J. "Public Attitudes Toward a Form of White Collar Crime." Social Problems, 4:228, Jan. 1957. Techniques used by meat packing companies, food industries and other companies to cheat the public. 3611

"People v. Sobiek (106 Cal. Rptr. 519): Punishing the Embezzling Partner." Hastings Law Journal, 25:1266, April 1974. 3612

(3) FORGERY

Ashton, H. M. "Multiple Forgeries." Journal of Forensic Science, 4:209, April 1959. 3613

Beck, A. "End of Automedacity?" Criminal Law Review, 1971:565, Oct. 1971. 3614

Bentley, D. J. "Documents in the Law of Forgery." Modern Law Review, 22:292, 1959. 3615

Black, D. A. "Forgery Above a Genuine Signature." Journal of Criminal Law and Criminology, 50:585, March-April 1960. 3616

"Check Forgeries: Rights, Duties and Liabilities of Payer and Collecting Banks Under the Uniform Commercial Code." Mississippi Law Journal, 43:311, 1972. 3617

"Checklist of Legal and Other Aspects of Art Forgery or 'The Gentle Art of Faking'." Record of the Association of the Bar of the City of New York, 29:512, May-June 1974. 3618

Cole, A. "Assassin Forger." Journal of Forensic Science, 11:272, July 1966. 3619

"Distinction Between Deceiving and Defrauding." Law Quarterly Review, 76:335, July 1960. 3620

"Drawing Check on Non-Existent Bank Account Held Forgery [In re Clemons (Ohio) 151 NE. 2d 553]." Harvard Law Review, 72:566, Jan. 1959. 3621

"Forgery--Use of Fictitious Name [Hubsch v. U.S. 256 F. 2d 820]." North Carolina Law Review, 37:200, Feb. 1958. 3622

"Forgery--Use of Fictitious or Assumed Name [Edge v. U.S. 270 F. 2d 837]." West Virginia Law Review, 62:393, June 1960. 3623

"Fraudulently Signing Own Name to Check Drawn on Bank Where No Account Is Maintained Constitutes Forgery [In re Clemons (OH) 151 NE. 2d 553]." Virginia Law Review, 45:286, March 1959. 3624

Hadden, T. "Intent in Forgery." Modern Law Review, 28:154, 286, March-May 1965. 3625

Harrison, Wilson R. Forgery Detection: A Practical Guide. New York: Praeger, 1964. Methods of forgers and simple detection techniques are described. 3626

________. "Forgery Detection for the Layman." Criminal Law Review, 1963:2, 168, 624, 765, Jan., March, Sept., Nov. 1963. 3627

McCall, C. C. and Grogan, H. J. "Rehabilitating Forgers." Crime and Delinquency, 20:263, July 1974. 3628

McDaniel, J. E. "Recent Developments in Forgery as Applied in the Bonds." ABC Sect. Ins. NCCL, 1970:58, 1970. 3629

McDonnell, J. B. "Rapid Decline of Privity in the Modern Law of Commercial Paper." Business Lawyer, 30:203, Nov. 1974. 3630

"Prescriptions Issued to Deceased and Fictitious Patients Are Forgeries Under New York Penal Law Although Signed with True Name of Issuing Doctor." Michigan Law Review, 64:513, Jan. 1966. 3631

Turner, J. W. C. "Intent to Defraud in Forgery." Criminal Law Review, 1963:465, July 1963. 3632

Whaley, D. J. "Forged Indorsements and the UCC's 'Holder'." Indiana Law Review, 6:45, 1972. 3633

________. "Forgery and the Holder in Due Course: The Commercial Paper Puzzle." Commercial Law Journal, 78:277, Aug. 1973. 3634

Worsley, M. D. L. "Falsity in the Law of Forgery." Criminal Law Review, 1959:100, Feb. 1959. 3635

Wurtenberger, T. "Criminal Damage to Art--A Criminological Study." DePaul Law Review, 14:83, autumn-winter 1964. 3636

G. ATTEMPTED CRIMES

"Attempt--Impossibility of Consummation of Complete Criminal Act Not a Bar to Conviction for Attempt [People v. Rojas, 10 Cal. Rptr. 465]." Villanova Law Review, 6:575, summer 1961. 3637

"Attempted Receiving of Stolen Property: Impossibility of Fact." California Law Review, 48:314, May 1960. 3638

"Attempts--The Damns Case and the General Attempt Statute." Wisconsin Law Review, 1960:516, May 1960. 3639

Brazier, R. "Reformation of Criminal Attempts." Modern Law Review, 37:329, May 1974. 3640

"Criminal Attempts: Linguistic Equations and Scholastic Camps." Journal of Urban Law, 47:841, 1969-70. 3641

"Should We Have a Law of Attempted Crime?" Law Quarterly Review, 85:28, Jan. 1969. 3642

Stuart, D. "Actus Reus in Attempts." Criminal Law Review, 1970:505, Sept. 1970. 3643

"Student Symposium on the Proposed California Criminal Code ... Attempts. . . . " UCLA Law Review, 19:525, April 1972. 3644

Williams, G. "Criminal Attempts--A Reply." Criminal Law Review, 1962:300, May 1962. 3645

H. CRIMES AGAINST JUSTICE

(1) PERJURY

"Attempted Perjury--The Rules of 'Legal' and 'Factual' Impossibility as Applied to the Law of Criminal Attempts [State v. Latiolas (LA) 74 S. 2d 148]." North Carolina Law Review, 33:641, June 1955. 3646

"Attorneys, and Subornation of Perjury." Maine Law Review, 26: 297, 1974. 3647

"Circumstantial Evidence Is Sufficient for False Swearing Conviction of Union Officer Filing Non-Communist Affidavit [Fisher v. U.S. 231 F. 2d 99]." Harvard Law Review, 70:383, Dec. 1956. 3648

"Criminal Law and Perjury in Kansas." Washburn Law Journal, 13:479, summer 1974. 3649

"Kind and Degree of Evidence Necessary to Convict of Perjury or Subornation." University of Florida Law Review, 10:77, spring 1957. 3650

"Lack of Miranda Warnings for Virtual Defendant Results in Suppression of Perjurious Testimony." Texas Law Review, 53:156, Dec. 1974. 3651

"Materiality of Questions and Not Answer Given in Testimony Constitutes Test for Perjury [U.S. v. Siegel, 263 F. 2d 530]." Harvard Law Review, 73:599, Jan. 1960. 3652

Murray, E. D. "Convictions Obtained by Perjured Testimony: A Comparative View." Ohio State Law Journal, 27:102, winter 1966. 3653

Pace, P. J. "Pressured into Perjury." Solicitors' Journal, 116: 606, Aug. 11, 1972. 3654

"Perjury." Brooklyn Law Review, 24:79, Dec. 1957. 3655

"Perjury and a Subjective Standard of Materiality [U.S. v. Icardi, 140 F. Supp 383]." Stanford Law Review, 9:574, May 1957. 3656

"Perjury and the Quantitative Evidence Rule." Missouri Law Review, 36:544, fall 1971. 3657

"Perjury--Materiality--Question of Law of Fact [People v. Clemente, 136 NYS 2d 202]." Brooklyn Law Review, 21:273, April 1955. 3658

"Perjury: The Forgotten Defense." Journal of Criminal and Criminology, 65:361, summer 1974. 3659

"Perjury--Witness Brought Before Grand Jury for Primary Purpose of Extracting Perjured Testimony [Brown v. U.S. 245 R. 2d 549]." Vanderbilt Law Review, 11:616, March 1958. 3660

"Proof of Perjury: The Two Witness Requirement." Southern California Law Review, 35:86, fall 1961. 3661

Sevilla, C. M. "Exclusionary Rule and Police Perjury." San Diego Law Review, 11:839, June 1974. 3662

"Statutory Immunity and the Perjury Exception." California Western Law Review, 10:428, winter 1974. 3663

(2) CONTEMPT

"Aggregating Multiple Contempts of Court: The Supreme Court Takes Another Step to Insure a Jury Trial." San Diego Law Review, 20:483, spring 1975. 3664

"Attorneys and the Summary Contempt Statute." Maine Law Review, 25:89, 1973. 3665

"Barnett Case and the Contempt Power [U.S. v. Barnett 84 Sup. Ct. 984]." New York University Intramural Law Review, 20:157, March 1965. 3666

"Contempt: How Far an Attorney May Go in Support of His Client's Position [Cooper v. Superior Ct. (Cal.) 368 P. 2d 107]." Southern California Law Review, 35:104, fall 1961. 3667

"Contempt of Court for Refusal to Testify: Power to Confine in Jail Until Testimony Is Given." Kansas Law Review, 10:433, March 1962. 3668

"Contempt Power in State Courts." Alabama Law Review, 26:655, fall 1974. 3669

"Contempt--Right of the Court to Punish Summarily [U.S. v. Galante and Mirra, 298 F. 2d 721]." North Dakota Law Review, 38:606, March 1962. 3670

Cotton, N. M. "Contempt Power--The Lifeblood of the Judiciary."

Loyola University Law Journal, 2:69, winter 1971. 3671

"Criminal Contempt: Necessity and Procedure Versus Fairness and Justice." Saskatchewan Law Review, 36:295, 1971-72. 3672

"Criminal Contempt--Right to a Public Trial [Levine v. U.S. 80 Sup. Ct. 1038]." Southwestern Law Journal, 15:427, 1960. 3673

"Criminal Law--Contempt--Conduct of Attorney During Course of Trial." Wisconsin Law Review, 1971-329, 1971. 3674

"Direct Criminal Contempt of Court--The Jury Requirement." St. Louis University Law Journal, 18:96, fall 1973. 3675

Dobbs, D. B. "Contempt of Court: A Survey." Cornell Law Review, 56:183, Jan. 1971. 3676

Gilmore, H. W. "Professional Responsibility Problems and Contempt in Advocacy." San Diego Law Review, 12:288, March 1975. 3677

Goldfarb, R. "Constitution and Contempt of Court." Michigan Law Review, 61:283, Dec. 1962. 3678

________. "Varieties of the Contempt Power." Syracuse Law Review, 13:44, fall 1961. 3679

Harnon, E. "Civil and Criminal Contempts of Court." Modern Law Review, 25:179, March 1972. 3680

Kuhns, R. B. "Limiting the Criminal Contempt Power: New Roles for the Prosecutor and the Grand Jury." Michigan Law Review, 73:483, Jan. 1975. 3681

Ricketts, R. N. "Direct Contempt in Oklahoma. Indirect Contempt in Oklahoma." Oklahoma Law Review, 26:359, Aug. 1973; 27:213, spring 1974. 3682

Riley, J. M. "Constitutional Limitations on Federal Contempt Proceedings." Loyola Law Review, 11:49, 1961-62. 3683

(3) BRIBERY

"Bribery--Offer to Give Money to Congressman's Political Party [U.S. v. Shirey, 79 Sup. Ct. 746]." Vanderbilt Law Review, 13:558, March 1960. 3684

"Control of Non-Governmental Corruption by Criminal Legislation." University of Pennsylvania Law Review, 108:848, April 1960. 3685

Crouchet, J. H. "Bribery and Graft." Military Law Review, 1964:85, July 1964. 3686

"Drafting an Effective Bribery Statute." American Journal of Criminal Law, 1:120, April 1972. 3687

"Federal Income Taxation--Public Policy and the Deductibility of Kickbacks Under 162 (c) (2)." Ohio State Law Journal, 35:686, 1974. 3688

Neely, W. E. "Gratuities--To Accept or Not Accept." JAG Journal, 20:68, Dec. 1965; Jan. 1966. 3689

"Offer of Political Contribution for Individual's Influence in Procuring Federal Job Held Criminal [U. S. v. Shirey, 79 Sup. Ct. 746]." Ohio State Law Journal, 20:961, autumn 1959. 3690

Stern, H. J. "Prosecutions of Local Political Corruption Under the Hobbs Act: The Unnecessary Distinction Between Bribery and Extortion." Seton Hall Law Review, 3:1, fall 1971. 3691

J. GENERAL CRIMINAL ACTIVITY

(1) GENERAL WORKS

"Accessory Before the Fact to Misdemeanor--A Legal Impossibility?" West Virginia Law Review, 74:402, Sept. 1972. 3692

"Accomplice Corroboration Requirement in Utah--A Need for Change." Utah Law Review, 1972:60, spring 1972. 3693

Bishop, S. J. "Damage to Property--Affinity with Other Criminal Offenses." New Law Journal, 122:910, Oct. 1972. 3694

Cosway, R. "Crime Compensation." Washington Law Review, 49: 551, fall 1974. 3695

Hadden, T. "Offenses of Violence: The Law and the Facts." Criminal Law Review, 1968:521, 1968. 3696

Oliver, A., and Finkelstein, I. "Report on Victimless Crime in New York State." New York Law Forum, 18:77, summer 1972. 3697

Ruby, C. C. "Obstructing a Police Officer." Criminal Law Quarterly, 15:375, Aug. 1973. 3698

Smith, A. B., and Hollack, Harriet. "Crimes Without Victims." Saturday Review, 54:27, Dec. 4, 1971. 3699

Sykes, Gresham W. Crime and Society. New York: Random House, 1964. Main topics: Social norms and criminal law, The state versus the accused, Society and its crimes, Society and its criminals, Crime and punishment, and Men in prison. 3700

Westbrook, J. W. "Crimes Without Plaintiffs." Baylor Law Review, 25:37, winter 1973. 3701

(2) CONSPIRACY

Abrams, N. "Conspiracy and Multi-Venue in Federal Criminal Prosecutions: The Crime Committed Formula." UCLA Law Review, 9:751, July 1962. 3702

Cameron, J. T. "Conspiracy and Intimidation: An Anti-Metaphysical Approach." Modern Law Review, 28:448, July 1965. 3703

"Conspiracy and the First Amendment." Yale Law Journal, 79:872, April 1970. 3704

"Conspiracy by Spouses Despite Concept of Unity of Husband and Wife." American Bar Association Journal, 42:162, Feb. 1956. Current trend to end the common law theory that man and wife are one, thereby incapable of conspiracy, and to treat man and wife as two separate individuals. 3705

"Conspiracy, Concealment and the Statute of Limitations." Yale Law Journal, 70:1311, July 1961. 3706

"Conspiracy--Consistency Rule [Eyman v. Deutsch (Ariz) 373 P. 2d 716]." West Virginia Law Review, 65:151, Feb. 1963. 3707

"Conspiracy in the Proposed Federal Criminal Code: Too Little Reform." Tulane Law Review, 47:1017, June 1973. 3708

"Criminal Law: The Conspiracy Hearsay Exception and Its Erratic Application." Dickinson Law Review, 76:728, summer 1972. 3709

"Defendant Cannot Be Convicted of Conspiracy to Assault Federal Officer Without Knowledge of His Victim's Federal Identity." Fordham Law Review, 43:128, Oct. 1974. 3710

Filvaroff, D. B. "Conspiracy and the First Amendment." University of Pennsylvania Law Review, 121:189, Dec. 1972. 3711

Forkosch, M. D. "Doctrine of Criminal Conspiracy and Its Modern Application to Labor." Texas Law Review, 40:303, Feb., April 1962. 3712

Johnson, P. E. "Unnecessary Crime of Conspiracy." Criminal Law Review, 61:1137, summer 1973. 3713

Lewis, M. B. "New Answers to an Old Problem: The Extra-Judicial Statement in Conspiracy--Type Prosecutions." John Marshall Journal of Practice and Procedure, 7:83, fall 1973. 3714

"Mass Demonstrations and Criminal Conspiracies." Hastings Law Journal, 16:465, Feb. 1965. 3715

O'Regan, R. S. "Duress and Criminal Conspiracies." Criminal Law Review, 1971:35, Jan. 1971. 3716

"People v. Pierce (Cal) 395 P. 2d 893, 61 California 2d 879." Connecticut Bar Journal, 39:492, September, 1965; Southern California Law Review, 38:705, summer 1965; UCLA Law Review, 12:1466, Aug. 1965; University of Cincinnati Law Review, 34:407, summer 1965. A California case deciding that in certain situations a husband and wife may conspire; discussion of the legal rule that a husband and wife cannot conspire because they became "one" when married. 3717

Perkins, R. M. "Act of One Conspirator." Hastings Law Journal, 26:337, Nov. 1974. 3718

Powell, C. M. "Conspiracy Preservations." Criminal Law Quarterly, 13:34, Dec. 1970. 3719

Samuels, A. "Criminal Conspiracy--Recent Developments." The New Law Journal, 121:301, April 8, 1971. 3720

Wessel, M. R. "Conspiracy Charge as a Weapon Against Organized Crime." Notre Dame Lawyer, 38:689, 1963. 3721

Yawn, M. T. "Conspiracy." Military Law Review, 51:211, Jan. 1971. 3722

Zellick, G. "Place of the Conspiracy." New Law Journal, 123:207, March 1, 1973. 3723

Zumwalt, W. J. "Conspiracy Confusion." Trial, 10:26, July-Aug. 1974. 3724

(3) ACCOMPLICES

"Accomplice Corroboration--Its Status in California." UCLA Law Review, 9:190, Jan. 1962. 3725

Andrews, J. A. "Reform in the Law of Complicity." Criminal Law Review, 1972:764, Dec. 1972. 3726

"Criminal Law--Accessory Before the Fact to Misdemeanor--A Legal Impossibility." West Virginia Law Review, 74:402, Sept. 1972. 3727

"Criminal Responsibility for Death of Co-Felon." Hastings Law Journal, 16:620, May 1965. 3728

Geraghty, J. M. "One Face of the Informer--The Approver." University Queens Law Journal, 5:66, April 1965. 3729

Heydon, J. D. "Corroboration of Accomplices." Criminal Law Review, 1973:264, May 1973. 3730

"Immunity Given to the Accomplice Witness." Drake Law Review, 21:331, Jan. 1972. 3731

"People v. Washington, (Cal) 402 P. 2d 130." Columbia Law Review, 65:1496, Dec. 1965; Fordham Law Review, 33:721, May 1965. Discusses court decision that in the perpetration of a felony (burglary), one accomplice who did not do the actual stag-ing cannot be convicted under the felony-murder doctrine. Comments on the case and numerous citations of the law in other states. 3732

"Procedural Rights of Juveniles--California Requirement of Corroboration of Accomplice Testimony Not Applicable to Wardship Proceedings in Juvenile Court." Santa Clara Lawyer, 15:881, summer, 1974. 3733

"Testimony of an Accomplice: California Definition of an Accomplice [People v. Raven (Cal) 275 P. 2d 626]." UCLA Law Review, 2:571, June 1955. 3734

(4) CONSENT--MISFORTUNE--NECESSITY--PROVOCATION

Bonds, A. B., Jr. "Law and the Climate of Consent." Cleveland-Marshal Law Review, 13:368, May 1964. 3735

"Consent, Liability and Guilt: A Study in Judicial Method." Stanford Law Review, 7:507, July 1955. 3736

Gibbons, M. M. "Consent." Law Journal, 114:186, March 20, 1964. 3737

Glatebrook, P. R. "Necessity Plea in English Criminal Law." Cambridge Law Journal, 30:87, April 1972. 3738

Hughes, G. "Two Views on Consent in Criminal Law." Modern Law Review, 26:233, May 1963. 3739

Powell, R. E. "Consent to Operative Procedures." Maryland Law Review, 21:189, summer 1961. 3740

"Psychiatric Evidence Ruled Admissible in Murder Prosecution to Determine Whether Defendants Acted in Heat of Passion." Dickinson Law Review, 77:435, winter 1973. 3741

Walker, E. S. "Silence Is Consent." Law Journal, 108:791, Dec. 1958. 3742

(5) MISTAKE

"Assault in the Third Degree--Mistake of Fact as a Defense [People v. Young, 183 NE. 2d 319]." Brooklyn Law Review, 29:141, Dec. 1962. 3743

Cetti, C. L. "Mistake of Fact and Mistake of Law as Defenses to a Prosecution for Bigamy." Mercer Law Review, 15:275, fall 1963. 3744

"Evidence: Proof Beyond a Reasonable Doubt in Civil Cases." University of Florida Law Review, 27:260, fall 1974. 3745

"Fair Comment and Fair Mistake--Extension of the Sullivan Precedent to Other Matters of Public Interest." Hastings Law Journal, 17:346, Dec. 1965. 3746

Johnson, E. P. "Trial: Speedy Trial: Delays Caused by Mistake or Oversight by the Government." JAG Journal, 26:261, spring 1972. 3747

"Mistake of Fact in Defense of Others [People v. Young (NY) 183 NE. 2d 319]." DePaul Law Review, 12:155, autumn, winter 1962. 3748

"Non Est Factum--A Fundamental or Radical Change?" University of Queens Law Journal, 7:440, Dec. 1972. 3749

(6) INSANITY

"Acquital by Reason of Insanity: Is Mandatory Commitment Constitutional?" University of Missouri at Kansas City Law Review, 39: 213, winter 1970-71. 3750

"Alcoholics and the Mentally Ill: Their Institutionalization and De-Institutionalization." Real Property, Probate and Trial Journal, 7:532, fall 1972. 3751

"Automatic Commitment of a Defendant Found Not Guilty by Reason of Insanity." Wisconsin Law Review, 1974:1203, 1974. 3752

Blinder, M. "Why It's Crazy for a Psychiatrist to Talk About Insanity." Catholic University Law Review, 23:769, summer 1974. 3753

Bowman, A. M. "Narcotic Addiction and Criminal Responsibility Under Durham." Georgia Law Journal, 53:1017, summer 1965. 3754

Brady, J. B. "Abolish the Insanity Defense?--NO!" Houston Law Review, 8:629, March 1971. 3755

Burt, R. A. "Of Mad Dogs and Scientists: The Perils of the 'Criminally Insane'." University of Pennsylvania Law Review, 123:258, Dec. 1974. 3756

Carr, J. L., and Linn, F. E. "Not Guilty by Reason of Insanity." California State Bar Journal, 39:349, May-June 1964. 3757

"Conditional Release from Mental Institutions Made Available to Persons Confined Under Criminal Statutes." Seton Hall Law Review, 6:128, fall 1974. 3758

"Criminal Law--Insanity Defense--District of Columbia Circuit Abandons the Durham 'Product' Formulation in Favor of the 'Substantial Capacity', Standard." New York University Law Review, 47:962, spring 1962. 3759

"Criminal Law--Reflections: Insanity Bifurcation, Burden of Proof." North Carolina Law Review, 50:917, June 1972. 3760

"Criminal Responsibility: New Test for Insanity [U.S. v. Currens 290 F. 2d 751]." Cornell Law Quarterly, 47:452, spring 1962. 3761

"Defenses of Insanity--Mental Disease and Defect in Durham Rule Defined [McDonald v. U.S. 312 F. 2d 847]." American University Law Review, 1962. 3762

Diamond, Bernard. "Criminal Responsibility of the Mentally Ill." Stanford Law Review, 14:59, Dec. 1961. Mens rea, the McNaughten Rule and the criminally insane; towards a better system of justice for the mentally ill. 3763

________. "From McNaughten to Currens and Beyond." California Law Review, 50:189, May 1962. A short explanation of psychiatry, the problems encountered, and the complexity of the study of mental illness. 3764

"Did McNaughten Need a Psychiatrist, A Lawyer or a Definition?" M. M. Belli, Medicines, Science and the Law, 11:25, Jan. 1971. 3765

"Drug Induced Insanity and Unconsciousness--A Clarification of California Law." Pepperdine Law Review, 1:442, 1974. 3766

"Due Process and Bifurcated Trials: A Double-Edged Sword." Northwestern University Law Review, 66:327, July-Aug. 1971. 3767

"Durham Court Changes the Insanity Rule." New England Law Review, 8:328, spring 1973. 3768

Fletcher, G. P. "Individualization of Excusing Conditions." Southern California Law Review, 47:1269, Aug. 1974. 3769

"Forensic Psychiatry: Uses and Limitations--A Symposium." Northwestern University Law Review, 57:1, March-April 1962. 3770

Goldstein, J., and Katz, J. R. "Abolish the 'Insanity Defense'--Why Not?" Yale Law Journal, 72:853, April 1963. 3771

Gray, J. W. R. "Purely Temporary Disturbance." Juridicial Review, 1974:227, Dec. 1974. 3772

Hardisty, J. H. "Mental Illness: A Legal Fiction." Washington Law Review, 48:735, Aug. 1973. 3773

Hofstadter, S. H. "McNaughten Renewed and Implemented." New Hampshire Bar Journal, 7:256, April 1965. 3774

Holliday, D. G. "Pretrial Mental Examinations Under Military Law: A Reexamination." Air Force Law Review, 16:14, fall 1974. 3775

Ibañez, R. A. "Criminal Responsibility: The Role of the Lawyer and the Psychiatrist in Structuring the Case for the Defense." Los Angeles Bar Bulletin, 41:486, Sept. 1966. 3776

"Insanity as a Defense: A Panel Discussion [Lumbard, Hays, Weintraub, Biggs, Wechsler, Kolb]." Federal Rules Decisions, 37:365, Aug. 1965. 3777

Lawrence, J. K. L. "Sanity: The Psychiatrico-Legal Communicative Gap." Ohio State Law Journal, 27:219, spring 1966. 3778

"Legal Standard for Determining Criminal Insanity; A Need for Reform." Drake Law Review, 20:353, Jan. 1971. 3779

Levine, W. R., and Bornstein, P. E. "Is the Sociopath Treatable? The Contribution of Psychiatry to a Legal Dilemma." Washington University Law Quarterly, 1972:693, fall 1972. 3780

Levinstein, S. R. "The Historical Development of Insanity as a Defense in Criminal Actions." Journal of Forensic Science, 14:275, July 1969. 3781

Lewin, T. N. "Mental Disorder and the Federal Indigent." South Dakota Law Review, 11:198, spring 1966. 3782

Lieberman, H. R. "Legal Significance of the 'Mental Illness' Criterion in the Civil Commitment Process." North Carolina Central Law Journal, 2:55, spring 1970. 3783

Logan, A. B. "May a Man Be Punished Because He Is Ill?" American Bar Association Journal, 52:932, Oct. 1966. 3784

Lynch, G. P. "Insanity Defense." Chicago Bar Record, 55:210, March-April 1974. 3785

"McNaughten Rule v. Irresistible Impulse Test." _Mercer Law Review,_ 14:418, spring 1963. 3786

Martin, G. A., and Edwards, J. L. J., and Bull, H. H. "Criminal Responsibility and Fitness to Stand Trial: Symposium." _Criminal Law Quarterly,_ 8:240, Jan. 1966. 3787

Moore, J. L., Jr. "McNaughten Is Dead--Or Is It?" _Houston Law Review,_ 3:58, spring-summer 1965. 3788-9

Mullock, P. "Responsibility, Propensity and Choice." _Mercer Law_ Review, 16:1, fall 1964. 3790

Nunez, P. K. "Mental Examinations of Criminal Defendants in Federal Courts." _San Diego Law Review,_ 9:838, June 1974. 3791

Platt, Anthony, and Diamond, Bernard L. "The Origins of 'Right and Wrong' Test of Criminal Responsibility." _California Law Review,_ 54:1227, Aug. 1966. Contents: Ancient doctrines of responsibility; Medieval concepts of responsibility; The "good and evil" test in English law; Concepts of responsibility in the U.S.--Children, 1800-1900, and the Insane, 1800-1843. 3792

Platt, G. M. "Proposal to Abolish the Federal Insanity Defense: A Critique." _California Western Law Review,_ 10:449, spring 1974. 3793

"Release from Confinement of Persons Acquitted by Reason of Insanity in New Jersey." _Rutgers Law Review,_ 27:160, fall 1973. 3794

Rosenberg, A. H. "Competency for Trial--Who Knows Best?" _Criminal Law Bulletin,_ 6:577, Dec. 1970. 3795

Samuels, A. "Mental Illness and the Law." _New Law Journal,_ 123: 277, March 22, 1973. 3796

Shadoan, G. "Raising the Insanity Defense: The Practical Side." _American Criminal Law Review,_ 10:533, spring 1972. 3797

Silverman, H. "Psychiatric Evidence in Criminal Law." _Criminal Law Quarterly,_ 14:145, Feb. 1972. 3798

Snoiffer, W. C. "Myth of McNaughten." _Oregon Law Review,_ 50: 41, fall 1970. 3799

"Sociopathic Criminal Offender: What To Do with Him?" _University of Cincinnati Law Review,_ 34:1, winter 1965. 3800

"Spirit of M'Naughten." _Gonzaga Law Review,_ 9:806, spring 1974. 3801

Szasz, Thomas S. Psychiatric Justice. New York: Macmillan, 1965. Furious blasts at the process of criminal law for those who need psychiatric help: we are denying constitutional rights to trial by sophisticated and insidious alliance between psychiatry and law. Replace psychiatrists as arbiters of who is competent to stand trial with competent lawyers, unfettered by psychiatric training and jargon, who will simply talk to the defendant to see if he can assist in his defense. 3802

"Texas Juries and the Insanity Defense." American Journal of Criminal Law, 2:251, winter 1974. 3803

"Texas Rejects M'Naughten." Houston Law Review, 11:946, May 1974. 3804

Walker, N. "Psychopathy in Law and Logic." Medical Science and Law, 5:3, Jan. 1965. 3805

Weintraub, Joseph. "Criminal Responsibility: Psychiatry Alone Cannot Determine It." American Bar Association Journal, 49:1075, 1963. Law is concerned with capacity, not insanity; distinction drawn between the bad and the sick; model penal code's provision examined; code resorts to social and ethical concepts; insanity shouldn't effect criminal accountability. 3806

Wingo, H. "Squaring McNaughten with Precedent--An Historical Note." South Carolina Law Review, 26:81, April 1974. 3807

"XYZ Syndrome and the Judicial System." North Carolina Central Law Review, 6:66, fall 1974. 3808

(7) INTOXICATION AND ADDICTION

Aaron, James E., and Safter, Albert J. The Police Officer and Alcoholism. Springfield, Ill.: Charles C. Thomas, 1963. 3809

"The Addiction Defense: Criminal Responsibility of an Addict Charged with Possession." University of Toledo Law Review, 5:388, winter 1974. 3810

Bennett, R. T. "Drug Addiction and Its Effect on Criminal Responsibility." Wake Forest Law Review, 9:179, March 1973. 3811

Berner, S. H. "Defense of Drunkenness--A Reconsideration." University of British Columbia Law Review, 6:309, Dec. 1971. 3812

Borkenstein, R. F. "Alcoholism and Law Enforcement." Crime and Delinquency, 9:84, Jan. 1963. 3813

"Criminal Intent and Knowledge As Requirements in Dangerous Drug

Cases." Montana Law Review, summer 1974. 3814

"Criminal Law: Alcoholism As a Defense." Marquette Law Review, 53:445, fall-winter 1970. 3815

"Criminal Punishment of Alcoholic for Public Drunkenness Held to Be Cruel and Unusual Under the 8th and 14th Amendments." Duke Law Journal, 1966:545, spring 1966. 3816

"Criminal Responsibility and the Drug Dependence Test--A Need for Judicial Clarification." Fordham Law Review, 42:361, Dec. 1973. 3817

Davies, D. L. "Is Alcoholism Really a Disease?" Contemporary Drug Problems, 3:197, summer 1974. 3818

"Driving Under the Influence of Alcohol." Journal of Forensic Medicine, 13:44, April-June 1966. 3819

Edwards, C. N. "Drug-Dependence: Legal Medicine and Social Regulation." Howard Law Journal, 18:107, 1973. 3820

Erwin, Richard E. Defense of Drunk Driving Cases, 2nd ed. San Francisco: Matthew Bender & Co., 1966. Chapters: Statutory law & judicial interpretation; Jeopardy and civil cases; Pretrial considerations; The arresting officer; Proper cross-examination; Pictures of accused taken or tape recordings made by police officers; Examining physician; Chemical tests for intoxication (all current tests discussed in detail). 3821

Fales, Edward D., Jr. "Catching Drunk Drivers Before They Kill You in Connecticut." Popular Science, 178:59, March 1961. 3822

Haddox, V. G.; Gross, B. H.; and Pollack, H. "Mental Competency to Stand Trial While Under the Influence of Drugs." Loyola University Law Review, (LA), 7:425, summer 1974. 3823

Hollopeter, C. "Trial of a 'Drunk-Driving' Case." Trial Lawyers Guide, 8:118, Nov. 1964. 3824

"Instructing the Jury on the Defense of Voluntary Intoxication in Tennessee." Tennessee Law Review, 39:479, spring 1971. 3825

"Intoxication and Specific Intent in Homicide Prosecution." Louisiana Law Review, 19:524, Feb. 1959. 3826

LaPlante, J. A. "Alcohol Testing: Some Recent Decisions Dealing with Implied Consent Statutes." Connecticut Bar Journal, 39:72, March 1965. 3827

Lovell, W. S. "Evidence in Oregon 'D.U.I.L.' Cases." Willamette Law Journal, 10:11, winter 1973. 3828

Lunter, G. W. "Effect of Drug Induced Intoxication on the Issue of Criminal Responsibility." Criminal Law Bulletin, 8:731, Nov. 1972. The overall problem regarding drug use and criminal responsibility; important decisions in the area reviewed, psychopharmacological issues analyzed; an excellent "short course" on the problems of prosecution and defense when drug use is involved. 3829

Marshall, M. B., and Reiter, J. H. "Confessions of a Drunk." American Bar Association Journal, 59:497, May 1973. 3830

Mason, G. R. "Implied Consent for Intoxication Tests." Wyoming Law Journal, 18:252, spring 1964. 3831

Murphy, A. A. "Defense of Voluntary Intoxication." Law Notes, 9:7, fall 1972. 3832

"Narcotic Addict's Lack of Mens Rea Not a Defense to Conviction for Illegal Possession of Narcotics." American Criminal Law Review, 12:219, summer 1974. 3833

Nash, Harvey. Alcohol and Caffeine. Springfield, Ill.: Charles C. Thomas, 1962. Psychological effects of the two drugs. 3834

Rivo, Julian D. "The Problem of the Drinking Driver." Police Chief, 32:14, Nov. 1965. Police problems with the large numbers of drunk drivers and resulting accidents. 3835

Rubin, E., and Lieber, C. S. "Alcoholism, Alcohol and Drugs." Science, 172:1097, June 1971. 3836

Ruffin, Roger S. "Intoxication Tests and the Bill of Rights: A New Look." California Western Law Review, Vol. II, 1-41, spring 1966. Constitutional limitations on the use of standardized test for motorists suspected of driving under the influence of alcohol. Several cases cited. 3837

Smith, K. J. M. "Drink, Drugs and Criminal Responsibility." New Law Journal, 124:129, Feb. 7, 1974. 3838

"Taking the Public Inebriate Out of California's Criminal Justice System." U.C.D. Law Review, 7:539, 1974. 3839

Tao, L. S. "Drunkenness and Criminal Law." Wayne Law Review, 13:530, spring 1967. 3840

"Trouble with Alcohol: Admissibility in Negligence Actions." Law and Social Order, 1970:304, 1970. 3841

"Uniform Alcoholism and Intoxication Treatment Act ... Decriminalization of Alcoholism--Alcoholism As a Defense to Criminal Liability." Washington Law Review, 50:755, June 1975. 3842

"Voluntary Intoxication As a Defense to Murder." Loyola Law Review, 47:880, June 1961. 3843

Woods, J. R. "Pretrial Release of Public Drunkenness Offenders in California." Santa Clara Lawyer, 15:81, fall 1974. 3844

(8) ENTRAPMENT

"Assertion of Inconsistent Defenses in Entrapment Cases." Iowa Law Review, 56:686, Feb. 1971. 3845

"Criminal Law--Defenses--Entrapment." North Dakota Law Review, 46:474, summer 1970. 3846

"Criminal Procedure: Entrapment Rationale Employed to Condemn Government's Furnishing of Contraband." Minnesota Law Review, 59:444, Dec. 1974. 3847

"Defense of Entrapment--Definition, Bases and Procedure." Texas Tech Law Reviews, 3:117, fall 1971. 3848

"Defense of Entrapment in Administrative Proceedings." Pepperdine Law Review, 1:316, 1974. 3849

Dix, G. E. "Undercover Investigations and Police Rule-Making." Texas Law Review, 53:203, Jan. 1975. 3850

"Due Process of Law and the Entrapment Defense." University of Illinois Law Review, 45:542, fall 1965. 3851

"Entrapment: A Critical Decision." Missouri Law Review, 37:633, fall 1972. 3852

"Entrapment: An Analysis of Disagreement." Boston University Law Review, 45:542, fall 1965. 3853

"The Entrapment Defense--A Reexamination." Mercer Law Review, 25:957, summer 1974. 3854

"Entrapment in the Federal Courts: Sixty Years of Frustration." New England Law Review, 10:179, fall 1974. 3855

Levy, J. C. "Police Entrapment--A Note on Recent Developments." Saskatchewan Law Review, 35:180, 1970-71. 3856

"New Statutory Defense of Entrapment." Brooklyn Law Review, 32:353, April 1966. 3857

Sagarin, E., and MacNamara, D. E. J. "Problem of Entrapment." Crime and Delinquency, 16:363, Oct. 1970. 3858

Seaton, R. "Entrapment Defense in Drug Cases." Journal of the Bar Association of the State of Kansas, 41:217, fall 1972. 3859

Watt, J. D. "Defense of Entrapment." Criminal Law Quarterly, 13:313, June 1971. 3860

(9) USE OF FORCE BY POLICE

Berger, M. "Law Enforcement Control: Checks and Balances for the Police System." Connecticut Law Review, 24:467, winter 1971-72. 3861

Brill, R. L. "Civil Liability of Police Officer for False Arrest." Chicago-Kent Police Law Reporter, 2:3, March 1969. 3862

Brown, D. "Police Offenses." University of Western Australia Law Review, 10:254, June 1972. 3863

Davis, K. C. "Approach to Legal Control of the Police." Texas Law Review, 52:703, April 1974. 3864

Harding, R. W., and Fahey, R. P. "Killings by Chicago Police, 1969-70: An Empirical Study." Southern California Law Review, 46:284, March 1973. 3865

"Injunctive Relief for Violations of Constitutional Rights by the Police." University of Colorado Law Review, 45:90, fall 1973. 3866

"Justifiable Use of Deadly Force by the Police: A Statutory Survey." William and Mary Law Review, 12:67, fall 1970. The statutorily sanctioned use of deadly force, primarily in areas of affecting arrest and preventing escape; Traces the defense of justification from common law to statutory law. 3867

Katz, M. "Patterns of Arrest and the Dangers of Public Visibility." Criminal Law Bulletin, 9:311, May 1973. 3868

"Law Enforcement Officer's Use of Deadly Force: Two Approaches." American Criminal Law Quarterly, 8:27, fall 1969. 3869

Leavy, J. "Self-Defense Against the Police." McGill Law Journal, 19:413, Nov. 1973. 3870

Mancke, J. B. "Removal, Suspension, or Demotion of a Municipal Police Officer: A Review and Analysis." Dickinson Law Review, 79:380, spring 1975. 3871

"Police Accountability in Wisconsin." Wisconsin Law Review, 1974: 1131, 1974. 3872

"Police Use of Deadly Force in Illinois." Chicago-Kent Law Review, 48:252, fall-winter 1971. 3873

"Police Use of Firearms in West Virginia--An Empirical Study." West Virginia Law Review, 75:166, Dec. 1972. 3874

"Reviewing Civilian Complaints of Police Misconduct--Some Answers and More Questions." Temple Law Quarterly, 48:89, fall 1974. 3875

"Use of Deadly Force in Arizona by Police Officers." Law and Social Order, 1973:481, 1973. 3876

Vanagunas, S. "Toward Checks and Balances of Police Authority." Marquette Law Review, 57:505, 1974. 3877

"Varieties of Police Policy: A Study of Police Policy Regarding the Use of Deadly Force in Los Angeles County." Loyola University Law Review, (LA), 6:1, Jan. 1973. 3878

Wellford, C. R. "Crime and the Police: A Multivariate Analysis." Criminology, 12:195, Aug. 1974. 3879

IV. CRIMINAL EVIDENCE (4000)

The literature in Part IV has been selected to offer a broad spectrum of topics on criminal evidence by leading scholars in specific subjects.

The conflicts between police and courts are discussed in several of the articles contained in the section on the exclusionary rule, which includes references that point out the trend of the U.S. Supreme Court to apply the entire Bill of Rights to the states through the due process clause of the Fourteenth Amendment. The rise of the exclusionary rules appears to exemplify this trend.

Hearsay is treated broadly to show the present status of the hearsay rules as interpreted throughout the United States.

As in parts III and V (on criminal law and on the administration of justice), articles that apply to various sections of the country are included. For example, literature on admissibility has been chosen to present the law as it applies not only to specific states, but to the states within a particular section of the country.

A. GENERAL WORKS

(1) BOOKS

Arthur, R. O. Scientific Investigation. Springfield, Ill.: Charles C. Thomas, 1970. 4000

Busch, Francis X. Law and Tactics in Jury Trials. Indianapolis: Bobbs-Merrill, 1959. 5 vols., general index. 4001

Cleary, Edward W. Law of Evidence. St. Paul, Minn.: West Pub. Co., 1971. 4002

Criminal Law Reporter. The Criminal Law Revolution and Its Aftermath, 1960-1971. Washington, D.C.: Bureau of National Affairs, 1972. 4003

Eastman Kodak Co. Criminal Evidence. Rochester, N.Y., 1959. 4004

Evans, William Edwin Dunn. The Chemistry of Death. Springfield, Ill.: Charles C. Thomas, 1963. The process of dying and the nature of somatic death as great clinical and chemical disguisers; the exterior signs of death from loss of movement to rigor mortis; the chemical changes associated with infraction of various tissues during life; the development of adipocere and its relationship to mummification; and many other topics. 4005

Felkenes, George T. Rules of Evidence. Albany, N.Y.: Delmar Publishers, 1974. 215pp. 4006

Ferguson, Robert, Jr. The Scientific Informer. Springfield, Ill. Charles C. Thomas, 1971. 4007

Fricke, Charles W., and Alarcon, Arthur L. California Criminal Evidence, 7th ed., rev. Los Angeles: Legal Book Store, 1966. Concise, practical volume of California evidence as laid down by statute and case decision. Critical comment on outmoded or illegal decisions. Includes complete text of the California Evidence Code. 4008

________, and Kolbrek, LeRoy M. Criminal Investigation. Los Angeles: Legal Book Store, 1962. 269pp. Text on investigation written by a trial judge and police officer and a college instructor in police science; emphasizes securing evidence and its proper presentation in court. 4009

George, James B. Constitutional Limitations on Evidence in Criminal Cases. Ann Arbor, Mich.: Institute of Continuing Legal Education, 1969. 4010

Harris, Raymond I. Outline of Death Investigation. Springfield, Ill.: Charles C. Thomas, 1962. This book is divided into the following categories: pictures for comparisons and explanation; charts for reference; forms to be used as guide and check list; glossary for quick reference; outlines to be used on the scene, and during investigation itself; and a short synopsis for general information. 4011

Houts, Marshall. Criminal Evidence. Springfield, Ill.: Charles C. Thomas, 1956. From evidence to proof; analysis of methods to establish facts. 4012

Iannarelli, Alfred Victor. The Innarelli System of Ear Detection. Brooklyn, N.Y.: Foundation Press, 1964. A system of anatomical classification and identification of the human ear to fulfill the obvious need for a supplementary method for positive identification of the individual. 4013

Inbau, F.; Aspen, M.; and Carrington, F. Evidence Law for the Police. Philadelphia: Chilton, 1972. 4014

Klein, Irving J. Law of Evidence for Police. St. Paul, Minn.: West Pub. Co., 1973. 4015

Klotter, John C., and Meier, Carl L. Criminal Evidence for Police. Cincinnati: W. H. Anderson Co., 1971. 4016

Lavine, Emanuel H. *Criminal Evidence.* Garden City, N.Y.: Garden City Pub. Co., 1930. The third degree; a detailed and appalling expose of police brutality. 4017

Louisell, David W. *Cases and Materials on Evidence.* Mineola, N.Y.: Foundation Press, 1968. 4018

________; Kaplan, John; and Waltz, Jon R. *Principles of Evidence and Proof.* Mineola, N.Y.: Foundation Press, 1968. 4019

McBaine, James P. *California Evidence Manual*, 2nd ed. St. Paul, Minn.: West Pub. Co., 1960. 4020

McCormick, Charles T. *Handbook of the Law of Evidence.* St. Paul, Minn.: West Pub. Co., 1954. 4021

Moenssens, Andre A.; Moses, Ray E.; and Inbau, Fred E. *Scientific Evidence in Criminal Cases.* Mineola, N.Y.: Foundation Press, 1973. 4022

National District Attorneys Assoc. *Confessions and Interrogations After Miranda: A Comprehensive Guideline of the Law.* Chicago: The Assoc., 1970. 4023

Newnan, Robert P. *Evidence.* Boston: Houghton-Mifflin, 1969. 4024

Nicholas, Clark A. *Applied Evidence.* Chicago: Callaghan & Co., 1928. 5 vols. 4025

O'Hara, Charles E. *Fundamentals of Criminal Investigation.* Springfield, Ill.: Charles C. Thomas, 1966. 4026

Rothblatt, Henry. *Handbook of Evidence for Criminal Trials.* Englewood Cliffs, N.J.: Prentice Hall, 1965. 4027

Rothstein, Paul F. *Evidence in a Nutshell.* St. Paul, Minn.: West Pub. Co., 1970. 4028

Southwestern Law Enforcement Institute. *Institute on Criminal Investigation, Dallas, 1962.* Springfield, Ill.: Charles C. Thomas, 1962, 132pp. Proceedings of the Institute on Homicide Investigation; problems faced by law enforcement officers in investigation of violent deaths. 4029

Stuckey, Gilbert B. *Evidence for the Law Enforcement Officer.* New York: McGraw-Hill, 1968. 4030

Sullivan, Francis. *Evidence: Cases and Materials.* Mineola, N.Y.: Foundation Press, 1968. 4031

Svensson, Arren, and Wendell, Otto. *Techniques of Crime Scene Investigation*, 2nd rev. ed. New York: American Elsevier Pub.

Co., 1965. 540pp. Practical field applications of scientific crime detection, such as crime scene search, search for and preservation of latent fingerprints, tool marks, weapons, and biological evidence are fully and interestingly covered. 4032

Waltz, Jon. Criminal Evidence. Chicago: Nelson-Hall, 1975. 4033

Weston, Paul B., and Wells, Kenneth M. Criminal Evidence for Police. Englewood Cliffs, N.J.: Prentice-Hall, 1971. 4034

Zimmerman, Charles. The Polygraph in Court. Auburndale, Mass.: BHF Printing Co., 1972. 4035

(2) ARTICLES

Adams, J. R. "Twin Codes of Evidence: Just What the System Ordered." South Dakota Law Review, 20: 228, spring 1975. 4036

"Alea's Participation as a Friend of the Court--Disclosure of Informant's Name." Police, 3-4: 26, 1971. 4037

"Brady v. Maryland and the Prosecutor's Duty to Disclose." University of Chicago Law Review, 40:112, fall 1972. 4038

Brown, Lawrence E. "Police Interrogation Dilemma." Police, 83: 75-77, 1964. 4039

"Bursey v. United States (466 F. 2d 1059): The First and Fifth Amendments in the Grand Jury Room." Hastings Law Journal, 24:915, April 1973. 4040

"California's Corpus Delicti Rule: The Case for Review and Clarification." University of California at Los Angeles Law Review, 20:1055, June 1973. 4041

Cohen, Stanley. "Legal Conditions Precedent to Admissibility of Fingerprint Evidence." Police Chief, 10:16, 1965. 4042

Cole, J. "Impeachment with Unconstitutionally Obtained Evidence: Coming to Grips with the Perjurous Defendant." Journal of Criminal Law, Criminology and Police Science, 3:1, 1971. 4043

Coleman, R. F., and Walls, H. J. "Evaluation of Scientific Evidence." Criminal Law Review, 1974:276, May 1974. 4044

"Constitutional Law--Evidence--Due Process Clause Bars States from Making Evidentiary Rulings Which Render Trial Fundamentally Unfair." Illinois Bar Journal, 62:158, Nov. 1973. 4045

"Constitutional Rules of Criminal Procedure and the Application of

Linkletter (Linkletter v. Walker, 85 Sup. Ct. 1731)." Journal of Public Law, 16:193, 1967. 4046

Davidson, R. B. "Who Is a Person Interested in Relation to the Law of Evidence?" Australian Lawyer, 6:33, April 1965. 4047

Davis, K. C. "Approach to Rules of Evidence for Non-Injury Cases." American Bar Association Journal, 50:723, Aug. 1964. 4048

De Garmo, J., Jr. "Must Identity of Informants Be on Record?" Law and Order, 4:80, 1972. 4049

"Exclusionary Rule in Context." North Carolina Law Review, 50: 1049, Aug. 1972. 4050

"Failure to Disclose Names and Addresses of Witnesses in Discovery Proceedings." Montana Law Review, 35:144, winter 1974. 4051

Gellhorn, E. "Rules of Evidence and Official Notice in Formal Administrative Hearings." Duke Law Journal, 1971:1, 1971. 4052

Green, T. F., Jr. "Evidence Symposium. Drafting Uniform Federal Rules of Evidence"; Roberts, E. F. "Preliminary Notes Towards a Study of Judicial Notice"; Ladd, M. "Some Observations on Credibility: Impeachment of Witnesses"; Burns, A. I. "Over-the Counter Quotations: Pink, Yellow, Green and White Sheets--A Gray Area in the Law of Evidence"; Strong, J. "Liberalizing the Authentication of Private Writings"; Cornell Law Quarterly, 52:177, winter 1967. 4053

"Informers and Probable Cause for Arrest." Hastings Law Journal, 11:211, Nov. 1959. 4054

"Judicial Integrity and Judicial Review: An Argument for Expanding the Scope of the Exclusionary Rule." University of California at Los Angeles Law Review, 20:1129, June 1973. 4055

Keatings, Richard H. "Evidence Code Still Needs Changes." The L. A. Daily Journal Report, Part II. March 20, 1967. Chairman of the California Law Revision Committee discusses the 1967 legislative recommendations covering personal injury damages awarded to married persons, imputed contributory negligence under the Vehicle Code, landlord and tenant law. 4056

Leonard, A. A. "Crime Reporting as a Police Management Tool." The Annals of the American Academy of Political and Social Science, 291:127-35, Jan. 1954. 4057

Levine, F. J., and Tapp, J. L. "Psychology of Criminal Identification: The Gap from Wade to Kirby (Kirby v. Illinois, 92 Sup. Ct. 1877)." University of Pennsylvania Law Review, 121:1079, May 1973. 4058

Levy, Albert. "The Drinking Man's Guide to Rules of Evidence." California Trial Lawyers Association Journal, 11:+, fall 1972. 4059

McKay, R. B. "Mapp v. Ohio, The Exclusionary Rule and the Right of Privacy." Arizona Law Review, 15:327, 1973. 4060

McKee, W. F. "Evidentiary Problems: Camera Surveillance of Sex Deviates." Law and Order, 8:72, 1972. 4061

Moore, J. W. "Congress, Evidence and Rulemaking." Yale Law Journal, 84:9, Nov. 1974. 4062

Patterson, L. R. "Types of Evidence: An Analysis." Vanderbilt Law Review, 19:1, Dec. 1965. 4063

"Proposed Federal Rules of Evidence: A Selected Bibliography." Federal Bar Journal, 33:96, winter 1974. 4064

Resnik, Reuben B., and Balter, Harry G. "Withholding Information from Law Bodies: Some Social Work and Legal Notes." Social Service Review, 8:677, Dec. 1934. Whether law enforcement agencies should be allowed to use social workers' case records as evidence against the suspected person or to help apprehend the suspects. 4065

"Rules of Evidence Applicable to Grand Juries." New York University Intramural Law Review, 20:13, Nov. 1964. 4066

Saltzburg, S. A. "Another Ground for Decision--Harmless Trial Court Errors." Temple Law Quarterly, 47:193, winter 1974. 4067

Sellin, Thorstein. "Criminal History of Released Prisoners." Journal of Criminal Law, Criminology and Police Science, 35: 223, Nov. 1944. Discusses use of fingerprint files of penal institutions for research purposes. 4068

"Special Evidence Edition." Arkansas Law Review, 27:171, summer 1973. Contents include: Judicial notice; Presumptions; Privileges; Witnesses; Opinions and expert testimony; Hearsay; Authentication and identification; Contents of writings, recordings, and photographs; and Demonstrative evidence. 4069

Smith, C. M., III, and Ehrhardt, C. W. "Proposed Code of Evidence." Florida Bar Journal, 48:13, Jan. 1974. 4070

"Validity and Relevancy Analysis: An Approach to the Admission of Evidence." Maine Law Review, 26:273, 1974. 4071

Wendorf, H. D. "Police Education and the Law of Evidence." Baylor Law Review, 17:245, fall 1965. 4072

Wingo, H. "Growing Disillusionment with the Exclusionary Rule." Southwestern Law Journal, 25:573, Oct. 1971. 4073

B. THE PROBLEM OF EVIDENCE

(1) ADMISSIBILITY

"Admissibility of Confessions Obtained Between Arrest and Arraignment." Dickinson Law Review, 79:309, winter 1975. 4074

"Admissibility of Evidence Obtained by Police Officers from the Person or Through Observation of the Person." Baylor Law Review, 17:408, summer-fall 1965. 4075

"Admissibility of Evidence Obtained from an Automobile." North Carolina Central Law Journal, 2:115, spring 1970. 4076

"Admissibility of Extrinsic Evidence in the Absence of Ambiguity." Marquette Law Review, 45:442, winter 1961-62. 4077

"Admissibility of Photographs of the Corpse in Homicide Cases." William & Mary Law Review, 7:137 Jan. 1966. 4978

"The Approximate Age of a Document." F. B. I. Law Enforcement Bulletin, 35:12, Feb. 1966. Techniques used to tell age, whether a document is official, or has been changed or added to, by analyzing paper, ink, typewriters, etc. 4079

Brereton, H. "Admissibility of Evidence of Microfilm Records." American Bar Association Journal, 59:500, May 1973. 4080

"Comment on the Exclusion of Evidence Wrongfully Obtained by Private Individuals." Utah Law Review, 1966:271, July 1966. 4081

Corboy, P. H. "Proof of Distance Objects Can Be Seen." Trial Lawyers Guide, 9:57, Feb. 1965. 4082

"Cumulative Evidence Rule and Harmless Error." Missouri Law Review, 40:79, winter 1975. 4083

Damaska, M. "Presentation of Evidence and Factfinding Precision." University of Pennsylvania Law Review, 123:1083, May 1975. 4084

Davidson, H. A. "Testimonial Capacity." Boston University Law Review, 39:172, spring 1959. 4085

"Evidence: Admissibility of Gruesome and Indecent Evidence in Oklahoma." Oklahoma Law Review, 17:333, Aug. 1964. 4086

"Evidence: Admission of Video Tape." Missouri Law Review, 38: 111, winter 1973. 4087

"Evidence--Gruesome Photographs of Corpse Admitted as Evidence." Texas Law Review, 40:284, Dec. 1961. 4088

"Evidence: Requisites of Admissibility of Sound Recordings." Oklahoma Law Review, 18:87, Feb. 1965. 4089

"Evidence: The Admissibility of Computer Printouts in Kansas." Washburn Law Journal, 8:330, spring 1969. 4090

"Evidence--Use of Scientific Methods of Identification--Voice Spectrograms Held Admissible." New York Law Forum, 18:779, winter 1973. 4091

"Footprinting of Infants." F.B.I. Law Enforcement Bulletin, 35:8, Oct. 1966. Describes and explains advantages of footprinting of infants at birth. 4092

Germann, A. C., ed. Footwear Evidence. Springfield: Charles C. Thomas, 1964. 88pp. 4093

"Gruesome Photographs Allowed in Evidence." Texas Law Review, 40:284, Dec. 1961. 4094

"Handwriting Samples--Treated as Genuine." Oregon Law Review, 41:154, fall 1962. 4095

Imwinkelreid, E. J. "Identification of Original, Real Evidence." Milwaukee Law Review, 61:145, summer 1973. 4096

Kamisar, Y. 'Dissent from the Miranda Dissents: Some Comments on the 'New' Fifth Amendment and the Old 'Voluntariness' Test (Miranda v. Arizona, 86 Sup. Ct. 1602)." Michigan Law Review, 65:59, Nov. 1966. 4097

Lang, James C. "In the Use of Non-testimonial Evidence from the Person." Oklahoma Bar Association Journal Quarterly Supplement, 367-375, June 1972. 4098

"Limitations on the Right to Use Evidence Pertaining to the Prior Sexual History of the Complaining Witness in Cases of Forcible Rape." Hofstra Law Review, 3:403, spring 1975. 4099

"Motion to Strike Out the Evidence in Virginia." William & Mary Law Review, 6:58, 1965. 4100

Murphy, H. "How to Win a Pedestrian's Case Without the Plaintiff and Without Eyewitnesses." Practical Lawyer, 11:67, Nov. 1965. 4101

Ormrod, R. "Scientific Evidence in Court." Criminal Law Review, 1968:240, May 1968. 4102

"Requisites of Admissibility of Sound Recordings." Okalhoma Law Review, 1968:240, May 1968. 4102

"Requisites of Admissibility of Sound Recordings." Oklahoma Law Review, 18:87, fall 1965. 4103

Russell, R. W. 'Radar Speedmeters in Court." Law Notes, 6:69, April 1970. 4104

"Schmerber vs. California." (86 Sup. Ct. 1826). Fordham Law Review, 35:131, Oct. 1966. 4105

Scott, Charles C. Photographic Evidence. Kansas City: Vernon Law Book Co., 1942. Supplement, 1955. 952pp. 4106

Seymour, W. E. "Admissibility of Police Movies of Drunk Drivers." Insurance Law Journal, 1966:754, Dec. 1966. 4107

Sheppard, C. A. 'Use of Photostatic Proof." Revue du Barreau de la Province de Québec, 25:3, Jan. 1965. 4108

Templar, G. "Admissibility of Evidence Secured by Eavesdropping Device." Washburn Law Journal, 5:174, spring 1966. 4109

Veldorale, V. C. "Principles of Corpus Delicti and the Evidence Pertaining Thereto." Temple Law Quarterly, 39:1, fall 1965. 4110

"Videotape Evidence: Technological Innovation in the Trial Process." Alabama Law Review, 36:228, April 1975. 4111

Villareal, Diego L. "The Admissibility of Evidence Obtained from an Automobile." North Carolina Central Law Journal, 2:115-125. 4112

'Witnesses--Imprisonment of the Material Witness for Failure to Give Bond." Nebraska Law Review, 40:503, April 1961. 4113

(2) EXPERIMENTS, DEMONSTRATIONS, EXHIBITS

Birnbaum, I. "Admissibility of Police Records, Photographs, and Movies." Trial Lawyers Quarterly, 8:48, spring-fall 1972. 4114

"Blackboard Jungle of Demonstrative Evidence: View of a Defense Attorney." Virginia Law Review, 48:913, June 1962. Blackboards have proved very effective as a device for showing a jury the dollar valuation of pain; discusses techniques and why they should not be condemned. 4115

"Bullets, Bad Florins, and Old Boots: A Report of the Indiana Trial Judge's Control Over Demonstrative Evidence." Notre Dame

<u>Lawyer</u>, 39:20, Dec. 1963. Discusses demonstrative evidence: how it affects juries, how it prejudices cases, how to admit it, and when. 4116

Cady, E. L., Jr. "Objections to Demonstrative Evidence." <u>Missouri Law Review,</u> 32:333, summer 1967. 4117

"Demonstrative Evidence--Admissibility of Motion Picture and Wig-Wag Signal." <u>Iowa Law Review,</u> 47:1138, summer 1962. Case study; established rules. 4118

"Exhibition of a Child in Court to Determine Paternity." <u>Washington University Law Quarterly</u>, 1973:245, winter 1973. 4119

"Experimental Evidence." <u>Cleveland-Marshall Law Review,</u> 11:453, spring 1962. 4120

Felkenes, George T. "Court Rules of Validity of Voice Recognition as Means of Identification." <u>Journal of California Law Enforcement</u>, 1:176-180, Jan.-March 1967. Summary and analysis of state case decisions on the issue of accepting evidence of voice identification; detailed discussion of California law on this subject. 4121

Fryd, C. F. M. "Examination of Inks on Documents." <u>Medicine, Science, and the Law,</u> 14:87, April 1974. 4122

Gordon, M. L. "Demonstrative Evidence: Past, Present and Future." <u>Wisconsin Bar Bulletin,</u> 32:11, fall 1959. 4123

Hare, F. H., Jr. "Demonstrative Evidence." <u>Alabama Law,</u> 27:193, April 1966. 4124

Kennelly, J. J. "Use of Demonstrative Evidence, Including Models." <u>Trial Lawyer's Guide,</u> 16:417, winter 1973. 4125

Kersta, L. G. "Speaker Recognition and Identification by Voiceprint." <u>Connecticut Bar Journal,</u> 40:586, Dec. 1966. 4126

Knepper, W. E. "Exhibits and Demonstrative Evidence." <u>Insurance Counsel Journal,</u> 30:133, Jan. 1963. 4127

Kornblum, G. O., and Rush, P. E. "Television in Courtroom and Classroom." <u>American Bar Association Journal,</u> 59:273, March 1973. 4128

Ladner, J. A. "Demonstrations and Experiments." <u>Trial Lawyer's</u> Guide, 3:1, Aug. 1959. 4129

MacFarland, B. A. "Photographic Evidence: Its Probative Value at Trial and the Judicial Discretion to Exclude It from Evidence." <u>Criminal Lawyer's Quarterly,</u> 16:149, fall 1974. 4130

"Opinion and Demonstrative Evidence: Automobile Accident Reconstruction." *Washburn Law Journal,* 14:264, spring 1975. 4131

Orfield, L. B. "Demonstrative Evidence in Federal Criminal Cases." *South Carolina Law Review,* 15:777, 1963. 4132

Perlman, P. "Demonstrative Evidence." *Kentucky State Bar Journal,* 33:5, Jan. 1969. Discusses cases involved in admissibility and use of picture evidence--photographs, motion pictures, x-rays, bodily demonstrations, medical charts, models and skeletons, surgery, prosthetic or orthopedic devices, maps, plates, and diagrams, and models. 4133

"Propriety of Demonstrative Evidence When Exploited by Trial Lawyers." *Alabama Law Review,* 18:447, spring 1966. 4134

Smith, L. J. "Plaintiff's Turn Behind the Movie Camera." *Trial,* 9:36, Nov.-Dec. 1973. 4135

Tabor, B. W. "Demonstrative Evidence." *J. B. A. Kansas,* 29:250, fall 1961. 4136

"Use of Gruesome Photographs in Criminal and Civil Cases in Montana." *Montana Law Review,* 30:247, spring 1969. Doctrines of illustrative and demonstrative evidence and the general admissibility of photographs. 4137

"Video Tape: A New Horizon in Evidence." *John Marshall Journal,* 4:339, spring 1971. 4138

"Videotape in the Courts: Its Use and Potential." *Rutgers Journal of Computers and Law,* 3:279, 1974. 4139

Wolf, A. J. "Aerial Photography as a Legal Tool." *American Bar Association Journal,* 52:543, June 1966. Aerial photographs included demonstrate the value of this technique; before and after an incident, skid mark measurements and contours, and picket lines are a few examples. 4140

(3) BEST EVIDENCE

Barney, T. M. "Protection of Documents in Criminal Tax Fraud Cases." *Taxes,* 44: 626, Sept. 1966. 4141

"Best Evidence and Authentication of Documents." *Loyola Law Review,* 21:450, spring 1975. 4142

"'Best Evidence' Rule in Tennessee." *Tennessee Law Review,* 38:97, fall 1970. 4143

Caldwell, B. B., and Smith, M. "Comparison and Identification of Adhesives on Questioned Documents." *Journal of Forensic Sci-*

ences, 11:28, Jan. 1966. 4144

Carter, J. J. "Civil Rules of Practice and Procedure." Alabama Law Review, 27:361, Oct. 1966. 4145

Cleary, E. W., and Strong, J. W. "Best Evidence Rule: An Evaluation in Context." Iowa Law Review, 51:825, summer 1966. 4146

Doulder, H. O. "Examination of a Document Case." Journal of Forensic Sciences, 10:433, Oct. 1965. 4147

"Evidence--Best Evidence Rule--The Law in Oregon." Oregon Law Review, 41:138, fall 1962, 30pp. Background of rule, how confusion got started, when the term was first used, Wigmore's four specific rules on best evidence, original document rule and exceptions. Suggests improvements of best evidence rule. 4148

Friedman, L. M. "Law, Rules and the Interpretation of Written Documents." Northwestern University Law Review, 59:751, Jan.-Feb. 1965. 4149

Gough, A. R. "Expungement of Adjudication Records of Juvenile and Adult Offenders: A Problem of Status." Washington University Law Quarterly, 1966:147, April 1966. 4150

Karst, K. L. "Files: Legal Controls over the Accuracy and Accessibility of Stored Personal Data." Law and Contemporary Problems, 31:342, spring 1966. 4151

Moore, W. C. "Age Determination of a Document." Nebraska State Bar Journal, 14:118, Oct. 1966. 4152

Osborn, P. A. "Trial of a Document Case." Journal of Forensic Sciences, 10:422, Oct. 1965. 4153

"Photostatic Copies and the Best Evidence Rule." Tennessee Law Review, 40:709, summer 1973. 4154

Walstead, E. N. "'Best Evidence' Rule." Wisconsin Bar Bulletin, 43:34, April 1970. 4155

"Where to Write for Marriage Records." Journal of Family Law, 5:93, spring 1965. 4156

C. JUDICIAL NOTICE

"Binding Effect of Judicial Notice Under the Common Knowledge Test." Baylor Law Review, 21:208, spring 1969. 4157

Currie, G. R. "Appellate Courts' Use of Facts Outside of the Record by Resort to Judicial Notice and Independent Investigation." Wisconsin Law Review, 1960:39, Jan. 1960. 4158

Davis, K. C. "Judicial Notice." Columbia Law Review, 55:945, Nov. 1955. 4159

Fins, H. G. "Judicial Notice--The Illinois Anomaly!" John Marshall Journal, 7:15, fall 1973. 4160

"Judicial Notice: Florida's New Look at Municipal Ordinances." University of Florida Law Review, 25:811, summer 1973. 4161

"Judicial Notice of Foreign Law." Vanderbilt Law Review, 18:1962, Oct. 1965. 4162

"Judicial Notice of Foreign Law." Washington Law Review, 38:802, winter 1963. 4163

"Judicial Notice of Scientific Facts." Cleveland-Marshall Law Review, 15:140, Jan. 1966. 4164

"Judicial Notice--Radar (Wilson v. State (Tex.) 328 SW 2d 311)." Southwest Law Journal, 14:394, summer 1960. 4165

"Judicial Notice Taken of Accuracy of Radar Speedmeter (State v. Dantonio (NJ) 115 A. 2d 35)." Rocky Mountain Law Review, 28: 277, Feb. 1956. 4166

"Judicial Recognition of Scientific Evidence in Criminal Cases." Utah Law Review, 8:313 [15pp.], winter 1963-64. Radar, breath intoxication devices, lie detectors, and psychiatric evidence; evaluates inconsistency of courts in accepting scientific evidence.
4167

Orfield, L. B. "Judicial Notice in Federal Criminal Procedure." Fordham Law Review, 31:503, fall 1963. 4168

Schlesinger, R. B. "Recurrent Problem in Transnational Litigation: The Effect of Failure to Invoke or Prove the Applicable Foreign Law." Cornell Law Review, 59:1, Nov. 1973. 4169

Slovenko, R. "Judicial Notice and 'Indisputables'." Cleveland-Marshall Law Review, 10:170, Jan. 1961. 4170

Stern, W. B. "Foreign Law in the Courts--Judicial Notice and Proof." California Law Review, 54:23, March 1957. 4171

"Utilization of Both Judicial and Official Notice by Administrative Agencies." Administrative Law Review, 10:333, summer 1964.
4172

Weinstein, J. B. "Judicial Notice and the Duty to Disclose Adverse

Information." Iowa Law Review, 51:807, summer 1966. 4173

D. TESTIMONY

(1) COMPETENCY OF WITNESSES

"Acts of Husband and Wife as Privileged Communications." (Pp vs. Melski (NY) 176 NE. 2d 81). North Dakota Law Review, 38: 133, Jan. 1962. 4174

Andrews, J. A. "Evidence of Children." Criminal Law Review, 1964:769, Nov. 1964. 4175

"Child Who Denied Belief in God Ruled Competent Witness (State vs. Walton (NJ) 179 A. 2d 78)." Notre Dame Law, 38:95, Dec. 1962. 4176

Cober, C. E. "Competency of a Defendant to Testify when Sued Under the Wrongful Death Statute." Mississippi Law Journal, 29:258, May 1958. 4177

"Compelled Testimony with Immunity: Applying the Standard of Use and Derivative Use." Southwestern Law Journal, 27:517, Aug. 1973. 4178

"Competency of Spouses to Testify Against Each Other in Criminal Trial--Compelling the Spouse to Testify." South Carolina Law Review, 16:615, 1964. 4179

"Competency of the Mentally Incompetent." (Pp vs. McCaughan (Cal) 317 P. 2d 974). Southern California Law Review, 32:65, fall 1958. 4180

"Competent Opinions and Privileges." Loyola Law Review, 21:422, spring 1975. 4181

"Dead Man Statutes: The Purposes, Effect and Future." Real Property, Probate and Trust Journal, 7:343, summer 1972. 4182

"Dead Man's Rule in Alabama." Alabama Law Review, 23:405, spring 1971. A Brief history of rules of disqualification of witnesses due to interest in the proceeding and the establishment of the 'Dead Man's Rule" in Alabama. Further case studies are made of the Alabama Rule. 4183

"Disqualification of a Witness for Perjury." University of Florida Law Review, 12:315, fall 1959. 4184

"Evidence--Credibility of Witnesses--Psychiatric Examination of Principal Witness in Murder Trial Denied." Ohio State Law

Journal, 29:505, spring, 1968. 4185

Henkel, W. "Competency, Compensability and Coroner's Courts." *Alberta Law Review,* 8:124, 1970. 4186

"Jencks Act: After Six Years." *New York University Law Review,* 38:1133, Dec. 1963. 4187

Kingston, C. R. "Law of Probabilities and the Credibility of Witnesses and Evidence." *Journal of Forensic Science,* 15:18, Jan. 1970. 4188

Lanham, D. "Payment to Witnesses and Contempt of Court." *Criminal Law Review,* 1975:144, March 1975. 4189

Lezak, M. D. "Some Psychological Limitations on Witness Reliability." *Maine Law Review,* 20:117, Nov. 1973. 4190

"Mentally Abnormal Witness: Challenges to His Competency and Credibility." *Rutgers Law Review,* 13:330, winter 1958. 4191

"Requirement of a Religious Belief for Competency of a Witness." *South Carolina Law Quarterly,* 11:548, summer 1959. 4192

Rothblatt, H. B. "Recognizing the Unreliable Witness." *Criminal Law Bulletin,* 10:246, April 1974. 4193

Samuels, A. "Prosecution Witness." *The New Law Journal,* 122:753, Aug. 17, 1972. 4194

Saxe, D. B. "Psychiatry, Psychoanalysis and the Credibility of Witnesses." *Notre Dame Lawyer,* 45:238, winter 1970. 4195

"Sex Offenses--Credibility of the Complaining Witness (*Wedmore* v. *State* (Ind) 143 NE. 2d 649)." *Iowa Law Review,* 43:650, summer 1958. 4196

Stafford, C. F. "Child As a Witness." *Washington Law Review,* 37:303, autumn 1962. 4197

Tarski, A. "Truth and Proof." *Scientific American,* 220:63070, June 1969. 4198

(2) FORM OF EXAMINATION

"Adverse Examination: A Consolidated Rule for the Hostile Witness in Texas." *Baylor Law Review,* 25:283, spring 1973. 4199

"Constitutional Rights of Witnesses in Federal Grand Jury Proceedings: *Bursey* v. *United States* (466 F 2d 1059)." *University of Pennsylvania Law Review,* 121:900, April 1973. 4200

Corboy, P. H. "Use of Written Authorities in Cross-Examination of Expert Witnesses." Trial Lawyer's Guide, 10:57, May 1966. 4201

Cotsirilos, G. J. "Cross-Examination in Criminal Cases." Trial Lawyer's Guide, 10:71, May 1966. 4202

Denrock, G. S. "Leading Questions." Criminal Law Quarterly, 6: 21, June 1963. 4203

Goff, C. E. "Argumentative Questions: Counsel, Protect Your Witness!" California State Bar Journal, 49:140, March-April 1974. 4204

Hagan, R. J. "Interviewing Witnesses in Criminal Cases." Brooklyn Law Review, 28:207, April 1962. 4205

Hinshaw, J. H. "Cross-Examination of Witnesses in Casualty Cases." Insurance Law Journal, 1958:482, June 1958. 4206

Jaworski, L. "Cross-Examination of Witnesses." Arkansas Law Review, 19:37, spring 1965. 4207

Jones, S. E. "Directivity vs. Nondirectivity: Implications of the Examination of Witnesses in Law for the Fact-Finding Interview." Journal of Communications, 19:64-75, March 1969. 4208

Judd, M. "Objectives, Motions, and Foundation Testimony." Cornell Law Quarterly, 43:543, summer 1958. 4209

Kornblum, G. O. "Preparation and Examination of Witnesses." Practical Lawyer, 17:11, May 1971. 4210

Margous, J. "Prosecutorial Cross-Examination: Limitations Upon the Sword of Justice." Journal of Criminal Law, 65:2, March 1974. 4211

Ordover, A. P. "Use of Written Direct Testimony in Jury Trials: A Proposal." Hofstra Law Review, 2:67, winter 1974. 4212

Orfield, L. B. "Examination of Witnesses in Federal Criminal Cases." Arizona Law Review, 4:215, spring 1963. 4213

Parnell, A. W. "Trial Judge's Suggestions on ... Preparation for Trial." Wisconsin Bar Bulletin, 39:12, fall 1966. 4214

Ratushny, E. "Basic Problems in Examination and Cross-Examination." Canadian Bar Review, 52:209, May 1974. 4215

"Recalling Witnesses in Criminal Cases." Scots Law Times, 1960: 161, October 1, 1960. 4216

Rothblatt, H. B. "Cross-Examination in Criminal Trials." Crim-

inal Law Bulletin, 10:5, Feb. 1974. 4217

Thomas, E. T. "Cross-Examination and Rehabilitation of Witnesses." *Defense Law Journal*, 14:247, 1965. 4218

"Trial Procedure and Examination of Witness." *Loyola Law Review*, 21:320, spring 1975. 4219

'Witnesses--Cross Examination--Right of Codefendants to Separate Cross-Examination." *Missouri Law Review*, 38:541, summer 1973. 4220

(3) OPINION RULE

Bertoch, M. J. "Admissibility of Opinions of the 'Experience' Expert." *International Society of Barristers Quarterly*, 5:22-27, July 1970. 4221

Coady, C. A. J. "Testimony and Observation." *American Philosophical Quarterly*, 10:149-157, April 1973. 4222

Doelle, B. "Opinion Evidence for Medical Experts." *Michigan State Bar Journal*, 32:9, April 1953. 4223

Grosman, B. A. "Testing Witness Reliability." *Criminal Law Quarterly*, 5:318, Nov. 1962. 4224

Hollies, J. H. 'Hearsay As the Basis of Opinion Evidence." *Criminal Law Quarterly*, 10:288, May 1968. 4225

Hudson, A. H. "Opinion Evidence of Intoxication." *Law Quarterly Review*, 77:166, April 1961. 4226

Juviler, M. "Psychiatric Opinions as to Credibility of Witnesses: A Suggested Approach." *California Law Review*, 48:648, Oct. 1960. 4227

Kinney, A. M., Jr. "Reexamination of the Ultimate Issue Rule." *University of Cincinnati Law Review*, 22:161, March 1953. 4228

Lacy, L. P. "Opinion Evidence or Facts?" *Washington and Lee Law Review*, 23:12, spring 1966. 4229

"Lay Opinion in Civil Cases--Speed of Motor Vehicles." *Villanova Law Review*, 4:245, winter 1958-59. 4230

McCormick, M. "Opinion Evidence in Iowa." *Drake Law Review*, 19:245, May 1970. 4231

Martindale, J. E. 'Intoxication and Opinion Evidence." *Trial Lawyer's Guide*, 8:102, Nov. 1964. 4232

"Opinion and Demonstrative Evidence." Washburn Law Journal, 14: 264, spring 1975. 4233

"Opinion Evidence--Competency of Infant Witness to Testify as to Identity and Speed of Automobile (Senecal v. Drollette (NY) 108 NE. 2d 602)." Brooklyn Law Review, 19:324, April 1953. 4234

"Opinion Testimony of Expert Witnesses: Oregon's New Rule." Oregon Law Review, 52:443, summer 1973. 4235

Pederson, L. D. "Opinion Evidence Rule in Oregon As It Relates to Cases Involving Medical Matters and Insanity." Oregon Law Review, 33:243, June 1954. 4236

Scott, W. L. "Proving State of Mind: Opinion Evidence." Los Angeles Bar Bulletin, 36:226, May 1961. 4237

Slovenko, R. "Opinion Rule and Wittgenstein's Tractatus." University of Miami Law Review, 14:1, fall 1959 4238

Stoebuck, W. B. "Opinions on Ultimate Facts: Status, Trends, and a Note of Caution." Denver Law Center Journal, 41:226, July-August, 1964. 4239

(4) EXPERT WITNESSES

Arnold, J. "Expert Witness." Manitoba Bar News, 38:330, Sept. 1972. 4240

Cantor, B. J. "Expert Witness." American Bar Association Journal, 52:946, Oct. 1966. 4241

Chambers, W. N. "Expert Textimony Regarding Paranoia." Florida Bar Journal 48:633, Oct. 1974. 4242

Clendenning, J. L. "Expert Testimony." Criminal Law Quarterly, 9:415, July 1967. 4243

Conrad, E. C. "Expert and Legal Certainty." Journal of Forensic Science, 9:445, Oct. 1964. 4244

Cook, C. M. "Role and Rights of the Expert Witness." Journal of Forensic Science, 9:456, Oct. 1964. 4245

Corboy, P. H. "Non-Medical Expert Witness." Trial Lawyer's Guide, 11:95, Aug. 1967. Explains sources for locating non-medical expert witnesses. Evidentiary fundamentals for opinion testimony and the nature of such testimony. An example of testimony by a non-medical expert is included. 4246

Couiser, E. G., Jr. "Expertise: The Expert and the Learned Treatise." Kansas Law Review, 17:167, Nov. 1968. 4247

"Courtroom Qualifications of Medical Witnesses." Trial, 6:59, June-July 1970. 4248

Diamond, B. L., and Louisell, D. W. "Psychiatrist as an Expert Witness: Some Ruminations and Speculations." Michigan Law Review, 63:1335, June 1965. 4249

Dieden, L., and Gasparich, C. "Psychiatric Evidence and Full Disclosure in the Criminal Trial." California Law Review, 52:543, Aug. 1964. 4250

"Discovery of Experts: A Historical Problem and a Proposed Solution." Minnesota Law Review, 53:785, March 1969. 4251

"Doctor in Court: Impartial Medical Testimony." Southern California Law Review, 40:728, summer 1967. 4252

"Evidence--Impeachment of Medical Expert--Use of Treatise Unknown to the Expert." Tennessee Law Review, 38:449, spring 1971. 4253

"Expert Opinion and the Ultimate Issue Doctrine (Shivers v. Carnaggio (MD) 165 A. 2d 898)." Maryland Law Review, 22:32, winter 1962. 4254

"Expert Witness: Hearsay vs. Opinion." Baylor Law Review, 24:108, winter 1972. 4255

"Expert Witnesses: Reasons for Opinion [Kavas v. Berry (Ohio) 134 NE. 2d 737]." Oklahoma Law Review, 11:323, Aug. 1958. 4256

Fowler, F. D. "Human Factors Analysis." Trial, 10:53, Nov.-Dec. 1974. 4257

Fricke, Charles W. Planning and Trying Cases. St. Paul, Minn.: West Pub. Co., 1952. 239pp. Problems of examination of witnesses through an interpreter: Comprehension of questions by the interpreter; Nature of the translation; Comprehension of questions by the witness; Legal aspect of official court interpreters. 4258

Gaines, I. D. "Psychologist as an Expert Witness." Wisconsin Bar Bulletin, 46:41, April 1973. 4259

Hammon, S. "Lawyer and the Expert." American Bar Association Journal, 49:254, March 1963. 4260

Hanson, N. R. "Expert Testimony." American Bar Association Journal, 49:254, March 1963. 4261

Harmon, R. "Use of Experts in Investigation." Journal of Air Law and Commerce, 40:441, summer 1974. 4262

Jackson, T. P. "Presenting Expert Testimony." Law Notes, 11:21, winter 1975. 4263

Karcher, J. T. "Cross-Examination of the Medical Expert." New Jersey State Bar Journal, 14:18-20, winter-Feb. 1970. 4264

Kornblum, G. O. "Expert as Witness and Consultant." Practicing Lawyer, 20:13, March 1974. 4265

Mehta, M. K. The Identification of Handwriting and the Cross Examination of Experts. Bombay: N.M. Tripathi, 1961. 287pp. Identification of handwriting as a science; importance of cross examination; forgeries, disguised writings; writing habits; and inks, additions, alterations, erasures and sequence of strokes. 4266

Meyer, B. S. "Some Problems Concerning Expert Witnesses." St. John's Law Review, 42:317, Jan. 1968. 4267

Moss, J. S. "Examination and Cross-Examination of Witnesses." South Texas Law Journal, 5:83, winter 1960. 4268

Murray, W. S. "Use of Interpreters in Court." North Dakota Law Review, 30:304, Oct. 1954. 4269

Perl, N. "The Expert and the Ultimate Issue." International Society of Barristers Quarterly, 5:9-21, July 1970. 4270

Pierson, W. D. "Abuses in the Use of Expert Testimony." Defense Law Journal, 9:117, fall 1961. 4271

Rheingord, P. D. "Basis of Medical Testimony." Trial Lawyer's Quarterly, spring-fall 1968. 4272

Rosenberg, A. H., and McGary, A. L. "Competency for Trial: The Making of an Expert." American Journal of Psychiatry, 128:1092-96, March 1972. 4273

Samuels, A. "Expert Forensic Evidence." Medical Science and Law, 14:17, Jan. 1974. 4274

Shellan, J. M. "Expert Witness in Narcotics Cases." Contemporary Drug, 2:81, spring 1973. 4275

Snyder, R. H. "Citations on the Use of Expert Testimony." J. B. A. Kansas, 29:306, May 1961. 4276

Thesiger, G. "Judge and the Expert Witness." Medicine Science and the Law, 15:3, Jan. 1975. 4277

"The Ultimate Issue Rule." Chicago-Kent Law Review, 40:147, fall 1963. 4278

"The Use of Learned Treatises on Cross-Examination of the Medical Expert...." Texas Tech Law Review, 6:237, fall 1974. 4279

Weihofen, H. "Disturbing the Experts." Washington University Law Quarterly, 1973:38, winter 1973. 4280

Zele, R. J. "Chiropractors as Expert Medical Witnesses." Cleveland State Law Review, 20:53, Jan. 1971. 4281

(5) IMPEACHMENT OF WITNESSES

"Admissibility of Evidence to Impeach Jury Verdicts." University of Miami Law Review, 22:729, spring 1968. 4282

"Adverse Party as a Witness." Arkansas Law Review, 17:136, summer 1963. 4283

"Adverse Spousal Testimony--Wife Compelled to Testify in Mann Act Prosecution (Wyatt v. U.S. 80 Supreme Court 901)." Vanderbilt Law Review, 14:643, March 1961. 4285

Amery, R. S. "Impeachment of Witnesses by Evidence of Prior Misconduct." Air Force JAG Law Review, 10:16, July-Aug. 1968. 4286

Andrews, J. A. "Issues as to the Credibility of Witnesses." Criminal Law Review, 1965:461, Aug. 1965. 4287

Bogart, J. H. "Criminal Procedure: Jencks Act: Right of Defense to Criminal Investigators' Notes for Impeachment Purposes." JAG Journal, 27:427, summer 1973. 4288

Brodsky, G. G. "Adverse Witnesses: Use of Previous Inconsistent Statements." Criminal Law Quarterly, 8:383, July 1966. 4289

Bull, H. H. "Hostile Witness." Criminal Law Quarterly, 4:384, March 1962. 4290

"Constitutional Law--Confrontation Clause--Prior Inconsistent Statements Inadmissible as Substantive Evidence Though Authorized by Statute." Wayne Law Review, 15:874, spring 1969. 4291

"Constitutional Law--Sixth Amendment--Admission of Prior Inconsistent Statements as Substantive Evidence Does Not Violate Right of Confrontation." Vanderbilt Law Review, 23:1365, Nov. 1970. 4292

"Direct Impeachment of an Adverse Party." Missouri Law Review, 35:271, spring 1970. 4293

"Due Process Challenge to Witness Coerced Statements Introduced for Impeachment Purposes." Temple Law Quarterly, 48:414, winter 1975. 4294

"Duty of the Prosecutor to Call Witnesses Whose Testimony Will Help the Accused to Establish His Innocence." Washington University Law Quarterly, 1966:68, fall 1966. 4295

"Evidence--Impeachment--Confession Taken in Violation of Miranda Rule (Miranda v. Arizona 86 Sup. Ct. 1602) Held Inadmissible for Impeachment Purposes." New York University Law Review, 42:722, Oct. 1967. 4296

"Evidence--Prior Inconsistent Statements of a Witness as Substantive Evidence." Wisconsin Law Review, 1970:202, 1970. 4297

"Evidence--Self-defense--Prior Acts of the Victim." Wisconsin Law Review, 1974:266, 1974. 4298

"Excluded Statements Collateral to Issue of Guilt May Be Used to Impeach Credibility of Defendant When They Vary from His Testimony or Direct." Houston Law Review, 4:144, spring-summer 1966. 4299

"Hearsay Witnesses Prior Statements and Criminal Justice in Illinois." University of Illinois Law Forum, 1974:675, 1974. 4300

"Impeaching a Defendant's Trial Testimony by Proof of Post-Arrest Silence." University of Pennsylvania Law Review, 123:940, April 1975. 4301

"Impeaching the Credibility of the Hearsay Declarant: The Foundation Prerequisite." UCLA Law Review, 22:452, Dec. 1974. 4302

"Impeachment by Prior Inconsistent Opinions." Missouri Law Review, 39:614, fall 1974. 4303

"Impeachment Exception to the Constitutional Exclusionary Rules." Columbia Law Review, 73:1476, Nov. 1973. 4304

"Impeachment Exception to the Exclusionary Rules." University of Chicago Law Review, 34:939, summer 1967. 4305

"Impeachment of a Defendant in a Criminal Case: The Door Is Open." University of Miami Law Review, 25:531, spring 1971. 4306

"Impeachment of Witness Called by Court." Wayne Law Review, 20:1385, spring 1974. 4307

Mueller, C. E. "Adverse Party Examinations." Trial Lawyer's Guide, 6:105, May 1962. 4308

Peltz, P. "More Than a Matter of Luck." New York Forum, 19:833, spring 1974. 4309

"Prior Inconsistent Statements As Substantive Evidence." Missouri

Law Review, 39:472, summer 1974. 4310

Reutingler, M. "Prior Inconsistent Statements: Presently Inconsistent Doctrine." Hastings Law Journal, 26:361, Nov. 1974. 4311

Schmertz, J. R., Jr., and Czapanskiy, K. S. "Bias Impeachment and the Proposed Federal Rules of Evidence." Georgia Law Journal, 61:257, Nov. 1972. 4312

"Specific Contradiction As a Mode of Impeachment." Idaho Law Review, 1:104, 1964. 4313

Thomas, R. C. "Rule Against Impeaching One's Own Witness: A Reconsideration." Missouri Law Review, 31:364, summer 1966. 4314

(6) LIE DETECTION DEVICES AND TECHNIQUES

"The Admissibility of Lie Detector Evidence." Aetna Insurance Co. v. Barnett Brothers 289 F. 2d 30, Georgia Bar Journal, 24:286, Nov. 1961. 4315

"Admissibility of Polygraph ('Lie Detector') Evidence Pursuant to Stipulation in Criminal Proceedings." Akron Law Review, 5: 235, spring 1972. 4316

"Admissibility of the Results of a Lie-Detector Test." Arizona Law Review, 5:76, fall 1963. In State v. Valdez, Arizona allowed lie-detectors: four safeguards established by Arizona Supreme Court for admitting this type of evidence. 4317

"Admitting Lie-Detector Results by Stipulation." State v. Valdez (Ariz) 371 P. 2d 894. Washington and Lee Law Review, 20:174, spring 1963. 4318

Blum, R. H., and Osterloh, W. "Polygraph Examination As a Means for Detecting Truth and Falsehood in Stories Presented by Police Informants." Journal of Criminal Law, 59:133, March 1968. 4319

Brasch, R. E. "Polygraph Confession." Willamette Law Journal, 9:54, March 1973. 4320

Bryan, William Joseph. Legal Aspects of Hypnosis. Springfield, Ill.: Charles C. Thomas, 1962. 304pp. 4321

Burkey, L. M. "Case Against the Polygraph." American Bar Association Journal, 51:855, spring 1965. 4322

Coghlan, J. P., Sr. "Lie Box Lies." Trial Lawyers Guide, 7:47, May 1963. 4323

"Confession to Polygraph Operator Prior to Actual Test Held Admissible." University of Richmond Law Review, 9:377, winter 1975. 4324

Cooke, R. E. "Truth, Statistics and the Polygraph." Police, 36-41, Nov.-Dec. 1968. 4325

"Emergence of the Polygraph as Trial." Columbia Law Review, 73: 1120, May 1973. 4326

"Evidence--Polygraph Evidence Is Inadmissible in Texas Despite Stipulation by the Parties." Texas Technological Law Review, 5:174, fall 1974. 4327

Falick, P. "Lie Detectors and the Right to Privacy." New York State Bar Journal, 40:102, Feb. 1961. 4328

Gall, J. C., Jr. "Case Against Narcointerrogation." Journal of Forensic Science, 7:29, Jan. 1962. 4329

Horvath, F. S., and Reid, J. E. "Polygraph Silent Answer Test." Journal of Criminal Law, 63:285, June 1972. 4330

"Hypnosis, Truth Drugs and the Polygraph: An Analysis of Their Use and Acceptance by the Courts." University of Florida Law Review, 21:541, spring 1969. 4331

Inbau, F. E., and Reid, J. E. "Lie-Detector Technique: A Reliable and Valuable Investigative Aid." American Bar Association Journal, 50:470, May 1964. 4332

Kaplan, A. G. "Lie Detector: An Analysis of Its Place in the Law of Evidence." Wayne Law Review, 10:381, winter 1964. 4333

Levin, M. "Lie Detectors Can Lie!" Labor Law Journal, 15:708, Nov. 1964. 4334

O'Connor, F. "That's the Man: A Sobering Study of Eyewitness Identification and the Polygraph." St. John's Law Review, 49:1, fall 1974. 4335

"Polygraph Evidence: The Case for Admissibility Upon Stipulation of the Parties." Tulsa Law Journal, 9:250, fall 1973. 4336

"Polygraph Revisited: An Argument for Admissibility." Criminal Law Bulletin, 6:63, March 1970; Suffolk University Law Review, 4:111, fall 1969. 4337

"Polygraph: Scientific v. Judicial Acceptance." University of Miami Law Review, 27:254, fall-winter 1972. 4338

"Problems Remaining for the 'Generally Accepted' Polygraph." Boston University Law Review, 53:375, March 1973. 4339

Radek, L. J. "Admissibility of Polygraph Results in Criminal Trials: A Case for the Status Quo." Loyola University Law Journal (Chicago) 3:289, summer 1972. 4340

"Role of the Polygraph in Our Judicial System." South Carolina Law Review, 20:804, 1968. 4341

Sadoff, R. L. "Psychiatric Involvement in the Search for Truth." American Bar Association Journal, 52:251, March 1966. 4342

Speiser, Stuart M. "Narcoanalysis--Using 'Truth Serums' in Legal Proceedings." Case and Comment, 72:11-15, Jan.-Feb. 1967. 4343

"United States v. Ridling (350 F. Supp. 90): The Polygraph Breaks Through the 'Twilight Zone'." Catholic University Law Review, 23:101, fall 1973. 4344

Use of Polygraphs as "Lie Detectors." Hearings before a Subcommittee on Government Operations, House of Representatives, Eighty-Eighth Congress, Second Session, April 10, 1964. Part III. Testimony of Army, Navy, and Air Force witnesses. 4345

________. ________, April 29 and 30, 1964. Part III. Panel discussion with scientists. 4346

________. ________, May 13, 1964. Part IV. Testimony of Post Office Department witnesses. 4347

________. ________, May 25, 1964. Part V. Testimony of Federal Bureau of Investigation Witnesses. 4348

________. ________, Aug. 19, 1964. Part VI. Testimony of Department of Defense witnesses. 4349

(7) CORROBORATION OF WITNESSES

"Accomplice Corroboration Requirement in Utah--A Need for Change." Utah Law Review, 1972:60, spring 1972. 4350

"Child's Evidence: Corroboration." Solicitor's Journal, 117:608, Aug. 17-24, 1973. An English case in which, on appeal, it was decided that the testimony of a nine-year-old child corroborating the testimony of a prosecutrix was not considered ample supporting evidence. 4351

"Corroborating Charges of Rape." Columbia Law Review, 67:1137, June 1967. 4352

"Corroboration in Rape Cases in New York--A Half Step Forward." Albany Law Review, 37:306, 1973. 4353

Cutts, J. A., III. "Corroboration of Confessions: The Opper Rule." Air Force JAG Law Review, 8:50, winter 1971. 4354

Dow, D. "Judicial Determination of Credibility in Jury-tried actions." Nebraska Law Review, 38:835, June 1959. 4355

"Effect of Perjury on Credibility of Witnesses in New York." Fordham Law Review, 38:835, June 1959. 4356

"Effect of Perjury on Credibility of Witnesses in New York." Fordham Law Review, 31:797, April 1963. 4357

"Evidence Against a Co-Accused." Law Journal, 115:446, July 2, 1965. 4358

Heydon, J. D. "Can Lies Corroborate?" Lawyer's Quarterly Review, 89:552, Oct. 1973. 4359

________. "Corroboration of Accomplices." Criminal Law Review, 1973:264, May 1973. 4360

Hubbard, P. C. "Corroboration of the Evidence of a Co-Prisoner." Criminal Law Review, 1958:728, Nov. 1958. 4361

"Nebraska's Corroboration Rule." Nebraska Law Review, 54:93, 1975. 4362

"Perjury--Evidence--The Two Witness Rule." May v. U.S. 280 F. 3d 555, Kansas Law Review, 10:475, March 1962. 4363

Pitler, R. M. "'Existentialism' and Corroboration of Sex Crimes in New York: A New Attempt to Limit 'If Someone Didn't See It, It Didn't Happen'." Syracuse Law Review, 24:1, 1973. The changes in the corroboration requirement in rape cases and sex crimes in New York in 1972; consideration of the reasonable underlying corroboration requirements. 4364

Savage, C. C. "Corroboration." Criminal Law Quarterly, 6:159, Nov. 1963. 4365

Sheppard, A. F. "Mutual Corroboration." Criminal Law Quarterly, 15:62, Dec. 1972. 4366

"Testimony As to Prior Identification of Defendant Held Admissible As Substantive Evidence but Insufficient Alone to Sustain Conviction, People v. Gould (California) 354 P. 2d 865." University of Pennsylvania Law Review, 190:1182, June 1961. 4367

Williams, G. O. "Corroboration--Sexual Cases." Criminal Law Review, 1962:662, Oct. 1962. 4368

Yahuda, J. "Unconscious Corroboration." New Law Journal, 116: 607, March 24, 1966. 4369

E. HEARSAY

(1) GENERAL CONSIDERATIONS

"Abolish the Rule Against Hearsay." *University of Pittsburgh Law Review*, 35:609, spring 1974. Attempts to promote serious discussion of abolishing the rule against hearsay; maintains that underlying the development of the rule is the assumption that human testimony is untrustworthy. Criticisms of the rule are that its exceptions are very complicated and difficult to apply and that it does not distinguish between reliable and unreliable hearsay. 4370

Cannon, J. J. "Hearsay Rule." *Juvenile Court Judges Journal*, 17:25, spring 1966. 4371

"Comparative Study of Hearsay Evidence Abroad." *International Law*, 4:156, Oct. 1969. 4372

"Criminal Defendant's Hearsay Evidence: Time for a Change." *Texas Law Review*, 47:250, Jan. 1969. 4373

"Criminal Law--Admissibility of Evidence--Relevant Facts--Hearsay --Res Gestae." *Michigan University Law Review*, 9:323, spring 1973. 4374

Cross, R. "Periphery of Hearsay." *Michigan University Review*, 7:1, May 1969. 4375

______. "Scope of the Rule Against Hearsay." *Law Quarterly Review*, 72:91, Jan. 1956. 4376

Davis, K. C. "Hearsay in Nonjury Cases." *Harvard Law Review*, 83:1362, April 1970. Argues that the proposed federal rules of evidence are needlessly ambiguous and should be altered to provide free admissibility of hearsay. 4377

Donnelly, R. C. "Hearsay Rule and Its Exceptions." *Minnesota Law Review*, 40:455, March 1956. 4378

Dow, D. "Criminal Hearsay Rules: Constitutional Issues." *Nebraska Law Review*, 53:425, 1974. 4379

"Evidentiary Use of a Witness' Prior Extra Judicial Statement." *University of Detroit Law Review*, 39:393, fall 1962. 4380

"Federal Confrontation: A Not Very Clear Say on Hearsay." *UCLA Law Review*, 13:366, Jan. 1966. 4381

Goldman, C. S. "Use of Learned Treatises in Canadian and United States Litigation." *University of Toronto Law Journal*, 24:423, autumn 1974. 4382

Hauselman, M. F. "Hearsay Evidence in Criminal Cases." Police Law Reporter. 2:3-14, July-Aug. 1969. 4383

"Hearsay and Confrontation: Can the Criminal Defendant's Rights Be Preserved under a Bifurcated Standard?" Washington and Lee Law Review, 32:243, winter 1975. 4384

"Hearsay Rule: The Law of Evidence's Swiss Cheese." Loyola Law Review, 21:279, spring 1975. 4385

Nokes, G. D. "Some Suggestions on Hearsay." Criminal Law Review, 1965:85, fall 1965. 4386

"Physician's Testimony--Hearsay Evidence or Expert Opinion: A Question of Professional Competence." Texas Law Review, 53: 296, Jan. 1975. 4387

Prince, J. "Policy Considerations and Changes in the Hearsay Rule." New York Law Forum, 19:761, spring 1974. 4388

"Prior Identification Evidence and the Hearsay Objection." Rocky Mountain Law Review, 30:332, April 1958. 4389

Reed, J. W. "What Is This Thing Called Hearsay." Michigan State Bar Journal, 36:17, March 1957. 4390

Strachan, B. "Hearsay Rules." New York Law Journal, 116:869, May 26, 1966. 4391

Symposium--Hearsay Evidence. "Foreword." E. M. Morgan; "What Is Hearsay?" C. C. Wheaton; "Spontaneous Statements and State of Mind." M. C. Slough; "Official Written Statements." W. E. Wallace; "Business Entries and the Like." C. V. Laughlin; "Admissions in the Uniform Rules: Are They Necessary?" J. L. Hetland, Jr.; "Probative Force of Hearsay." J. B. Weinstein; "Affidavits, Depositions, and Prior Testimony, Dying Declarations, Confessions, Judgments as Evidence, Pedigree, Reputation, Voter's Statements, Recitals in Ancient Documents, Commercial Lists, Learned Treatises." Iowa Law Review, 46:207, winter 1961. 4392

Teasdale, J. P. "Hearsay and Gone Tomorrow." New Law Journal, 124:61, Jan. 17, 1974. 4393

Tribe, L. H. "Triangulating Hearsay." Harvard Law Review, 87: 957, May 1974. 4394

Weinstein, J. B. "Alternatives to the Present Hearsay Rules." Federal Rules Decisions, 44:375, Aug. 1968. 4395

Younger, I. "A Brief for Exception to Rule Against Hearsay." New York Law Journal, 163:1+, March 27, 1970. 4396

(2) CONFESSIONS AND ADMISSIONS

"Admissibility of Confessions and Statements." Criminal Law Quarterly, 5:35, June 1962. 4397

"Admission of Extrajudicial Third Party Confessions." Kansas Law Review, 11:275, Dec. 1962. 4398

"Admissions and the Admissibility of Exculpary Statements." Victoria University of Wellington Law Review, 5:82, fall 1968. 4399

"Admissions to Agents." Missouri Law Review, 40:55, winter 1975. 4400

"Adoptive Admissions, Arrest and the Privilege Against Self-Incrimination: A Suggested Constitutional Imperative." University of Chicago Law Review, 31:556, spring 1964. 4401

Bell, G. M. "Admissions Arising Out of Compromise--Are They Relevant?" Texas Law Review, 31:239, Feb. 1953. 4402

"Effect of the Introduction of Exculpatory Statements in a Criminal Procedure." Baylor Law Review, 26:79, winter 1974. 4403

"Evidence--Silence as an Admission of Guilt--Admissibility Criticized." Missouri Law Review, 39:264, spring 1974. 4404

"Evidence--The Use of Prior Uncounseled Convictions for Impeachment." DePaul Law Review (LA) 6:429, Jan. 1973. 4405

"Evidentiary Use of the Express Admissions of Infant Parties." Georgia State Bar Journal, 3:122, Aug. 1966. 4406

Fisch, E. L. "Extra-Judicial Admissions." Syracuse Law Review, 4:90, fall 1952. 4407

Heller, S. L. "Admissions by Acquaintance." Miami Law Review, 15:161, winter 1960. 4408

Hooper, A. "Admissibility of Exculpatory Statements." Osgoode Hall Law Journal, 11:295, Aug. 1973. 4409

Morgan, E. M. "Admissions." UCLA Law Review, 1:18, Dec. 1953. 4410

Newark, M., and Samuels, A. "Confessions." The New Law Journal, 119:570, 609, June 19-26, 1969. English legal history through the present as to admission of confessions. 4411

"Party's Testimony As Judicial Admission." Western Reserve Law Review, 5:398, summer 1954. 4412

"Res Gestae--Extra Judicial Declarations of Co-Conspirators." Sapet vs. State (Tex), 266 SW. 2d 154. Texas Law Review, 3: 138, July 1952. 4413

Savage, C. C. "Admissions in Criminal Cases." Criminal Law Quarterly, 5:49, June 1962. 4414

Scoble, C. N. "Admissions." South Africa Law Journal, 69:273, Aug. 1952. 4415

Smith, P. "Dangerous Silence." New Law Journal, 123:661, July 12, 1973. 4416

Stewart, D. J. "Admissibility and Probable Value of an Accused's Subsequent Statements of Intent." Washburn Law Journal, 8:313, spring 1969. 4417

"Tacit Criminal Admissions." University of Pennsylvania Law Review, 112:210, Dec. 1963. 4418

"Vicarious Admissions and Utterances." Marquette Law Review, 47:84, summer 1963. 4419

"Voluntary Incriminating Statements Made Subsequent to an Illegal Arrest--A Proposed Modification of the Exclusionary Rule." Dickinson Law Review, 71:573, summer 1967. 4420

Wall, P. M. "Judicial Admissions: Their Use in Criminal Trials." Journal of Criminal Law, Criminology, and Police Science, 53: 15, March 1962. 4421

(3) REPUTED AND FORMER TESTIMONY

"Admissibility of Prior Testimony of Unavailable Witness [People v. Pickett (Mich.) 63 NW 2d 681]." UCLA Law Review, 2:138, Dec. 1954. 4422

Baldinger, M. L. "Admissibility of Reproduced Records in Evidence." Journal of the Bar Association of the District of Columbia, 19:461, Oct. 1952. 4423

Beaver, J. E., and Biggs, P. W. "Attending Witnesses' Prior Declarations as Evidence: Theory vs. Reality." Indiana Legal Forum, 3:309, spring 1970. 4424

"Clark's Notes of Evidence as Evidence." Solicitor's Journal, 109: 60, Jan. 22, 1965. 4425

Donahue, J. E. "Former Testimony." Military Law Review, 21:1, 1966. 4426

"Evidence--Hearsay--A Witness' Prior Written Statement Not Made

Under Oath Is Admissible As Substantive Evidence." Georgia Law Review, 1:137, fall 1966. 4427

"Evidence--Out of Court Statement As Non-Hearsay." Mississippi Law Journal, 43:122, 1972. 4428

"Evidence--Whether Witness' Prior Voluntary Testimony Constitutes Waiver of Privilege of Self-Incrimination in Second Trial of Same Case." Dickinson Law Review, 73:80, fall 1968. 4429

"Hearsay Rule--Exception for Former Testimony." Wolf v. United Airlines, Inc., 191 F. 2d 818. Columbia Law Review, 52:666, May 1952. 4430

Kennelly, J. J., and Harte, W. J. "Production of Documents by Categories." Trial Lawyer's Guide, 9:73, Feb. 1965. 4431

"Objections to Former Testimony." Indiana Law Journal, 35:454, summer 1960. 4432

"Reported Testimony Exception." State v. Storm (Montana) 265 P. 2d 971. Kansas Law Review, 3:374, May 1955. 4433

"Use of Former Testimony as Substantive Evidence in Criminal Cases." Montana Law Review, 30:201, spring 1969. 4434

"Use of Reported Testimony in Subsequent Cases." Western Reserve Law Review, 11:471, June 1960. 4435

(4) IMPLIED ADMISSION AND ACCUSATORY STATEMENTS

"Admissibility of Adoptive Admissions." New York University Law Review, 29:1266, June 1954. 4436

"Admissibility of Self-Serving Declaration." Arkansas Law Review, 14:105, winter 1959-1960. 4437

"Admission by Silence in Civil Cases." Syracuse Law Review, 17: 507, spring 1966. 4438

Ball, Joseph A. "Conduct as Hearsay." Los Angeles Bar Bulletin, 41:558, Oct. 1966. 4439

Brody, A. "Admissions Implied from Silence, Evasion and Equivocation in Massachusetts Criminal Cases." Boston University Law Review, 42:46, winter 1962. 4440

Cestaro, G. T. "Admission by Silence of Written Matter: A Comment on Evidence and Public Policy." Chicago-Kent Law Review, 39:138, Oct. 1962. 4441

"Criminal Law--Fifth Amendment--Use of the Silence of the Accused

Before Trial to Impeach Testimony Is Constitutionally Impermissible." Maryland Law Review, 33:363, 1973. 4442

"Evidence--Exclusion and Suppression--Silence of Defendant When Arrested May Not Be Used to Impeach His Testimony." Harvard Law Review, 87:882, fall 1974. 4443

"Exclusion of Self-Serving Declarations." Michigan Law Review, 61: 1306, May 1963. 4444

Finman, T. "Implied Assertions As Hearsay: Some Criticisms of the Uniform Rules of Evidence." Stanford Law Review, 14:682, July 1962. 4445

Holtman, D. R. "Squire Marsden in Connecticut: Non-Assertive Conduct As Hearsay." Connecticut Bar Journal, 40:27, March 1966. 4446

"Miranda Decision and Its Effects on the Tacit Admissions Rule in Pennsylvania (Miranda v. Arizona, 86 Supreme Court 1962)." University of Pittsburgh Law Review, 28:77, Oct. 1966. 4447

Nokes, G. D. "Self-Serving Conduct." Corke v. Corke 2 WLR 110. Modern Law Review, 21:289, May 1958. 4448

"Physicians and Surgeons--Extrajudicial Admissions of the Defendant." Granwood v. Harris (Oklahoma), 362 P. 2d 85. Washburn Law Journal, 1:615, spring 1962. 4449

Reilly, J. J. "Non-Verbal Statements: Observations on a Unique Concept Employed by Military Courts." JAG Journal, 25:24, July-Aug. 1970. 4450

"Silence--An Admission of Guilt." De Paul Law Review, 11:307, summer 1962. 4451

"Silence--Can It Waive a Constitutional Right?" Washburn Law Journal, 10:321, winter 1971. 4452

"Silence of an Accused As Evidence of Guilt." Arkansas Law Review, 13:123, spring 1959. 4453

"Tacit Admissions and Miranda." Tennessee Law Review, 36:566, spring 1969. 4454

Weinberg, M. "Implied Assertions and the Scope of the Hearsay Rule." Michigan University Law Review, 9:268, summer 1973. 4455

(5) STATEMENTS AGAINST INTEREST

"Admissibility of Declarations Against Penal Interest." Dickinson

Law Review, 79:189, fall 1974. 4456

"Co-parties: Use of Admissions and Declarations Against Interest." John Marshall Journal, 3:364, spring 1970 4457

"Declaration Against Interest." Modern Law Review, 25:458, July 1962. 4458

"Declaration Against Interest: A Critical Review of the Unavailability Requirement." Cornell Law Quarterly, 52:301 4459

"Declaration Against Penal Interest: A Time for Review." Connecticut Bar Journal, 44:276, June 1970. 4460

"Declaration Against Penal Interest Exception to the Hearsay Rule, McGrain v. Horn (Ind) 183 NE 2d 206." De Paul Law Review, 12:232, spring-summer 1963. 4461

"Declarations Against Interest--An Exception to the Hearsay Rule." Syracuse Law Review, 18:61, fall 1966. 4462

"Declarations Against Interest--Rules of Admissibility." Northwestern University Law Review, 62:934, Jan.-Feb. 1968. 4463

"Declarations Against Penal Interests As an Exception to the Hearsay Rule." St. Louis University Law Journal, 7:335, spring 1963. 4464

"Declarations by Third Persons in Presence of a Party--Hearsay Aspects, Past, Present and Future." Wyoming Law Journal, 19:43, 1965. 4465

"Evidence--Admissibility of Declarants Against Penal Interest." Fordham Law Review, 39:136, Oct. 1970. 4466

"Evidence--Exceptions to Hearsay Rule--Declarations Against Penal Interest Admissible." New York Law Forum. 16:504, 1970. 4467

Fine, J. "Declarations Against Penal Interest in New York: Carte Blanche?" Syracuse Law Review, 21:1095, summer 1970. 4468

"Self-Serving Declaration and Declaration Against Interest." Brown v. McConnell (PA) 93 A. 2d 96, University of Detroit Law Journal, 16:154, March 1953. 4469

"Statement Against Penal Interest As an Exception to the Hearsay Rule." University of Pittsburgh Law Review, 26:129, Oct. 1964. 4470

"The Unavailability Requirement for Declarations Against Interest--Should It Be Retained?" Missouri Law Review, 39:461, summer 1974. 4471

(6) DYING DECLARATIONS

"Admissibility of Dying Declarants." Fordham Law Review, 38:509, March 1970. 4472

"Dying Declarations [Cummings v. Illinois Central Railroad Co. (Mo.). 269 SW 2d 111]." Missouri Law Review, 20:99, Jan. 1955. 4473

"Dying Declarations in Louisiana Law." Louisiana Law Review, 22: 651 [24pp.]. April 1962. Three aspects: (1) exceptions to the hearsay rule, (2) general rules of evidence applied, (3) procedural aspects. 4474

"Dying Declarations--Instructions by the Trial Court." Nebraska Law Review, 32:461, March 1953. 4475

"Evidence--Necessary Exception to Hearsay Rule--Declarations of Decedent Admissible When No Other Witnesses." Mercer Law Review, 14:445, spring 1963. 4476

Iacovitti, Joseph M. "The Affiliations Between Pennsylvania's Abortion Laws and Dying Declarations." North Carolina Central Law Journal, 2:214-218, fall 1971. 4477

Quick, C. W. "Some Reflections on Dying Declarations." Howard Law Journal, 6:109, June 1960. 4478

Shaw, M. M. "Dying Declaration." Trial Lawyer's Guide, 5:73, Feb. 1961. 4479

"Should the Admissibility of Dying Declarations in Evidence Be Limited to Homicide Cases?" West Virginia Law Review, 61: 132, Feb. 1956. 4480

(7) BUSINESS RECORDS

"Admissibility of Computer Printouts." North Carolina Law Review, 52:903, March 1974. 4481

"Admissibility of Hospital Records." Albany Law Review, 37:579, 1973. 4482

"Admissibility of Hospital Records Under Section 327.25, Wisconsin Statutes." Marquette Law Review, 49:801, May 1966. 4483

"Admission of Printed Material As an Exception to the Hearsay Rule." Baylor Law Review, 19:280, spring 1967. 4484

"Business Records As Evidence in Colorado." University of Colorado Law Review, 35:221, winter 1963. 4485

Button, J. J. "Official Records Exception to the Hearsay Rule in California." Santa Clara Law, 6:1, fall 1965. 4486

"Evidence--Exception to Hearsay Rule--Writings, Records, Entries, and Memoranda Made in the Regular Course of Business." Georgia Bar Journal, 25:314 [5pp], fall 1963. Discusses a court case, cites Georgia rule on writings and six items involving the rules, and discusses four federal issues which courts have allowed. 4487

"Exception to Hearsay Rule--Federal Business Records Act." Washburn Law Journal, 2:176, winter 1962. 4488

"The Federal Shop Book Rule--Admissibility of Hospital Records." West Virginia Law Review, 65:229, April 1963. 4489

"Hearsay--Admissibility of Hospital Records." North Carolina Law Review, 41:621, spring 1963. North Carolina rule and the possibility of more frequent use of hospital records. 4490

"Hospital Accident Reports: Admissibility and Privilege." Dickinson Law Review, 79:493, spring 1975. 4491

Murray, C. J. "Admissibility of Hospital Records--A Continuing Problem." Texas Bar Journal, 29:163, March 1966. 4492

"Official Records Exception to the Hearsay Rule in California." Santa Clara Lawyer, 6:1, fall 1965. 4493

(8) PHYSICAL OR MENTAL CONDITION

"Admissibility of a Death Certificate Entry Indicating Secondary Cause of Violent Death--Problems of Hearsay, Expertise, Foundation and Ultimate Fact Rule." Rutgers Law Review, 25:207, spring 1971. 4494

"Admissibility of Expressions of Pain and Suffering." Michigan Law Review, 51:902, April 1953. 4495

"Admissibility of Testimony by an Attending Physician to a Hearsay Statement Made by His Patient Concerning Causal Facts of the Injury [Shell Oil Co. v. Industrial Commission (Ill.), 119 NE. 2d 224]." Illinois Bar Journal, 43:320, Jan. 1955. 4496

"Commonwealth v. McCusker (Pa.) 292 A. 2d 286--The Use of Psychiatric Testimony in Pennsylvania Homicide Trials." Temple Law Quarterly, 47:156, fall 1973. 4497

Huckabee, H. M. "Resolving the Problem of Dominance of Psychiatrists in Criminal Responsibility Decisions: A Proposal." Southwestern Law Journal, 27:790, Dec. 1973. 4498

"Medical Testimony and the Hearsay Rule." *Washington University Law Quarterly*, 1964:192, April 1964. 4499

Nordstrom, Niles. *The Rights and Rewards of the Medical Witness and Dental Appraiser.* Springfield, Ill.: Charles C. Thomas, 1962. 104pp. Methods of arriving at workable, friendly relationships in the personal injury field. Discusses problems of medical men as witnesses and of lawyers who are presenting the claims of doctors' patients in courts. 4500

"State of Mind and Physical Condition As a Hearsay Exception." *Oklahoma Law Review*, 14:75, Feb. 1961. 4501

"Statements of Symptoms to a Treating Physician As Substantive Evidence [Peterson v. Richfield Playa, Inc. (Minn) 89 NW. 2d 712]." *Minnesota Law Review*, 43:145, Nov. 1958. 4502

Younger, I. "Statements of Physical Condition As an Exception to the Rule Against Hearsay." *New York Law Forum*, 19:777, spring 1974. 4503

(9) SPONTANEOUS UTTERANCES

"Excited Utterances--Requirement That the Utterance Explain the Exciting Event [Murphy Auto Parts Co. v. Ball, 249 F. 2d 508]." *New York University Law Review*, 34:166, Jan. 1959. 4504

Hardman, T. P. "Spontaneous Declarations (res gestae)." *West Virginia Law Review*, 56:1, Feb. 1954. 4505

Quick, C. W. "Hearsay, Excitement, Necessity and the Uniform Rules: A Reappraisal of Rule 63 (4)." *Wayne Law Review*, 6:204, spring 1960. 4506

"Res Gestae and Spontaneous Exclamations." Murphy Auto Parts Co. v. Ball, 249 F. 2d 508. *Arkansas Law Review*, 12:405, fall 1958. 4507

"Res Gestae in New York." *New York University Intramural Law Review*, 8:115, Jan. 1953. 4508

"Spontaneous Declarations [Murphy Auto Parts Co. v. Ball, 249 F. 2d 508]." *Tulane Law Review*, 32:775, June 1958. 4509

"Spontaneous Declarations [People v. Marks (NY), 160 NE. 2d 26]." *Cornell Law Quarterly*, 45:810, summer 1960. 4510

(10) MISCELLANEOUS

"Evidence--Admission of Statistical Surveys Under Learned Treatise

Exception to Hearsay Rule." Tennessee Law Review, 40:759, summer 1973. 4511

"Evidence of Habit and Custom in Massachusetts Civil Cases." Boston University Law Review, 33:205, April 1953. 4512

Garland, N. M., and Snow, D. C. "Co-Conspirators Exception to the Hearsay Rule: Procedural Implementation and Confrontation Clause Requirements." Journal of Criminal Law, 63:1, March 1972. 4513

"Habit and Custom--Proving What Was Done on a Particular Occasion [Boldridge v. Matthew (Pa.) 106 A. 2d 809]." University of Pittsburgh Law Review, 16:201, winter 1955. 4514

"Habit Evidence in California Negligence Cases." UCLA Intramural Law Review, 1952:1, June 1952. 4515

"Opinion Poll Evidence [Sears, Roebuck and Co. v. All State Life Insurance Co., 246 F. 2d 161]." Georgia Bar Journal, 20:566, May 1958. 4516

"Past Recollection Recorded: The 'Forward-Looking' Federal Rules of Evidence Lean Backwards." Notre Dame Lawyer, 50:737, April 1975. 4517

Seidelson, D. E. "State of Mind Exception to the Hearsay Rule." Duquesne Law Review, 13:251, winter 1974. 4518

Tapper, C. "Evidence from Computers." Georgia Law Review, 8:562, spring 1974. 4519

"Testimony from 'Present Memory Refreshed'; Accused Right to Examine Documents Used to Refresh Witness' Memory." Loyola Law Review, 20:214, 1973-74. 4520

F. CIRCUMSTANTIAL EVIDENCE

(1) USED INFERENTIALLY

"Admissibility of Affadivits Used to Refresh Present Recollection of Witness." Maryland Law Review, 34:649, 1974. 4521

"Admissibility of Testimonial By-Products of a Physical Test." University of Miami Law Review, 24:50, fall 1969. 4522

"Constitutional Law--Mere Evidence Rule As a Constitutional Standard." De Paul Law Review, 16:215, autumn-winter 1966. 4523

Davidson, R. B. "Imputations Against Prosecution Witnesses."

Australian Lawyer, 14:133, summer. 4524

"Directed Verdicts--Inferences from Circumstantial Evidence." Nebraska Law Review, 34:102, Nov. 1954. 4525

"Drawing an Inference from the Failure to Produce a Knowledgeable Witness: Evidentiary and Constitutional Considerations." California Law Review, 61:1422, Dec. 1973. 4526

"Evidentiary Value of the Presumption Against Suicide [Kettlewell v. Presidential Insurance Co. (Ill.), 122 NE. 2d 817]." Illinois Bar Journal, 43:674, April 1955. 4527

Feldman, S. M. "Difference Between the Pennsylvania and Federal Tests of Sufficiency of Circumstantial Evidence of Negligence and the Choice of Law in Federal Diversity Cases." Dickinson Law Review, 72:409, spring 1968. 4528

Goldstein, A. H., Jr. "Krulewitch Warning: Guilty by Association." Georgetown Law Journal, 54:133, fall 1965. 4529

Greenberg, A. H. "Inferences from Refusal to Answer Questions Concerning Communist Affiliation." Los Angeles Bar Bulletin, 29:37, Nov. 1953. 4530

Liddle, T. H., III. "Mathematical and Statistical Probability As a Test of Circumstantial Evidence." Case Western Reserve Law Review, 19:254, Jan. 1968. 4531

"Proof of Deed by Circumstantial Evidence." Baylor Law Review, 20:167, spring 1968. 4532

Sebastian, Raymond F. "Destruction of Evidence--A Rationale for Blood Tests Without an Arrest." Stanford Law Review, 18:243-255, Nov. 1965. California police use of blood samples to determine intoxication; reviews legality as evidence under the Fourth Amendment. 4533

"Sufficiency--Effect of Testimony of Party Contrary to His Testimony at Prior Trial." California Law Review, 42:176, spring 1954. 4534

"Use of Voice Prints to Establish Probable Cause Held Admissible." Santa Clara Lawyer, 14:194, fall 1973. 4535

(2) PROOF OF OTHER CRIMES

"Admissibility of Evidence of Other Crimes in a Criminal Prosecution [Day v. Commonwealth (Va.), 86 SE. 2d 23]." Ohio State Law Journal, 17:351, summer 1966. 4536

"Admissibility of Prior Convictions to Impeach a Defendent-Witness." South Dakota Law Review, 15:160, winter 1970. 4537

"California's Use of Prior Convictions to Impeach a Criminal Defendant." University of San Francisco Law Review, 9:491, winter 1975. 4538

"Constitutional Problems Inherent in the Admissibility of Prior Record Conviction Evidence for the Purpose of Impeaching the Credibility of the Defendant Witness." University of Cincinnati Law Review, 37:168, winter 1968. 4539

"Conviction upon Plea of Nolo Contendere as Impeaching Evidence." Arkansas Law Review, 21:124, spring 1967. 4540

"Criminal Action--Admissibility of Prior Similar Offenses [Commonwealth v. Boulden (Pa.), 116 A. 2d 867]." University of Pittsburgh Law Review, 17:302, winter 1956. 4541

"Criminal Law--Admissibility of Evidence of Unconnected Crimes [People v. Mikka (Ill.), 131 NE. 2d 79]." Notre Dame Lawyer, 31:717, Aug. 1956. 4542

"Criminal Law--Evidence--Prior Crime Evidence Admissible Only When Relevant to Crime Charged." Florida State University Law Review, 2:197, winter 1974. 4543

"Criminal Law: Proof of Former Convictions." Oklahoma Law Review, 24:372, Aug. 1971. 4544

"Developments in Evidence of Other Crimes." University of Michigan Journal of Law, 7:535, spring 1974. 4545

"Evidence: Admissibility of Similar Offenses as Evidence of Identity in a Criminal Trial." Washburn Law Journal, 14:367, spring 1975. 4546

"Evidence--Proof of Particular Facts--Evidence That Defendant May Have Committed Similar Crimes Is Admissible to Prove Corpus Delicti of Murder." Harvard Law Review, 87:1074, March 1974. 4547

"Exclusion of Prior Acquittals: An Attack on the 'Prosecutor's Delight'." UCLA Law Review, 21:892, fall 1974. 4548

McGavan, C. "Impeachment of Criminal Defendants by Prior Convictions." Law and Social Order, 1970:1, 1970. 4549

McMahon, W. J. "Relevancy of Similar Offenses or Acts of Misconduct." JAG Journal, 1954:3, Dec. 1954. 4550

"Other Crimes Evidence at Trial: Of Balancing and Other Matters." Yale Law Journal, 70:763, April 1916. 4551

"Other Crimes Evidence in Louisiana--To Show Knowledge, Intent, System, etc. in the Case in Chief. To Attack the Credibility of the Defendant on Cross-Examination." Louisiana Law Review, 33:614, summer 1973. 4552

"Other Crimes Evidence to Prove Intent in Rape Cases." Loyola Law Review, 19:751, fall 1973. 4553

"Prior Crimes Used to Show Specific Intent and Identity." Marquette Law Review, 50:133, Aug. 1966. 4554

"Prior Criminal Convictions to Impeach Credibility in Oklahoma." Oklahoma Law Review, 19:430, Nov. 1966. 4555

"Use of Evidence of Prior Acts of Misconduct." JAG Journal, 18: 248, April 1964. 4556

"Use of Prior Conviction and Reputation to Show Defendant's Bad Character." Idaho Law Review, 1:90, 1964. 4557

"Use of Prior Convictions to Impeach the Credibility of the Criminal Defendant." West Virginia Law Review, 71:160, fall 1969. 4558

"Use of Prior Crimes to Affect Credibility and Penalty in Pennsylvania." University of Pennsylvania Law Review, 113:382, Jan. 1965. 4559

"Use of Record of Criminal Conviction in Subsequent Civil Action Arising from the Same Facts As the Prosecution." Michigan Law Review, 64:702, Feb. 1966. 4560

Wood, Q. H. "Evidence of Previous Convictions." JAG Journal, 1954:5, March 1954. 4561

(3) PROOF OF CHARACTER

Boller, R. R. "Proof of Defendant's Character." Military Law Review, 64:37, spring 1974. 4562

"Character Evidence." Loyola Law Review, 21:405, spring 1975. 4563

"Character Evidence--The Rules of Admissibility in Criminal Cases in Kentucky." Kentucky Law Journal, 61:693, 1972-73. 4564

"Character in Evidence." Baylor Law Review, 14:59, winter 1962. 4565

"Constitutional Law--Evidence--Use of Miranda--Violative Confessions for Impeachment Purposes." West Virginia Law Review, 74:187, Nov.-Jan. 1971-72. 4566

Curley, R. M. "Reputation of a Witness for Truth and Veracity in Civil and Criminal Cases." Marquette Law Review, 46:353, winter 1962-63. 4567

Falknor, J. F., and Steffen, D. T. "Evidence of Character: From Its 'Crucible of the Community' to the 'Couch of the Psychiatrist'." University of Pennsylvania Law Review, 102:980, June 1954. 4568

Friedmen, G. H. L. "Character." Solicitor Quarterly, 1:211, July 1962. 4569

Hiner, W. E. "Reputation Evidence As a Basis for Reasonable Doubt." JAG Journal, 1954:13, Feb. 1954. 4570

"Impugning Character of Prosecution Witness." Solicitor's Journal, 113:864, Nov. 14, 1969. Reviews the history of that portion of the Criminal Justice Act of 1898 which refers to the fact that the character of the defendant may not be brought up in court unless he has by the nature of his defense involved imputations on the character of the prosecutor or the witnesses for the prosecution. 4571

Lawson, R. G. "Credibility and Character: A Different Look at an Interminable Problem." Notre Dame Lawyer, 50:758, June 1975. 4572

"Necessity That Spontaneous Declaration Relates to the Exciting Event and Spontaneous Declaration of an Agent Admissible to Prove Scope of Employment [Murphy Auto Parts Co. v. Ball (Colo.), 249 F. 2d 508]." California Law Review, 47:939, Dec. 1959. 4573

O'Donoghue, F. "Imputations on the Character of Prosecution Witnesses." Modern Law Review, 29:492, spring 1966. 4574

"Spontaneous Exclamation Improperly Admitted to Prove Agency [Murphy Auto Parts Co. v. Ball, 294 F. 2d 508]." Washington & Lee Law Review, 16:47, spring 1959. 4575

"Testimony Showing Insured's Good Character Held Sufficient to Raise Jury Question Despite Uncontradicted Evidence of Fraudulent Misrepresentation in Insurance Application [Lawyer v. Life Insurance Co. of Georgia, 82, S.E. 2d 281]." Georgia Bar Journal, 17:386, Feb. 1955. 4576

"Use of Bad Character and Prior Convictions to Impeach a Defendant-Witness." Fordham Law Review, 34:107, Oct. 1975. 4577

G. EXCLUSIONARY RULES

(1) SELF-INCRIMINATION

Aronson, R. H. "Should the Privilege Against Self-Incrimination Apply to Compelled Psychiatric Examinations?" Stanford Law Review, 26:55, Nov. 1973. 4578

Berry, F. D., Jr. "Self-Incrimination and the Compulsory Mental Examination: A. Proposal." Arizona Law Review, 15:919, 1973. 4579

"Breathalyzer--Elements of the Offense--Criminal Code S. 237 (1)." Saskatchewan Law Review, 36:483, 1971-72. 4580

"Changing Standards for Compulsory Mental Examinations." Wisconsin Law Review, 1969:200, 1969. 4581

Cohen, B. "Case for Admitting Evidence of Refusal to Take a Breath Test." Texas Tech Law Review, 6:927, spring 1975. 4582

"Constitutional Law--Admissibility of the Results of a Blood Test for Intoxication in a Criminal Proceeding." Connecticut Bar Journal, 41:125, March 1967. 4583

"Constitutional Law--Self-Incrimination--Production of Client's Work Papers in Possession of Attorney May Be Compelled When Client Has Never Been in Physical Possession." Fordham Law Review, 42:197, Oct. 1973. 4584

"Constitutionally Privileged False Statements." Stanford Law Review, 22:783, April 1970. 4585

"Criminal Law--Self-Incrimination--The Fifth Amendment Protects a Witness Who Refuses to Testify for Fear of Self-Incrimination under the Laws of a Foreign Jurisdiction." Rutgers Camden Law Journal, 5:146, fall 1971. 4586

Dionisopoulos, P. A. "New Dimensions to the Privilege Against Self-Incrimination: The Supreme Court and the Fifth Amendment." Chicago-Kent Law Review, 44:1, spring 1967. 4587

Dorn, D., and Erwin, G. D. "Privilege Against Self-Incrimination in Nebraska." Nebraska Law Review, 44:783, July 1965. 4588

"Exclusionary Rule Under Attack." University of Baltimore Law Review, 4:89, fall 1974. 4589

Givens, R. A. "Reconciling the Fifth Amendment with the Need for More Effective Law Enforcement." American Bar Association Journal, 52:443, May 1966. 4590

"Griffin v. California (85 Supreme Court 1229): Comment on Accussed's Failure to Testify Prohibited by the Fifth Amendment." Dickinson Law Review, 70:98, fall 1965. 4591

Hechtkopf, E. A. "Constitutional Law: Self-Incrimination: Sufficiency of Use and Derivative--Use Immunity to Compel Testimony of a Witness over a Claim of the Privilege Against Self-Incrimination." JAG Journal, 24:401, summer 1973. 4592

"Immunity and the Self-Incrimination Clause." American Journal of Criminal Law, 2:29, fall 1973. 4593

"In Re Gault (87 Sup. Ct. 1428) and the Privilege Against Self-Incrimination in Juvenile Court." Marquette Law Review, 51:68, summer 1967. 4594

Jacobs, R. C. "Miranda: The Right to Silence." Trial, 11:69, March-April 1975. 4595

Kuh, R. H. "Rest of Us in the 'Policing the Police' Controversy." Journal of Criminal Law, Criminology and Police Science, 57:224, Sept. 1966. 4596

McClemens, J. H. "Admissibility of Self-Incriminatory Evidence." Australian Law Journal, 45:57, fall 1971. 4597

MacKenna, B. J. M. "Police Interrogation." New Law Journal, 120:665, July 16, 1970. Interrogation and the rule against self-incrimination. 4598

"Mental Examinations of Defendants Who Plead Insanity: Problems of Self-Incrimination." Temple Law Quarterly, 40:366, spring-summer 1967. 4599

"Miranda Without Warning: Derivative Evidence As Forbidden Fruit." Brooklyn Law Review, 41:325, fall 1974. 4600

"Need to Repeat Miranda Warnings at Subsequent Interrogations." Washburn Law Journal, 12:222, winter 1973. 4601

"New Texas Self-Incrimination Privilege and the Breathalyzer Statute." Houston Law Review, 10:903, May 1973. 4602

"Papers Privacy and the Fourth and Fifth Amendments: A Constitutional Analysis." Northwestern University Law Review, 69:626, Sept.-Oct. 1974. 4603

Payne, J. D. "Privilege Against Self-Incrimination." Ottawa Law Review, 2:461, spring 1968. 4604

"Privilege Against Self-Incrimination: The Scope and Application of Miranda." University of Missouri at Kansas City Law Review, 37:260, summer 1969. 4605

"Probation Revocation: Pre-trial Revocation and Due Process." Dickinson Law Review, 79:177, fall 1974. 4606

"Procedural Protections of the Criminal Defendant--A Reevaluation of the Privilege Against Self-Incrimination and the Rule Excluding Evidence of Propensity to Commit Crime." Harvard Law Review, 78:426, Dec. 1964. 4607

Schaeffer, W. V. "Police Interrogations and the Privilege Against Self-Incrimination." Northwestern University Law Review, 61: 506, Sept.-Oct. 1966. 4608

"Scope of the Taint Under the Exclusionary Rule of the Fifth Amendment Privilege Against Self-Incrimination." University of Pennsylvania Law Review, 114:570, fall 1966. 4609

"Self-Incrimination and the Breathalyzer." Saskatchewan Law Review, 36:22, 1971-72. 4610

"Self-Incrimination: Testimonial vs. Non-Testimonial Evidence." Denver Law Journal, 43:501, fall 1966. 4611

"Status of Voiceprints As Admissible Evidence." Syracuse Law Review, 24:1261, 1973. 4612

Stenning, P. C. "Breathalyzer Reference." Criminal Law Quarterly, 12:394, Oct. 1970. 4613

"Suspect's Confusion About Miranda Rights." Ohio State Law Journal, 36:220, 1975. 4614

"Tacit Criminal Admissions in Light of the Expanding Privilege Against Self-Incrimination." Cornell Law Quarterly, 52:355, winter 1962. 4615

Wendell, G. D. "Compulsory Immunity Legislation and the Fifth Amendment Privilege: New Developments and New Confusion." St. Louis University Law Review, 10:327, spring 1966. 4616

"What Price Immunity? The Pressing Need for Protection Against the Abuse of Immunity Grants." University of San Fernando Valley Law Review, 3:83, 1974. 4617

(2) ILLEGALLY OBTAINED EVIDENCE

"Admissibility of Evidence Seized by Privileged University Officials in Violation of Fourth Amendment Standards." Cornell Law Review, 56:507, Feb. 1971. 4618

"Admitting the Inadmissible: The Warning of Miranda." Baylor Law Review, 23:639, fall 1971. 4619

"Antidote for the Fruit of the Poisonous Tree." Baylor Law Review, 21:316, summer 1969. 4620

Beeson, R. D., and James, R. R. "Searches by Private Individuals: Admissible Windfalls." Air Force JAG Law Review, 15: 19, Sept. 1973. Requirements for the admissibility of illegally obtained evidence by private individuals considered by many to be a gap in the exclusionary rule; development of the exclusionary rule in federal court is also discussed. 4621

Boas, M. S. "Impact of the Dorado, [People v. Dorado, 62, A. C. 350], Lopez [In re Lopez 62 A. C. 380] and Griffin [Griffin v. California 85 Sup. Court 1229] Cases on Administrative Law." Los Angeles Bar Bulletin, 40:473, Aug. 1965. 4622

Brodsky, J. A. "Terry and the Pirates: Constitutionality of Airport Searches and Seizures." Kentucky Law Journal, 62:623, 1973-74. 4623

"Circumventing the Exclusionary Rule." University of Florida Review, 15:427, fall-winter 1962. 4624

"Constitutional Law--Impeachment by Unconstitutionally Obtained Evidence--The Erosion of the Exclusionary Rule." Ohio State Law Journal, 34:706, 1973. 4625

"Constitutional Law: Schmerber v. California (86 Sup. Ct. 1826): Blood and the Constitution." Tulsa Law Journal, 4:246, June 1967. 4626

"Criminal Procedure--Fourth Amendment Vitality of Wong Sun v. U.S., 83 Supreme Court 407." Rutgers Law Review, 19:140, fall 1964. 4627

"Evidence Suppression by the Prosecution and Police in Criminal Trials." Baylor Law Review, 17:400, summer-fall 1965. 4628

"Exclusionary Rule and the Question of Standing." Georgetown Law Journal, 50:585, spring 1962. Discusses background, what was necessary before the Jones decision; California and the exclusionary rule, People v. Calum; and the Federal viewpoint after Jones. 4629

"Exclusionary Rule of Illegally Obtained Evidence: Its Development and Application." Southern California Law Review, 35:64, fall 1961. 4630

"Federal Cause of Action Against a Municipality for Fourth Amendment Violations by Its Agents." George Washington Law Review, 42:850, May 1974. 4631

Frankel, Lionel H. "Search and Seizure and the Organized Bar: A Proposal." American Bar Association Journal, 53:806-7, Sept. 1967. 4632

Graham, Kenneth W., Jr. "What Is 'Custodial Interrogation'?: California's Anticipatory Application of Miranda v. Arizona." UCLA Law Review, 14:59, Nov. 1966. Detailed discussion of the constitutional basis of the decision, when the Miranda protection operates, custody detention, and "custodial interrogation." 4633

Grave, D. G. "Suppression of Illegally Obtained Evidence: The Standing Requirement on Its Last Leg." Catholic University Law Review, 67:1529, Dec. 1967. 4634

Gray, J. W. R. "Chalmers and After: Police Interrogation and the Trial Within a Trial." Juridical Review, 1970:1, April 1970. 4635

Heydan, J. D. "Illegally Obtained Evidence." Criminal Law Review, 1973:603, Oct.-Nov. 1973. 4636

"Impeachment of a Defendant--Witness by the Use of Illegally Obtained Statements: From Walder to Harris (Harris v. New York 91 Sup. Ct. 643)--The Exception Becomes the Rule." Syracuse Law Review, 22:685, 1971. 4637

La Prade, C. "Alternative to the Exclusionary Rule Presently Administered Under the Fourth Amendment." Connecticut Bar Journal, 48:100, June 1974. 4638

Maguire, R. F. "How to UnPoison the Fruit--The Fourth Amendment and the Exclusionary Rule." Journal of Criminal Law, Criminology, and Police Science, 55:307, Sept. 1964. 4639

Miller, R. W. "Confession Confusion." Marquette Law Review, 49:715, May 1966. 4640

Oberman, G. W. and Finkel, K. "Constitutional Arguments Against 'Stop and Frisk'." Criminal Law Bulletin, 3:441, Sept. 1967. 4641

"Police Coercion of Witnesses." Washington University Law Quarterly, 1973:865, fall 1973. 4642

"Pretrial Exclusionary Evidence Rulings." Wisconsin Law Review, 1967:738, summer 1967. 4643

Quinn, J. "Effect of Police Rule Making on the Scope of the Fourth Amendment." Journal of Urban Law, 52:25, Aug. 1974. 4644

"Review of Present Law on the Admission of Illegally Obtained Evidence in Our State and Federal Courts." Wyoming Law Journal, 13:166, winter 1959. 4645

Richardson, J. R. "Law and Policy: Emphasis on Exclusionary Rules of Evidence." Kentucky Law Journal, 53:663, summer 1965. 4646

"Selective Detention and the Exclusionary Rule." University of Chicago Law Review, 34:158, autumn 1966. 4647

Sevilla, C. M. "Exclusionary Rule and Police Perjury." San Diego Law Review, 11:839, June 1974. 4648

Smythe, B. "Police Investigations and the Rules of Evidence." Solicitor's Journal, 117:78, Oct. 1973. 4649

"Survey of the Expanded Exclusionary Rule." George Washington Law Review, 32:193, Dec. 1963. 4650

Thompson, J. R. "Detention After Arrest and In-Custody Investigation: Some Exclusionary Principles." University of Illinois Law Forum, 1966:390, summer 1966. 4651

Trager, D. G. "Law of Standing Under the Fourth Amendment." Brooklyn Law Review, 41:421, winter 1975. 4652

"Trends in Legal Commentary on the Exclusionary Rule." Journal of Criminal Law and Criminology, 65:373, summer 1974. 4653

(3) SEARCHES AND SEIZURES

"Administrative Search Warrants." Minnesota Law Review, 58:607, March 1974. 4654

"Administrative Searches and the Fourth Amendment." Missouri Law Review, 30:612, fall 1965. 4655

"Admissibility of Illegally Seized Evidence." North Dakota Law Review, 38:117, June 1962. 4656

"Admission of Illegally Obtained Evidence." Hastings Law Journal, 5:227, spring 1954. 4657

"Admission of Illegally Seized Evidence--The Federal Exclusionary Rule--An Historical Analysis." University of Detroit Law Journal, 38:635, June 1961. The Jones decision and the Leveson vs. Florida case; Police are not hindered by the exclusionary rule, as they get the information they need anyway. 4658

"Aftermath of Mapp v. Ohio." Brooklyn Law Review, 29:98, Dec. 1962. Discusses the Mapp decision, retroactivity, appeals, 4th v. 14th amendments, Rodin Doctrine, Fruit of the Poisonous Tree Doctrine, civil cases, electronic eavesdropping, and wiretapping. 4659

"Airline Searches." Florida Bar Journal, 47:707, Dec. 1973. Balancing the government's interest in searches for concealed weapons with the invasion of privacy. 4660

"Airport Search and Seizure--Has the Fourth Amendment Become Excess Baggage for Travellers?" Santa Clara Lawyer, 14:169, fall 1973. 4661

"Automobile Inventory Search and Cady v. Dombrowski." Villanova Law Review, 20:147, Nov. 1974. 4662

"Automobile Searches and the Fourth Amendment." Chicago-Kent Law Review, 47:232, fall-winter 1970. 4663

"Automobile Spot Checks and the Fourth Amendment." Rutgers Camden Law Journal, 6:85, summer 1974. 4664

Berkman, B. A. "Aftermath of Mapp v. Ohio--Search and Seizure and the Exclusionary Rule." Trial Lawyers Quarterly, 5:67, winter 1968. 4665

"Blood Tests and the Bill of Rights--Breithaupt Revisited." Hasting Law Journal, 17:139, Oct. 1965. 4666

"California Supreme Court Creates a New Exception to the Search Warrant Requirement: People v. Sirhan [(Calif.) 497 P. 2d 1121]." Southwestern Law Journal, 27:385, May 1973. 4667

Carrington, F. "Chimel v. California (89 Sup. Ct. 2034), A Police Response." Notre Dame Lawyer, 45:559, summer 1970. 4668

"Chimel v. California (89 Sup. Ct. 2034): A Potential Roadblock to Justice Searches." UCLA Law Review, 17:626, Feb. 1970. 4669

"Chimel v. California (89 Sup. Ct. 2034)--Its Effect on Search and Seizure." New Mexico Law Review, 2:308, July 1972. 4670

"Concept of Privacy and the Fourth Amendment." University of Michigan Journal of Law References, 6:154, fall 1972. 4671

"Consent Search." Chicago-Kent Police Law Report, 2:25, July-Aug. 1969. 4672

"Constitutional Criminal Procedure--Stop and Frisk--Reliable Informants." Tulsa Law Review, 47:893, April 1973. 4673

"Constitutional Law--Eavesdropping by Warrantless Federal Agents Concealed in an Informant's Home Is Not an Unreasonable Search and Seizure." Texas Law Review, 48:1188, June 1970. 4674

"Constitutional Law--Electronic Surveillance and the Fourth Amendment: Warrant Required for Wiretapping of Domestic Subversives." De Paul Law Review, 22:430, winter 1972. 4675

"Constitutional Law--Electronic Surveillance and the Supreme Court: A Move Back?" De Paul Law Review, 21:806, spring 1972. 4676

"Constitutional Law--Electronic Surveillance by Bugged Agents Is Not a Search and Seizure Within the Fourth Amenement." Albany Law Review, 36:451, winter 1972. 4677

"Constitutional Law--Search and Seizure--Evidence Stolen by Private Individuals with Intent to Aid the Government Held Inadmissible in Administrative Proceedings." New York University Law Review, 44:206, March 1969. 4678

"Constitutional Law--Search and Seizure--Hearsay as Grounds for Probable Cause." Case Western Reserve Law Review, 21:135, Nov. 1969. 4679

"Constitutional Law--Search and Seizure--Home Visits by Welfare Workers Held to be Searches Requiring Warrants Under the Fourth Amendment." New York University Law Review, 45:168, March 1970. 4680

"Constitutional Law--Search and Seizure--Police May Conduct Limited Search for Weapons in Course of Field Investigation Without Probable Cause for Arrest." Vanderbilt Law Review, 21:1109, Nov. 1968. 4681

"Constitutional Standards for Stop and Frisk: Guidelines and Implementation." California Western Law Review, 5:265, spring 1969. 4682

"Constitutionality of the 1973 Airport Searches: A Factual Analysis." University of San Francisco Law Review, 8:172, fall 1973. 4683

"Criminal Law--Evidence Obtained by Private Individuals Without Government Assistance Through Illegal Search and Seizure Is Admissible in State Criminal Proceedings." Drake Law Review, 19:476, May 1970. 4684

"Criminal Law--Search Warrant--Heroin Seized in Backyard Incident to Arrest of Defendant in His Apartment Held Admissible in Evidence." Florida State University Law Review, 1:169, winter 1973. 4685

"Criminal Procedure--Protective Search Incident to Warrantless, In-Custody Arrest Constitutionally Limited to Pat-Down of Outer Clothing." Texas Law Review, 51:1241, Aug. 1973. 4686

"Criminal Procedure--Search and Seizure--Prospective Search Warrants." Wayne Law Review, 19:1339, July 1973. 4687

"Criminal Procedure--Stop and Frisk on Basis of Tip by Unidentified Informant Held Valid." Syracuse Law Review, 24:839, 1973. 4688

"Criminal Procedure--Stop and Frisk: Warrantless Car Searches--

Adams v. Williams (92 Sup. Ct. 1921)." Denver Law Journal, 50:243, 1973. 4689

Cross, John C., and Harney, Malachi L. The Informer in Law Enforcement. Springfield, Ill.: Charles C. Thomas, 1960, 96pp. 4690

"Custodial Search Incident to Arrest: Siding with the Street Cop." Capital University Law Review, 3:266, 1974. 4691

Delgado, R. "College Searches and Seizures: Students, Privacy, and the Fourth Amendment." Hastings Law Journal, 26:57, summer 1974. 4692

Dempsey, Michael D. "Suppression of Evidence: Giles v. State." UCLA Law Review, 14:670, Jan. 1967. Giles arose from the current hodge-podge of case law dealing with suppression and illustrates the need for a single, clearly articulated standard in this area. 4693

"Eavesdropping, Wiretapping, and the Law of Search and Seizure--Some Implications of the Katz (Katz v. U.S. 88 Sup. Ct. 507) Decision." Arizona Law Review, 9:428, spring 1968. 4694

"Effect of 'Stop and Frisk' in Defeating the Purpose of the Exclusionary Rule." Howard Law Journal, 15:440, spring 1969. 4695

"Effect of the Fourth Amendment on Arrests Without a Warrant." Louisiana Law Review, 26:789, June 1966. 4696

Fabricant, N. "Probable Cause and the Confidential Informant." Criminal Law Bulletin, 1:1, Feb. 1965. 4697

"Federal Standard: The New State Law of Search and Seizure?" Arkansas Law Review, 19:329, March 1966. 4698

"Fourth and Fifth Amendments--Dimensions of an Intimate Relationship." UCLA Law Review, 13:857, March 1966. 4699

Frels, K. "Search and Seizure in the Public Schools." Houston Law Review, 11:876, May 1974. 4700

Gilligan, F. A. "Probable Cause and the Informer." Military Law Review, 60:1, summer 1973. 4701

Green, Sharon. "Forcible Administration of Blood Tests: Schmerber v. California." UCLA Law Review, 14:680-692, Jan. 1967. Also discusses unreasonable search and seizure. 4702

Haley, A. "In Search of Reason at the Border." Hawaii Bar Journal, 10:101, winter 1974. 4703

Hartman, P. "Admissibility of Evidence Obtained by Illegal Search and Seizure Under the United States Constitution." Modern Law Review, 28:298, May 1965. 4704

"Inadmissibility of Illegally Obtained Evidence in State Criminal Proceedings." North Carolina Law Review, 40:314, fall 1962. 4705

"Informer's Word As the Basis for Probable Cause in the Federal Courts." California Law Review, 53:840, Aug. 1965. 4706

"Inventory Search of an Offender Arrested for a Minor Traffic Violation: Its Scope and Constitutional Requirements." Boston Law Review, 53:858, July 1973. 4707

Irons, R. S. "Burger Court: Discord in Search and Seizure." University of Richmond Law Review, 8:433, spring 1974. 4708

"Jackson v. Denno [84 Supreme Court 1774] Does Not Apply to Searches and Seizures." Houston Law Review, 4:139, spring-summer, 1966. 4709

Knox, W. A. "Some Thoughts on the Scope of the Fourth Amendment and Standing to Challenge Searches and Seizures." Missouri Law Review, 40:1, winter 1975. 4710

Lambert, J. L. "Police Powers to Stop and Frisk." The New Law Journal, 124:476, May 1974. 4711

"Lawful Custodial Arrest for a Traffic Violation Justifies a Full Search of the Arrestee." Houston Law Review, 11:1283, July 1974. 4712

Leigt, L. H. "Recent Developments in the Law of Search and Seizure." Modern Law Review, 33:268, May 1970. 4713

Liacos, P. J. "Criminal Law: Search Incident to Arrest: Probable Cause Revisited. Standing to Challenge Illegally Obtained Evidence. The Right to Confrontation." Atlanta Law Journal, 33: 200, 1970. 4714

Louisell, David W. "'Informed Consent': Does It Have Real Meaning?" J. D. California Trial Lawyers Association Journal, 11: 37-51, fall 1972. 4715

McGinley, P. W., and Dawns, S. F. "Airport Searches and Seizures--A Reasonable Approach." Fordham Law Review, 41:293, Dec. 1972. 4716

Nedrud, D. R. "Outline of Arrest, Search and Seizure." Tulsa Law Journal, 5:154, May 1968. 4717

"Non-Arrest Automobile Stops: Unconstitutional Seizures of the

Person." Stanford Law Review, 25:865, June 1973. 4718

"Non-Usable Amounts of Narcotics: The Residual Dilemma." South Western University Law Review, 6:224, spring 1970. 4719

"Oral Search Warrants: A New Standard of Warrant Availability." UCLA Law Review, 21:691-718, Dec. 1973. 4720

Percy, C. H. "Legacy of No-Knock: Drug Law Enforcement Abuse." Contemporary Drug Problems, 3:3, spring 1974. 4721

"Person Who Consents to a Search Need Not Know He May Refuse." American Journal of Criminal Law, 2:349, winter 1974. 4722

"Private Party Searches and Seizures--A Province of the Fifth Amendment." University of San Francisco Law Review, 3:459, Oct. 1968. 4723

"Probable Cause for Warrantless Arrests Pursuant to Statewide Police Pickup: Directives." Baylor Law Review, 25:697-703, fall 1973. 4724

"Restricting the Scope of Searches Incident to Arrest: United States v. Robinson (471 F. 2d 1082)." Virginia Law Review, 59:724, April 1973. 4725

Rintamaki, J. "Plain View Searching." Military Law Review, 60: 25, spring 1973. 4726

Rotenberg, D. L. "Searching the Person to be Seized." Ohio State Law Journal, 35:56, 1974. 4727

"Scope Limitations for Searches Incident to Arrest." Southwestern Law Journal, 23:959, Dec. 1969. 4728

"Search and Seizure--A Constitutional Standard for South Carolina." South Carolina Law Review, 17:687, 1965. 4729

"Search and Seizure by Private Parties: An Exception to the Exclusionary Rule." Land and Water Law Review, 5:653, 1970. 4730

"Search and Seizure--Evidence Obtained Illegally Not Admissible in Federal or State Courts." Arkansas Law Review, 15:445, fall 1961. 4731

"Search and Seizure--Miranda Warnings Necessary to Valid Consent." Dickinson Law Review, 77:569, spring 1973. 4732

"Search and Seizure of an Automobile Incident to an Arrest for an Offense Other Than a Vehicle Violation." Missouri Law Review, 31:436, summer 1966. 4733

"Search and Seizure of Private Papers: Fourth and Fifth Amendment Considerations." Loyola University Law Review, (L. A.), 6:274, July 1973. 4734

"Search Warrants and Administrative Area Searches." Gonzaga Law Review, 3:172, spring 1968. 4735

"Searches by School Officials: The Diminishing Fourth Amendment." Santa Clara Lawyer, 14:118, fall 1973. 4736

"Seizure of Property as Evidence, Its Unlawful Retention and Suggested Remedies of the Owner." Wyoming Law Journal, 19:172, winter 1965. 4737

Sheffield, J. F. "Illegal Searches and Arrests of Aliens; The Evolving Standard." Los Angeles Bar Bulletin, 49:375, July 1974. 4738

Shiner, Amy. "Police Helicopter Surveillance." Arizona Law Review, 15:145, 1973. Examines three surveillance programs utilizing police helicopters, then considers whether police operations of helicopters for surveillance violates a general constitutional right of privacy, whether it constitutes a taking of property under the Fourth Amendment, or whether it infringes upon the constitutional right of others to be free from unreasonable searches and seizures under the Fourth Amendment. 4739

"Standing and the Fourth Amendment." University of Cincinnati Law Review, 6:131, fall 1969. 4740

"Standing to Object to an Unlawful Search and Seizure." Washington University Law Quarterly, 1965:488, Dec. 1965. 4741

"Stop and Frisk." Northwestern University Law Review, 63:837, Jan.-Feb. 1969. 4742

"Stop and Frisk: Police Protection or Police State." New York University Intramural Law Review, 21:180, March 1966. 4743

"Terry v. Ohio 88 Supreme Court 1868." Brooklyn Law Review, 35:147, fall 1968; Loyola Law Review, 15:155, 1968-69. 4744

"Third Party Consent to Search and Seizure." St. John Law Review, 41:82, July 1966. 4745

Thomas, D. A. "Arrest and Search." Criminal Law Review, 1966: 481, Sept. 1966. 4746

________; Balmer, H. R.; and Williams, D. G. T. "Law of Search and Seizure." Criminal Law Review, 1967:3, Jan. 1967. 4747

"Unexcited View of United States v. Calandra." Chicago-Kent Law Review, 51:212, summer 1974. 4748

"United States v. Robinson: Chipping Away at the Fourth Amendment." Ohio Northern Law Review, 1:334, 1974. 4749

"Unlawful Search and Seizure--Evidence Obtained Thereby Not Admissible in State Courts." West Virginia Law Review, 64:83, Dec. 1961. The exclusionary rule, while solving one problem, has created many by confusing the law; discusses Mapp, Rodin, William v. Ball, Irvine v. California, and Weeks v. U.S. 4750

"Unreasonable Private Searches and Seizures and the Exclusionary Rule." American-University Law Review, 16:403, June 1967. 4751

"Valid Consent to Search and Determined by Standard of Voluntariness." American Criminal Law Review, 12:231, summer 1974. 4752

"Validity of Warrantless Searches Under the Occupational Safety and Health Act of 1970." North Carolina Law Review, 53:722, April 1975. 4753

Wallenstein, D. "Consent Searches." Criminal Law Bulletin, 4: 509, Nov. 1968. 4754

"Warrantless Searches and Seizures of Automobiles." Ohio State Law Journal, 36:190, 1975. 4755

(4) CONFESSIONS AND ADMISSIONS

"A Dissent from the Miranda Dissents: Some Comments on the New Fifth Amendment and the Old 'Voluntariness' Test." Michigan Law Review, 65:59, 1966. Discusses arguments and criticisms of the Miranda v. Arizona decision in 1966; includes a brief history of the use of confessions by police and court treatment of confessions. Valuable footnotes. 4756

"Admissibility of Confession of Co-Defendant." Journal of Criminal Law, 60:195, June 1969. 4757

"Admissibility of Evidence--Confessions--Admissions of a Defendant Which Are Inadmissible in the Prosecutor's Direct Case Because of Failure to Give the Miranda Warnings May Be Used to Impeach the Defendant's Direct Testimony Where Admissions Satisfy Legal Standards of Truthfullness." University of Cincinnati Law Review, 40:350, summer 1971. 4758

"Admissions of Confessions Obtained by Trickery." American Bar Association Journal, 50:648, July 1964. 4759

"Aftermath of Miranda--The Courts Grapple with Burden of Proof." West Virginia Law Review, 71:180, Feb. 1969. 4760

"Analysis of the Procedures Used to Determine the Voluntariness of Confessions: and a Solution." South Dakota Law Review, 11:70, winter 1966. 4761

"Applying the Harmless Error Rule to a Confession Obtained in Violation of Miranda--The Oklahoma View." Oklahoma Law Review, 28:370, spring 1975. 4762

Beale, C. H. "Corpus Delicti: A Confession Cannot Stand Alone." JAG Journal, 1958-59:11, Dec. 1958-Jan. 1959. 4763

"Burton v. U.S. 88 Supreme Court 1620." Brooklyn Law Review, 35:139, fall 1968; Missouri Law, 35:125, winter 1970; Washburn Law Journal, 8:381, spring 1969. Detailed analyses of the Burton Case including the rationale of the court and probable reverberations concerning admissibility of a co-defendants confession. 4764

"Co-Defendant's Confessions." Columbia Journal of Law and Social Problems, 3:80, June 1967. 4765

"Confessions and Their Uncertainty." Loyola Law Review, 14:166, 1967-1968. 4766

"Confessions by the Accused--Does Miranda Relate to Reality?" Kentucky Law Journal, 62:794, 1973-74. 4767

"Confessions of Juveniles." Willamette Law Journal, 5:66, spring 1968. 4768

"Confessions--Rights to Counsel--The Impact of Miranda in Missouri." St. Louis University Law Journal, 17:572, summer 1973. The effect of Miranda on interrogation has not been devastating; courts tend to apply the provisions of Miranda cases less strictly than was predicted in 1966. 4769

"Constitutional Attacks on a Guilty Plea Motivated by a Coerced Confession." Temple Law Quarterly, 44:426, spring 1971. 4770

"Constitutional Law--Criminal Law--Confessions Need Not Be Voluntary Beyond a Reasonable Doubt Prior to Being Admitted into Evidence." Loyola University Law Journal (Chicago), 3:433, summer 1972. 4771

Cooper, A. M. "Admissibility of Confessions." Criminal Law Quarterly, 1:46, May 1958. 4772

Cray, E. "Criminal Interrogations and Confessions: The Ethical Imperative." Wisconsin Law Review, 1968:173, 1968. 4773

"Criminal Law--Admissibility of Confessions or Admissions of Accused Obtained During Custodial Interrogation by Non-Police Personnel: Are the Miranda Warnings Required?" Mississippi

Law Journal, 40:139 Dec. 1968. 4774

"Criminal Law--Confessions--Government Can Satisfy Its Burden of Proving Waiver of Miranda Rights by Showing Warnings Given, Signed Waiver, and Proof of Defendant's Capacity to Understand the Warnings." Vanderbilt Law Review, 26:1069, Oct. 1973. 4775

"Criminal Law--Confessions--Probable Cause--Confession Obtained After Illegal Search and Seizure Admissible If Voluntary and Made After Miranda Warnings Given; Information Insufficient to Constitute Probable Cause to Search Residence May Constitute Probable Cause to Search Vehicle." Florida State University Law Review, 1:533, summer 1973. The Case of Jetmore v. State (275 So. ID 61) (Florida 4th District Court App. 1973), and the arguments of the defense, may cause a line of demarcation between automobile search probable cause and probable cause in general. 4776

"Criminal Procedure--Lowering the Standard for Defendant's Understanding of His Miranda Rights." North Carolina Law Review, 52:454, Dec. 1973. 4777

"Defense, Dignity, Reliability: The Control of Police Interrogation." Southern California Law Review, 39:92, 1966. 4778

"Due Process and the Rule of the Trial Judge in Determining the Voluntariness of a Confession--A New Constitutional Rule." Southwestern Law Journal, 18:729, Dec. 1964. 4779

Edwards, H. L. "Effects of 'Miranda' (Miranda v. Arizona, 86 Supreme Court 1602) on the Work of the Federal Bureau of Investigation." American Criminal Law Quarterly, 5:159, summer 1967. 4780

"Everything But the Truth--Narco-Analysis and Its Effect Upon Confessions." Temple Law Quarterly, 31:359, summer 1958. 4781

"Evidence: Confessions and Admissions." Oklahoma Law Review, 14:209, May 1961. 4782

"Examination of the Rights to a Voluntariness Hearing." Journal of Criminal Law, 53:30, March 1972. 4783

"Exclusion of Evidence Found As a Result of a Coerced Confession." California Law Review, 50:723, Oct. 1962. 4784

Fabricant, N. "Comments on Miranda v. Arizona, [86 Supreme Court 1602 and Johnson v. New Jersey, 86 Supreme Court 177]." Criminal Law Bulletin, 2:3, July-Aug. 1966. 4785

Gandara, D. "Admissibility of Confessions in Federal Prosecutions...." Georgetown Law Journal, 63:305, Nov. 1974. 4786

Gangi, W. "Confessions: Historical Perspective and a Proposal." Houston Law Review, 10:1687, July 1973. 4787

________. "Critical View of the Modern Confession Rule: Some Observations on Key Confession Cases." Arkansas Law Review, 21:1, spring 1974. 4788

George, B. J., Jr. "Fruits of Miranda (86 Supreme Court 1602): Scope of the Exclusionary Rule." University of Colorado Law Review, 39:478, summer 1967. 4789

Hoffman, W. E. "Wiretapping, Confessions and Physical Evidence Under the United States Supreme Court and Statutes." New England Law Review, 5:17, fall 1969. 4790

"Illegal Delay in Arraignment--Admissibility of Confession." Brooklyn Law Review, 28:342, April 1962. 4791

"Intoxicated Confessions: A New Haven in Miranda (Miranda v. Arizona 86 Supreme Court 1602)." Stanford Law Review, 20:1269, June 1968. 4792

Little, H. E. "Confessions and Admissions: Test for Prejudice: Application of the Harmless--Error Doctrine to Constitutionally Infirm Confessions." JAG Journal, 27:299, spring 1973. 4793

Milledge, S. "Escobedo [Escobedo v. Illinois, 84 Supreme Court 1758]--Toward Eliminating Coerced Confessions." University of Miami Law Review, 19:415, May 1966. 4794

"Miranda and Its Progeny--Application and Limitation of the Warren Court's Legacy." Syracuse Law Review, 21:232, fall 1969. 4795

"Miranda v. Arizona: Incustody Interrogation; An Examination of the New Rules Further Defining the Suspect's Rights." Dickinson Law Review, 71:116. 4796

Morrissey, F. J., Jr. "Escobedo's European Ancestors [Escobedo v. Illinois 84 Supreme Court 7158]." American Bar Association Journal, 52:723, Aug. 1966. 4797

"The New Definition: A Fifth Amendment Right to Counsel." UCLA Law Review, 14:604, Jan. 1967. Miranda v. Arizona, Escobedo v. Illinois, People v. Dorado, and other cases dealing with the Fifth Amendment. 4798

Pope, W. L. "Escobedo Then Miranda and Now Johnson v. United States." Federal Rules Decisions, 40:351, spring 1966. 4799

"Ramifications of the McNabb Rule." De Paul Law Review, 8:410, spring-summer 1959. 4800

Ratushny, E. J. "Unravelling Confessions." Criminal Law Quarterly, 13:453, Sept. 1971. 4801

Roe, W. J. "Quantium of Proof Required in Confessions." Gonzaga Law Review, 6:35, fall 1970. 4802

Rogge, O. J. "Proof by Confession." Villanova Law Review, 12:1, fall 1966. 4803

"Role of a Jury in Determining the Voluntariness of a Confession." Michigan Law Review, 63:381, Dec. 1964. 4804

Saltzbrug, S. A. "Standards of Proof and Preliminary Questions of Fact." Stanford Law Review, 27:271, Jan. 1975. 4805

"Silence As an Admission of Guilt--Admissibility Criticized." Missouri Law Review, 39:264, spring 1974. 4806

Slough, M. C. "Confessions and Admissions." Fordham Law Review, 28:96, spring 1959. 4807

Smith, J. V. "Threshold Question in Applying Miranda: What Constitutes Custodial Interrogation?" South Carolina Law Review, 25:699, Feb. 1974. 4808

Spanogle, J. A. "Immunity Through Confession." Vanderbilt Law Review, 18:37, Dec. 1964. 4809

Sterling, D. L. "Police Interrogation and the Psychology of Confession." Journal of Public Law, 14:25, 1965. 4810

Stevens, G. N. "Confessions and Criminal Procedure--A Proposal." Washington Law Review, 34:542, winter 1959. 4811

Stevens, H. A. "Confession and Confusion." New York County Lawyers Association Bar Bulletin, 23:145, 1965-66. 4812

Sutherland, A. E. "Crime and Confession." Harvard Law Review, 79:21, Nov. 1965. 4813

________. "Justice Black on Counsel and Non-Voluntary Confessions." UCLA Law Review, 14:536, Jan. 1967. 4814

"Threatened Loss of Private Economic Benefits Can Be Sufficient Coercion To Render Confession Involuntary." Fordham Law Review, 43:466, Dec. 1974. 4815

Williamson, P. "With Regard to Statements." New Law Journal, 166:1225, Aug. 25, 1966. 4816

H. PRIVILEGED COMMUNICATIONS

(1) GENERAL

"Adultery Privilege." University of Toronto Faculty of Law Review, 31:107, Aug. 1973. 4817

Berger, R. "Executive Privilege v. Congressional Inquiry." UCLA Law Review, 12:1044, May 1965. 4818

"Confidential Relationships: Does the Law Require Silence Outside the Court Room?" Utah Law Review, 6:380, spring 1959. 4819

"Current Status of Confidential Communication Privileges in Georgia." Georgia State Bar Journal, 2:356, fall 1966. 4820

"Drug Bounty Programs: A Misguided Approach to the Narcotics Problem." Southern California Law Review, 47:1575, Aug. 1974. 4821

Evans, T. W. "New Freedom of Speech in Politics." New York Law Forum, 10:333, Sept. 1964. 4822

"Evidence--Privileged Communications." Suffolk University Law Review, 6:184, fall 1971. 4823

"Federal Recess of Evidence and the Law Privileges." Wayne Law Review, 15:1287, summer 1969. 4824

Freedman, M. H. "Where the Bodies Are Buried: The Adversary System and the Obligation of Confidentiality." Criminal Law Bulletin, 10:979, Dec. 1974. 4825

"Future of Testimonial Privilege in Bankruptcy Proceedings." Southern California Law Review, 48:92, Oct. 1974. 4826

"Hospital Accident Reports: Admissibility and Privilege." Dickinson Law Review, 79:493, spring 1975. 4827

Jacob, J., and Jacob, R. "Confidential Communications." New Law Journal, 119:133, Feb. 6, 1969. 4828

"Judicial Supervision of Non-Statutory Immunity." Journal of Criminal Law and Criminology, 65:334, summer 1974. 4829

Lee, G. A. "Professional Witnesses and Privileged Communications." Northern Ireland Legal Quarterly, 16:79, March 1965. 4830

Louisell, D. W., and Crippin, B. M., Jr. "Evidentiary Privileges." Minnesota Law Review, 40:413, March 1956. 4831

Marshall, T. K. "Privileged Occasions and Professional Secrecy." Medicine, Science and the Law, 6:68, April 1966. 4832

"Privilege Doctrine and the Proposed Federal Rules of Evidence." Syracuse Law Review, 24:1173, summer 1973. 4833

"Privileged Communication--The Personal Privilege." Military Law Review, 37:155, July 1967. 4834

"Privileged Communications: A Case by Case Approach." Maine Law Review, 23:443, 1971. History and survey of privileged communications and discussion of those applicable in Maine. 4835

"Privileged Communications in Colorado--A Summary and Analysis of Colorado's Revised Statutes. Annotated Section 154-1-7 (1963)." University of Colorado Law Review, 37:388, spring 1965. 4836

"Rule 67--Production, Privilege and Waiver." Baylor Law Review, 16:202, spring 1964. 4837

"Symposium: Evidentiary Privileges in Illinois. Introduction: Physician-Patient Privilege, Priest-Penitant Privilege, Attorney-Client Privilege, Marital Privileges, Privileges to Protect the Government." Chicago-Kent Law Review, 46:35, spring-summer 1969. 4838

"Symposium: Evidentiary Privileges of Non-Disclosure." Connecticut Bar Journal, 33:170, June 1959. 4839

"Use of In-Camera Hearings in Ruling on the Informer Privilege." University of Michigan Journal of Law Reform, 8:151, fall 1974. 4840

Welch, E. W. "Classified Information and the Courts." Federal Bar Journal, 31:360, fall 1972. 4841

(2) ATTORNEY-CLIENT

"Attorney and His Client's Privileges." Yale Law Journal, 74:539, Jan. 1965. 4842

"Attorney-Client Privilege." Oklahoma Law Review, 27:704, fall 1974. 4843

"The Attorney-Client Privilege and the Corporate Client." Corporation Journal, 26:147-150, Sept.-Nov. 1970. 4844

"Attorney-Client Privilege in Multiple Party Situations." Columbia Journal of Law and Social Problems, 8:179, winter 1972. 4845

"Attorney-Client Privilege: The Remedy of Corrupt." Wisconsin Law Review, 1968:1192, 1968. 4846

"Attorney in Possession of Evidence Incriminating His Client." Washington and Lee Law Review, 25:133, spring 1968. 4847

Comerton, E. A. "Legal Professional Privilege in England Today." Northern Ireland Legal Quarterly, 15:510, Dec. 1964. 4848

"Evidence--Attorney-Client Privilege--The Identity of the Client." Kentucky Law Journal, 59:229, 1970-71. 4849

"False Claims Not Within Attorney-Client Privilege." Maryland Law Review, 21:270, summer 1961. Discusses a case in which the court ruled that a communication with an attorney previously consulted in a matter is not a privilege when the client persists in a suit after being informed by that attorney that it clearly would be based on a dishonest cause of action. 4850

"Fruits of the Attorney-Client Privilege: Incriminating Evidence and Conflicting Duties." Duquesne University Law Review, 3:239, spring 1961. 4851

Gardner, J. A. "Agency Problems in the Law of Attorney-Client Privilege." University of Detroit Law Journal, 42:105, 253, 473, Oct. 1964-April 1965. 4852

"Government Interceptions of Attorney-Client Communications." New York University Law Review, 49:87, April 1974. 4853

Heydon, J. D. "Legal Professional Privilege and Third Parties." Modern Law Review, 37:601, Nov. 1974. 4854

Jox, M. L. "Attorney-Client Privileges: Application to a Corporate Client." Washburn Law Journal, 3:33, winter 1963. 4855

Lasky, M. "Lawyer-Client Privilege." Journal of the State Bar of California, 38:427, July-Aug. 1963. 4856

Rifkind, S. H. "Access to Client and Adversary--A Plea." Record, 22:566, Oct. 1967. 4857

Rylaarsdam, W. F. "Disclosure of Lay Expert Witness Reports--Discovery vs. the Work Product and Attorney-Client Privileges." Los Angeles Bar Bulletin, 48:336, July 1973. 4858

Steinhaus, R. Z. "Attorney-Client Privilege ... Recent Invasions." Louisiana Bar Journal, 14:9, May 1966. 4859

Thomas, R. C. "Lawyer-Client Privilege." Tulsa Law Journal, 10:130, 1974. 4860

(3) DOCTOR-PATIENT

"Accelerated Waiver of the Physician-Patient Privilege." Washington Law Review, 42:1107, June 1967. 4861

"Attorney May Waive Physician-Patient Privilege on Behalf of Absent Client." Syracuse Law Review, 13:604, summer 1962. Discusses a decision by the appellate court in New York, overruling the Civil Practices Act, which rules an attorney may waive physician-patient privilege. 4862

Baldwin, R. W. "Confidentiality Between Physician and Patient." Maryland Law Review, 22:181, summer 1962. 4863

Fisher, R. M. "Psychotherapeutic Professions and the Law of Privileged Communications." Wayne Law Review, 10:609, summer 1964. 4864

Flemming, J. G. "Patient or His Victim: The Therapists Dilemma." California Law Review, 62:1025, May 1974. 4865

Foulke, D. 'Doctor's Duty to Secrecy." Law Journal, 115:673, Oct. 8, 1965. 4866

Freedman, A. M. "Looking Over the Doctor's Shoulder." Trial, 11:29, Jan.-Feb. 1975. 4867

Horty, F. "Court's Need Can Impose Limits on Physician-Patient Privilege." Modern Hospital, 113:54-61, Aug. 1969. 4868

O'Neill, M. "Ohio's Physician-Patient Privilege in Personal Injury Case--Time for Reform." Western Reserve Law Review, 16:334, March 1965. 4869

"Patient-Physician Privilege in the Discovery Process." South Dakota Law Review, 17:188, winter 1972. 4870

"Physician-Patient Privilege." North Carolina Law Review, 41:672, spring 1963. Discusses the concept of judges requiring disclosure to minimize the evils of physician-patient privilege and problems in appellate procedures. 4871

"Physician-Patient Privilege--A Need to Revise the Arizona Law." Arizona Law Review, 6:292, spring 1965. 4872

"Physician-Patient Privilege in Colorado." University of Colorado Law Review, 37:349, spring 1965. 4873

"Physician-Patient Privilege--Some Reflections." Drake Law Review, 14:83, May 1965. 4874

"Physician's Breach of Confidentiality Gives Rise to Patient's Action for Damages." Cumberland-Samford Law Review, 5:169, spring 1974. 4875

"Privileged Communications--Abrogation of the Physician-Patient Privilege to Protect the Battered Child." De Paul Law Review, 15:453, spring-summer 1966. 4876

Robitscher, J. B. "Doctor's Privileged Communications, Public Life and History's Rights." Cleveland Marshall Law Review, 17:199, May 1968. 4877

Stewart, J. J. "Waiver of the Physician-Patient Privilege in Personal Injury Litigation." The Forum, 2:16, Oct. 1966. 4878

Tortorella, A. N. "Physician-Patient Privileged Communications." Trial, 9:59, March-April 1973. 4879

(4) PRIEST-PENITENT

Blaes, E. A. "Penitent Privilege Under the New Code." Journal of the Bar Association of the State of Kansas, 33:279, winter 1964. 4880

"Defamation Privilege in Internal Affairs of Religious Societies." Cleveland Marshall Law Review, 15:356, May 1959. 4881

"Evidence: 'Is There a Time to Keep Silence?'--The Priest-Penitent Privilege in Oklahoma." Oklahoma Law Review, 27:258, spring 1974. 4882

"Evidence--Privileged Communications--Confession to Minister Deemed Inadmissible in Federal Criminal Proceeding [Mullen v. U.S. 263 F. 2d. 275]." Virginia Law Review, 45:599, May 1959. 4883

Hogan, E. A., Jr. "Modern Problem on Privilege of the Confessional." Loyola Law Review, 6:1, 1951. 4884

Kuhlmann, F. L. "Communications to Clergymen--When Are They Privileged?" Valparaiso University Law Review, 2:265, spring 1968. 4885

Manley, D. L. "Privileged Communications. Patient, Penitent, Client, and Spouse in New York; A Prize-Winning Essay." New York State Bar Association Bulletin, 21:288, July 1949. 4886

"Priest-Penitent Privilege in South Carolina--Background and Development." South Carolina Law Quarterly, 12:440, spring 1960. 4887

"Privileged Communications--Some Recent Developments." Vanderbilt Law Review, 5:590, April 1952. 4888

"Privileged Communications to Clergymen." Catholic Lawyer, 1:199, July 1955. 4889

"Sacerdotal Privilege in English Law." Law Times, 221:268, May 25, 1965. 4890

Stoyles, R. L. "Dilemma of the Constitutionality of the Priest-Penitent Privilege--the Application of the Revision Clauses." University of Pittsburgh Law Review, 29:27, Oct. 1967. 4891

(5) TESTIMONY OF SPOUSES

Black, C. L., Jr. "Marital and Physician Privilege: A Reprint of a Letter to a Congressman." Duke Law Journal, 1975:45, March 1975. 4892

"Confession to Wife." Solicitors' Journal, 106:807, Oct. 12, 1962. 4893

"Evidence--Confidential Communications Between Husband and Wife--Acts Committed in Presence of Third Parties Presumptively Not Privileged [People v. Melski, New York, 176 NE 2d 81]." Albany Law Review, 26:340, June 1962. 4894

"Evidence: Spouse Testifying As Personal Representative." Oklahoma Law Review, 15:191, May 1962. 4895

"Husband-Wife Evidentiary Privilege in Criminal Proceedings." Journal of Criminal Law, Criminology & Police Science, 52:74, May-June 1961. 4896

"Husband-Wife Evidentiary Privilege: The Power of the Federal Courts to See a Rational Solution." St. Louis University Law Journal, 17:107, fall 1972. 4897

"Husband-Wife Privilege in Kansas; The Effect of the New Kansas Rules of Evidence." Washburn Law Journal, 6:144, fall 1966. 4897a

"Husband-Wife Testimony in Ohio." Western Reserve Law Review, 591, June 1963. 4898

"Marital Privileges and the Right to Testify." University of Chicago Law Review, 34:196, autumn 1966. 4899

"Privilege for Marital Communications in New Mexico." Natural Resources Journal, 4:123, May 1964. 4900

"Privileged Communications Between Husband and Wife." Tennessee Law Review, 41:943, summer 1974. 4901

Samuels, A. "Husband and Wife in the Law of Evidence." Law Journal, 113, 84, Feb. 8, 1963. 4902

Sevier, C. B. "Husband and Wife Privilege--Rules of Evidence."

JAG Journal, 20:15, July-Aug. 1965. 4903

"Spousal Testimony." Brooklyn Law Review, 28:259, April 1962. 4904

"Witnesses--Competency--Acts of Husband and Wife As Privileged Communication [People v. Meleski (NY) 176 NE 2d 81]." North Dakota Law Review, 38:133, Jan. 1962. 4905

"Witnesses--Competency of Spouses to Testify Against Each Other in Criminal Trial--Compelling the Spouse to Testify." South Carolina Law Review, 16:615, 1964. 4906

Yahuda, J. "Communication Between Husband and Wife." Law Times, 233:479, Aug. 31, 1962. 4907

(6) JOURNALISTS' PRIVILEGES

"Act to Protect Confidential Sources of News Media." Harvard Journal on Legislation, 6:341, March 1969. 4908

Beaver, J. E. "Newsman's Code, the Claim of Privilege and Everyman's Rights to Evidence." Oregon Law Review, 47:243, April 1968. 4909

Cades, J. R. "Power of the Courts to Protect Journalists' Confidential Sources of Information: An Examination of Proposed Shield Legislation." Hawaii Bar Journal, 11:35, summer 1974. 4910

"Constitutional Protection for the Newsman's Work Product." Harvard Civil Rights-Civil Liberties Law Review, 6:119, Dec. 1970. 4911

"Degree of Privilege Afforded the Press in South Carolina in Publication of Quasi-Judicial Proceedings." South Carolina Law Quarterly, 7:644, summer 1955. 4912

Dixon, R. G. "Newsman's Privilege by Federal Legislation: Within Congressional Power." Hastings Constitutional Law Quarterly, 1:39, spring 1974. 4913

"Evidence--Privileged Communications--Journalist Must Reveal News Source in Pretrial Examination When Information Is Material to Plaintiff's Claim [Garland v. Torre, 257 F. 2d 545]." Harvard Law Review, 72:768, Feb. 1959. 4914

Gallup, E. H., Jr. "Further Consideration of a Privilege for Newsman." Albany Law Review, 14:16, Jan. 1950. 4915

Goldsworthy, P. J. "Claim to Secrecy of New Source: A Journalistic Privilege?" Osgood Hall Law Journal, 9:157, Aug. 1971. 4916

Goodale, J. C. "Branzburg v. Hayes and the Developing Privilege for Newsmen." Hastings Law Journal, 26:709, Jan. 1975. 4917

Gordon, David. "The Confidences Newsmen Must Keep." Columbia Journalism Review, 10:15, Nov.-Dec. 1971. 4918

Graham, Fred P., and London, Jack C. "The Federal Shield Law We Need: Legislation to Protect Reporters' News Sources and Confidential Information Now Is Before Congress; What Kind of Bill Might Be Adopted?" Columbia Journalism Review, 11:26, March-April 1973. 4919

"Journalist and His Confidential Informants--Should They Be Privileged from Compulsory Disclosure?" Temple Law Quarterly, 32:432, summer 1959. 4920

"Journalist and His Confidential Source: Should A Testimonial Privilege Be Allowed?" Nebraska Law Review, 35:562, 1956. 4921

Nadelmann, K. H. "Newspaper Privilege and Extortion by Abuse of Legal Process." Columbia Law Review, 54:359, March 1954. 4922

"Newsman--Source Privilege: A Foundation in Policy for Recognition at Common Law." Florida Law Review, 26:453, spring 1974. 4923

"Newsman's Privilege: A Survey of the Law in California." Pacific Law Journal, 4:880, July 1973. 4924

"Newsmen's Privilege and the Constitution." South Carolina Law Review, 23:436, 1971. 4925

"Newspaper Immunity from Disclosure of Sources." Faculty of Law Review, University of Toronto, 17:141, April 1959. 4926

"Newspaper Reporter's Confidential Sources of Information--Are They Constitutionally Protected? [Garland v. Torre, 259 F. 2d 5451]." Buffalo Law Review, 8:294, winter 1959. 4927

"Newspaperman's Privilege As to Sources." New York University Intermural Law Review, 13:120, March 1958. 4928

"Right of a Newsman to Refrain from Divulging Sources of His Information." Virginia Law Review, 36:61, Feb. 1950. 4929

"State Abridgment of Newsman's Right of Access to News of Government Held Unconstitutional." Cumberland-Samford Law Review, 5:124, spring 1974. 4930

(7) ACCOUNTANT-CLIENT

"Accountant-Client Privilege: Where Does It Exist and How Far Does It Extend?" Journal of Taxation, 30:308, May 1969. 4931

"Accountants, Privileged Communications, and Section of the Internal Revenue Code." St. Louis University Law Journal, 10:252, winter 1965. 4932

"Caich v. United States (93 Supreme Court 611): The Supreme Court Takes a Fresh Look at the Accountant-Client Privilege--Or Does It?" Kentucky Law Journal, 62:263, 1973-74. 4933

"Evidence--Privileged Communications--Accountant and Client." North Carolina Law Review, 46:419, Feb. 1968. 4934

Helstein, R. S. "Privileged Communication for CPA's: An Analysis of the Laws Relating to Account-Client Privilege and the Merits of Such Laws." Journal of Accountancy, 130:39, Dec. 1970. 4935

Jentz, G. A. "Accountant Privileged Communications: Is It a Dying Concept Under the New Federal Rules of Evidence?" American Business Law Journal, 11:149, fall 1973. 4936

Tigue, J. J., Jr. "Accountant-Client Communications." Tax Counselor's Quarterly, 12:1, March 1968. 4937

(8) PSYCHOLOGIST/PSYCHOANALYST-PATIENT

Fox, R. G. "Professional Confidences and the Psychologist." Tasmania University Law Review, 3:12, Dec. 1968. 4938

Fox, S. J. "Psychotherapy and the Legal Privilege." Massachusetts Law Quarterly, 53:307, 1968. 4939

"Liability of Psychotherapist for Failure to Warn of Homicide Threatened by Patient." Vanderbilt Law Review, 28:631, April 1975. 4940

Love, G. H., and Yanity, G. J. "Psychotherapy and the Law." Medical Trial Technique Quarterly, 20:405, spring 1974. 4941

"Psychiatrist-Patient Privilege--A Need for the Retention and Future Crime Exception." Iowa Law Review, 52:1170, June 1967. 4942

"Psychotherapists' Privilege." Washburn Law Journal, 12:297, spring 1973. 4943

Slovenko, R. "Psychotherapist-Patient Testimonial Privilege: A Picture of Misguided Hope." Catholic University Law Review, 23:649, summer 1974. 4944

"Underprivileged Communications: Extension of the Psychotherapist-Patient Privilege to Patients of Psychiatric Social Workers." California Law Review, 61:1050, June 1973. 4945

(9) GOVERNMENTAL AND MISCELLANEOUS PRIVILEGES

Bender, L. "Review of Privileged Communications As Applied to Tax Fraud Proceedings." Tulane Tax Institute, 23:237, 1974. 4946

Coburn, D. R. "Child-Parent Communications: Spare the Privileges and Spoil the Child." Dickinson Law Review, 74:599, summer 1970. Existing privileges and a basis for the privilege of child-parent communications with an injury vs. benefit discussion. 4947

"Constitutional Rights of Criminal Defendants: The Identity of Informers." The John Marshall Journal of Practice and Procedure, 8:401, spring 1975. 4948

"Disclosure of Informant's Identity--The Substantive and Procedural Balance Tests." Albany Law Review, 39:561, 1975. 4949

Ehrherdt, Charles W. "Privileged Communications by the Drug User in Federal Courts." Journal of Drug Issues, 3:356, summer 1973. 4950

"Evidence: Government Privilege to Refuse to Disclose Contents of Official Documents in Federal Courts." Cornell Law Quarterly, 41:737, summer 1956. 4951

"Evidence--Privilege--Right of Third Person to Assert Privilege as to Accident Report Made (10 WA) Confidential by Statute [Sprague v. Brodus (A) 60 NW 2d 850]." Michigan Law Review, 52:1061, May 1954. 4952

"Evidence--Privilege--Use of Privileged Accident Report to Refresh Officer's Recollection [Wallace v. Skrzychi (Mich.) 61 NW 2d 106]." Michigan Law Review, 52:1063, May 1954. 4953

"Government's Privilege to Withhold the Identity of Informers, As Applied to Decoys [Roviars v. U.S. 77 Supreme Court 623]." Georgia Bar Journal, 20:562, May 1958. 4954

Hayes, J. L. "Disclosure of Informers: The Accused's Right." Connecticut Bar Journal, 48:91, June 1974. 4955

"Informer's Privilege in Criminal Cases." University of Illinois Law Forum, 1967:665, fall 1967. 4956

"Jencks Rule Held Applicable to Administrative Hearings [NLRB v. Adhesive Products Corp. 258 F. 2d 403]." Syracuse Law Review, 10:353, spring 1959. 4957

Miles, C. W. "Right of the President of the United States to Withhold Executive Information." Maryland State Bar Association, 59:230, 1954. 4958

Parry, C. "Legislatures and Secrecy." Harvard Law Review, 67:737, March 1954. 4959

"Policing the Executive Privilege." University of Michigan Journal of Law References, 5:568, spring 1972. 4960

Remington, F. J. "Police Investigation and the Privilege Against Self-Incrimination." Wisconsin Bar Bulletin, 26:7-8, 63-4, Dec. 1953. 4961

Robinson, W. P. "Testimonial Privilege and the School Guidance Counselor." Syracuse Law Review, 25:911, fall 1974. 4962

Ryan, K. W. "Police Reports and Privilege in Civil Actions." Australian Law Journal, 30:627, April 1957. 4963

"Use of In-Camera Hearings in Rulings on the Informer Privilege." University of Michigan Journal of Law Reform, 8:151, fall 1974. 4964

J. PRESUMPTIONS

"Abrogation of Criminal Statutory Presumptions." Suffolk University Law Review, 4:161, fall 1970. 4965

"Application of the Deadly Weapons Presumption in West Virginia." West Virginia Law Review, 75:287, April 1973. 4966

Brakel, S. J. "Presumption, Bias and Incompetency in the Criminal Process." Wisconsin Law Review, 1974:1105, 1974. 4967

"California Evidence Code: Presumptions." California Law Review, 53:1439, Dec. 1965. 4968

Collins, L., and Livingston, D. K. "Aspects of Conclusive Evidence Clauses." Journal of Business Law, 1974:212, July 1974. 4969

"Conflicting Presumptions: An Evaluation of the Solution Proposed by Uniform Rule 15." Villanova Law Review, 10:324, winter 1965. 4970

"Constitutional Law--Due Process and Equal Protection--Effect of Irrebuttable Statutory Presumptions." Georgia State Bar Journal, 10:484, Feb. 1974. 4971

"Criminal Presumption and Inference Instructions." Willamette Law Journal, 6:497, Dec. 1970. 4972

"Criminal Statutory Presumptions and the Reasonable Doubt Standard of Proof: Is Due Process Overdue?" St. Louis University Law Journal, 19:223, winter 1974. 4973

"Evidence--Presumptions--Application of the Deadly Weapons Presumption in West Virginia." West Virginia Law Review, 75:287, April 1973. The practical effect of the deadly weapons presumption is to place upon the defendant the burden of persuading the jury that malice is non-existent. This article reviews the history and effectiveness of such a presumption. 4974

Hug, J. P. "Presumptions and Inferences in Criminal Law." Military Law Review, 56:81, Spring 1972. 4975

"Irrebuttable Presumption Doctrine in the Supreme Court." Harvard Law Review, 87:1534, May 1974. 4976

"Law of Rebuttable Presumptions in Maine." Maine Law Review, 23:175, 1971. 4977

"Mere Evidence Rule: Need for Re-Evaluation." Cleveland State Law Review, 20:361, May 1971. 4978

"Presumption Arising Out of the 'No Eye Witness Rule'." Insurance Law Journal, 1962:85, fall 1962. 4979

"Presumption of Guilt from Proof of Possessions." Texas Law Review, 40:287, Dec. 1961. 4980

"Presumptions in Texas: A Study in Irrational Jury Control." Texas Law Review, 52:1329, Nov. 1974. 4981

"Presumptions--The Uniform Rules in the Federal Courts." Duke Law Journal, 1964:867, autumn 1964. 4982

"Some Problems of Presumptions: The South Carolina Problems." South Carolina Law Quarterly, 14:538, summer 1962. 4983

"Statutory Criminal Presumptions: A Compulsion to Testify." UCLA Law Review, 5:11, fall 1973. 4984

"Statutory Presumptions." Notre Dame Lawyer, 37:390, March 1962. 4985

"Statutory Presumptions of Due Care in Wrongful Death Action." Michigan Law Review, 60:510, fall 1962. 4986

Stumbo, J. E. "Presumptions--A View at Chaos." Washburn Law Journal, 3:182, spring 1964. 4987

Subrin, H. S. "Presumptions and Their Treatment Under the Law of Ohio." Ohio State Law Journal, 26:175, spring 1965. 4988

Weinstock, S. L., and Chase, H. J. "The Presumption of the Due Care in California." Hastings Law Journal, 4:124, spring 1953. 4989

"What Is the Law of Rebuttable Presumptions in Maine?" Maine Law Review, 16:226, 1964. 4990

V. ADMINISTRATION OF JUSTICE (5000)

Part V deals with procedures in criminal justice from the time the investigation focuses on a suspect to the final completion of the appellate processes. The materials presented cover not only the various procedures before, during and after trial but also such diverse topics as the grand jury, jurisdiction, extraordinary writs, plea bargaining and some of the theories underlying these subjects.

Of special interest is the section on the rights of the accused. The authors have sought to present an impartial view of the entire field by selection of well-written articles and books on each topic which may be of interest to those in all sections of the United States.

A. GENERAL WORKS AND REFERENCES

(1) BOOKS

Alexander, Franz, and Stuab, Hugo. The Criminal, the Judge and the Public. New York: Macmillan, 1931. Psychoanalytical knowledge applied to the criminal personality. The criminal mind is as legitimate an objective for psychological investigation as the neurotic or the normal individual. 5000

Ancel, Marc. Social Defense: A Modern Approach to Criminal Problems. New York: Schocken Books, 1965. 5001

Bramlett, B. Role Strain and the Administration of Justice. Ann Arbor: University Microfilms, 1972. 5002

Clark, W. Clarks Criminal Procedure. St. Paul, Minn.: West Pub. Co., 1918. 5003

The Constitution of the United States: Analysis and Interpretation--1963. Washington, D.C.: U.S. Gov. Printing Office, 1964. 5004

Cooper, Frank E. State Administrative Law. Indianapolis: Bobbs-Merrill, 1965. 2 vols. Analyzes all relevant state statutory and case law of the past ten years in light of the Revised Model State Administrative Act. 5005

Felkenes, G. T. Criminal Law and Procedure: Text and Cases. Englewood Cliffs, N.J.: Prentice-Hall, 1976. 430pp. 5006

Fricke, Charles W., and Alarcon, Arthur L. California Criminal Procedure, 6th ed. Los Angeles: Legal Book Store, 1965. A basic text in the broad field of criminal procedure and the administration of criminal justice, with hundreds of rules and case citations. Search warrants, statute of limitations, the grand jury, dismissals, trials and special judicial proceedings are exhaustively discussed. 5007

George, B. J. Constitutional Limitations. Ann Arbor, Mich.: Institute of Continuing Legal Education, 1967. 5008

Gibbons, Don C. Changing the Lawbreaker: The Treatment of Delinquents and Criminals. Englewood Cliffs, N.J.: Prentice-Hall, 1965. Identifies factors which compel individuals to break the law. Typology of juvenile delinquents and criminals based on a pattern of social roles, described as occurring within "definitional dimensions" of offensive behavior, interactional setting, self-image, and attitudes. 5009

Hall, Livingston, and Kamisar, Yale. Modern Criminal Procedure. St. Paul, Minn.: West Pub. Co., 1966. Case book on rapid change in the constitutional criminal field. Arrest, search and seizure, police interrogations and confessions, and coerced, induced and negotiated guilty pleas are treated in a comprehensive manner. Articles of prominent officials in the legal field included. 5010

Hartung, Frank E. Crime, Law and Society. Detroit: Wayne State University Press, 1965. 5011

Housel, Theodore W., and Walser, Guy O. Defending and Prosecuting Federal Criminal Cases, 2nd ed. Buffalo, N.Y.: Dennis and Co., 1946. Practice and procedures; topics range from crimes the federal courts take cognizance of through the trial and appeals to the federal use of pardons, paroles, and habeas corpus. 5012

Houts, M. From Arrest to Release. Springfield, Ill.: Charles C. Thomas, 1958. 5013

Israel, J. H. Criminal Procedure in a Nutshell: Constitutional Limitations. St. Paul, Minn.: West Pub. Co., 1971. 5014

Kerlen, D. Anglo-American Criminal Justice. New York: Oxford University Press, 1967. 5015

Lasson, Nelson B. The History and Development of the Fourth Amendment to the United States Constitution. Baltimore: Johns Hopkins Press, 1937. Part of the university's studies in Historical and Political Science, prepared under the direction of the departments of history, political economy, and political science. 5016

Lorton, J. Justice and the Press. Boston: Beacon Press, 1966. 5017

Louisell, David W. Modern Discovery in California. San Francisco: Berkeley Press, 1963. Realistic, practical and concise guide to modern rules of discovery in both criminal and civil cases in California. The philosophy of discovery, its history and the dilemma in California are included. A section on recent developments in California is of special interest to the entire field of law enforcement. 5018

Matza, David. Delinquency and Drift. New York: John Wiley, 1964. Contrasts the classical school of criminology, which emphasizes crime in relation to legal structure, with the positive school, which looks at the criminal actor in an effort to discover the causes of criminal behavior. 5019

Miller, F. W. Prosecution: The Decision to Charge a Suspect with a Crime. Mineola, N. Y.: Foundation Press, 1971. 5020

Murphy, W. F. Wiretapping on Trial: A Case Study of the Judicial Process. New York: Random House, 1965. 5021

Newman, Edwin S. Police, the Law and Personal Freedom. New York: Oceana Publications, 1964. Discusses: (1) police methods and practices--requirements for a legal arrest, search and seizure, development of evidence, etc.; (2) the proper procedures for a fair trial; (3) habeas corpus in terms applicable to the citizen. 5022

Ringel, William E. Searches and Seizures, Arrests and Confessions. New York: Clark Boardman, 1972. 5023

Shulman, Harry M. Juvenile Delinquency in American Society. New York: Harper, 1961. Organized crime and prostitution related to the central problems of delinquency; also legal aspects, extent, psychological and physiological bases of delinquency; typologies of delinquent behavior based on degrees of overtness, personalization, social conventionalism, and social goal orientation. 5024

U. S. Justice Dept. Handbook of Search and Seizure. Washington, D. C.: U. S. Gov. Printing Office, 1971. 5025

Vedder, Clyde B., and Kay, Barbara A. Penology: A Realistic Approach. Springfield, Ill.: Charles C. Thomas, 1964. 5026

Weston, P. B. The Administration of Justice. Englewood Cliffs, N. J.: Prentice-Hall, 1972. 5027

(2) ARTICLES

Abram, M. B. "Access to the Judicial Process." Georgia Law Review, 6:247, winter 1972. 5028

"Access to the Civil Courts: The Need for Continuing Reform." Albany Law Review, 37:135, 1972. 5029

Ace, G. "In Hot Blood; Suspects and Their Rights." Saturday Review, 51:3, June 6, 1968. 5030

Altschuler, A. W. "Defense Attorney's Role in Plea Bargaining." Yale Law Journal, 84:1179, May 1975. 5031

"Another Confession Problem; Unjoining the Joint Trial." Time, 86:31, Dec. 24, 1965. Explains California's attack on joint trials in which a confession by one defendant incriminates the other "unconfessed" defendant. 5032

"Are Too Many Getting Acquitted?" New Law Journal, 124:624, July 4, 1974. 5033

Ashford, A. A., and Risinger, D. M. "Presumptions, Assumptions, and Due Process in Criminal Cases: A Theoretical Overview." Yale Law Journal, 79:165, Dec. 1969. 5034

Atkinson, D. N., and Dunn, J. A., Jr. "Impact of Expenditures on the Operation of the Criminal Justice System." Washburn Law Journal, 12:269, spring 1973. 5035

Baier, P. R., and Lesinski, T. J. "In Aid of the Judicial Process: A Proposal for Curricular and Student Involvement." Judicature, 56:100, Oct. 1972. 5036

"Balance Sheet on Justice." Nation, 213:166, Sept. 6, 1971. 5037

Ball, George H. "Labor and the Law: A Challenge by Ball." New York Times, Magazine, Oct. 28, 1945. The laws of the land should be enforced equally against all law breakers. Labor demonstration and pickets which the court upholds as free speech and the right to peaceable assembly are a lot of bunk. When labor unions picket or go on strike and commit beatings or destroy property or block thoroughfares, they are in violation of the law. 5038

Burger, W. "State of the Judiciary-1975." American Bar Association Journal, 61:439, April 1975. 5039

Cleveland, A. G. "Role of the Bar in Judicial System Improvements." Georgia State Bar Journal, 11:90, Oct. 1974. 5040

Cohn, A. W. "Training in the Criminal Justice Nonsystem." Federal Probation, 38:32, June 1974. 5041

"Criminal Sentencing: An Overview of Procedures and Alternatives."

Mississippi Law Journal, 45:782, June 1974. 5042

Culhane, James E. "California Enacts Legislation to Aid Victims of Criminal Violence." Stanford Law Review, 18:266, Nov. 1965. Also discusses similar statutes in Britain, New Zealand, and a recently proposed federal statute. 5043

Dam, K. W. "Class Actions: Efficiency Compensation, Deterrence and Conflict of Interest." Journal of Legal Studies, 4:47, Jan. 1975. 5044

Damaska, M. "Structures of Authority and Comparative Criminal Procedure." Yale Law Journal, 84:480, Jan. 1975. 5045

Dash, S. "Crime Law Enforcement and Justice: The Prospects for Reform." Federal Bar Journal, 26:244, summer 1966. 5046

______. "Means and Methods Employed in Criminal Law." Criminal Law Bulletin, 10:57, summer 1974. 5047

Desmond, C. S. "Courts, the Public and the Law Explosion." Georgetown Law Journal, 54:777, spring 1966. 5048

"An End to Copping." Time, 87:54, June 24, 1966. "Deals" made between judges and the accused (a guilty plea assures a relatively light sentence), save time and money but federal Judge Edward Weinfield states that it is wrong. 5049

Erickson, W. H. "History of the Tripod of Justice." Milwaukee Law Review, 64:79, spring 1974. 5050

"Fair Trial, Free Press, the Contempt Power: Its Historic and Modern Application." Suffolk University Law Review, 3:384, summer 1969. 5051

Felkenes, G. T. "The Prosecutor: A Look at Reality." Southwestern University Law Review, 1:98, spring 1975. 5052

Finley, R. C. "Who Is on Trial--The Police? The Courts? or the Criminally Accused?" Journal of Criminal Law, Criminology and Police Science, 57:238, Sept.-Dec. 1966. 5053

Fortas, Abraham. "Criminal Justice 'Without Pity'." Trial Lawyers Quarterly, 9:9, 1973. 5054

France, J. G. "Judicial Reorganization--A Solution to Congestion." Dickinson Law Review, 68:143, winter 1963-64. 5055

Frankel, M. E. "Search for Truth--An Umpireal View." Record 30:14, Jan.-Feb. 1975. 5056

Friedman, L. N. "Notes Toward a History of American Justice." Buffalo Law Review, 24:111, fall 1974. 5057

Friendly, Henry J. "The Bill of Rights as a Code of Criminal Procedure." California Law Review, 53:929, Oct. 1965. Text of the 1965 Morrison Lecture to the State Bar of California on Sept. 23, 1965, on criminal procedure. 5058

Gallo, Jon J. "Removal of Federal Judges--New Alternatives to an Old Problem: Chandler v. Judicial Council of the Tenth Circuit." UCLA Law Review, 13:1385, 1966. 5059

Galzell, J. A. "Rudiments of State Level Judicial Management." Chicago-Kent Law Review, 47:169, fall-winter 1970. 5060

Geis, Gilbert. "Experimental Design and the Law: A Prospectus for Research on Victim-Compensation in California." California Western Law Review, 2:85, spring 1966. Comparative analysis of 60 persons or families who during 1965 and 1966 are granted compensation under provisions of the new statute as contrasted to 60 persons or families who would have been granted such compensation during 1963 and 1964 had the law been in effect. 5061

Gerard, Eleanor J. "Model Crime Prevention Division." Journal of Criminal Law, Criminology and Police Science, 34:344, Jan. 1944. 5062

Ginsberg, M. "Rural Criminal Justice: An Overview." American Journal of Criminal Law, 3:35, summer 1974. 5063

Godbold, J. C. "Bite Your Own Bullets." Alabama Lawyer, 34:143, April 1973. 5064

Goff, C. E. "Is Lady Justice a Blind Date?" American Bar Association Journal, 59:851, Aug. 1973. 5065

Goldberg, A. J. "Equal Justice for the Poor Too." New York Times Magazine, March 15, 1964. Far too often, money--or the lack of it--can be the deciding factor in a courtroom; calls for insuring proper representation and justice for all. 5066

______. "Role of Law in a Free Society." Georgia Law Review, 7:403, spring 1973. 5067

"Government Lawyer Looks at the Crime Problem; Fourth Amendment and Administration of Criminal Justice." U.S. News and World Report, 57:74, Sept. 28, 1964. Police are hampered by revised rules on arrests, investigations, and criminal trials which expand the rights of criminals, restrict the police and make convictions in local trials easily upset in federal courts. 5068

Griswold, E. N. "Judicial Process." Federal Bar Journal, 31:309, fall 1972. 5069

_______. "When Newsmen Become Newsmakers; Problem of Publicity Before and During a Trial." Saturday Review, 47:21, Oct. 24, 1964. Reply, W. O'Neil, 47:21, Nov. 21, 1964. The case for a measure of restraint on the press to assure a defendant a fair trial; Public statements, public appearances and release of evidence are inappropriate and disciplinary measures should be taken against violators. 5070

Hagan, J. "Parameters of Criminal Prosecution: An Application of Path Analysis to a Problem of Criminal Justice." Journal of Criminal Law and Criminology, 65:536, Dec. 1974. 5071

Harlan, J. M. "Bills of Rights and the Constitution." American Bar Association Journal, 50:918, Oct. 1964. 5072

Hazard, G. C. "Commission Introduces New Standards of Judicial Administration." American Bar Association Journal, 60:912, Aug. 1974. 5073

Heflin, H. "Judicial System Improvement." Washburn Law Journal, 13:1, winter 1974. Excellent article on the improvements in the court system in Alabama by that state's chief justice. 5074

_______. "State of the Judiciary." Alabama Lawyer, 35:500, Oct. 1974. 5075

"How Equal Is Justice?" Newsweek, 80:97, Oct. 30, 1972. 5076

Ingraham, B. L. "Impact of Argersinger (Argersinger v. Hamlin, 92 Sup. Ct. 2006)--One Year Later." Law and Society Review, 8:615, Dec. 1974. 5077

Jewitt, R. "Law Is No Respecter of Persons." Christian Century, 90:1116, Nov. 14, 1973. 5078

Jordan, V. E., Jr. "System Propagates Crime." Crime and Delinquency. 20:233, July 1974. 5079

Judice, C. R. "Texas Judicial System: Historical Development and Efforts Toward Court Modernization." South Texas Law Journal, 14:295, 1973. 5080

"Judicial Inquiry Commission: Successor to the Judicial Commission of Alabama." Alabama Lawyer, 35:289, July 1974. 5081

"Judicial Intervention in Trials." Washburn University Law Quarterly, 1973:843, fall 1973. 5082

"Justice: Blind or Impartial." North Carolina Central Law Journal, 4:168, fall 1972. 5083

"Justice on Trial." Christianity Today, 14:29, Oct. 24, 1969. 5084

"Justice Overdue: Speedy Trial for the Potential Defendant." Stanford Law Review, 5:95, Dec. 1952. 5085

Kaplan, V. "Equal Justice in an Unequal World: Equality for the Negro--The Problem of Special Treatment." Northwestern University Law Review, 61:363, July-Aug. 1966. 5086

Katzenbach, N. deB. "Free Press and Fair Trial." Vital Speeches of the Day, 31:518, June 15, 1965. 5087

Kooken, D. L. "Post War Influence Upon Criminal Investigation." Journal of Criminal Law, Criminology and Police Science, 35: 426, March 1945. Increasing awareness of rights and privileges under the Constitution; new patterns of criminal behavior can be expected after the war. The police must beware of practices which bring criticism by the public. 5088

Landes, W. M. "Legality and Reality: Some Evidence on Criminal Procedure." Journal of Legal Studies, 3:287, June 1974. 5089

Levin, M. A. "Delay in Five Criminal Courts." Journal of Legal Studies, 4:83, Jan. 1975. 5090

Lewis, A. "Case of Trial by Press." New York Times Magazine, March 1, 1964. 5091

Lewis, N. "Litigants in Person and Unrepresented Defendants." Modern Law Review, 25:494, summer 1974. 5092

Lindsay, John V. "Bar and Reforming the Criminal Justice System." Record, 28:193, March 1973. 5093

Lumbard, J. Edward. "The Administration of Criminal Justice: Some Problems and Their Resolution." American Bar Association Journal, 49:840, Sept. 1963. Discusses federal leadership in clarifying individual rights, the necessity for improved police training and instruction, wiretapping, counsel and appeals proceedings. 5094

McGowan, C. "Toward Better Court Organization." American Bar Association Journal, Nov. 1973. 5095

Motley, C. B. "'Law and Order' and Criminal Justice System." Journal of Criminal Law and Criminology, 64:259, Sept. 1973. 5096

Murray, F. D. "ABA Standards--The Judge's Function Report." Pennsylvania Bar Association Quarterly, 44:7, Oct. 1972. 5097

Nagel, S., and Weitzman, L. J. "Double Standard of American Justice." Society, 9:18, March 1972. 5098

Palmer, L. I. "Implementing the Obligation of Advocacy in Review of Criminal Convictions." Journal of Criminal Law and Criminology, 65:267, summer 1974. 5099

Parness, J. A. "Concept of a Unified Court System." DePaul Law Review, 24:1, fall 1974. 5100

Philbin, E. J. "Justice: A Lady in Distress." San Diego Law Review, 10:280, Feb. 1973. 5101

Piggins, Edward S. "Are We Handcuffing Law Enforcement?" Vital Speeches of the Day, 24:441, May 1, 1958. Detroit Commissioner of Police on court decisions and actions which hamper police. 5102

Posner, R. A. "Economic Approach to Legal Procedure and Judicial Administration." Journal of Legal Studies, 2:398, June 1973. 5103

"Press or Trial; S. Sheppard Case Before Supreme Court." Time, 87:64, March 11, 1966. The murder case; influencing a jury by an unfavorable press. 5104

Prettyman, E. B. "Qualities of Victory; Justice." Nation's Business, 50:40, June 1962. Justice defined in its historical context, compared and contrasted with our ideals. 5105

"Price of Justice: The Cost of Trying a Suspected Murderer." Time, 100:74, Nov. 20, 1974. 5106

"The Price of Liberty [review of Allan Barth's Price of Liberty]." Saturday Review, 44:27, Oct. 7, 1961. Personal liberty is being imperiled for the sake of order; discusses arrest, wiretapping, bugging, search and seizure, entrapment, and the right to counsel. 5107

"Push to Streamline the Courts." Illustrated: Business World, p. 46, Dec. 4, 1971. 5108

Pye, A. K. "The Supreme Court and the Police: Fact and Fiction." Journal of Criminal Law, Criminology and Police Science, 57:238, Sept.-Dec. 1966. 5109

Reder, M. W. "Citizen Rights and the Cost of Law Enforcement." Journal of Legal Studies, 3:435, June 1974. 5110

Reed, J. H. "Operational Research and the Courts." Judicature, 56:67, Aug.-Sept. 1972. 5111

Riccio, L. J. "Model for Court Resource Planning." The Judicial System Journal, 1:49, March 1975. 5112

"Rights of Society v. Rights of the Individual in the Administration of Criminal Law." Duquesne University Law Review, 3:73, fall 1964. 5113

"Rights of the Accused." F.B.I. Law Enforcement Bulletin, 35:21, Sept. 1966. Supreme Court ruling in the cases of Miranda v. Arizona, Vigners v. New York, Westover v. U.S., and California v. Steward. In these decisions the court describes the manner in which an accused must be warned of his right to silence and to counsel. 5114

"Rights of the Criminal." National Review, 20:535, June 4, 1968. 5115

Robinson, Richard M. "The Criminal Justice Act of 1964: A Step Toward Equal Justice in the Federal Courts." University of Florida Law Review, 13:606, spring 1966. Discusses the provisions of the 1964 Council Justice Act and evaluates its strengths and weaknesses. 5116

Rosett, A. "Discretion, Severity and Legality in Criminal Justice." Southern California Law Review, 46:12, Dec. 1972. 5117

Schlusberg, M. D. "Due Process: The Supreme Court Gets Turned on and Tuned In." American Business Law Journal, 6:501, fall 1968. 5118

Senna, J. J. "Criminal Justice Higher Education--Its Growth and Other Directions." Crime and Delinquency, 20:389, Oct. 1974. 5119

Smith, C. "Challenge of Law in a Changing Society." Juvenile Justice, 23:12, Aug. 1972. 5120

Star, J. "Jam-up: Crisis in Our Criminal Courts." Look, 35:32, March 23, 1971. 5121

Stone, Donald C. "The Police Attack Crime." National Civic Review, 24:39, Jan. 1935. A thorough overhauling of police methods and criminal procedure urged at round table conference. 5122

Stuart, C., and Stuart, D. D. "Metaphoric View of the Criminal Process." American Journal of Criminal Law, 3:17, summer 1974. 5123

Summers, M. R. "Tilted Scales of Criminal Justice: The Plight of the Indigent Defendant." Criminal Law Bulletin, 5:508, Nov. 1969. 5124

Tauro, G. J. "State of the Judiciary." Massachusetts Law Quarterly, 57:209, summer 1972. 5125

Thompson, J. R. "The Supreme Court and the Police: 1968?" Journal of Criminal Law, Criminology and Police Science, 57: 238, Sept.-Dec. 1966. 5126

"TRB from Washington: One-Eyed Justice." New Republic, 163:4, Oct. 31, 1970. 5127

"Trial by Newspapers; Case of Sam Sheppard." Time, 84:44, July 24, 1964. Explains why Dr. Sam Sheppard was freed from prison after ten years by U. S. District Judge Carl A. Weinman. 5128

Vorenberg, J. "President's Commission on Law Enforcement and Administration of Justice: Organization and Goals." American Criminal Law Quarterly, 4:118, spring 1966 5129

Wagner, W. J. "Crime and the Law: Sociologico-Legal Observations." Catholic Lawyer, 20:177, summer 1974. 5130

Wasby, S. L. "Getting the Message Across--Communicating Court Decisions to the Police." The Justice System Journal, 1:29, winter 1974. 5131

Weigel, Stanley A. "Some Reflections on Civil Disobedience, Riots, and Law." Lincoln Law Review, 1:1, Dec. 1965. Address to an audience of lawyers and judges; the conflict between constitutional rights and the enforcement of the law. 5132

Weinstein, J. B. "Role of the Chief Judge in a Modern System of Justice." Record, 28:291, April 1973. 5133

"We've Been Asked Who Enforces High-Court Rule." U.S. News and World Report, 36:92, May 28, 1954. 5134

Wittman, D. "Two Views of Procedure." Journal of Legal Studies, 3:249, Jan. 1974. 5135

Wright, J. Skelly. "A Judge's View: The News Media and Criminal Justice." American Bar Association Journal, 50:1125, 1964. The threat posed by the news media to an accused person's right to a fair trial exemplified by the Oswald incident and the Ruby trial and the coverage of the Lindbergh case a generation ago. 5136

Wyzanski, C. E., Jr. "Equal Justice Through Law." Tulane Law Review, 47:951, June 1973. 5137

Zeisel, H. "Reflections on Experimental Techniques in the Law." Journal of Legal Studies, 2:107, Jan. 1973. 5138

B. RIGHTS OF ACCUSED

(1) SPEEDY TRIAL

Amsterdam, A. G. "Speedy Criminal Trial: Rights and Remedies."

Stanford Law Review, 27:525, Feb. 1975. 5139

Campbell, W. J. "Delays in Criminal Cases." Federal Rules Decisions, 55:229, Sept. 1972. 5140

Clark, T. C. "Sixth Amendment and the Law of the Land." Saint Louis University Law Journal, 8:1, fall 1963. 5141

Comisky, M. "Slow Justice Is Preferable to Speedy Injustice." Pennsylvania Bar Association Quarterly, 44:23, Oct. 1972. 5142

"Constitutional Guarantee of Speedy Trial." Indiana Law Review, 8:414, 1974. 5143

"Constitutional Law--Prisoner's Right to a Speedy Trial in Another Jurisdiction." Washburn Law Journal, 9:153, fall 1969. 5144-5

"Constitutional Law--Right to Speedy Trial--Post Indictment Delay." New York Law Forum, 18:997, spring 1973. 5146

"Criminal Law--Right to Speedy Trial--Waiver [Ex Parte State Attorney General (Alabama 52 So. (2d) 158)]." Alabama Law Review, 4:112, fall 1951. 5147

Curtiss, W. D. "Achieving Prompt Criminal Trials in New York." New York State Bar Journal, 44:517, Dec. 1972. 5148

Desmond, C. S. "Should It Take Thirty-Four Months for a Trial?" New York Times Magazine, p29+, Dec. 8, 1963. Advocates abolishing the jury, except in criminal cases, to clear the court's calenders. 5149

"Excessive Delay in the Courts: Toward a Continuance Policy Relating to Counsel and Parties." Cleveland State Law Review, 21:118, Sept. 1972. 5150

"Experiment in Justice Without Delay." Judicature, 52:334, March 1969. 5151

Foster, J. "Speedier Justice in Britain; We Reformed Our Laws in the 19th Century and the U.S. Didn't." U.S. News and World Report, 58:43, March 22, 1965. Compares crime and law enforcement in Britain and United States. 5152

Fuld, S. H. "Gordian Knot: Congestion and Delay in Our Courts." New York State Bar Journal, 39:488, Dec. 1967. 5153

Godblod, J. C. "Speedy Trial--Major Surgery for a National Ill." Alabama Law Review, 24:265, spring 1972. 5154

Gross, S. E. "Denial of the Right to a Speedy Trial: Strict Remedy for an Uncertain Doctrine." The Justice System Journal, 1:73, winter 1974. 5155

"Impact of Speedy Trial Provisions: A Tentative Appraisal." Columbia Journal of Law and Social Problems, 8:356, spring 1972. 5156

"Implementation of the Speedy Trial Guarantee in Louisiana." Louisiana Law Review, 33:568, summer 1973. 5157

"Military Courts System Takes the Initiative with the Issue of Speedy Trial." Capital University Law Review, 3:292, 1974. 5158

"Obligation of Securing a Speedy Trial." Wyoming Law Journal, 11: 44, fall 1956. 5159

"Right of Accused to a Speedy Trial [In re Gregory (OK) 309 P. 2d 1083]." Oklahoma Law Review, 10:447, Nov. 1957. 5160

"Right to a Speedy Trial: Ohio Follows the Trend." University of Cincinnati Law Review, 43:610, 1974. 5161

Rudenstein, D. S. "Right to a Speedy Trial: Barker v. Wingo (92 S. Ct. 2182) in the Lower Courts." University of Illinois Law Forum, 1975:11, 1975. 5162

Scandur, L. "Traffic Courts; Cash Register Justice." Nation, 198: 144, Feb. 10, 1964. Thirty million traffic summonses were issued by the nation's police in 1963, all but a few disposed of by cafeteria-line justice and mass pronouncements of guilty from the bench. 5163

"Speedy Trial Guarantee: Criteria and Confusion in Interpreting Its Violation." DePaul Law Review, 22:839, summer 1973. 5164

"Speedy Trial Guarantees in Pennsylvania: The Impact of Rule 1100." Dickinson Law Review, 78:755, summer 1974. 5165

"Speedy Trial. Protection for Criminal Defendants Under Indiana's Amended Criminal Rule 4." Valparaiso University Law Review, 8:683, spring 1974. 5166

"Speedy Trial Schemes and Criminal Justice Delay." Cornell Law Review, 57:794, May 1972. 5167

Torvestad, R. J. "Speedy Trial in Military Law." Air Force JAG Law Review, 8:33, May-June 1966. 5168

"Trial Delay Indemnity--Insuring Our Criminal Justice Machinery." Notre Dame Law, 48:936, April 1973. 5109

Wallace, G. "Speedier Justice (and: Trial by Ambush)." Australian Law Journal, 35:124, Aug. 1961. 5170

Waybright, R. J. "Justice Without Delay." Florida Bar Journal, 42:1132, Nov. 1968. 5171

Weidberg, L. E. "Calendar Congestion--Insolvable?" Plaintiff's Advocate, 6:72, July 1962. 5172

Wideikis, J. R. 'Rejection of the Compensatory Remedy with Respect to the Right to a Speedy Trial: The Conclusion of the Marion (U.S. v. Marion, 92 Supreme Court 455)--Barker (Barker v. Wingo, 92 Supreme Court 2182)--Strunk (U.S. v. Strunk, 467 F. 2d 969) Triology." John Marshall Journal; 7: 253, spring 1974. 5173

Yackle, L. W. "Taking Stock of Detainer Statutes." Loyola University Law Review (LA), 8:88, fall 1975. 5174

Zeisel, H. "Delay by the Parties and Delay by the Courts." Journal of Legal Education, 15:27, 1962. 5175

(2) PUBLIC TRIAL

"Accused's Right to a Public Trial." Columbia Law Review, 49: 110, Jan. 1949. Examines the different views now held regarding the extent to which the public may be excluded from criminal proceedings without infringing the accused's right to a public trial. 5176

"Aftermath of Sheppard (Sheppard v. Maxwell, 86 Supreme Court 1507): Some Proposed Solutions to the Free Press-Fair Trial Controversy." Journal of Criminal Law, Criminology and Police Science, 59:234, June 1968. 5177

Ainsworth, R. A., Jr. "Fair Trial--Free Press." Federal Rules Decisions, 45:417, Feb. 1969. 5178

"American Bar Association Suggests an Answer to the 'Fair Trial-Free Press' Dilemma." Duke Law Journal, 1967:593, June 1967. 5179

"Arizona Fair Trial--Free Press Dilemma at the Preliminary Hearing Stage." Arizona Law Review, 9:466, spring 1968. 5180

Beavers v. Haubert, 198 U.S. 77, 87 (1905). Constitutional right of the accused to a speedy trial is not violated with proceeding to change jurisdiction. 5181

Cohen, N. P. "Trial in Absentia 'Reexamined'." Tennessee Law Review, 40:155, winter 1973. 5182

"Constitutional Law--Criminal Trial--Right of the Press to Demand Admittance After Defendant Has Waived Public Trial." Southern California Law Review, 30:340, April 1957. Kirstowsky v. Superior Court 143 Cal. App. 2d 745 (1956). After defendant waived public trial, the press sought a writ of mandamus to compel the Superior Court to vacate the order. In this case the writ was denied. 5183

"Constitutional Law--Pretrial Publicity--The Milwaukee 14." Wisconsin Law Review, 1970:209, 1970. 5184

"Constitutional Law--Sixth Amendment--Right to Public Trial." Southern California Law Review, 23:91, Dec. 1949. U.S. v. Kobli 1972 Fed. (2d) 919 (1949); indiscriminate exclusion of the public from the courtroom was held a deprivation of the defendant's right to a public trial under the Sixth Amendment. 5185

"Courts: The Right of the Public to a Public Trial." UCLA Law Review, 4:475, April 1957. The secret trial has always been the mark of despotism. 5186

"Criminal Law: Fair Trial and Free Press: Oklahoma's Compact of Understanding and Guidelines for Reporting." Oklahoma Law Review, 22:174, May 1969. 5187

"Criminal Law: Newspaper Publicity of Criminal News in Oklahoma." Oklahoma Law Review, 22:180, May 1969. 5188

Erickson, W. H. "How Can Trial Disruptions Be Curbed?" Pennsylvania Bar Association Quarterly, 44:15, Oct. 1972. 5189

"Exclusion of the Press From a 'Public Trial'." Oklahoma Law Review, 10:320, Aug. 1957. 5190

"Free Press--Fair Trial Controversy--An Empirical Approach." Connecticut Law Review, 2:351, winter 1969-70. 5191

"'Gag Order', Exclusion of the Press's Right to Information." Albany Law Review, 39:317, 1975. 5192

Kalven, H., Jr. "Concept of the Public Forum Cox v. Louisiana (85 Supreme Court 476)." Supreme Court Review, 1965:1, 1965. 5193

Lewis, S. R. "Right to Public Trial [Tanksley v. United States, 145 F. 2d 58]." Boston University Law Review, 25:145, April 1945. 5194

Lowe, R. G. "Right of the Accused to Public Trial in Oklahoma." The Journal--Oklahoma Bar Association, 25:585, Mar. 27, 1954. 5195

Martel, John S. "Fair Trial v. Free Press in Criminal Trials." California Law Review, 47:366, May 1959. The case, Shepard v. Florida, 341 U.S. 50 (1951), illustrates the inevitable conflict of two constitutionally protected rights, fair trial and free press; analysis of situation within each of the two major divisions. 5196

"News and the Accused." Prospectus, 3:95, Dec. 1969. 5197

"Perils of Being Too Public, Pauling v. National Review." Time, 87:80, April 29, 1966. In the question of free discussion as opposed to an individual's reputation, using biochemist Linus Pauling's libel suit as an example, the Supreme court is in favor of freedom of public discussion. 5198

Pollard v. United States, 352 U.S. 354 (1957). Rights of accused to be informed in open court of every action taken against him until he is lawfully sentenced. 5199

"Public Trial--Exclusion of the Public--Interests Protected." Connecticut Bar Journal, 27:239, June 1953. 5200

"Public Trial in Criminal Cases." Michigan Law Review, 52:128, Nov. 1953. 5201

Rawlings, M. E. "Constitutional Balance Between Fair Trials and Free Press." Drake Law Review, 17:1, Dec. 1967. 5202

Reardon, P. C. "Fair Trial--Free Press." Marquette Law Review, 52:547, winter 1969. 5203

"Right of an Individual Other Than the Criminally Accused to Petition for a Public Trial." Washington University Law Quarterly, 1972: 580, summer 1972. 5204

"Right to a Public Trial." Journal of Criminal Law, Criminology and Police Science, 41:782, April 1959. 5205

"Right to a Public Trial in California: Whose Right?" California Western Law Review, 5:287, spring 1969. 5206

"Right to a Public Trial in Criminal Cases." New York University Law Review, 41:1138, Dec. 1966. 5207

"Right to Public Trial--Exclusion of Public from Federal Courtroom, United States v. Kobli, 172 F. 2d 919." Minnesota Law Review, 33:662, May 1949. 5208

"Right to Public Trial--Secret Trials Constitute Denial of Due Process Under Fourteenth Amendment [In re Oliver, 68 Supreme Court 499]." Minnesota Law Review, 33:71, Dec. 1948. 5209

Seymour, W. N., Jr. "Trial by Television." New York State Bar Journal, 40:19, Jan. 1968. 5210

Simon, David. "Criminal Law--Public Trial: Power of a Court to Exclude the Press and General Public from a Criminal Trial." UCLA Law Review, 2:567, June 1955. People v. Jelke 308 New York 56; 123 N.E. 2d 769, (1954); the trial judge made order, on his own motion and over defendant's objection, excluding the general public and the press from the courtroom on grounds that public decency compelled the exclusion. (Defendant charged with pimping.) Upheld. 5211

Stewart, R. B. "Trial by the Press." Military Law Review, 43:37, Jan. 1969. 5212

Tauro, G. J. "Fair Trial Free Press Revisited." American Bar Association Journal, 55:417, May 1969. 5213

Ware, W. M. "Journalistic Media and for Trial." Cleveland State Law Review, 18:440, Sept. 1969. 5214

Younger, E. J. "Fair Trial, Free Press, and the Man in the Middle." American Bar Association Journal, 56:127, Feb. 1970. 5215

(3) COUNSEL

Adam, S. "Right of an Accused to Counsel." Illinois Bar Journal, 54:308, Dec. 1965. 5216

"Adequate Representation for Defendants in Federal Criminal Cases: Appointment of Counsel Under the Criminal Justice Act of 1964." New York University Law Review, 41:758, Oct. 1966. 5217

"Administration of Criminal Justice: A Student Symposium." Louisiana Law Review, 26:666, April-June 1966. 5218

Alder, J. E. "Representation Before Tribunals." Public Law, 1972:278, winter 1972. 5219

"Appointed Counsel Must Actually and Substantially Assist the Client in Determining Whether or Not to Plead Guilty." Journal of Urban Law, 51:564, Feb. 1974. 5220

"Argersinger v. Hamlin (92 Supreme Court 2006): A Demand for Change in Administration of Criminal Justice." Montana Law Review, 35:157, winter 1974. 5221

"Argersinger v. Hamlin (92 Supreme Court 2006) and the Collateral Use of Prior Misdemeanor Convictions of Indigents Unrepresented by Counsel at Trial." Ohio State Law Journal, 35:168, 1974. 5222

"Assistance to the Indigent Person Charged with Crime." Georgia State Bar Journal, 2:197, Nov. 1965. 5223

"Assuring the Right to an Adequately Prepared Defense." Journal of Criminal Law and Criminology, 65:302, summer 1974. 5224

"Attorney's Lack of Pretrial Investigation Constitutes Ineffective Assistance of Counsel but Burden Is on Defendant to Prove Prejudice Requiring Reversal." Fordham Law Review, 43:310, Nov. 1974. 5225

"Balance Sheet of Appointed Counsel in Louisiana Criminal Cases." <u>Louisiana Law Review,</u> 34:88, fall 1973. 5226

Bazelon, P. L. "Defective Assistance of Counsel." <u>University of Cincinnati Law Review,</u> 42:1, 1973. 5227

Benenson, A. "Lawyer in the Juvenile Court." <u>Journal of the Bar Association of the State of Kansas,</u> 38:15, spring 1969. 5228

Bird, J. T. "Representation of Indigent Criminal Defendants in Kentucky." <u>Kentucky Law Journal,</u> 53:478, spring 1965. 5229

Bloom, M. T. "Justice for the Poor; Public Defender System." <u>Reader's Digest,</u> 86:126, April 1965. Examples from the L.A. Defender's Office substantiate the argument. 5230

Bluth, W. H. "Legal Services for Inmates: Coopting the Jailhouse Lawyer." <u>Capital University Law Review,</u> 1:59, 1972. 5231

Brickman, L. "Of Arterial Passageways Through the Legal Process: The Right of Universal Access to Courts and Lawyering Services." <u>New York University Law Review,</u> 48:595, Oct. 1973. 5232

"California Constitution and Counsel at Pretrial Lineups: Disneyland Claims or Deadly Serious Business." <u>Pepperdine Law Review,</u> 2:83, 1974. 5233

Clark, T. C. "Gideon Revisited." <u>Arizona Law Review,</u> 15:343, 1973. 5234

"Confessions--Right to Counsel--The Impact of Miranda in Missouri." <u>Saint Louis University Law Journal,</u> 17:572, summer 1973. 5235

"Constitutional Law--Attorney and Client--Right to Counsel." <u>Case Western Reserve Law Review,</u> 19:1107, June 1968. 5236

"Constitutional Law--Criminal Procedure--Counsel Required at Line-up only if Formal Judicial Proceedings Have Been Initiated." <u>Tulane Law Review,</u> 47:899, April 1973. 5237

"Constitutional Law--Fourteenth Amendment Due Process--Representation by Counsel at Trial Is Prerequisite to the Imposition of any Sentence of Imprisonment Absent Valid Waiver." <u>Villanova Law Review,</u> 18:750, March 1973. 5238

"Constitutional Law--No Imprisonment for Any Defendant Who Has Not Had or Waived the Assistance of Counsel at His Trial, Regardless of the Classification of the Criminal Offense Charged." <u>Duke Law Review,</u> 77:176, fall 1972. 5239

"Constitutional Law: Prison 'No-Assistance' Regulations and the

Jailhouse Lawyer." Duke Law Journal, 1968:343, April 1968. 5240

"Constitutional Law--Right to Appointed Counsel--Indigent Misdemeanant." Duquesne Law Review, 12:115, fall 1973. 5241

"Constitutional Law--Self-representation in Criminal Trials--The Pro Se Defendant." Wake Forest Law Review, 9:265, March 1973. 5242

"Criminal Law: Applying the Harmless Error Rule to a Confession Obtained in Violation of Miranda-The Oklahoma View." Oklahoma Law Review, 28:37, spring 1975. 5243

"Criminal Law Appointment of Counsel, Constitutional and Statutory Guarantees Are Not Violated by the Appointment of Counsel Other than that Requested by Defendant." UCLA Law Review, 5:74, fall 1973. 5244

"Criminal Law: Remarks of the Trial Judge to the Defense Attorney." Missouri Law Review, 39:252, spring 1974. 5245

"Criminal Law--Right to Counsel--The Sixth Amendment Right to Counsel Does Not Require Presence of Defense Counsel at Post Indictment Photographic Displays." American Journal of Criminal Law, 3:105, summer 1974. 5246

"Criminal Law--Right to Counsel Extended to Any Imprisonable Offense--Reverberations to Gideon's Trumpet." Memphis State University Law Review, 3:156, fall 1972. 5247

"Criminal Law: The Night of Self-representation." Washburn Law Journal, 12:257, winter 1973. 5248

"Criminal Procedure--Effective Assistance of Counsel--Appointed Counsel Must Actually and Substantially Assist His Client in Determining Whether or Not to Plead Guilty." Journal of Urban Law, 51:564, fall 1974. 5249

Edwards, G. "Interrogation of Criminal Defendants--Some Views on Miranda v. Arizona (86 Supreme Court 1602)." Fordham Law Review, 35:169, Dec. 1966. 5250

"Effective Assistance of Counsel in Plea Bargaining: What Is the Standard?" Duquesne Law Review, 12:321, winter 1973. 5251

Elison, L. M. "Assigned Counsel in Montana: The Law and the Practice." Montana Law Review, 26:1, fall 1964. 5252

"Extension of the Sixth Amendment Right to Counsel--the Road from Wade to Ash [U.S. v. Ash No. 22, 340 (D.C. Cir. March 1, 1972]." University of Richmond Law Review, 7:139, fall 1972. 5253

Finer, J. J. "Ineffective Assistance of Counsel." *Cornell Law Review,* 58:1077, June 1973. 5254

"Gideon's Encore." *University of Miami Law Review,* 26:828, summer 1972. 5255

Goldberg, N. E., and Hartman, M. J. "Help for the Indigent Accused: The Effect of Argersinger (Argersinger v. Hamlin 92 Sup. Ct. 2006)." *NLADA Briefcase,* 30:203, June 1972. 5256

"Government Can Satisfy Its Burdens of Proving Waiver of Miranda Rights by Showing Warnings Given, Signed Waiver and Proof of Defendant's Capacity to Understand the Warnings." *Vanderbilt Law Review,* 26:1069, Oct. 1973. 5257

Grunis, A. D. "Incompetence of Defense Counsel in Criminal Cases." *Criminal Law Quarterly,* 16:288, May 1974. 5258

Homans, W. P., Jr. "Legal Services Program--Defense of the Accused." *Massachusetts Law Quarterly,* 51:329, Dec. 1966. 5259

Indigent's Right to Counsel in California: People v. Shipman, [(California), 397 P. 2d 993]." *UCLA Law Review,* 13:446, Jan. 1966. Shipman held that an indigent coram nobis petitioner was constitutionally entitled to counsel at a hearing on his petition. 5260

"Indigent's Dissatisfaction with Assigned Counsel." *Cleveland State Law Review,* 22:157, winter 1973. 5261

Katin, E. "Advocate as Lawmaker: Luis Kutner and the Struggle for Due Process." *University of Miami Law Review,* 23:397, winter-spring 1969. 5262

Katz, L. R. "Gideon's Trumpet: Mournful and Muffled." *Iowa Law Review,* 55:523, Feb. 1970. 5263

Kaus, O. M., and Mallen, R. E. "Misguiding Hand of Counsel-Reflections on 'Criminal Malpractice'." *UCLA Law Review,* 21:1191, June 1974. 5264

Kittel, N. G. "Defense of the Poor: A Study in Public Parsimony and Private Poverty." *Indiana Law Journal,* 45:90, fall 1969. 5265

Lane, L. J. "Lawyer for the Defense in Mass Arrests." *American Criminal Law Quarterly,* 7:242, summer 1969. 5266

Lehman, P. S. "Juvenile's Right to Counsel in a Delinquency Hearing." *Juvenile Court Judge's Journal,* 17:53, summer 1966. 5267

Lewis, H. "American Lawyers: Gideon's Army." Cornell Law Quarterly, 50:155, winter 1965. 5268

"Lowering the Standard for Defendant's Understanding of His Miranda Rights." North Carolina Law Review, 52:454, Dec. 1973. 5269

Matheny, M. D. "Role of Court-Appointed Attorney." Texas Bar Journal, 36:789, summer 1973. 5270

Mather, L. M. "Some Determinants of the Method of Case Disposition: Decision-Making by Public Defenders in Los Angeles." Law and Society Review, 8:187, winter 1974. 5271

Monaghan, H. P. "Gideon's Army: Student Soldiers." Boston University Law Review, 45:445, fall 1965. 5272

Nagel, S. S. "Effects of Alternative Types of Counsel on Criminal Justice Procedure Treatment." Indiana Law Journal, 48:404, spring 1973. 5273

Nichols, L. B. "ABA Standards: What They Can Mean to the Criminal Defense Lawyer." Law Notes, 11:25, winter 1975. 5274

"Non-Lawyer Counsel at Special Court-Martials and the Sixth Amendment." California Western Law Review, Vol. II, 121, spring 1966. A private was tried before a special Army court-martial for violation of the Uniform Code of Military Justice; precedents and impact of this case on law. 5275

O'Brien, D. M. "Implementing Justice: The National Defender Project." Valparaiso University Law Review, 1:320, spring 1967. 5276

Parker, F. J. "Legal Aid for the Poor; New Directions." America, 121:421, Nov. 8, 1969. 5277

Pollitt, D. H. "Counsel for the Unpopular Cause: The 'Hazard of Being Undone'." North Carolina Law Review, 43:9, Dec. 1964. 5278

"Preindictment Identification Confrontations Without Presence of Counsel Held Constitutionally Permitted." Indiana Law Review, 365, 1972. 5279

"Pretrial Right to Counsel." Stanford Law Review, 26:399, Jan. 1974. 5280

"Right of an Accused to Proceed Without Counsel." Minnesota Law Review, 49:1133, May 1965. 5281

"Right of Self Representation." Washburn Law Journal, 12:257, winter 1973. 5282

"Right to Counsel: A New Standard." Southwestern Law Journal, 27:406, May 1965. 5283

"Right to Counsel: A Perspective." William and Mary Law Review, 7:80, Jan. 1974. 5284

"Right to Counsel and Due Process in Probation Revocation Proceedings: Gagnon v. Scarpelli (93 Sup. Ct. 1956)." Cleveland State Law Review, 23:151, winter 1974. 5285

"Right to Counsel at Pretrial Lineups." University of Missouri at Kansas City Law Review, 42:251, winter 1973. 5286

"Right to Counsel Does Not Extend to Preindictment Identification Proceedings." Syracuse Law Review, 24:845, 1973. 5287

"Right to Counsel in Criminal Cases." Cleveland-Marshall Law Review, 15:152, Jan. 1966. 5288

"Right to Counsel on All Appeals." Houston Law Review, 11:725, March 1974. 5289

"Right to Counsel: Repayment of Cost of Court-Appointed Counsel As a Condition of Probation." Marquette Law Review, 56:551, spring 1973. 5290

"Right to Counsel: The Argersinger (Argersinger v. Hamlin, 92 Sup. Ct. 2006)--Kirby (Kirby v. Illinois, 92 Sup. Ct. 1877) Dichotomy." South Carolina Law Review, 25:292, 1973. 5291

"Right to Free Transcript." Hastings Law Journal, 17:113, Oct. 1965. Transcripts essential to safeguard defendant's liberty. As the concept of due process expands, so must the right to free transcript. 5292

"Right to 'No Trial' and the Right to 'No Counsel'." Valparaiso University Law Review, 4:163, fall 1969. 5293

Samuels, G. "Justice in the Courtroom, Can the Poor Get It? Public Defender System." Saturday Review, 49:25+, Jan. 29, 1966. 5294

"Self-Representation in Criminal Trials--The Pro Se Defendant." Wake Forest Law Review, 9:265, March 1973. 5295

Silverstein, Lee. Defense of the Poor in Criminal Cases in American Courts: A Field Study and Report, vol. I. Chicago: American Bar Foundation, 1965. 280pp. Various methods in state use for the defense of the poor defendant; compares four systems (assigned counsel, public, private, or public-private defender systems) and presents a list of conclusions and recommendations. 5296

"Sixth Amendment Does Not Grant Accused the Right to Counsel at Pre-Trial Photographic Display." Vanderbilt Law Review, 26: 1323, Nov. 1973. 5297

Strazzella, J. A. "Ineffective Identification Counsel: Cognizability Under the Exclusionary Rule." Temple Law Quarterly, 48:241, winter 1975. 5298

Summers, M. R. "Defending the Poor: The Assigned Counsel System in Milwaukee County." Wisconsin Law Review, 1969:525, 1969. 5299

Taylor, J. G., and others. "Analysis of Defense Counsel in the Processing of Felony Defendants in San Diego, California." Denver Law Journal, 49:233, 1972. 5300

"United States v. Davis (442 F. 2d 72): A Muddling of the Effective Assistance of Counsel Rule." Utah Law Review, 1972:127, spring 1972. 5301

"Wade-Gilbert Exclusionary Rules Held Not to Apply to Pre-Indictment Showup." Fordham Law Review, 41:1063, May 1973. 5302

"Where to After Gideon? Question of Right to Counsel Covering Miscellaneous." Time, 81-88, Dec. 16, 1966. Gideon decision requiring all courts to provide lawyers for indigent felons is being challenged to cover indigent misdemeanants also by Justice Potter Stewart; pros and cons of the decision are briefly discussed. 5303

Wigner, S. "Bail and Civil Rights." Law in Transition Quarterly, 2:111, spring 1965. 5304

Wilson, P. E. "Right of the Accused to Effective Counsel: The Military View." Kansas Law Review, 14:593, May 1966. 5305

Zander, M. "Departmental Committee Report: Legal Aid in Criminal Proceedings." Modern Law Review, 29:639, Nov. 1966. 5306

________. "Unrepresented Defendants in Magistrates Courts, 1972." The New Law Journal, 122:1041, Nov. 23, 1972. 5307

________, and Glaser, C. "Study in Representation." The New Law Journal, 117:815, July 27, 1967. 5308

(4) JURY TRIAL

"Aggregating Indirect Criminal Contempts of Court--Right to Jury Trial." Wayne Law Review, 20:891, March 1974. 5309

"Aggregation of Sentences: Obtaining Jury Trials for Petty Offenders." <u>Iowa Law Review</u>, 59:615, Feb. 1974. 5310

"Apodaca v. Oregon (92 Sup Ct. 1628): New Support for Oregon's Non-Unanimous Jury Rule." <u>Willamette Law Journal</u>, 9:155, March 1973. 5311

Arnold, M. S. "Law and Fact in the Medieval Jury Trial: Out of Sight, Out of Mind." <u>American Journal of Legal History</u>, 18: 267, Oct. 1974. 5312

Ashman, A., and McConnell, J. "Trial by Jury: The New Irrelevant Right?" <u>Southwestern Law Journal</u>, 27:436, Aug. 1973. 5313

"Availability of Criminal Jury Trials Under the Sixth Amendment." <u>University of Chicago Law Review</u>, 32:311, winter 1965. Explores ideas about juries gathered from selected cases to develop a workable theory for availability. 5314

Babcock, B. A. "Voir Dire: Preserving 'Its Wonderful Power'." <u>Stanford Law Review</u>, 27:545, Feb. 1975. 5315

"Backward, Run Backward; Supreme Court's Decision on Jury Verdicts." <u>National Review</u>, 24:629, June 9, 1972. 5316

Bermant, G. "Fish Out of Water: A Brief Overview of Social and Psychological Concerns About Videotaped Trials." <u>Hastings Law Journal</u>, 26:999, Feb. 1975. 5317

"Burger Court and the Confrontation Clause: A Return to the Fair Trial Rule." <u>John Marshall Journal</u>, 7:136, fall 1973. 5318

"Case Study of the Peremptory Challenge: A Subtle Strike at Equal Protection and Due Process." <u>St. Louis University Law Journal</u>, 18:662, summer 1974. 5319

Clark, T. C. "American Jury: A Justification." <u>Valparaiso University Law Review</u>, 1:1, fall 1966. 5320

"Congress, the Court and Jury Selection: A Critique of Titles I and II of the Civil Rights Bill of 1966." <u>Vanderbilt Law Review</u>, 52:1069, Oct. 1966. 5321

"Constitutional Law--Federal Juvenile Delinquency Act--Waiver of Jury Trial Held Unconstitutional As a Prerequisite to Treatment as Juvenile." <u>New York University Law Review</u>, 43:769, Oct. 1968. 5322

"Constitutional Law--Fourteenth Amendment Entitles Defendants Charged with Serious Crimes in State Courts to Trial by Jury." <u>Vanderbilt Law Review</u>, 21:1099, Nov. 1972. 5323

"Constitutional Law--Juvenile's Right to Trial by Jury." <u>Tennessee Law Review</u>, 39:508, spring 1972. 5324

"Constitutional Law--Retroactive Application of the Jury Trial Requirement." <u>Dickinson Law Review</u>, 74:556, spring 1970. 5325

"Constitutional Law--Sixth Amendment--Exclusion from Jury Selection of Residents of the Judicial District Where a Crime Is Committed Held Unconstitutional As a Denial of the Right to a Jury from the Vicinage." <u>Fordham Urban Law Journal</u>, 2:395, winter 1974. 5326

"Constitutional Law--Trial by Jury--Unanimity in Criminal Trials." <u>Case Western Reserve Law Review</u>, 24:227, fall 1972. 5327

"Criminal Law: Pretrial Publicity--Threat to Trial by Jury." <u>Oklahoma Law Review</u>, 22:165, May 1969. 5328

"Does the Sixth Amendment Require a Jury of the Vicinage of State Criminal Trials? A Functional Approach." <u>Rutgers Camden Law Journal</u>, 5:514, spring 1974. 5329

Edelman, J. "Trial Brief on Behalf of the American Jury System." <u>Trial Lawyers Quarterly</u>, 3:26, winter 1965-66. 5330

"Efficacy of a Charge of Venue in Protecting a Defendant's Right to an Impartial Jury." <u>Notre Dame Law</u>, 42:925, Symposium, 1967. 5331

"Empirical Study of Six and Twelve-Member Jury Decision Making." <u>University of Michigan Journal of Law Reform</u>, 6:712, spring 1973. 5322

"Expendable Resource: Studies to Improve Juror Utilization." <u>The Justice System Journal</u>, 1:39, winter 1974. 5333

Fisher, J. J. "Federal Jury." <u>St. Mary's Law Journal</u>, 5:1, spring 1973. 5334

Goldberg, N. E., and Hartman, M. J. "Requiem for the American Jury." <u>NLADA Briefcase</u>, 30:210, June 1972. 5335

"Half a Jury Better Than None; Supreme Court Ruling on Size of Jury." <u>Time</u>, 96:42, June 6, 1970. 5336

Hall, R. A. "Trial by Judge or Jury." <u>Solicitor's Journal</u>, 110: 42, Jan. 21, 1966. 5337

Hallworth, G. L. "Myth of the Jury Trial; Analysis of the Miranda v. Arizona Decision." <u>Commonweal</u>, 90:161, April 25, 1968. 5338

Harris, R. "Annals of Law: Supreme Court's Decision on Jury Trials." New Yorker, 48:117, Dec. 16, 1972. 5339

Hart, R. A. "Selection of Federal Jurors: A Discussion of Proposed Changes; The Case for Federal Jury Reform." American Bar Association Journal, 53:128, Feb. 1967. 5340

Higley, D. A. "Constitutional Law: Trial by Jury: The Judge's Authority to Deny the Accused's Request to Be Tried by the Court Alone." JAG Journal, 27:412, summer 1973. 5341

"Impartial Jury--Twentieth Century Dilemma: Some Solutions to the Conflict Between Free Press and Fair Trial." Cornell Law Quarterly, 51:306, winter 1966. 5342

"Incorporation Doctrine: Sixth Amendment Trial by Jury." Howard Law Journal, 15:164, fall 1968. 5343

"Juries and the Death Penalty." Nation, 206:814, June 24, 1968. 5344

"Juries and the Rules of Evidence." Criminal Law Review, 1973: 208, April 1973. 5345

"Jury Selection and the Equal Protection Clause." UCLA-Alaska Law Review, 2:141, spring 1973. 5346

"Jury Trial Waiver." Willamette Law Journal, 4:97, spring 1966. 5347

Knittel, E., and Seiler, D. "Merits of Trial by Jury." Cambridge Law Journal, 30:316, Nov. 1972. 5348

Kramer, C. "Psychology of a Jury Trial." Practical Lawyer, 16:61, April 1970. 5349

Levine, H. I. "Restrictions on the Right of Trial by Jury in Illinois." Illinois Bar Journal, 51:802, June 1963. 5350

Maisel, A. Q. "Right to Trial by Jury." Reader's Digest, 82:121, Jan. 1963. History, advantages and disadvantages of trial by jury. 5351

Murtagh, J. M. "Case for Trial by Jury." America, 125:309, Oct. 23, 1971. 5352

Nanes, A. S. "Jury System Reform." Current History, 61:92, Aug. 1971. 5353

O'Reilley, K. F. "Why Some Juries Fail." Journal of the Bar Association of the District of Columbia, 41:69, Jan.-June 1974. 5354

"People v. Culhane: A Discussion of Challenge for Cause in Jury Selection." Albany Law Review, 39:156, 1974. 5355

Plutchek, R., and Schwartz, A. K. "Jury Selection: Folklore or Science?" Criminal Law Bulletin, 1:3, May 1965. 5356

Powell, L. F., Jr. "Jury Trial of Crimes." Washington and Lee Law Review, 23:1, spring 1966. 5357

Riane, L. L. "Fair and Impartial Trial by Jury in the United States and in England." American Bar Association Journal, 50:232, March 1964. Constrasts the two systems; the framework of the study is the NATO Status of Forces Agreement and a resolution of the U. S. Senate dealing with American servicemen stationed abroad. 5358

Richards, R. "New Look at Our Jury System." Florida Bar Journal, 41:93, Feb. 1967. 5359

"Right to a Non-jury Trial." Harvard Law Review, 74:1176, April 1961. Issues in a civil action not constitutionally given by a jury. Deals with following questions: Is there a constitutional right to a non-jury trial of certain issues? If not, is there a court-created right? How did such a court-created right develop? What effect did the establishment of merged procedures have on non-jury trials? What is role of court in non-jury trial? 5360

"Right to an Impartial Federal Jury in the Event of Prejudicial Pretrial Publicity." Columbia Law Review, 53:651, May 1953. Where the source of the publicity is the prosecutor, the accused should be accorded a continuance until the publicity subsides, or a change of venue, if he desires one. 5361

Rosenblatt, J. C. "Six Member Juries in Criminal Cases: Legal and Psychological Considerations." New York State Bar Journal, 46:259, June 1974. 5362

Rothblatt, H. B. "Voir Dire." Law Notes, 10:1, Feb. 1974. 5363

"Sequestering Sanity." New Republic, 164:14, Feb. 20, 1971. 5364

"Should Juries Nullify Bad Laws?" Current, 101:101, Nov. 1968. 5365

Simon, C. K. "Juror in New York City: Attitudes and Experiences." American Bar Association Journal, 61:207, Feb. 1975. 5366

"Sixth Amendment and the Right to a Trial by a Jury of the Vicenage." Washington and Lee Law Review, 31:399, summer 1974. 5367

"Smaller Juries and Non-Unanimity: Analysis and Proposed Revision of the Ohio Jury System." University of Cincinnati Law Review, 43:583, 1974. 5368

Stever, A. "Case Against the Jury (A Brief Without Citations)." New York State Bar Journal, 47:101, Feb. 1975. 5369

Strodtbeck, Fred L. "Social Status in Jury Deliberations." American Sociological Review, 22:713, Dec. 1957. 5370

"Taking Note of Note Taking." Columbia Journal of Law and Social Problems, 10:565, summer 1974. 5371

"This Month's Feature: The Question of Revising the Jury System." Congressional Digest, 50:193, Aug. 1971. 5372

Trautman, P. A. "Serving Substantial Justice--A Dilemma." Washington Law Review, 40:270, June 1965. 5373

"Voir Dire Examination As to Fundamental Rules of Law." Louisiana Law Review, 33:449, spring 1973. 5374

"Voir Dire in Federal Criminal Trials: Protecting the Defendant's Right to an Impartial Jury." Indiana Law Journal, 48:269, winter 1973. 5375

Westen, P. "Compulsory Process Clause." Michigan Law Review, 26:297, Nov. 1974. 5376

Wilson, F. W. "Use of Jurors." Federal Rules Decisions, 62:211, May 1974. 5377

Zeisel, A., and Diamond, S. S. "'Convincing Empirical Evidence' on the Six Member Jury." University of Chicago Law Review, 41:281, winter 1974. 5378

(5) CONFRONTATION

"Admission in an Accomplice's Trial of a Principal's Oral Out-of Court Confession Implicating the Accomplice Does Not Violate the Accomplice's Sixth Amendment Right of Confrontation." American Journal of Criminal Law, 2:75, Feb. 1973. 5379

"Burger Court and the Confrontation Clause: A Return to the Fair Trial Rule." John Marshall Journal, 7:136, fall 1973. 5380

Carlson, R. L. "Argument to the Jury and the Constitutional Right of Confrontation." Criminal Law Bulletin, 9:293, May 1973. 5381

"Confrontation and the Hearsay Rule." Yale Law Journal, 75:1434, July 1966. Pointer v. Texas, 380 U. S. 400 (1904); in this case the court read into the 10th Amendment the confrontation clause of the Sixth Amendment, making no distinction. 5382

"Constitutional Law--Unruly Criminal Defendants Disrupting Court

Proceedings: Right to the Court to Remove, Gag, or Shackle Defendants Versus Right of Defendants to Be Present at and Participate in Their Trial." Wake Forest Law Review, 6:499, May 1970. 5383

"Criminal Procedure--Confrontation of Witnesses: Witness' Repeated Claim of Fifth Amendment Privilege in Presence of Jury Denied Defendant's Sixth Amendment Right to Confront Witness." Washington Law Review, 44:474, winter 1969. 5384

"Criminal Procedure--Sixth Amendment Right of Confrontation Made Obligations in State Prosecutions." North Carolina Law Review, 44:173, Dec. 1965. 5385

"Defendant's Sixth Amendment Right to Confrontation Out Weighs State's Policy of Protecting a Juvenile Offender." University of Cincinnati Law Review, 43:647, 1974. 5386

"Evidence: The Right of Confrontation--Exceptions to the Hearsay Rule and the Scope of the Confrontation Clause." Missouri Law Review, 40:150, winter 1975. 5387

Felts v. Murphy, 201 U.S. 123, 130 (1906). 5388

Frank v. Mangum, 237 U.S. 309, 343 (1915). Accused may waive his right to be present when the jury renders its verdict; this is not a denial of due process. 5389

Geraghty, J. M. "Another Face of the Informer--The Police Spy." University of Queensland Law Journal, 5:170, April 1966. 5390

Howard v. Kentucky, 200 U.S. 164 (1906). 5391

Kirby v. United States, 714 U.S. 47 (1899). 5392

Liacos, P. J. "Right of Confrontation and the Hearsay Rule: Another Look." American Trial Lawyers Law Journal, 34:153, 1972. 5393

Phillips, J. J. "Confrontation Clause and the Scope of the Unavailability Requirement." University of Michigan Journal of Law, 6:327, winter 1973. 5394

Richards, R. "New Look at Our System." Florida Bar Journal, 41:93, Feb. 1967. 5395

"Right to a Non-Jury Trial." Harvard Law Review, 74:1176, April 1961. 5396/7

"Right to Confrontation Paramount to Anonymity of Juvenile Offenders." Mercer Law Review, 26:343, fall 1974. 5398

"Uncertain Relationship Between the Hearsay Rule and the Confrontation Clause." Texas Law Review, 52:1167, Aug. 1974. 5399

(6) PRODUCING WITNESSES

Avins, A. "Right to Be a Witness and the Fourteenth Amendment." Missouri Law Review, 131:471, fall 1966. 5400

Christian, A. D. "Right to Compulsory Process." JAG Journal, 19:31, Nov.-Dec. 1964. 5401

"Constitutional Law--Fourth Amendment: A Grand Jury Witness May Not Refuse to Testify by Invoking the Exclusionary Rule As a Bar to Questions Based on Evidence Obtained from an Illegal Search and Seizure in Violation of His Fourth Amendment Rights." Brooklyn Law Review, 41:134, summer 1974. 5402

"Criminal Defendant's Hearsay Evidence: Time for a Change." Texas Law Review, 47:250, Jan. 1969. 5403

Kramer, R. A. "Service of Process by Mail--A Proposed Revision." California State Bar Journal, 48:249, May-June 1973. 5404

Lind, E. A.; Thibaut, J.; and Walker, L. "Discovery and Presentation of Evidence in Adversary and Nonadversary Proceedings." Michigan Law Review, 71:1129, May 1973. 5405

"Police Coercion of Witnesses." Washington University Law Quarterly, 1973:865, fall 1973. 5406

"Severn v. Adidas Sportschuhfabriken (109 Cal. Rptr. 328): A Modern View of Immunity from Process." California Western Law Review, 10:646, spring 1974. 5407

"To Take the Stand or Not to Take the Stand: The Dilemma of the Defendant with a Criminal Record." Columbia Journal of Law and Social Problems, 4:215, July 1968. 5408

Tobin, D. B. "Foreign Subpoena: A Proposal for Improvement." Georgetown Law Journal, 62:1531, July 1974. 5409

Westen, P. "Compulsory Process Clause." Michigan Law Review, 73:71, Nov. 1974. 5410

"Witness Immunity Statues in Illinois--Time for a Change." John Marshall Journal, 7:175, fall 1973. 5411

"Witness: Securing the Appearance of Material Witnesses from Within the State for Criminal Proceedings in Oklahoma." Oklahoma Law Review, 27:297, spring 1974. 5412

(7) SELF-INCRIMINATION

"Advice to Assert the Privilege Against Self-Incrimination Crime or Constitutional Mandate?" California Law Review, 53:611, May 1965. 5413

"Aftermath of Miranda--The Courts Grapple with Burden of Proof." West Virginia Law Review, 71:180, Feb. 1969. 5414

"Alabama Standards Concerning Comment by Counsel on the Failure of an Accused to Take the Stand." Alabama Law, 17:321, spring 1965. 5415

"Application of Miranda v. Arizona to Motor Vehicle Violations." Missouri Law Review, 38:652, fall 1973. 5416

Aronson, R. H. "Should the Privilege Against Self Incrimination Apply to Compelled Psychiatric Examination?" Stanford Law Review, 26:55, Nov. 1973. 5417

Berry, F. D., Jr. "Self-Incrimination and the Compulsory Mental Examination: A Proposal." Arizona Law Review, 15:919, 1973. 5418

Bittker, B. I. "Taxing Income from Unlawful Activities." Case Western Reserve Law Review, 25:130, fall 1974. 5419

"Books and Records and the Privilege Against Self-Incrimination." Brooklyn Law Review, 33:70, fall 1966. 5420

Buchanan, G. S. "Privilege Against Self-Incrimination: To What Extent Should It Protect a State Employee or Professional License Against the Loss of His State-Created Status?" Houston Law Review, 7:297, Jan. 1970. 5421

"Bursey v. United States (466 F. 2d 1059): The First and Fifth Amendments in the Grand Jury Room." Hastings Law Journal, 24:915, April 1973. 5422

Chamberlain, Park. "Has the Fifth Amendment Become a Menace to Human Rights?" National Review, 362, April 19, 1966. The murder in 1955 of Emmett Gill is cited as an example of the misuse of the Fifth Amendment. The accused invoked the Fifth Amendment and refused to testify and were acquitted. Suggestions for tighter reins on the use of the Fifth Amendment. 5423

Cohen, M. B. "Case for Admitting Evidence of Refusal to Take a Breath Test." Texas Tech Law Review, 6:927, spring 1975. 5424

"Comment at Trial Upon Accused's Exercise of Right to Remain Silent During Police Interrogation." University of Toledo Law

Review, 5:381, winter 1974. 5425

"Compelled Production of Taxpayer's Records from Possession of Accountant Does Not Violate Taxpayer's Right Against Compulsory Self-Incrimination." Georgia State Bar Journal, 10:648, May 1974. 5426

"Compelled Testimony with Immunity: Applying the Standard of Use and Derivative Use." Southwestern Law Journal, 27:517, Aug. 1973. 5427

"Confession of Error." Utah Law Review, 1968:286, May 1968. 5428

"Constitutional Law: Another Limitation on the Mandate of Miranda v. Arizona and Further Erosion of the Exclusionary Rule." University of Florida Law Review, 27:302, fall 1974. 5429

"Constitutional Law--Burden of Proof at Voluntariness Hearing to Determine the Admissibility of a Confession." Duquesne Law Review, 11:81, fall 1972. 5430

"Constitutional Law--Comment on Defendant's Failure to Testify--Harmless Error." Case Western Reserve Law Review, 19:757, April 1968. 5431

"Constitutional Law--Fifth Amendment--Compelled Testimony-Use and Derivative Use Immunity." Duquesne Law Review, 11:714, summer 1973. 5432

"Constitutional Law--Hit and Run Statutes and the Privilege Against Self-Incrimination." Arkansas Law Review, 26:81, spring 1972. 5433

"Constitutional Law--Miranda Rules Are Not Applicable to Simple Misdemeanor Prosecutions, Though Evidence of Coercion, Threats, Promises or Other Wrongful Inducement May Render Accused's Statements Inadmissible." Drake Law Review, 22:184, Sept. 1972. 5434

"Constitutional Law--Privilege Against Self-Incrimination." Baylor Law Review, 25:181, winter 1973. 5435

"Constitutional Law--Privilege Against Self-Incrimination--Application of Miranda v. Arizona to Motor Vehicle Violations." Missouri Law Review, 38:652, fall 1973. 5436

"Constitutional Law--Privilege Against Self-Incrimination Does Not Prevent Compulsory Mental Examination in Criminal Sexual Psychopathy Proceeding." Ohio State Law Journal, 30:866, fall 1969. 5437

"Constitutional Law: Schmerber v. California (86 Sup. Ct. 1826):

Blood and the Constitution." Tulsa Law Journal, 4:246, June 1967. 5438

"Constitutional Law: Self-Incrimination and Court Granted Immunity in Civil Litigation." Oklahoma Law Review, 27:243, spring 1974. 5439

"Constitutional Law--Self-Incrimination--Information Obtained Through Mandatory Disclosure Statutes Held Subject to Fifth Amendment Protection." University of Richmond Law Review, 7:371, winter 1972. 5440

"Constitutional Law--Self-Incrimination--Use and Derivative Use Immunity Is Coexistensive with the Privilege Against Self-Incrimination and May Be Used to Compel Testimony." Memphis State University Law Review, 3:151, fall 1972. 5441

"Constitutional Law--Self-Incrimination--Voluntariness--In a Preliminary Hearing to Determine Voluntariness of a Confession, a Judge Need Only Apply the Preponderance of Evidence Test." University of Cincinnati Law Review, 41:504, 1972. 5442

"Constitutional Law: Testimonial Immunity Adopted in Kastigar v. United States ... to Supplant Prior Federal Immunity Grants." Loyola University Law Journal, (Chicago), 4:193, winter 1973. 5443

"Constitutional Law--The Fifth and Fourteenth Amendments--Comment at Trial Upon Accused's Exercise of Right to Remain Silent During Police Interrogation." University of Toledo Law Review, 5: 381, winter 1974. 5444

"Constitutional Law: The Taxpayer's Surrender of Books and Records." Tulane Law Review, 48:160, Dec. 1973. 5445

"Constitutional Law: Use of Voice Exemplars in Investigations Upheld." Mercer Law Review, 25:365, winter 1974. 5446

"Constitutional Ramifications of the Police Line-Up." Villanova Law Review, 12:135, fall 1966. 5447

"Constitutionality of Administrative or Statutory Sanctions Upon the Exercise of the Privilege Against Self-Incrimination." Fordham Law Review, 36:593, March 1968. 5448

"Constitutionally Privileged False Statements." Stanford Law Review, 22:783, April 1970. 5449

"Criminal Defendants: Maintaining the Appearance of Innocence." Missouri Law Review, 37:660, fall 1972. 5450

"Criminal Immunity in Florida." University of Florida Law Review, 16:475, winter 1963. 5451

"The Fifth Amendment and Silence as Admissible Conduct Evidence." California Western Law Review, 2:140, spring 1966. Discusses People v. Wilson: Theoretical considerations and the extent of constitutional protection. 5452

"Fifth Amendment Does Not Protect Federal Grand Jury Witnesses from Being Compelled to Give Testimony Which Would Incriminate Them in a Foreign Jurisdiction." Texas International Law Journal, 8:262, spring 1973. 5453

"Fifth Amendment Privilege in Criminal Tax Investigations: Miranda and the Omnibus Crime Act." Temple Law Quarterly, 42:255, spring 1969. 5454

"Fifth Amendment Rights of a Client Regarding Documents Held by His Attorney." Duke Law Journal, 1973:1080, Dec. 1973. 5455

"Fifth Amendment--Suspect's Confusion About Miranda Rights." Ohio State Law Journal, 36:220, 1975. 5456

Fink, A. B., Jr. "Privilege Against Self-Incrimination--A Critical Reappraisal." Western Reserve Law Review, 13:722, Sept. 1962. 5457

Fisk, J. J. J. "Compulsory Testimony of the Congressional Witness and the Fifth Amendment." Oklahoma Law Review, 15:151, May 1962. 5458

Friendly, H. J. "Fifth Amendment: The Case for a Constitutional Change." Pennsylvania Bar Association Quarterly, 40:524, June 1969. 5459

"Garner v. United States [No. 71-1219 (9th Cir., June 5, 1972)]: Self-Incrimination and the Use of Tax Returns in Nontax Criminal Prosecution--The Ninth Circuit Attempts a Balancing Act." Hastings Law Journal, 24:959, April 1973. 5460

"Guilt by Physiology: The Constitutionality of Tests to Determine Predisposition to Violent Behavior." Southern California Law Review, 48:489, Nov. 1974. 5461

Hechtkopf, E. A. "Constitutional Law: Self-Incrimination: Sufficiency of Use and Derivative Use Immunity to Compel Testimony of a Witness Over a Claim of the Privilege Against Self-Incrimination." JAG Journal, 27:401, summer 1973. 5462

"Immunity From Prosecution and the Fifth Amendment: An Analysis of Constitutional Standards." Vanderbilt Law Review, 25:1207, Nov. 1, 1972. 5463

"Impeaching a Defendant's Trial Testimony by Proof of Post Arrest Silence." University of Pennsylvania Law Review, 123:940, April 1975. 5464

"In re Gault (87 Sup. Ct. 1428) and the Privilege Against Self-Incrimination in Juvenile Court." Marquette Law Review, 51:68, summer 1967. 5465

"Indigent's Right to Counsel in Civil Cases." Fordham Law Review, 43:989, April 1975. 5466

"Interrogation of Juveniles: The Right to a Parent's Presence." Dickinson Law Review, 77:543, spring 1973. 5467

"Joinder of Courts as a Violation of an Accused's Right to Remain Silent." Temple Law Quarterly, 41:458, summer 1968. 5468

"Kastigor v. United States (92 Sup. Ct. 1653): Compulsory Witness Immunity and the Fifth Amendment." John Marshall Journal, 6:120, fall 1972. 5469

"Kastigor v. United States (92 Sup. Ct. 1653): The Required Scope of Immunity." Virginia Law Review, 58:1099, Sept. 1972. 5470

Lipton, P. P. "Partnership Records Lose Fifth Amendment Protection." Tax Adviser, 5:454, Aug. 1974. 5471

McKay, R. B. "Self-Incrimination and the New Privacy." Supreme Court Review, 1967:193, 1967. 5472

"Marchetti (Marchetti v. U.S. 88 Sup. Ct. 697): Federal Registration and the Fifth Amendment." Ohio State Law Journal, 29:771, summer 1968. 5473

Martin, G. A. "Privilege Against Self-Incrimination Endangered." Canadian Bar Journal, 5:6, Feb. 1962. 5474

Mascolo, E. G. "Use at Trial of Suppression Hearing Admissions: An Erosion of the Privilege Against Self-Incrimination." Dickinson Law Review, 72:1, fall 1967. 5475

Meltzer, B. D. "Privileges Against Self-Incrimination and the Hit-and-Run Opinions." Supreme Court Review, 1971:1, 1971. 5476

"Mental Examinations of Defendants Who Plead Insanity: Problems of Self-Incrimination." Temple Law Quarterly, 40:366, spring-summer 1967. 5477

Miranda v. State of Arizona (86 Supreme Court 1602)--"The Fifth Amendment Enters the Police Station." DePaul Law Review, 16:138, autumn-winter 1966. 5478

"Miranda Without Warning: Derivative Evidence as Forbidden Fruit." Brooklyn Law Review, 41:325, fall 1974. 5479

"Need to Repeat Miranda Warnings at Subsequent Interrogations." Washburn Law Journal, 12:222, winter 1973. 5480

Payne, J. D. "Privilege Against Self-Incrimination." Ottawa Law Review, 2:461, spring 1968. 5481

Pieck, M. "Accused's Privilege Against Self-Incrimination in the Civil Law." American Journal of Comparative Law, 11:585, autumn 1962. 5482

"Police Coercion and Witnesses." Washington University Law Quarterly, 1973:865, fall 1973. 5483

"Pre-Trial Psychiatric Examination: A Conflict with the Privilege Against Self-Incrimination." Criminal Law Bulletin, 5:497, Nov. 1969; Syracuse Law Review, 20:738, spring 1969. 5484

"Probation Revocation: Pre-Trial Revocation and Due Process." Dickinson Law Review, 79:177, fall 1974. 5485

"Protection of Privacy by the Privilege Against Self-Incrimination: A Doctrine Laid to Rest?" Iowa Law Review, 59:1336, June 1974. 5486

"Public Official: Consequences of Refusal to Testify." Kansas Law Review, 16:541, June 1968. 5487

"Re-examination of Defense Witness Immunity: A New Use for Kastigor (Kastigor v. U. S. 92 Sup. Ct. 1653)." Harvard Journal on Legislation, 10:74, Dec. 1972. 5488

"Registration Statutes and the Privilege Against Self-Incrimination." Northwestern University Law Review, 63:398, July-Aug. 1968. 5489

"Required Information and the Privilege Against Self-Incrimination." Columbia Law Review, 65:681, April 1965. The government's need for information and the individual's basic privilege against incriminating himself. 5490

"Requirement of a Grand Jury Witness to Produce Voice Exemplars or Handwriting Specimens Does Not Violate His Fourth and Fifth Amendment Rights." Journal of Urban Law, 51:136, Aug. 1973. 5491

"Requiring a Criminal Defendant to Submit to a Government Psychiatric Examination: An Invasion of the Privilege Against Self-Incrimination." Harvard Law Review, 88:648, Jan. 1970. 5492

Rintala, William T. "The Mere Evidence Rule: Limitations on Seizure Under the Fourth Amendment." California Law Review, 54:1, 20:5, Dec. 1966. Recent court decisions; discussion of the Fifth and Fourth Amendments to the Constitution is especially valuable. 5493

"Search and Seizure of Private Papers: Fourth and Fifth Amendment Considerations." Loyola University Law Review, (LA), 6:274, July 1973. 5494

"Self-Incrimination and the States: Striking the Balance." Yale Law Journal, 73:1491, July 1964. Malloy v. Hogan 32 U.S.L. Week 4507 (U.S. June 15, 1964); indicates court's awareness of the need to limit state power to protect the individual. Analysis of the dual sovereignty doctrine. 5495

"Self-Incrimination Privilege: Barrier to Criminal Discovery?" California Law Review, 51:138, March 1963. Jones v. Superior Court, 372 P. 2d 919 (1962); D.A. was allowed to discover the names and addresses of the witnesses defendant intended to use in defense. Examination of the privilege against self-incrimination. 5496

"Self-Incrimination: Privilege, Immunity and Comment in Bar Disciplinary Proceedings." Michigan Law Review, 72:84, Nov. 1973. 5497

"Silence of Defendant When Arrested May Not Be Used to Impeach His Testimony." Harvard Law Review, 87:882, Feb. 1974. 5498

Smith, J. V. "Threshold Question in Applying Miranda: What Constitutes Custodial Interrogation?" South Carolina Law Review, 25:699, Feb. 1974. 5499

Smith, T. M., and McCollom, W. G. "Counterdiscovery in Criminal Cases: Fifth Amendment Privileges Abridged." American Bar Association Journal, 54:256, March 1968. 5500

"Standing to Object to the Admission of Evidence Obtained in Violation of Another's Fifth and Sixth Amendment Rights: People v. Varnum (Cal) 427, P. 2d 772." UCLA Law Review, 15:1060, April 1968. 5501

"State Immunity Statutes in Constitutional Perspective." Duke Law Journal, 1968:311, April 1968. 5502

"Statutory Criminal Presumptions: A Compulsion to Testify." University of West Los Angeles Law Review, 5:11, fall 1973. 5503

"Statutory Immunity and the Perjury Exception." California Western Law Review, 10:428, winter 1974. 5504

"Tacit Admissions and Miranda." Tennessee Law Review, 36:566, spring 1969. 5505

"Tax Investigations and the Privilege Against Self-Incrimination." Suffolk University Law Review, 52:322, March 1966. 5506

"Texas Self-Incrimination Privilege and the Breathalyzer Statute." Houston Law Review, 10:903, May 1973. 5507

"Threatened Loss of Private Economic Benefits Can Be Sufficient Coercion to Render Confession Involuntary." Fordham Law Review, 43:466, Dec. 1973. 5508

"Unitary Criminal Proceeding: Denial of the Privilege Against Self-Incrimination." Washington and Lee Law Review, 25:287, fall 1968. 5509

"Use of the Privilege Against Self-Incrimination in Civil Litigation." Virginia Law Review, 52:322, March 1966. 5510

"Waiver of the Fifth: What Level of Incrimination?" Southwestern Law Journal, 26:589, Aug. 1972. 5511

"Waiver of the Privilege Against Self-Incrimination." Stanford Law Review, 14:811, July 1962. Examines the waiver concept and assesses its value. 5512

"What Price Immunity? The Pressing Need for Protection Against the Abuse of Immunity Grants." University of San Fernando Valley Law Review, 3:83, 1974. 5513

Wilder, M. S. "Prosecution Discovery and the Privilege Against Self-Incrimination." American Criminal Law Quarterly, 6:3, fall 1967. 5514

(8) SEARCH AND SEIZURE

"Administrative Inspection and the Fourth Amendment--A Rationale." Columbia Law Review, 65:288, Feb. 1965. Frank v. Maryland 359, U.S. 360 (1959); constitutional law of criminal search and seizure not generally applicable to administrative inspections. 5515

"Airport Searches and the Right to Travel: Some Constitutional Questions." Cleveland State Law Review, 23:90, winter 1974. 5516

"Airport Security: Piracy Within the Terminal?" Valparaiso University Law Review, 8:85, fall 1973. 5517

"Area Search Warrants in Border Areas: Almeida-Sanchez and Camara." Yale Law Journal, 84:355, Dec. 1974. 5518

Armentano, P. N. "Standards for Probable Cause Under the Fourth Amendment." Connecticut Bar Journal, 44:137, June 1970. 5519

"Arson Investigations and the Fourth Amendment." Washington and Lee Law Review, 30:133, spring 1973. 5520

"Automobile License Checks and the Fourth Amendment." Virginia Law Review, 60:666, April 1974. 5521

"Automobile Spot Checks and the Fourth Amendment." Rutgers Camden Law Journal, 6:85, summer 1974. 5522

Bacigal, R. J. "Emergency Exception to the Fourth Amendment." University of Richmond Law Review, 9:249, winter 1975. 5523

"Back on the Road Again--The Mobility Exception of the 70's." Loyola University Law Review, (LA), 7:55, Sept. 1974. 5524

Balmer, H. R. "Law of Search and Seizure: Further Ground for Rationalization." Criminal Law Review, 1967:3, Jan. 1967. 5525

Beeson, R. D., and James, R. R. "Searches by Private Individuals: Admissible Windfalls." Air Force JAG Law Review, 15: 91, Sept. 1973. 5526

Berner, B. G. "Search and Seizure: Status and Methodology." Valparaiso University Law Review, 8:471, spring 1974. 5527

"Broadening the Scope of a Search Incident to Custodial Arrest: The Burger Court's Retreat from Chimel." Emory Law Journal, 24: 151, winter 1975. 5528

"California Pat-Down: A Touching Experience." UCLA--Alaska Law Review, 1:119, spring 1972. 5529

"Cause to Search and Seize." Louisiana Law Review, 26:802, June 1966. 5530

"Chimel v. California (89 Sup. Ct. 2034)--Its Effect on Search and Seizure." New Mexico Law Review, 2:308, July 1972. 5531

"Concept of Privacy and the Fourth Amendment." University of Michigan Journal of Law References, 6:154, fall 1972. 5532

"Confusing the Confusion: Automobile Search and Seizure Takes a New Turn." Houston Law Review, 12:460, Jan. 1975. 5533

"Constitutional Criminal Procedure--Search and Seizure--Airport Weapons Search Based on Less Than Probable Cause." Tulane Law Review, 48:703, April 1974. 5534

"Constitutional Law: Airport Searches and the Exclusionary Rule--Valid Police Work or Prosecution by Windfall?" University of Florida Law Review, 26:329, winter 1974. 5535

"Constitutional Law--Due Process--Delineation of Procedures Used in Seizing Obscene Films." Journal of Urban Law, 47:746, 1969-70. 5536

"Constitutional Law--Fourth Amendment--Federal Grand Jury Witness Who Has Been Granted Transactional Immunity Can Move to Suppress Evidence Seized from Him in Violation of the Fourth Amendment." Ohio State Law Journal, 34:450, 1973. 5537

"Constitutional Law: Fourth Amendment: Marijuana Seized in 'Pat-Down' Incident to Traffic Violation Inadmissible in Subsequent Criminal Prosecution." Minnesota Law Review, 57:414, Dec. 1972. 5538

"Constitutional Law--Fourth Amendment Protection Against Unreasonable Searches and Seizures Extended to Aliens on Foreign Soil." Tulsa Law Journal, 10:479, 1975. 5539

"Constitutional Law--Fourth Amendment--Right to Be Free of Warrantless Searches at the Border." Journal of Urban Law, 51: 556, Feb. 1974. 5540

"Constitutional Law: Fourth Amendment--Search and Seizure--Carefully Defined Warrentless Administrative Inspections Are Permitted Under Federal Gun Control Act of 1968." Catholic University Law Review, 22:496, winter 1973. 5541

"Constitutional Law--Fourth Amendment--The 'Search All Persons' Power--Does Presence Really Equal Probable Cause?" Cornell Law Review, 58:614, March 1973. 5542

"Constitutional Law--Full Custody Arrest Held Reasonable Basis for Complete Search of the Person." Cumberland-Samford Law Review, 5:130, spring 1974. 5543

"Constitutional Law--Grand Jury Witness May Not Assert Fourth Amendment Exclusionary Rule." Kansas Law Review, 22:629, summer 1974. 5544

"Constitutional Law--Impeachment by Unconstitutionally Obtained Evidence--The Erosion of the Exclusionary Rule." Ohio State Law Journal, 34:706, 1973. 5545

"Constitutional Law--Search and Seizure--Carroll Doctrine for Warrantless Search Extended to Chattel Consigned to Common Carriers." Fordham Law Review, 41:1034, May 1973. 5546

"Constitutional Law--Search and Seizure--Judicial Limitations on Warrantless Border Searches Made Without Probable Cause Make Fourth Amendment Rights of Travelers Uncertain." Vanderbilt Law Review, 27:523, April 1974. 5547

"Constitutional Law--Search and Seizure--Limiting the Permissible

Scope of Search Incident to an Arrest." Villanova Law Review, 15:242, fall 1969. 5548

"Constitutional Law--Search and Seizure--No Knock Entry Held Reasonable in Virginia When Exigencies Present." University of Richmond Law Review, 7:565, spring 1973. 5549

"Constitutional Law--Search and Seizures--The Reasonableness Standard for Warrantless Searches and Seizures Is Applied to an Airport Security Case." Texas Tech Law Review, 5:166, fall 1973. 5550

"Constitutional Law--Search Incident to a Lawful Arrest." New York Law Forum, 20:381, fall 1974. 5551

"Constitutional Law: The Balancing Procedure Applied in Search and Seizure." University of Missouri-Kansas City Law Review, 43: 98, fall 1974. 5552

"Constitutional Law--The President May Not Authorize Electronic Surveillance in Domestic Security Cases Without Compliance with Fourth Amendment Requirements." Dickinson Law Review, 77: 166, fall 1972. 5553

"Constitutional Standards for Applying the Plain View Doctrine." St. Mary's Law Journal, 6:725, fall 1974. 5554

Cook, J. G. "Warrantless Search Incident to Arrest." Alabama Law Review, 24:607, summer 1972. 5555

"Criminal Law: Criminal Search Incident to Lawful Arrest." Washburn Law Journal, 14:158, winter 1975. 5556

"Criminal Law--Search and Seizure--A Separate Living Unit within a Multi-Unit Dwelling Is Entitled to Protection Against Unreasonable Searches." Mississippi Law Journal, 44:298, April 1973. 5557

"Criminal Law--Search and Seizure--Mere Presence in an Airport Is a Factor in Justifying a Frisk--Skyjacking Danger Justifies Extension of Scope of Frisk Beyond 'Pat-down'." Catholic University Law Review, 23:157-63, fall 1973. 5558

"Criminal Law--Search and Seizure--The Mere Possibility of a Conspiracy to Assassinate Political Leaders Obviates the Need for a Search Warrant." Rutgers Camden Law Journal, 4:432, spring 1973. 5559

"Criminal Law--Search and Seizures--Arrest--Motor Vehicle Exception to Warrant Requirements--Limits?" Akron Law Review, 7:343-52, winter 1974. 5560

"Criminal Law: The Inventory Search After Arrest for a Minor

Traffic Violation." Oklahoma Law Review, 27:693, fall 1974. 5561

"Criminal Procedure--Grand Juries--Exclusionary Rule in Search and Seizure Cases Does Not Apply to Grand Jury Proceedings." Vanderbilt Law Review, 27:560, April 1974. 5562

"Criminal Procedure--Refusal to Consent to a Search." Tennessee Law Review, 40:100, fall 1972. 5563

"Criminal Procedure--Search and Seizures--Fourth Amendment Held Not to Require That One Giving Permission for a Consent Search Be Informed That He Has the Right to Withhold His Consent." Indiana Law Review, 68:189, 1973. 5564

"Criminal Procedure--Search and Seizure--Prospective Search Warrants." Wayne Law Review, 19:1339, July 1973. 5565

"Criminal Procedure--Third Party Consent Searches." Tennessee Law Review, 41:923, summer 1974. 5566

Dalbey, D. J.; Hotis, J. B.; and Mintz, J. A. "Search of the Person." Criminal Law Bulletin, 2:13, Nov. 1966. 5567

Danenberg, R. V. "Administrative Searches and the Right to Privacy in the United States." International and Comparative Law Quarterly, 23:169, Jan. 1974. 5568

Davis, Rex D. Federal Searches and Seizures. Springfield, Ill.: Charles C. Thomas, 1964. Presents federal rules relating to search and seizure in an orderly, easily understood manner. 5569

Delgado, R. "College Searches and Seizures: Students' Privacy and the Fourth Amendment." Hastings Law Journal, 26:57, Sept. 1974. 5570

Dudley, R. H. "Another Tool for Off-Base Searches--The Search Warrant." JAG Journal, 19:43, Nov.-Dec. 1964. 5571

"Effective Consent to Search and Seizure." University of Pennsylvania Law Review, 113:260, Dec. 1964. 5572

Eggers, H. C. "Specificity Required in Military Search Warrants." Military Law Review, 61:1, summer 1973. 5573

"Evidence--Exclusion and Suppression--Silence of Defendant When Arrested May Not Be Used to Impeach His Testimony." Harvard Law Review, 87:882, Feb. 1974. 5574

"Evidentiary Searches: The Rule and the Reason." Georgetown Law Journal, 54:593, winter 1966. 5575

"Extent of the Border." Hastings Constitutional Law Quarterly, 1: 235, spring 1974. 5576

Felkenes, G. T. "Right of Privacy and Police Surveillance by Aircraft." Journal of Police Science and Administration, 1:345, Sept. 1973. 5577

"Foreign Security Surveillance and the Fourth Amendment." Harvard Law Review, 87:976, March 1974. 5578

Forkosch, M. D. "Constitutional Right to Challenge the Content of Affidavits in Warrants Issued Under the Fourth Amendment." Ohio State Law Journal, 34:297, 1973. 5579

"Fourth Amendment and the Exclusionary Rule in Civil Cases." Denver Law Journal, 43:511, fall 1966. 5580

"Fourth Amendment Application to Semi-Public Areas. Smayda v. U.S. (352 F. 2d 251)." Hastings Law Journal, 17:835, May 1966. Fourth Amendment did not proscribe the clandestine surveillance of public restrooms by police officers. 5581

"Fourth Amendment Applications to Searches Conducted by Immigration Officials." Albany Law Review, 38:962, 1974 (Supp.). 5582

"Freedom of the Road: Public Safety v. Private Right." DePaul Law Review, 14:381, spring-summer 1965. 5583

Frels, K. "Search and Seizure in the Public Schools." Houston Law Review, 11:876, May 1974. 5584

"Fresh Look at Stale Probable Cause: Examing the Timeliness Requirement of the Fourth Amendment." Iowa Law Review, 59: 1308, June 1974. 5585

"Fresh Look at the Suppressed Evidence Rule." Brooklyn Law Review, 34:269, winter 1968. 5586

"From Bags to Body Cavities: The Law of Border Search." Columbia Law Review, 74:53, Jan. 1974. 5587

"From Private Places to Personal Privacy: A Post-Katz (Katz v. U.S. 88 Sup. Ct. 507), Study of Fourth Amendment Protection." New York University Law Review, 43:968, Nov. 1968. 5588

"Fruit of the Poisonous Tree--A Plea for Relevant Criteria." University of Pennsylvania Law Review, 115:1136, May 1967. 5589

Gilligan, F. A. "Search of Premises, Vehicles, and the Individual Incident to Apprehension." Military Law Review, 61:89, summer, 1973. 5590

"Government Access to Bank Records." Yale Law Journal, 83:1439, June 1974. 5591

Gutterman, M. "Person Aggrieved: Standing to Suppress Illegally Seized Evidence in Transition." Emory Law Journal, 23:111, winter 1974. 5592

Haley, A. "In Search of Reason at the Border." Hawaii Bar Journal, 10:101, winter 1974. 5593

Heller, D. "Conflict of Laws: The Drug Possession Offense and the Fourth Amendment." Oklahoma Law Review, 26:317, Aug. 1973. 5594

Hotis, J. B. "Search of Motor Vehicles." Dickinson Law Review, 73:363, spring 1969. 5595

"Immigration and Naturalization 'Dragnet': Warrantless Seizures of Aliens--Due Process or Discrimination?" Suffolk Law Review, 4:805, spring 1970. 5596

"Informant's Tip as the Basis for Probable Cause: Modified Aguilar Standard." San Diego Law Review, 20:363, spring 1975. 5597

"Inventory Search of an Offender Arrested for a Minor Traffic Violation: Its Scope and Constitutional Requirements." Boston University Law Review, 53:858, July 1973. 5598

Jesmore, K. L. "Courthouse Search." UCLA Law Review, 21:797, Feb. 1974. 5599

Judice, C. R. "Probable Cause in Search Warrants: The Issuing Magistrate's View." Texas Bar Journal, 35:703, Aug. 1972. 5600

Kaplan, J. "Limits of the Exclusionary Rule." Stanford Law Review, 26:1027, May 1974. 5601

"Katz and the Fourth Amendment: A Reasonable Expectation of Privacy or a Man's Home Is His Fort." Cleveland State Law Review, 23:63, winter 1974. 5602

"Key Ruling on Police Power." U.S. News, 75:55, Dec. 24, 1973. 5603

Larkin, M. A. "Search Authorized by a Commanding Officer: The Requirement of Probable Cause." JAG Journal, 20:3, July-Aug. 1966. 5604

"Lawful Custodial Arrest for a Traffic Violation Justified a Full Search of the Arrestee." Houston Law Review, 11:1283, July 1974. 5605

"Legislative Approach to the Fourth Amendment." Nebraska Law Review, 45:148, Jan. 1966. 5606

"License to Frisk." Newsweek, 82:20, Dec. 1973. 5607

McGinley, P. W., and Dowens, S. F. "Airport Searches and Seizures--A Reasonable Approach." Fordham Law Review, 41: 293, Dec. 1972. 5608

Miles, J. G., Jr., and Wefing, J. B. "Automobile Search and the Fourth Amendment: A Troubled Relationship." Seton Hall Law Review, 4:105, fall-winter 1972. 5609

"Motor Vehicle Exception to Warrant Requirement--Limits?" Akron Law Review, 7:343, winter 1974. 5610

Nagel, Stuart S. "Testing the Effects of Excluding Illegally Seized Evidence." Wisconsin Law Review, 1965:283, spring 1965. Illustrates some methodological problems in testing and gives substantive findings of a study. 5611

Nasst, A. T. "The Scope of Search Incident to Arrest for Minor Offenses." Southwestern University Law Review, 7:383, summer 1975. 5612

Nedrud, D. R. "Outline of Arrest, Search, and Seizure." Tulsa Law Journal, 5:154, May 1968. 5613

"Nonarrest Automobile Stops: Unconstitutional Seizures of the Person." Stanford Law Review, 25:865, Dec. 1973. 5614

"Oral Search Warrants: A New Standard of Warrant Availability." UCLA Law Review, 21:691, Dec. 1973. 5615

"People v. McKinnon [(Cal) 500 P. 2d 1097]: Warrantless Search of Effects Enlarged in Scope." Southwestern University Law Review, 5:286, summer 1973. 5616

"Permissable Search of Premises Incidental to a Lawful Arrest." Temple Law Quarterly, 43:180, winter 1970. 5617

"Plain View--Anything But Plain: Coolidge Divides the Lower Courts." Loyola University Law Review (Louisiana), 7:489, Sept. 1974. 5618

"Police Helicopter Surveillance." Arizona Law Review, 15:145, 1973. 5619

"Probable Cause for Warrantless Arrests Pursuant to Statewide Police 'Pick-Up' Directives." Baylor Law Review, 25:697, fall 1973. 5620

Quintana, W. A. "Erosion of the Fourth Amendment Exclusionary

Rule." Howard Law Journal, 17:805, 1973. 5621

"Recent Assault on the Barricade Against Police Intrusion: The Exclusionary Rule." Kentucky Bar Journal, 38:46, April 1974. 5622

"Recent Developments in Search and Seizure." Texas Bar Journal, 28:93, Feb. 1965. 5623

"Relevance of the Absent Party's Whereabouts in Third Party Consent Searches." Boston University Law Review, 53:1087, Nov. 1973. 5624

"Restricting the Scope of Searches Incident to Arrest: United States v. Robinson." Virginia Law Review, 59:724, April 1973. 5625

Rintamaki, J. "Plain View Searching." Military Law Review, 60: 25, spring 1973. 5626

Rotenberg, D. L. "Searching for the Person to Be Seized." Ohio State Law Journal, 35:56, 1974. 5627

Rothstein, M. A., and Rothstein, L. F. "Administrative Searches and Seizures: What Happened to Camara and See?" Washington Law Review, 50:341, Feb. 1975. 5628

Schoenfeld, M. "'Stop and Frisk' Law is Unconstitutional." Syracuse Law Review, 17:627, summer 1966. 5629

"Scope of Searches Incident to Traffic Arrests in California: Rejecting the Federal Rule." University of San Francisco Law Review, 9:317, fall 1974. 5630

"Search and Seizure." Northwestern University Law Review, 59:611, Nov.-Dec. 1964. 5631

"Search and Seizure Incident to a Traffic Offense." Memphis State University Law Review, 4:530, spring 1974. 5632

"Search and Seizure Incident to Arrests for Minor Traffic Violations in Illinois, 1960." University of Illinois Law Forum, 440, fall 1960. 5633

"Search and Seizure of Private Papers: Fourth and Fifth Amendment Considerations." Loyola University Law Review (LA), 6:274, July 1973. 5634

"Search and Seizure--Totality of Circumstances May Provide Probable Cause for Arrest and Search Absent a Valid Warrant." Santa Clara Lawyer, 13:339, winter 1972. 5635

"Search Incident to Arrest: A Line Is Drawn." Missouri Law Review, 34:231, spring 1970. 5636

"Search Incident to Arrest for Minor Traffic Violations." American Criminal Law Review, 11:801, spring 1973. 5637

"Search Incident to Arrest for Traffic Violations, 1959." Wisconsin Law Review, 347, March 1959. 5638

"Search Warrant Affidavits--The Constitutional Restraints." Drake Law Review, 23:623, June 1974. 5639

"Searches and Seizures--Electronic Devices--Misplaced Confidence." University of Richmond Law Review, 4:134, fall 1969. 5640

"Searches Incident to Arrest: The Expending Exception to the Warrant Requirements." Georgetown Law Journal, 63:223, Oct. 1974. 5641

Seneker, Carl J., II. "Methods of Challenging Searches and Seizures in California." California Law Review, 54:10170, 1966. The present search law of California is given; covers: Challenging a search & seizure before the trial; Challenging the Search & seizure at trial and on appeal; the present law in practice; the proposed law. 5642

Souris, T. "Stop and Frisk or Arrest and Search--The Use and Misuse of Euphemisms." Journal of Criminal Law, Criminology and Police Science, 57:251, Sept. 1960. 5643

"Standing to Contest Searches and Seizures." Mississippi Law Journal, 46:147, winter 1975. 5644

"Terry Revisited and the Law of Stop and Frisk in Texas." Southwestern Law Journal, 27:490, Aug. 1973. 5645/6

"Third Party Consent to Search and Seizure." University of Chicago Law Review, 33:797, summer 1966. Examination of third party consent to search and seizure with a view towards reconciling the individual's interest with society's interest; both can be accommodated by disallowing searches on basis of consent by a "third party" except in those cases when he is actually the agent of the nonconsenting party and is empowered to authorize a search. 5647

Thornton, W. J. "Justice in Chains." National Review, 25:311, March 16, 1973. 5648

"Tossings and Traffic; Question of Lawful Arrest Establishing the Authority to Search; Supreme Court Decision." Time, 102:74, Dec. 24, 1973. 5649

"Trends in Legal Commentary on the Exclusionary Rule." Journal of Criminal Law, 65:373, Sept. 1974. 5650

"United States Supreme Court and the Law of Search and Seizure."

St. Louis University Law Journal, 9:549, summer 1965. 5651

"United States v. Robinson (94 Sup. Ct. 467) and Gustofson v. Florida (94 Sup. Ct. 488): The United States Supreme Court Clarification of Search Incident to Arrest." South Dakota Law Review, 19: 494, spring 1974. 5652

"Use of Evidence Obtained During a Search and Seizure Consented To by the Defendant's Spouse." University of Illinois Law Forum, 1964:653, fall 1964. 5653

"Valid Consent to Search Determined by Standard of Voluntariness." American Criminal Law Review, 12:231, summer 1974. 5654

"Valid Consent to Search Does Not Require Knowledge of the Constitutionally Protected Right to Refuse." Gonzaga Law Review, 9: 845, spring 1974. 5655

"Warrantless Searches and Seizures of Automobiles." Harvard Law Review, 87:835, Feb. 1974. 5656

"Warrantless Searches in Light of Chimel (Chimel v. California, 89 Sup. Ct. 2304); A Return to the Original Understanding." Arizona Law Review, 11:457, fall 1969. 5657

"Warrantless Searches--The Worm Has Turned Again." Baylor Law Review, 22:39, winter 1970. 5658

"Warrantless Searches Under Anti-Hijacking Program." Baylor Law Review, 26:604, fall 1974. 5659

Wefing, J. B., and Miles, J. G., Jr. "Consent Searches and the Fourth Amendment: Voluntariness and Third Party Problems." Seton Hall Law Review, 5:211, winter 1974. 5660

Weinreb, L. L. "Generalities of the Fourth Amendment." University of Chicago Law Review, 42:74, fall 1974. 5661

Weisgall, J. M. "Stop, Search, and Seize: The Emerging Doctrine of Founded Suspicion." University of San Francisco Law Review, 9:219, fall 1974. 5662

Young, D. J. "Searches and Seizures in Juvenile Proceedings." Juvenile Justice, 25:26, May 1974. 5663

(9) INFORMANTS

"Constitutional Criminal Procedure--Stop and Frisk--Reliable Informants." Tulane Law Review, 47:893, April 1973. 5664

"Constitutional Rights of Criminal Defendants: The Identity of Informers." The John Marshall Journal of Practice and Procedure, 8:401, spring 1975. 5665

"Criminal Law: An Expansion of the Terry Rule; Reasonable Ground for a Stop and Frisk; Use of Uncorroborated Informant; Probable Cause to Arrest; Possession of a Firearm--Connecticut Law." Catholic University Law Review, 22:702, spring 1973. 5666

"Criminal Procedure--Stop and Frisk on Basis of Tip by Unidentified Informant Held Valid." Syracuse Law Review, 24:839, 1973. 5667

"Evidence--Search and Seizure--Probable Cause: When an Informer's Tip Is Used to Obtain a Search Warrant." Missouri Law Review, 37:538, summer 1972. 5668

Gilligan, F. A. "Probable Cause and the Informer." Military Law Review, 60:1, Spring 1973. 5669

Hatchett, J. W. "Discovering the Identity of the Informer." Florida Bar Journal, 46:644, Dec. 1972. 5670

"Informant's Tip and Terry's 'Reasonable Conclusion'--A Modified Standard." Texas Tech Law Review, 4:167, fall 1972. 5671

"Informant's Tip As the Basis for Probable Cause: Modified Aguilar Standards." San Diego Law Review, 20:363, spring 1975. 5672

"Informer's Privilege in Criminal Cases." University of Illinois Law Forum, 1967:665, fall 1967. 5673

"Informer's Tip as Probable Cause for Search or Arrest." Cornell Law Review, 54:958, July 1969. 5674

"Predicates of Suspicion: Stop and Frisk or an Informant's Tip--Extending Terry to Possessory Offenses." Notre Dame Law Review, 49:127, fall 1972. 5675

"Probable Cause and the Confidential Informer in the United States Supreme Court." University of Missouri-Kansas City, 37:352, summer 1969. 5676

Rebell, M. A. "Undisclosed Informant and the Fourth Amendment; A Search for Meaningful Standards." Yale Law Journal, 81:703, March 1972. 5677

"Reliability of the First-Time Informant." American Journal of Criminal Law, 1:283, Oct. 1972. 5678

"Rule of Reputation in Establishing Probable Cause for Arrest and Search." Washington University Law Quarterly, 1969:339, summer 1969. 5679

"Unrevealed Informants and the Fourth Amendment." Tennessee Law Review, 40:75, fall 1972. 5680

(10) WIRETAPPING

Admissibility of Wiretap Cases in Federal Criminal Cases." Texas Law Review, 41:617, May 1963. 5681

"Admissibility of Wiretap Evidence in Criminal Cases." University of Florida Law Review, 16:120, summer 1963. 5682

Aspen, M. E. "Court-Ordered Wiretapping: An Experiment in Illinois." DePaul Law Review, 15:15, autumn-winter 1965. 5683

Bartan, W. V. "Law Enforcement Wiretap Policy in the United States." Criminal Law Bulletin, 2:15, Jan.-Feb. 1966. 5684

Chorney, N. M. "Wiretapping and Electronic Eavesdropping." Criminal Law Quarterly, 7:434, Feb. 1965. 5685

"Cleaning Up a Dirty Business: Resolving the Power of the Executive to Authorize Wiretaps without Procuring Prior Judicial Approval." American University Law Review, 21:757, Sept. 1972. 5686

Cohen, C. "Poisonous Tree; Electronic Surveillance of Private Citizens by Government Agencies." Nation, 212:231, Feb. 22, 1971. 5687

"Consent to Electronic Surveillance by a Party to a Conversation: A Different Approach." Tulsa Law Journal, 10:386, 1975. 5688

"Constitutional Law--Electronic Surveillance and the Fourth Amendment: Warrant Required for Wiretapping of Domestic Subversives." DePaul Law Review, 22:430, winter 1972. 5689

"Constitutional Law--Electronic Surveillance and the Supreme Court: A Move Back." DePaul Law Review, 21:806, spring 1972. 5690

"Constitutional Law--Electronic Surveillance by Bugged Agents--Is Electronic Surveillance by Bugged Agents a Search and Seizure within the Fourth Amendment?" Villanova Law Review, 9:144, Dec. 1972. 5691

"Constitutional Law--Interception or Disclosure of Communications: Authorization by Courts or Public Officers." University of Missouri at Kansas City Law Review, 36:90, winter 1968. 5692

"Constitutional Law--Requirements for a Valid Electronic Surveillance Statute." Wake Forest Law Review, 9:144, Dec. 1972. 5693

"Constitutional Law--Right to Privacy--Electronic Surveillance." West Virginia Law Review, 76:228, Feb. 1974. 5694

"Constitutional Law--Search and Seizure--Electronic Eavesdropping Procedures Authorized by Title III of the Omnibus Crime Control and Safe Streets Act of 1968 Violate the Fourth Amendment." Vanderbilt Law Review, 26:177, Jan. 1973. 5695

"Constitutional Law: The Applicability of the Fourth Amendment's Search and Seizure Protection to Electronic Eavesdropping." Tulsa Law Journal, 6:187, March 1970. 5696

"Constitutional Law: The Validity of Eavesdropping Under the Fourth Amendment." Marquette Law Review, 51:96, summer 1967. 5697

"Court and Electronic Surveillance: To Bug or Not to Bug--What Is the Exception?" St. John's Law Review, 47:76, Oct. 1972. 5698

Courtney, J. "Electronic Eavesdropping, Wiretapping and Your Right to Privacy." Federal Communications Bar Journal, 26:1, 1973. 5699

Cranwell, J. L. "Judicial Finetuning of Electronic Surveillance." Seton Hall Law Review, 6:225, winter 1975. 5700

"Criminal Law--Wiretapping--Consenting Party of Conversation Recorded by Police Without Warrant Required to Verify at Trial Consent to Recording Prior to Its Admission Against Other Party to Conversation." Florida State University Law Review, 2:188, winter 1974. 5701

"Criminal Procedure--Discovery by Defendant of Results of Prosecution's Unlawful Electronic Surveillance." Loyola Law Review, 16:184, 1969-70. 5702

"Criminal Procedure--Electronic Surveillance." Loyola Law Review, 16:199, 1969-70. 5703

"Criminal Procedure--Search and Seizure--Electronic Eavesdropping --Abortion: Recording of Voluntary Conversation Between Police Agent and Defendant Admissible in Evidence." Washington Law Review, 45:411, April 1970. 5704

Dash, S. "Remarks on the Attorney General's Program on Wiretapping." Federal Rules Decisions, 32:114, March 1963. Nationwide study of wiretapping and electronic eavesdropping sponsored by the Pennsylvania Bar Association Endowment. 5705

Dershawitz, A. M. "Wiretaps and National Security; Question of Constitutionality of Warrantless Taps." Commentary, 53:56, Jan. 1972. 5706

"Eavesdropping in New York: 1968 Legislation." Syracuse Law Review, 20:601, spring 1969. 5707

"Electronic Eavesdropping: A Victim's Primer." Notre Dame Law Review, 49:162, Oct. 1973. 5708

"Electronic Eavesdropping--Fourth Amendment National Security Cases--The President Need Not Obtain a Warrant to Wiretap in National Security Cases." Loyola University Law Review (LA), 7:622, Sept. 1974. 5709

"Electronic Eavesdropping Procedures Authorized by Title III of the Omnibus Crime Control and Safe Streets Act of 1968 Violates the Fourth Amendment." Vanderbilt Law Review, 26:177, Jan. 1973. 5710

"Electronic Surveillance and the Fourth Amendment." Chicago-Kent Law Review, 2:12, June 1969. 5711

"Electronic Surveillance by Law Enforcement Officers." Northwestern University Law Review, 64:63, March-April 1969. 5712

"Federal Decisions on the Constitutionality of Electronic Surveillance Legislation." American Criminal Law Review, 11:629, spring 1973. 5713

"Federal Wiretap Law and the Grand Jury." Houston Law Review, 10:1156, July 1973. 5714

"Federal Wiretap Law--Needed--Weapon Against Organized Crime." DePaul Law Review, 13:98, autumn-winter 1963. 5715

Fly, A. "New Taps on Freedom; Title III of the Omnibus Crime Control and Safe Streets Act of 1968." Nation, 208:697, June 2, 1969. 5716

"Fourth Amendment Held to Require Search Warrant for Wiretapping in Domestic National Security Cases." Indiana Law Review, 6:314, 1972. 5717

"Fourth Amendment Limitations on Eavesdropping and Wiretapping." Cleveland-Marshall Law Review, 16:467, Sept. 1967. 5718

Greenwalt, K. "Consent Problem in Wiretapping and Eavesdropping: Surreptitious Monitoring with the Consent of a Participant in a Conversation." Columbia Law Review, 68:189, Feb. 1968. 5719

Henzi, F. "Electronic Eavesdropping." Illinois Bar Journal, 56:938, July 1968. 5720

House, F. O. "Use of Wiretap Evidence in Trials by Court-Martials." JAG Bulletin, 5:9, May-June 1963. 5721

"Inadmissibility of Wiretap Evidence in State Courts." Duke Law Journal, 1968:1008, Oct. 1968. 5722

Kaplan, J. "Limits of the Exclusionary Rule." Stanford Law Review, 26:1927, May 1974. 5723

Katzenbach, N. D. "Approach to the Problems of Wiretapping." Federal Rules Decisions, 32:107, March 1963. Why federal legislation appears necessary, and the legislation proposed by the Dept. of Justice. 5724

Kennedy, Robert F. "Attorney General's Opinion on Wiretaps." The New York Times, 21, 80, June 3, 1962. Wiretapping is the only way certain criminals may be prosecuted; legislation should permit it. The wiretap law has been on the books since 1934, and bills have been introduced to change it almost every year. 5725

Kent, R. J. "Wiretapping: Morality and Legality." Houston Law Review, 2:285, winter 1965. 5726

King, D. B., and Batt, M. A. "Wiretapping and Electronic Surveillance: A Neglected Constitutional Consideration." Dickinson Law Review, 66:17, fall 1961. 5727

Lumbard, J. E. "Lawyers' Responsibility for Due Process and Law Enforcement." Syracuse Law Review, 14:431, summer 1961. 5728

"Minimization of Wire Interception: Pre-Search Guidelines and Post Search Remedies." Stanford Law Review, 26:1411, June 1974. 5729

Musmanno, M. J. "Wiretapping: A Judge's View." Criminal Law Bulletin, 2:16, Dec. 1966. 5730

Nelson, G. "Warrantless Bugs: The Invisible Pest." Trial, 11:64, March-April 1975. 5731

Nesson, R. "Aspects of the Executive's Power Over National Security Matters: Secrecy Classification and Foreign Intelligence Wiretaps." Indiana Law Journal, 49:399, spring 1974. 5732

"New Approach to Double Jeopardy." Hastings Law Journal, 10:188, Nov. 1958. Green v. United States, 355 U.S. 193 (1957); where a defendant is convicted of a lesser crime than charged, but on appeal that conviction is reversed and a new trial ordered, a trial of the higher charge would be double jeopardy. 5733

"New Curb on Bugging; Supreme Court Decision." Time, 100:30, July 3, 1972. 5734

"New Look at Wiretapping; Pro and Con Discussion." Senior Scholastic, 96:10, Feb. 9, 1970. 5735

"One Party's Consent to Electronic Surveillance." University of Miami Law Review, 24:194, fall 1969. 5736

Orfield, L. B. "Wiretapping in Federal Criminal Cases." Texas Law Review, 42:983, Oct. 1964. 5737

"Overruling Mitchell; Legalities of Electronic Eavesdropping." Time, 97:58, April 19, 1971. 5738

"Permissible Eavesdropping Under the Berger and Katz Standards." University of Toledo Law Review, 1969:419, spring 1969. 5739

Pitter, R. M. "Eavesdropping and Wiretapping--The Aftermath of Katz (Katz v. U. S. 88 Sup. Ct. 507) and Kaiser (people v. Kaiser (NY) 233, N. E. 2d 818): A Comment." Brooklyn Law Review, 34:223, winter 1968. 5740

Pollak, L. H. "Wiretapping." New Republic, 142:13, May 16, 1960. 5741

"Right to Privacy: Actions in Intrusion for Electronic Eavesdrop and Wiretap." Journal of Urban Law, 51:79, Aug. 1973. 5742

Ryan, E. F. "United States Electronic Eavesdrop Cases." University of Toronto Law Journal, 19:68, 1969. 5743

Schwartz, H. "Electronic Eavesdropping--What the Supreme Court Did Not Do." Criminal Law Bulletin, 4:83, March 1968. 5744

________. "Legitimation of Electronic Eavesdropping: The Politics of Law and Order." Michigan Law Review, 67:455, Jan. 1969. 5745

________. "Wiretapping Problem Today." Criminal Law Bulletin, 2:3, Dec. 1966. 5746

Scoular, R. F. "Wiretapping and Eavesdropping Constitutional Development from Olmstead to Katz (Katz v. U. S. 88 Sup. Ct. 507)." St. Louis University Law Journal, 12:513, summer 1968. 5747

Shattuck, J. H. F. "National Security Wiretaps." Criminal Law Bulletin, 11:7, Jan.-Feb. 1975. 5748

Silver, E. S. "People's Case for Wiretapping." American Criminal Law Quarterly, 1:15, May 1963. 5749

________. "The Wiretapping-Eavesdropping Problem: A Prosecutor's View." Minnesota Law Review, 44:835, 1960. Study by Samuel Dash: The problems of private wiretapping; The so-called abuses in law enforcement tapping (The number of taps, The safeguards surrounding court order, Police corruption, The myth about gambling); The need for law enforcement tapping; Concluding observations. 5750

Sklar, A. "Now They Bug the Courthouse." *Nation,* 216:653, May 21, 1973. 5751

Sullivan, F. C. "Wiretapping and Eavesdropping: A Review of the Current Law." *Hastings Law Journal,* 18:59, Nov. 1966. 5752

"Supreme Court Decision: Tighter Limits Now on Wiretapping." *U.S. News,* 73:45, July 3, 1972. 5753

Swire, J. B. "Eavesdropping and Electronic Surveillance: An Approach for a State Legislature." *Harvard Journal on Legislation,* 4:23, Dec. 1966. 5754

Theoharis, A. G. "National Security Justification for Electronic Eavesdropping: An Elusive Exception." *Wayne Law Review,* 14:749, summer 1968. 5755

________. "Thirty Years of Wiretapping." *Nation,* 212:744, June 14, 1971. 5756

"Turmoil on Taps; Question of Use Against Radical Protestors." *Time,* 99:56, March 6, 1972. 5757

"Untapped; Supreme Court Ruling." *Newsweek,* 80:17, July 3, 1972. 5758

Walsh, J. H. "Key to Legal Bugging." *Florida Bar Journal,* 47:366, June 1973. 5759

"Ways and Means of Bugging." *Time,* 101:28, May 28, 1973. 5760

Weinstein, D. R. "Court Order System of Regulating Electronic Eavesdropping Under State Enabling Legislation." *Connecticut Law Review,* 2:250, Winter 1969-70. 5761

Williams, Edward Bennett. "The Wiretapping-Eavesdropping Problem: A Defense Counsel's View." *Minnesota Law Review,* 44:855, 1960. 5762

"Wiretap Evidence from the Viewpoint of the Law Enforcement Officer." *Wyoming Law Journal,* 17:49, fall 1962. 5763

"Wiretapping and Domestic Security Cases." *Loyola Law Review,* 20:199, 1973-74. 5764

"Wiretapping and Eavesdropping: A Case Analysis." *Tennessee Law Review,* 36:362, winter 1969. 5765

"Wiretapping and Electronic Surveillance--Title III of the Crime

Control Act of 1968." Rutgers Law Review, 23:319, winter 1969. 5766

"Wiretapping: The Need for Congressional Action--The Dodd Proposal As Meeting This Need." St. Louis University Law Journal, 6:436, spring 1961. 5767

"Wiretapping Wipe-out." Time, 99:34, March 27, 1972. 5768

"Wiretaps--Admissibility Notwithstanding the Federal Communications Act." Albany Law Review, 27:141, Jan. 1963. 5769

"Witness Before Grand Jury Summoned to Testify Under Compulsion Is Entitled to Notice of Wiretapping Conducted Against Him Before He Is Committed to Jail for Civil Contempt for Refusing to Answer Grand Jury's Questions." Indiana Law Review, 6:614, March 1973. 5770

(11) DOUBLE JEOPARDY

Bray, J. M. "Evidence of Prior Uncharged Offenses and the Growth of Constitutional Restrictions." University of Miami Law Review, 28:489, spring 1974. 5771

Carr, J. G. "Effect of Double Jeopardy Clause on Juvenile Proceedings." University of Toledo Law Review, 6:1, fall 1974. 5772

"Civil Rights--Double Jeopardy--Grant of Mistrial for Marginally Improper Conduct of Defense Counsel Is Error and Bars Reprosecution Under Fifth Amendment." Harvard Law Review, 82:1752, June 1969. 5773

"Constitutional Law--Criminal Procedure--Double Jeopardy Clause Requires That Punishment Already Exacted Must Be Fully 'Credited' in Imposing Sentence Upon a New Conviction for the Same Offense. Neither Double Jeopardy Clause Nor Equal Protection Clause Impose Absolute Bar to More Severe Sentence Upon Reconviction but Due Process Requires That Judges Set Forth Factual Data Supporting More Severe Sentences." Villanova Law Review, 15:751, spring 1970. 5774

"Constitutional Law--Criminal Law--Double Jeopardy--Two Sovereignties Rule (Bartkus v. Illinois, 79 Supreme Court 676)." University of Cincinnati Law Review, 28:518, fall 1959. 5775

"Constitutional Law--Cruel and Unusual Punishment--Status As a Crime (Robinson v. California, 82 Supreme Court 1417)." Brooklyn Law Review, 29:139, Dec. 1962. 5776

"Constitutional Law--District Court Must Have Jurisdiction Over First Trial to Constitute Jeopardy, (U.S. v. Sabella 272 F. 2d

206)." DePaul Law Review, 9:257, spring-summer 1960. 5777

"Constitutional Law--Double Jeopardy and the Constitutionality of Trial De Novo in Superior Court." Wake Forest Law Review, 9:566, Dec. 1973. 5778

"Constitutional Law--Double Jeopardy--Benton v. Maryland (89 Sup. Ct. 2056) Applies Retroactively to State Criminal Convictions." Vanderbilt Law Review, 23:835, 1973. 5779

"Constitutional Law--Double Jeopardy Clause of the Fifth Amendment --Doctrine of Dual Sovereignty." Duquesne Law Review, 12: 365, winter 1973. 5780

"Constitutional Law--Double Jeopardy Incorporated to the States." Arkansas Law Review, 24:110, spring 1970. 5781

"Constitutional Law: Double Jeopardy--Premeditated Murder and Felony Murder Treated As One Offense Under the Theory of Continuing Jeopardy." Mercer Law Review, 24:679, spring 1973. 5782

"Constitutional Law--Double Jeopardy--Prosecutions by Both a City and a State for an Identical Offense As a Violation of the Prohibition Against Double Jeopardy." Michigan Law Review, 68:336, Dec. 1969. 5783

"Constitutional Law--Double Jeopardy--State Prosecution Barred After Federal Prosecution for Same Offense--Burden on State to Show Substantially Different Interests from Those of Initial Prosecuting Jurisdiction." Villanova Law Review, 18:491, Feb. 1973. 5784

"Constitutional Law: Juvenile Courts and Double Jeopardy--An Opportunity for Change." University of Florida Law Review, 26: 603, spring 1974. 5785

Craig, W. L. "Double Jeopardy and Cumulative Sentencing in the Military." Georgetown Law Journal, 48:43, fall 1959. 5786

"Criminal Law--Double Jeopardy and Due Process--Protection Against a Harsher Sentencing on Retrial." Rutgers Camden Law Journal, 4:138, fall 1972. 5787

"Criminal Law--Double Jeopardy--Arbitrary Acquittal by Trial Court, (In re United States 286 F. 2d 556)." Iowa Law Review, 47: 527, winter 1972. 5788

"Criminal Law--Double Jeopardy (Green v. U.S. 78 Supreme Court 221)." Journal of Bar Association of the State of Kansas, 27: 219, Nov. 1958. 5789

"Criminal Law--Double Jeopardy--Multiple Attaches--Submission and

Acceptance of Prior Trial Record, [Nolan v. Court of General Sessions (NY) 181 N.E. 2d 751]." Brooklyn Law Review, 29: 147, Nov. 1962. 5790

"Criminal Law--Double Jeopardy--Multiple Transgressing from a Single Act [Bennett v. State (Maryland) 82 A. 2d 815]." West Virginia Law Review, 65:54, Dec. 1962. 5791

"Criminal Law--Double Jeopardy--Should 'Offense' Be Defined in Terms of Substantive Law?" Missouri Law Review, 38:523, summer 1973. 5792

"Criminal Law--Double Jeopardy--Tennessee Strict Variance Rule Permits a Second Trial for the Same Offense If the Acquittal in the First Trial Was Due to a Material Variance Between the Indictment and the Proof." Memphis State University Law Review, 3:390, spring 1973. 5793

"Criminal Law--Jury Imposed Harsher Sentence on Retrial Held to Be Unconstitutional." Dickinson Law Review, 78:597, spring 1974. 5794

"Criminal Law--Successive State Prosecutions of the Same Individual for Crimes Arising Out of the Same Occurrence but Which Involve Multiple Victims Do Not Violate the Fourteenth Amendment." Notre Dame Law Review, 44:293, Dec. 1968. 5795

"Criminal Procedure--Double Jeopardy--Trial Courts Granted Broad Discretion to Determine 'Manifest Necessity' for Mistrial." Rutgers Law Review, 26:682, spring 1973. 5796

"Criminal Procedure: Search and Seizure--The Right to a Speedy Trial, Double Jeopardy, Sentencing." Annual Survey of American Law, 1973-74:379, spring 1974. 5797

"Criminal Procedure--The Same Transaction Test--Is It Really Double Jeopardy?" Wayne Law Review, 20:1377, Sept. 1974. 5798

"Defendant in Jeopardy--Is Virginia Unique?" Wake Forest Law Review, 7:130, fall 1972. 5799

"Double Jeopardy: A New Trial After Appellant's Reversal for Insufficient Evidence." University of Chicago Law Review, 31:365, winter 1964. Examines critically the waiver theory by which the court reaches the conclusion, and proposes a new approach for the analysis of the double jeopardy implications of a new trial after appellate reversal, which avoids this anomaly. 5800

"Double Jeopardy: A Protection or an Empty Promise?" Florida Law Review, 25:838, summer 1973. 5801

"Double Jeopardy: A Vanishing Constitutional Right." Howard Law

Journal, 14:360, summer 1968. 5802

"Double Jeopardy--Acquittal of Federal Crime Does Not Bar Subsequent Trial in State Court for State Criminal Offense Arising Out of Same Act, (People v. Lo Cicero, 230 N.Y.S. 2d 384)." Fordham Law Review, 31:587, Feb. 1963. 5803

"Double Jeopardy and Collateral Estoppel." Criminal Law Bulletin, 4:406, Sept. 1968. 5804

"Double Jeopardy and Dual Sovereigns." Indiana Law Journal, 35: 444, summer 1960. 5805

"Double Jeopardy and Due Process." University of Miami Law Review, 23:531, winter-spring 1969. 5806

"Double Jeopardy and Due Process." Journal of Criminal Law, 59: 247, June 1968. 5807

"Double Jeopardy and Due Process in the Juvenile Courts." University of Pittsburgh Law Review, 29:756, June 1968. 5808

"Double Jeopardy and Hung Juries: United States v. Costellanos (478 F. 2d 749)." Rutgers Camden Law Journal, 5:218, winter 1974. 5809

"Double Jeopardy and the Doctrine of Manifest Necessity." New York University Intramural Law Review, 20:189, March 1965. 5810

"Double Jeopardy and the Identity of Offenses." Louisiana Law Review, 21:615, April 1961. 5811

"Double Jeopardy and the Waiver of Jurisdiction in California's Juvenile Courts." Stanford Law Review, 24:874, May 1972. 5812

"Double Jeopardy--Attaches Where Court Erroneously Directs Verdict of Acquittal During Presentation of Government's Case, (Fong Foo v. U.S. 82 Supreme Court 621)." Maryland Law Review, 22:168, spring 1962. 5813

"Double Jeopardy Clause: Refining the Constitutional Proscription Against Successive Criminal Prosecutions." UCLA Law Review, 19:804, June 1972. 5814

"Double Jeopardy in Federal Criminal Cases." Houston Law Review, 11:1277, July 1974. 5815

"Double Jeopardy in Missouri--The Future Under Collateral Estoppel." St. Louis University Law Journal, 16:636, March 1972. 5816

"Double Jeopardy--Its History, Rationale and Future." Dickinson Law Review, 70:377, spring 1966. 5817

"Double Jeopardy: Mistrial Declared Without the Consent of Defendant As a Bar to Reprosecution." Maryland Law Review, 33:211, 1973. 5818

"Double Jeopardy: The Reprosecution Problem." Harvard Law Review, 77:1272, May 1964. 5819

"Double Jeopardy--The 'Same Evidence Test' Applied." Louisiana Law Review, 33:474, spring 1973. 5820

"Double Jeopardy Where Both City and State Prosecute the Same Act." Washington Law Review, 38:819, winter 1963. 5821

"Dual Meaning of One Offense." Baylor Law Review, 20:218, spring 1968. 5822

"Expanding Double Jeopardy: Collateral Estoppel and the Evidentiary Use of Prior Crimes of Which the Defendant Has Been Acquitted." Florida State University Law Review, 2:511, summer 1974. 5823

"Federal and State Prosecution for Same Offense." West Virginia Law Review, 62:164, Feb. 1960. 5824

"Former Jeopardy." Kansas Law Review, 9:438, May 1961. 5825

Frels, J. C. "Double Jeopardy, the Aftermath of Waller and Ashe, a Continuing Confusion." South Texas Law Journal, 15:37, 1974. 5826

Friendland, M. L. "Double Jeopardy and the Division of Legislative Authority in Canada." University of Toronto Law Journal, 17: 66, 1967. 5827

"Government Appeals of 'Dismissals' in Criminal Cases." Harvard Law Review, 87:1822, June 1974. 5828

Harrison, H. R. "Federalism and Double Jeopardy: A Study in the Frustration of Human Rights." University of Miami Law Review, 17:306, spring 1963. 5829

"Increased Sentence by a Jury Permitted at Retrial Following a Successful Appeal or Collateral Attack of an Erroneous Conviction." Emory Law Journal, 23:879, summer 1974. 5830

"Jurisdiction and Double Jeopardy." Rutgers Law Review, 16:597, spring 1962. 5831

"Juvenile Court: Due Process, Double Jeopardy and the Florida Waiver Procedures." University of Florida Law Review, 26: 300, winter 1974. 5832

"Juvenile Law--Double Jeopardy." University of Richmond Law Review, 8:601, spring 1974. 5833

Kimmelman, W. M. "Double Jeopardy: A Political Perspective." Cumberland-Samford Law Review, 5:369, winter 1975. 5834

"Limits of the Concurrent Sentence Doctrine As a Jurisdictional Bar --The Fifth Amendment's Double Jeopardy Protection Applied to the States." Northwestern University Law Review, 65:123, March-April 1970. 5835

Loewry, A. F. "Supreme Court Revisits Palko v. Connecticut." Connecticut Bar Journal, 40:408, Sept. 1966. 5836

"Misdemeanor Conviction at Preliminary Hearing Held a Bar to Subsequent Felony Prosecution Upon Double Jeopardy Principles." University of Richmond Law Review, 9:330, winter 1975. 5837

"Mistrial and Double Jeopardy." New York University Law Review, 49:937, Nov. 1974. 5838

"Multiple Prosecution; Federalism v. Individual Rights." University of Florida Law Review, 20:353, winter 1968. 5839

"Multiple Prosecutions When Conduct Constitutes More Than One Offense." Ohio Northern Law Review, 2:23, 1974. 5840

Newman, L. "Double Jeopardy and the Problem of Successive Prosecutions: A Suggested Solution." Southern California Law Review, 34:252, spring 1961. Relationship between the double jeopardy doctrine and successive prosecutions by state and federal authorities; suggests a solution for the difficulties. 5841

"One Transaction--One Conviction--The Texas Doctrine of Carving." Baylor Law Review, 25:623, fall 1973. 5842

Rudstein, D. S. "Double Jeopardy in Juvenile Proceedings." William and Mary Law Review, 14:266, winter 1972. 5843

Sears, R. W. "Illinois Double Jeopardy Act: An Empty Gesture." Journal of Criminal Law, Criminology and Police Science, 51: 236, July-Aug. 1960. 5844

Sigler, J. A. "History of Double Jeopardy." American Journal of Legal History, 7:283, Oct. 1963. 5845

Stim, M. "Problems in Double Jeopardy." Criminal Law Review, 7:14, 1961. 5846

"Successive Prosecutions by State and Federal Governments for Offenses Arising Out of the Same Act." Minnesota Law Review, 44:534, Jan. 1960. 5847

"Twice in Jeopardy." Yale Law Journal, 25:262, Dec. 1965. Examines the most popular offense-definition tests, and reconstructs them to conform to the policies of the double jeopardy prohibition. 5848

(12) UNNECESSARY RESTRAINT--CRUEL AND UNUSUAL PUNISHMENT

Block, M. K., and Lind, C. R. "Crime and Punishment Reconsidered." Journal of Legal Studies, 4:241, Jan. 1975. 5849

Chauncey, R. "Deterrence: Certainty, Severity and Sky Jacking." Criminology, 12:447, fall 1975. 5850

"Constitutional Law--Conditions of Confinement and the Eighth Amendment." University of Toledo Law Review, 4:262, winter 1973. 5851

"Constitutional Law: Criminal Punishment of Alcoholic for Public Drunkenness Held to be Cruel and Unusual Under the Eighth and Fourteenth Amendments." Duke Law Journal, 1966:45, spring 1966. 5852

"Constitutional Law--Criminal Sanctions Against the Narcotics Addict (Robinson v. California, 82 Supreme Court 1417)." Tulane Law Review, 37:119, Dec. 1962. 5853

"Constitutional Law--Cruel and Unusual Punishment--Criminality of a Status (Robinson v. California, 82 Supreme Court 1417)." North Carolina Law Review, 41:244, winter 1963. 5854

"Constitutional Law--Cruel or Unusual Punishment--Indeterminate Sentence With No Maximum Term for a Second Offense of Indecent Exposure Is so Disportionate to the Crime As to Violate the Cruel and Unusual Punishment Provision of the California Constitution." Loyola University (LA), 6:416, July 1973. 5855

"Constitutional Law--Eighth Amendment--Statutory Penalty for Possession of Marijuana Violates Cruel and Unusual Punishments Clause." Mississippi Law Journal, 45:1297, Nov. 1974. 5856

"Constitutional Law--Imprisonment for the 'Crime' of Narcotics Addiction. Held Unconstitutional as Cruel and Unusual Punishment [Robinson v. California, 82 Supreme Court 1417]." University of Pennsylvania Law Review, 111:122, Nov. 1962. 5857

"Constitutional Law: Punishment for Narcotic Addiction Held Cruel and Unusual [Robinson v. California, 82 Supreme Court 1417]." California Law Review, 51:219, March 1963. Robinson v. California, 370 U. S. 660 (1962); addiction clause of Section 11721 is unconstitutional. 5858

"Constitutional Prohibition Against Cruel and Unusual Punishment--Its Present Significance." Vanderbilt Law Review, 4:680, April 1951. 5859

"Contempt--Cruel and Unusual Punishment--Discretion of Trial Judge, [Kenimer v. State (Georgia) 63 S.E. (2d) 280]." Georgia Bar Journal, 14:233, Nov. 1951; West Virginia Law Review, 53:179, Feb. 1951. 5860

Core, N. S. "Liberty and Punishment." New Republic, 161:26, Nov. 1, 1969. 5861

"Criminal Law--Behavior Modification in Prison and the Eighth Amendment." University of Toledo Law Review, 6:252, fall 1974. 5862

"Cruel and Unusual Punishment Clause and the Substantive Criminal Law." Harvard Law Review, 79:635, Jan. 1960. Discusses principles, historical context, cruelly excessive punishment, and Robinson v. California, 370 U.S. 660 (1962). 5863

"Cruel and Unusual Punishment in California: New Problems in Fitting Punishment to Crimes." San Diego Law Review, 3:145, 1974. 5864

"Cruel and Unusual Punishment: Of Straps and Strips Cells." Catholic Lawyer, 19:200, summer 1973. 5865

"Death Penalty: A Cruel and Unusual Punishment." Southwestern Law Review, 27:298, May 1973. 5866

"Deportation as Cruel and Unusual Punishment After Furman v. Georgia." University of San Fernando Valley Law Review, 3:27, 1974. 5867

"Effectiveness of the Eighth Amendment--An Appraisal of Cruel and Unusual Punishment." New York University Law Review, 36:846, April 1961. 5868

Ex Parte Kemmler, 136 (1890). Held--Punishments are cruel when they involve torture or a lingering death; but the punishment of death is not cruel, within the meaning of that word used in the Constitution. 5869

"Finding the Death Penalty Cruel and Unusual." University of Missouri-Kansas City Law Review, 43:162, winter 1974. 5870

"5-Year Maximum Sentences: Does the Punishment Fit the Crime? Pro and Con Discussion." Senior Scholastic, 92:14, April 4, 1968. 5871

"Florida Death Penalty: A Lack of Discretion?" University of Miami Law Review, 28:723, spring 1974. 5872

Fox, S. J. "Philosophy and Principles of Punishment in the Juvenile Court." Family Law Quarterly, 8:373, winter 1974. 5873

Francis v. Resweber, 329 U.S. 459 (1947). 5874

Goldfarb, R. "Prison: The National Poorhouse." New Republic, 161:115, Nov. 1, 1969. 5875

"Indiana Habitual Criminal Statute Not Punishment for Status, [U.S. v. Dowd, 271 F. 2d 292]." DePaul Law Review, 9:261, spring-summer 1960. 5876

McAninch, W. S. "Penal Incarceration and Cruel and Unusual Punishments." South Carolina Law Review, 25:579, Nov. 1973. 5877

McKane v. Durston, 153 U.S. 684 (1894). 5878

Packer, H. L. "Making the Punishment Fit the Crime." Harvard Law Review, 77:1071, April 1964. Author believes death penalty for rape is unconstitutional. 5879

"Recidivist Statutes and the Eighth Amendment: A Disproportional Analysis." Washington University Law Quarterly, 1974:147, 1974. 5880

"Revival of the Eighth Amendment: Development of Cruel Punishment Doctrine by the Supreme Court." Stanford Law Review, 16:996, July 1964. 5881

Troy v. Dulles, 356 U.S. 86 (1958). Held--the death penalty does not violate the constitutional prohibition of cruel punishment, but the existence of the death penalty is not a license to the governor to devise any punishment short of death within the limit of his imagination. 5882

"Unjust and Unequal; the Problem of Excessive Sentences for Criminal Offenders." Nation, 207:708, Dec. 30, 1960. 5883

Vance, C. S. "Death Penalty After Furman." Notre Dame Lawyer, 48:850, April 1973. 5884

Wilkerson v. Utah, 99 U.S. 130 (1879). Held--in a conviction of a crime punishable by death it was within the authority of the court to prescribe the mode of execution. 5885

C. LAW OF ARREST

(1) GENERAL

"Admissibility of Confessions Made Subsequent to an Illegal Arrest;

Wong Sun v. United States Revisited." Journal of Criminal Law, 61:207, June 1970. 5886

"Application of Deadly Force to Effectuate an Arrest." Washburn Law Journal, 5:262, spring 1966. 5887

"Appropriateness of Deadly Force." Howard Law Journal, 15:306, winter 1969. 5888

"Arrest: A General View." Criminal Law Review, 1960:639, Dec. 1966. 5889

"Arrest Record and New York City Public Hiring: An Evaluation." Columbia Journal of Law and Social Problems, 9:442, spring 1973. 5890

"Arrest Records--Protecting the Innocent Misuse of Arrest Records." Tulane Law Review, 48:629, April 1974. 5891

Aspen, M. E. "Arrest and Arrest Alternatives: Recent Trends." University of Illinois Law Forum, 1966:241, summer 1966. 5892

Barrett, Edward J. "Police Practices and the Law--From Arrest to Release of Charge." California Law Review, 50:11, 1962. Role of police and prosecuting officials in determining which persons arrested for serious offenses shall be brought before court. 5893

"Branded: Arrest Records of the Unconvicted." Mississippi Law Journal, 44:928, Nov. 1973. 5894

Brownlie, I. "Interrogation in Depth: The Compton and Parker Reports." Modern Law Review, 35:501, Sept. 1972. 5895

Buckley, R. S. "Volunteer Mass or Multiple Arrest Panel." Briefcase, 28:39, Nov. 1969. 5896

Carey, W. J. "Arrest to Arraignment." Illinois Bar Journal, 47: 24, Oct. 1958 (supplement.) 5897

Chevigny, P. G. "Right to Resist an Unlawful Arrest." Yale Law Journal, 78:1128, June 1969. 5898

"Civil Arrest in North Carolina." North Carolina Central Law Journal, 3:87, fall 1971. 5899

"Civil Liability for Illegal Arrests and Confinements in California." Hastings Law Journal, 19:974, March 1968. 5900

"Civil Liability of Peace Officers for Wounding or Killing." University of Cincinnati Law Review, 28:488, fall 1959. 5901

"Civil Liability of Police for False Arrest." Northwestern University Law Review, 64:229, May-June 1969. 5902

Clark, R. S. "Overmastering Physical Force: Regina v. Larsonneur Revisited." Criminal Law Quarterly, 14:413, Sept. 1972. 5903

"Constitutional Law--Full Custody Arrest Held Reasonable Basis for Complete Search of the Person." Cumberland-Samford Law Review, 5:130, spring 1974. 5904

"Constitutional Law--Miranda Warnings to Juveniles in New Jersey: The Worst of Both Worlds Revisited." Rutgers Law Review, 26:358, winter 1973. 5905

"Constitutional Law--Search and Seizure--A Full Search of the Arrestee's Person Incident to a Lawful Custodial Arrest Is Always a Reasonable Search Under the Fourth Amendment." University of Cincinnati Law Review, 43:438, 1974. 5906

"Criminal Law--Arrest--The Right to Resist Unlawful Arrest." National Resources Journal, 7:119, Jan. 1976. 5907

"Criminal Law: Personal Searches Incident to Traffic Arrests--No Nexus Necessary?" University of Florida Law Review, 25:239, fall 1972. 5908

"Criminal Law--Probable Cause--Profane Response to Police Officer's Command to Stop Constituted Probable Cause for Disorderly Conduct Arrest." Rutgers Camden Law Journal, 4:160, fall 1972. 5909

"Criminal Law: The Issuance of Arrest Warrants by Persons Other than Magistrates." Oklahoma Law Review, 26:273, May 1973. 5910

"Criminal Law: The Right to Resist an Unlawful Arrest: An Outdated Concept?" Tulsa Law Journal, 3:40, Jan. 1960. 5911

"Criminal Procedure--Protective Search Incident to Warrantless, In-Custody Arrest Constitutionally Limited to Pat-down of Outer Clothing." Texas Law Review, 51:1241, Aug. 1973. 5912

"Criminal Procedure: Searches Incident to a Lawful Arrest Limited to the Area Within Reach of the Arrestee." Duke Law Journal, 69:1084, Oct. 1969. 5913

"Davidson v. Dill [(Colo) 503 P. 2d 157]: A Compelling State Interest in Retaining Arrest Records." University of Pittsburgh Law Review, 35:205, fall 1973. 5914

Dodds, R. H., and Dempsey, R. R. "Civil Disorders: The Impact of Mass Arrests on the Criminal Justice System." Brooklyn

Law Review, 35:355, spring 1969. 5915

Douglas, W. O. "Vagrancy and Arrest on Suspicion." Yale Law Journal, 70:1, Nov. 1960. How our system can be designed to dispense justice to vagabonds as well as to corporate clients. 5916

"Dragnet Arrests: Court Says No." U.S. News, 66:12, May 5, 1969. 5917

"Expungement of Arrest Records: Police Retention of Data v. Individual Freedom from Governmental Interference." Rutgers Camden Law Journal, 4:378, spring 1973. 5918

"Expungement or Restriction of Arrest Records." Cleveland State Law Review, 23:23, winter 1974. 5919

"Expungement v. Retention of Arrest Records." University of Missouri at Kansas City Law Review, 41:106, fall 1972. 5920

Fitzgerald, D. J. "Arrest of a Motor-Car." Criminal Law Review, 1965:23, Jan. 1965. 5921

Gilligan, F. A. "Search of Premises, Vehicles, and the Individual Incident to Apprehension." Military Law Review, 61:89, summer 1973. 5922

"Informer's Tip as Probable Cause for Search or Arrest." Cornell Law Review, 54:958, July 1969. 5923

"Interrogations in New Haven: The Impact of Miranda (Miranda v. Arizona, 86 Sup. Ct. 1602)." Yale Law Journal, 76:1519, June 1967. 5924

Jacobs, D. H. "Erasure of Criminal Arrest Records: The Connecticut Statute." Connecticut Bar Journal, 47:2, March 1973. 5925

Katz, M. "Patterns of Arrest and the Dangers of Public Visibility." Criminal Law Bulletin, 9:311, May 1973. 5926

Kolbrek, Leroy M., and Porter, George W. The Law of Arrest Search and Seizure. Los Angeles: Legal Book Store, 1965. First definitive work on the intricate rules of the California law of search and seizure; for the officer who works in the field, the narcotics agent, the detective, and the prosecutor. 5927

La Fave, Wayne R. Arrest: The Decision to Take a Suspect Into Custody. Boston: Little, Brown and Co., 1965. Analysis of field data obtained in the American Bar Foundation Survey of the Administration of Criminal Justice. Discusses laws on arrests with a warrant and arrests without a warrant. 5928

________. "Case by Case Adjudication versus Standardized Procedures: The Robinson Dilemma." Supreme Court Review, 1974: 127, 1974. 5929

________. "'Street Encounters' and the Constitution: Terry (Terry v. Ohio, 88 Supt. Ct. 1868) Sileron v. New York, 88 Sup. Ct. 1889) Peters (Peters v. New York, 88 Sup. Ct. 1889) and Beyond." Michigan Law Review, 67:40, Nov. 1968. 5930

Lambert, J. L. "Reasonable Cause of Arrest." Public Law, 1973: 285, winter 1973. 5931

"Law and Police Practice: Restrictions in the Law of Arrest." Northwestern University Law Review, 52:2, 1957. The public makes the work of the police more difficult and unpleasant by a captious attitude and failure to support police efforts to modernize the laws of arrest. False arrest suits, summons and citation procedures, and delay between arrest and arraignment are also discussed. 5932

"Law of Arrest: Constitutionality of Detention and Frisk Acts." Northwestern University Law Review, 59:641, Nov.-Dec. 1964. 5933

"Law of Arrest." Mercer Law Review, 17:300, fall 1965. 5934

"Law of Arrest in Texas." Baylor Law Review, 17:303, summer-fall 1965. 5935

"Law of Arrest in Virginia." Washington and Lee Law Review, 21: 249, fall 1964. 5936

"Law of Citizen's Arrest." Columbia Law Review, 65:502, March 1965. Circumstances under which a citizen should be authorized to make an arrest, the acts that are necessary to effect a valid arrest; the degree of force that can be employed; and the standard of care to which an arrester will be held. 5937

"Lawful Custodial Arrest for a Traffic Violation Justifies a Full Search of the Arrestee." Houston Law Review, 11:1283, July 1974. 5938

Leigh, L. H. "Powers of Arrest in Relation to Vagrancy and Related Offenses." Criminal Law Review, 1974:157, March 1974. 5939

McDonald, M. C. "Use of Force by Police to Effect Lawful Arrest." Criminal Law Quarterly, 9:435, July 1967. 5940

Merrill, M. H. "Escobedo-Miranda Syndrome and the Municipal Judge." Oklahoma Bar Association Journal, 40:943, April 26, 1969. 5941

Meyer, K. G. "Arrest Under the New Kansas Criminal Code." Kansas Law Review, 20:685, summer 1972. 5942

"Miranda and Minor Offenses." Arizona Law Review, 14:766, 1972. 5943

"Motor Vehicle Exception to Warrant Requirement--Limits?" Akron Law Review, 7:343, winter 1974. 5944

Moylan, C. E., Jr. "Hearsay and Probable Cause: An Aguilar and Spinelli Primer." Mercer Law Review, 25:741, summer 1974. 5945

Munro, C. R. "Without Miranda: The Legality of Police Detention." New Law Journal, 125:137, Feb. 6, 1975. 5946

"Obstruction of Justice--Illegal Arrest--Third Party's Right to Interfere with a Peace Officer Arrest." St. Louis University Law Journal, 18:283, winter 1973. 5947

"Police Records of Arrest: A Brief for the Right to Remove Them from Police Files." St. Louis University Law Journal, 17:263, winter 1972. 5948

"Pre-Arrest Delays and the Right to Speedy Arrest: Apologia Pro Vita Ross." Arizona Law Review, 11:770, winter 1969. 5949

"Private Person's Duty to Assist the Police in Arrest." Wyoming Law Journal, 13:72, fall 1958. 5950

"Regulation of Motorists and the Law of Arrest." South Dakota Law Review, 9:198, spring 1964. 5951

"Removing the Stigma of Arrest: The Courts, the Legislatures and Unconvicted Arrestees." Washington Law Review, 47:659, Aug. 1972. 5952

"Right to Resist an Unlawful Arrest Amended." North Carolina Central Law Journal, 2:125, spring 1970. 5953

Robinsen, C. D. "Alternatives to Arrest of Lesser Offenders." Crime and Delinquency, 11:8, Jan. 1965. 5954

Ruby, C. C. "Obstructing a Police Officer." Criminal Law Quarterly, 15:375, Aug. 1973. 5955

Rummel, B. "Right of Law Enforcement Officers to Use Deadly Force to Effect an Arrest." New York Law Forum, 14:749, winter, 1968. 5956

Schirott, J. R., and Kolor, R. D. "False Arrest: Good Faith a Defense to Section 1983 Actions." Insurance Law Journal, 1974: 213, April 1974. 5957

Scurlock, J. "Arrest in Missouri." University of Kansas City Law Review, 29:117, summer 1961. 5958

Steele, W. W., Jr. "Proposal to Legitimate Arrest for Investigation." Southwestern Law Journal, 27:415, Aug. 1973. 5959

"Stop and Frisk: Dilemma for the Courts." Southern California Law Review, 41:161, fall 1967. 5960

Teb, G. L. "Detention for Interrogation." Melbourne University Law Review, 9:11, May 1973. 5961

Thomas, D. A. "Arrest: A General View." Criminal Law Review, 1966:639, Dec. 1966. 5962

"United States v. Robinson: Chipping Away at the Fourth Amendment." Ohio Northern Law Review, 1:334, 1974. 5963

"United States v. Robinson: Toward a Neutered Principle of the Exclusionary Rule." University of San Francisco Law Review, 8: 777, spring 1974. 5964

"Use of Deadly Force by a Peace Officer in the Apprehension of a Person in Flight." University of Pittsburgh Law Review, 21: 132, Oct. 1959. 5965

"Use of Deadly Force in the Apprehension of Fugitives from Arrest." McGill Law Journal, 14:293, June 1968. 5966

Vallow, Herbert Phillip. Police Arrest and Search. Springfield, Ill.: Charles C. Thomas, 1962. 5967

"What Are Reasonable Grounds for Arrest?" Chicago-Kent Law Review, 42:101, fall 1965. 5968

Witt, J. W. "Non-Coercive Interrogation and the Administration of Criminal Justice: The Impact of Miranda on Police Effectuality." Journal of Criminal Law, 64:320, Sept. 1973. 5969

(2) ARRESTS WITH WARRANTS

"Criminal Procedure--Protection Accorded the Officer Who Arrests Under a Defective Warrant." Kentucky Law Journal, 42:120, Nov. 1953. 5970

"Constitutional Requirements for Authority to Issue Warrants." Washington University Law Quarterly, 1972:777, fall 1972. 5971

Ford, Patrick H. "Constitutional Law--Criminal Procedure--Searches and Seizures--Fictitious Names (John Doe) Warrants." Southern California Law Review, 2:520, 1937-38. Elliott v. Haskins, 20 Cal. App. 2d 591 (1937); held--a fictitious name warrant is valid and constitutional. 5972

Grant, J. A. C. "Search and Seizure in California." Southern California Law Review, 15:139, Jan. 1942. 5973

Higgins, G. V. "Warrants Upon Warrants: The Pen Register and Probable Cause Under Omnibus Crime Control." Journal of Criminal Law, 60:455, Dec. 1969. 5974

Miller, F. W., and Tiffany, L. P. "Prosecutor Dominance of the Warrant Decision: A Study of Current Practices." Washington University Law Quarterly, 1964:1, Feb. 1964. 5975

Thomas, D. A. "Execution of Warrants of Arrest." Criminal Law Review, 1962:520, Aug.-Sept. 1962. 5976

Walter, Robert H. K. "Some Proposals for Modernizing the Law of Arrest." California Law Review, 39:96 at 112, March 1951. Covers: Extending use of summons and citations; Right to search for deadly weapons; Permissible force; Arresting without possession of issued warrant; Release by police without charging; False arrest suits. 5977

"When Is an Arrest Warrant Required?" St. Louis University Law Review, 8:415, spring 1964. 5978

(3) ARRESTS WITHOUT WARRANTS

"Arrest Procedure: Right to Use Force to Arrest During a Riot." Kentucky Law Journal, 57:290, winter 1968-1969. 5979

"Arrest Without a Warrant in New England." Boston University Law Review, 40:58, winter 1969. 5980

"Arrest Without Warrant in Delaware." Dickinson Law Review, 68:308, spring 1964. 5981

"Arrest Without Warrant in Iowa." Drake Law Review, 19:441, May 1970. 5982

"Arrest Without Warrant in Wisconsin." Wisconsin Law Review, 1959:489, May 1959. 5983

"Circumstances Justifying Police Entry into Dwelling of Innocent Third Party." University of British Columbia Law Review, 9:197, 1974. 5984

Cook, J. G. "Warrantless Searches Incident to Arrest." Alabama Law Review, 24:607, summer 1972. 5985

"Criminal Law--Arrest by Police Officer Without Warrant Requirement That Misdemeanor Be Committed in Arresting Officer's

Presence. [People v. Caliente (NY) 187 N.E. 2d 550]." St. John's Law Review, 37:367, May 1963. 5986

"Criminal Law--Arrest Without a Warrant--Informer's Tip Is Probable Cause [Draper v. U.S. 79 Supreme Court 329]." Catholic University Law Review, 8:117, May 1959. 5987

"Criminal Law--Arrest Without a Warrant--Probable Cause [Henry v. U.S. 80 Supreme Court 168]." Loyola Law Review, 10:116, 1959-1960. 5988

"Criminal Law: Informers and Probable Cause for Arrest, [Draper v. U.S. 79 Supreme Court 329]." Hastings Law Journal, 11: 211, Nov. 1959. 5989

"Criminal Law: Misdemeanors Arrest Without a Warrant [Shirley v. State (Oklahoma) 321 P. 2d 981]." Oklahoma Law Review, 12: 154, Feb. 1959. 5990

"Criminal Law--Peace Officer's Authority Extended for Misdemeanor Arrest Without a Warrant, [People v. Foster (NY), 176 N.E. 2d 397]." Syracuse Law Review, 13:320, winter 1961. 5991

"Criminal Law--Probable Cause of Arresting Officer in Making an Arrest Without a Warrant." New York Law Forum, 5:287, July 1959. 5992

"Criminal Law--Warrantless Search of the Person Incident to a Lawful Arrest." Tennessee Law Review, 41:932, summer 1974. 5993

Evans, G. "Arrests Without Warrant in Victoria." Law Institute Journal, 46:507, Dec. 1972. 5994

"Evolution of the Police Officer's Right to Arrest Without a Warrant in Colorado." Denver Law Journal, 43:366, summer 1966. 5995

Maclean, H. "Arrest Without Warrant." Law Journal, 111:184, March 24, 1961. 5996

"Police Power to Stop, Frisk, and Question Suspicious Persons." Columbia Law Review, 65:848, 1965. Discusses cases, traditional law of arrest and informal detention, the Uniform Arrest Act and constitutionality of informal detention. 5997

"Probable Cause at the Initial Appearance in Warrantless Arrest." Southern California Law Review, 45:1128, fall 1972. 5998

"Probable Cause for Warrantless Arrests Pursuant to Statewide Police 'Pick-up' Directives." Baylor Law Review, 25:697, fall 1973. 5999

"Searches Incident to Arrest: The Expanding Exception to the Warrant Requirement." Georgetown Law Journal, 63:223, Oct. 1974. 6000

Taylor, Richard W.; Barnett, Elliott B.; and Tresolini, R. "Arrest Without a Warrant: Extent and Social Implication." Journal of Criminal Law, Criminology and Police Science, 46:187, July-Aug. 1955. Public ignorance of what constitutes a legal arrest, warrant arrest and what legal aspects must be considered before making an arrest. 6001

"Washington Law of Arrest Without Warrant--Incidental Search." Washington Law Review, 36:501, winter 1961. 6002

(4) BAIL

"Administration of Bail and Pretrial Freedom in Texas." Texas Law Review, 43:356, Feb. 1965. 6003

"Administration of Pretrial Release and Detention: A Proposal for Unification." Yale Law Journal, 83:153, Nov. 1973. 6004

"Analysis of the Citation System in Evanston, Illinois: Its Value, Constitutionality and Viability." Journal of Criminal Law, 65: 75, March 1974. 6005

"Answer to the Problem of Bail: A Proposal in Need of Confirmation." Columbia Journal of Law and Social Problems, 9:394, spring 1973. 6006

Ares, Charles E. "The Manhattan Bail Project: An Interim Report on the Use of Pretrial Parole." New York University Law Review, 67-95, Jan. 1963. 6007

"Bail--An Examination of Release on Recognizance." Mississippi Law Journal, 39:303, March 1968. 6008

"Bail and Bail Bondsmen: Need for Reform in Kentucky." Kentucky Law Journal, 61:601, 1972-1973. 6009

"Bail and Recognizance." in American Jurisprudence, vol. 8 (Rochester, N.Y.: Lawyer's Cooperative Pub. Co., 1963). 6010

"Bail as a Matter of Right...." Hastings Law Journal, 26:559, Nov. 1974. 6011

"Bail in Capital Cases After Furman (Furman v. Georgia, 92 Sup. Ct. 2726): A Process Question." Rutgers Camden Law Journal, 4:326, spring 1973. 6012

"Bail in the United States: A System in Need of Reform." Hastings Law Journal, 20:380, Nov. 1968. 6013

"Bail or Jail." Record, 91:11, Jan. 1964. 6014

"Bail or Jail: Toward an Alternative." University of Florida Law Review, 21:59, summer 1968. 6015

"Bail: Right or Privilege?" University of San Fernando Valley Law Review, 3:159, 1974. 6016

"Bail System: Is It Acceptable?" Ohio State Law Journal, 29:1005, fall 1968. 6017

"Bail: The Need for Reconsideration." Northwestern University Law Review, 59:678, Nov.-Dec. 1964. 6018

Bakakos, P. "Bail in Capital Cases." Chicago Bar Record, 56:164, Nov.-Dec. 1974. 6019

Berger, M. "Bail in Missouri Revisited." University of Missouri-Kansas City Law Review, 43:40, fall 1974. 6020

"Beyond the Bail System: A Proposal for Pre-Trial Release in California." California Law Review, 57:1112, Nov. 1969. 6021

Bogomolny, R. L., and Sonnenreich, M. R. "Bail Reform Act of 1966: Administrative Tail Wagging and Other Legal Problems." Arizona Law Review, 11:201, summer 1969. 6022

Bottomley, A. K. "Granting of Bail: Principles and Practice." Modern Law Review, 31:40, Jan. 1968. 6023

"Compensatory Pretrial Detention." Gonzaga Law Review, 9:203, fall 1973. 6024

"Constitutional Controversy of a Juvenile's Right to Bail in Juvenile Preadjudication Proceedings." Hastings Constitutional Law Quarterly, 1:215, spring 1974. 6025

"Crimes While on Bail; The Hunt for a Remedy." U.S. News, 66:42, Feb. 17, 1969. 6026

"Criminal Law--Bail--Capital Offense Exception to Constitutional Bail Guarantee Unaffected by Abolition of Death Penalty." Mississippi Law Journal, 44:565, June 1973. 6027

"Criminal Procedure--Preventive Detention in New Mexico." New Mexico Law Review, 4:247, May 1974. 6028

Cromwell, P. F., and Rios, O. G. "Bond Supervision: Implementing the Federal Bail Reform Act." Federal Probation, 38:30, Dec. 1974. 6029

Fabricant, N. "Bail as a Preferred Freedom and the Failures of New York's Revision." Buffalo Law Review, 18:303, 1968-69. 6030

Foote, Caleb. "The Bail System and Equal Justice." *Federal Probation,* 19:43, Sept. 1955. 6031

________. "Coming Constitutional Crises in Bail." *University of Pennsylvania Law Review,* 113:959, May 1965. 6032

________. "A Study of the Administration of Bail in New York." *University of Pennsylvania Studies in Law Administration,* 106: 707, 1958. 6033

Freed, Daniel J., and Wald, Patricia M. "Bail in the United States: 1964." *A Report to the National Conference on Bail and Criminal Justice.* Washington, D. C., May 27-29, 1964. 6034

"Furman v. Georgia (92 Sup. Ct. 2726): Will the Death of Capital Punishment Mean a New Life for Bail?" *Hofstra Law Review,* 2:432, winter 1974. 6035

Galafarb, Ronald. *Ransom: A Critique of the American Bail System.* New York: Harper & Row, 1965. 6036

Galligan, D. "Working Paper on Bail." *Modern Law Review,* 38: 59, Jan. 1975. 6037

"Game of Bail." *Time,* 101:54, Jan. 15, 1973. 6038

Goldstein, A. S. "Jail Before Trial." *New Republic,* 160:15, March 8, 1969. 6039

Haemmel, W. G. "Tennessee Bail Bond System: The Search for a Better Answer." *Memphis State University Law Review,* 3:39, fall 1972. 6040

Hall, L. "Subsequent Misconduct as Ground for Forfeiture of the Right to Release on Bail--A Proposal." *New York Law Forum,* 15:873, winter 1969. 6041

Hangisto, R. D., and Levine, C. "Workable Alternatives to the Present Bail System." *California State Bar Journal,* 47:577, Nov.-Dec. 1972. 6042

Harris, B. "Bail--The Case for Reform." *News Law Journal,* 124:332, April 11, 1974. 6043

Hermann, D. H. J. "Preventive Detention, a Scientific View of Man, and State Power." *University of Illinois Law Forum,* 1973: 673, 1973. 6044

Hickey, J. P. "Preventive Detention and the Crime of Being Dangerous." *Georgia Law Journal,* 58:287, Nov. 1969. 6045

Hindelang, M. J. "Unconstitutional Administration of Bail: Bellamy v. The Judges of New York City. On the Methodological Rigor of the Bellamy Memorandum: A Study of the Effect of Pretrial Detention on the Outcome of a Criminal Case." Criminal Law Bulletin, 8:459, July-Aug. 1972. 6046

Hunter, E. B. "Bail Reform Act of 1966." University of Missouri-Kansas City Law Review, 40:295, spring 1972. 6047

"Institution of Bail as Related to Indigent Defendants." Louisiana Law Review, 21:627, April 1961. 6048

Just, B. "Bail and Pretrial Detention in the District of Columbia: An Empirical Analysis." Howard Law Journal, 17:844, 1973. 6049

"Juveniles Right to Bail in Oregon." Oregon Law Review, 47:194, Feb. 1968. 6050

Kamin, A. "Bail Administration in Illinois." Illinois Bar Journal, 53:674, April 1965. 6051

Kennedy, P. M. "VISTA Volunteers Bring About Successful Bail Reform Project in Baltimore." American Bar Association Journal, 54:1093, 1965. 6052

Kennedy, R. F. "Criminal Justice." William and Mary Law Review, 5:167, 1964. 6053

Landes, Eugene A., Jr. "A Survey of Bail in the United States: Historical Development Problems, Reforms, and Importance to the Legal Profession." Police, 10:54, July-Aug. 1966. Continuation of a two-part article. 6054

Landes, W. M. "Bail System: An Economic Approach." Journal of Legal Studies, 2:79, Jan. 1973. 6055

Leahy, E. R., and Pound, J. B. "Bail Reform--The Search for Constitutional Realism." Duquesne Law Review, 11:14, fall 1972. 6056

McCarthy, D. J., Jr. "Practical Results of Bail Reform." Federal Probation, 29:10, Sept. 1965. 6057

McWilliams, P. K. "Law of Bail." Criminal Law Quarterly, 9:1, Sept. 1966. 6058

Meyer, H. H. "Constitutionality of Pretrial Detention." Georgetown Law Journal, 60:1139, May-June 1972. 6059

Mitchell, J. N. "Bail Reform and the Constitutionality of Pretrial Detention." Virginia Law Review, 55:1223, Nov. 1969. 6060

Molinari, J. B. "Admission to Bail in California--To Bail or Not to Bail." California State Bar Journal, 49:366, July-Aug. 1974. 6061

Moriarty, F. V. "Pretrial Release Succeeds in Santa Clara County." American Bar Association Journal, 61:861, July 1965. 6062

Mosk, S. "Purpose of Bail in the Administration of Justice." Chicago Bar Record, 54:183, Jan. 1973. 6063

Mostyn, F. E. "Bail and the Presumption of Innocence." Law Society's Gazette, 61:799, Dec. 1964. 6064

Paulsen, M. G. "Pretrial Release in the United States." Columbia Law Review, 66:109, Jan. 1966. Bail system in the U. S. 6065

"Post Conviction Bail: The Application of an Unjust and Outmoded System--A Case for Reform." New York Law Forum, 15:889, winter 1969. 6066

"Presumption of Guilt? Legal Experts Discuss Pretrial Detention." Newsweek, 74:67, Nov. 10, 1969. 6067

"Pretrial Release of an Accused in Ohio--A Proposed Revision of Ohio Bail Laws." University of Cincinnati Law Review, 41:423, 1972. 6068

"Pretrial Release Under California Penal Code Section 853. 6: An Examination of Citation Release." California Law Review, 60: 1339, Sept. 1972. 6069

"Preventive Detention and the Proposed Amendments to the Bail Reform Act of 1966." William and Mary Law Review, 11:525, winter 1969. 6070

"Prison Discipline and the Eighth Amendment: Out of the Quagmire?" American Journal of Criminal Law, 1:4, Feb. 1972. 6071

Proceedings and Interim Report of the National Conference on Bail and Criminal Justice. Washington: United States Department of Justice, 1965. 6072

Rice, P. R., and Gallagher, M. C. "Alternative to Professional Bail Bonding: A 10% Cash Deposit for Connecticut." Connecticut Law Review, 5:143, fall 1972. 6073

"Right to Bail for Juveniles." Chicago-Kent Law Review, 48:99, spring 1971. 6074

"Roll v. Larson: The Right to Bail in Capital Cases After Furman." Utah Law Review, 1974:421, summer 1974. 6075

Rolls, W. R. "Bail in the United States." Michigan State Bar Journal, 48:28, Jan. 1969. 6076

Samuels, A. "Bail Principles." New Law Journal, 116:1269, Sept. 8, 1966. 6077

Samuels, Gertrude. "Bail: Justice for Far from All." The New York Times Magazine, Aug. 19, 1962. 6078

Sanduffer, W. C. "Article of Faith Abolishes Bail in Oregon." Oregon Law Review, 53:273, spring 1974. 6079

Scott, R. E. "Bail Fact Finding Projects at San Francisco." Federal Probation, 30:39, Dec. 1966. 6080

Semaan, A. A. "Bail. Examining Trials. Magistrate Justice and Cooperation Courts, Right to Counsel in Magistrate Courts." Texas Bar Journal, 29:245, April 1966. 6081

Silverstein, L. "Bail in the State Courts--A Field Study and Report." Minnesota Law Review, 50:621, March 1966. 6082

Smith, T. "New Approach to the Bail Practice." Federal Probation, March 1965. 6083

Sturz, H. "Alternative to the Bail System." Federal Probation, 26:49, Dec. 1962. 6084

________. "Manhattan Bail Project." Brief Case, 21:21, Oct. 1962. 6085

Subin, H. "Bail for the Rich, Jail for the Poor." Nation, 208:363, March 24, 1969. 6086

"Trends in Own Recognizance Release: From Manhattan to California." Pacific Law Journal, 5:675, July 1974. 6087

Treuhaft, R. E. "Abolition of Bail in Misdemeanor Cases." Law in Transition, 19:55, summer 1955. 6088

Villagran, J. A. "Mastodon of Bail." University of San Fernando Valley Law Review, 4:35, spring 1975. 6089

Wald, P. M., and Freed, D. J. "Bail Reform Act of 1966: A Practitioner's Primer." American Bar Association Journal, 52:940, Oct. 1966. Explains the changes in the bail system by outlining the provisions of the act and by clarifying defense counsel's larger role in securing his client's pretrial release. 6090

Watt, D. "Judicial Interim Release." Criminal Law Quarterly, 16:27, 1973. 6091

Wice, P. B. "Bail Reform in American Cities." Criminal Law Bulletin, 9:770, Nov. 1973. 6092

Younger, E. J. "It's Time to Forfeit Bail." Southwestern University Law Review, 5:262, summer 1973. 6093

D. JURISDICTION

Abraham, H. J., and Lader, P. C. "Supreme Court and the Preemption Question." Kentucky Law Journal, 53:289, winter 1964-65. 6094

"Admiralty-Jurisdiction Over Airplane Crashes on Navigable Waters." Wayne Law Review, 18:1569, spring 1972. 6095

"Alabama's Nonresident-Jurisdiction Statutes: The Reach of the Long Arm." Alabama Law Review, 24:777, summer 1972. 6096

Alders, M. S. "Transfer of Jurisdiction from Juvenile to Criminal Court." Crime and Delinquency, 19:519, Oct. 1973. 6097

Blume, W. W. "Place of Trial of Criminal Cases--Constitutional Vicinage and Venue." Michigan Law Review, 43:59, Aug. 1949. 6098

Boucher, G. V. "Crimes of U.S. Servicemen Overseas: Does the Constitution Follow the Flag?" University of Detroit Law Journal, 35:1, Oct. 1957. 6099

Boyle, R. P. P. "Jurisdiction Over Crimes Committed in Flight: An International Convention." American Criminal Law Quarterly, 3:68, winter 1965. 6100

Bubany, C. P. "Constitutional Question Appellate Jurisdiction: The Albatross Hangs Heavy Still." Missouri Law Review, 39:299, summer 1974. 6101

"Change of Venue in Criminal Cases: The Defendant's Right to Specify the County of Transfer." Stanford Law Review, 26:131, Nov. 1973. 6102

Cheatham, E. E. "Does Federal or State Law Apply in International Transaction?" New York County Lawyers Association Bar Bulletin, 23:200, 1965-66. 6103

"Civil Rights--Extraterritorial Operation of Bill of Rights Guaranties [Reed v. Covert, 77 Supreme Court 1222]." Southwestern Law Journal, 4:341, fall 1965. 6104

"Collateral Attack for Lack of Subject Matter Jurisdiction." California Law Review, 52:623, Aug. 1964. Examines cases preceding Durfee v. Duke to determine what rule the Supreme Court has developed as a compromise between the conflicting policies underlying res judicata and collateral attack, and Durfee (375 U.S. 106 1963). 6105

"Conflict of Laws--Limitation on 'Any Act' Within the Scope of the Oklahoma Long Arm Statute." Tulsa Law Journal, 5:87, Jan. 1968. 6106

"Constitutional Law--Equal Protection--Necessity of Standards in Statute Allowing Probate Court to Waive Jurisdiction of a Minor to Circuit Court." Journal of Urban Law, 50:782, May 1973. 6107

"Constitutional Law: Military Jurisdiction Over Inactive Reservists." JAG Journal, 27:129, fall 1972. 6108

"Courts-Martial Jurisdiction and Civilian Defendants: Constitutional Restrictions [Reid v. Covert, 77 Supreme Court 1222]." Duke Law Journal, 7:155, spring 1958. 6109

"Criminal Jurisdiction over Non-Trust Lands Within the Limits of Indian Reservations." Willamette Law Journal, 9:288, June 1973. 6110

"Criminal Law--Infants--Jurisdictional Determination of a Teenage Offender." North Dakota Law Review, 43:351, winter 1967. 6111

"Criminal Law--Place of Crime Determines Jurisdiction as Well as Venue." Dickinson Law Review, 77:561, spring 1973. 6112

Curtiss, W. D. "Extraterritorial Law Enforcement in New York." Cornell Law Quarterly, 50:34, fall 1964. 6113

Davis, S. M. "Jurisdictional Dilemma of the Juvenile Court." North Carolina Law Review, 51:195, Dec. 1972. 6114

Dobbs, D. B. "Trial Court Error As an Excess of Jurisdiction." Texas Law Review, 43:854, July 1965. 6115

"Double Jeopardy and the Waiver of Jurisdiction in California's Juvenile Courts." Stanford Law Review, 24:874, May 1972. 6116

"Due Process and Waiver of Juvenile Court Jurisdiction." Washington and Lee Law Review, 30:591, fall 1973. 6117

Ellis, E. M. "Jurisdiction of General Sessions Courts in Tennessee to Try and Determine Criminal Cases." Tennessee Law Review, 36:458, spring 1969. 6118

Empson, P. D. "Application of Criminal Law to Acts Committed Outside the Jurisdiction." American Criminal Law Quarterly, 6:32, fall 1967. 6119

"Extension of County Jurisdiction Over Indian Reservations in California: Public Law 280 and the Ninth Circuit." Hastings Law Journal, 25:1451, May 1974. 6120

"Extradition: Concurrent Jurisdiction and the Uncertainty of Prosecution in the Requested Nation." Wayne Law Review, 14:1181, fall 1968. 6121

"Federal Venue for Aliens: The Presumption of Nonresidency." California Western International Law Journal, 3:417, May 1973. 6122

Forde, K. M. "Emergence of Metropolitan Centers as Litigation Centers for the 'Big Case': New Concepts in Federal and State Court Jurisdiction." John Marshall Journal, 2:1, fall 1968. 6123

Foster, G. W., Jr. "Judicial Economy: Fairness and Convenience of Place of Trial: Long-arm Jurisdiction in District Courts." Federal Rules Decisions, 47:73, July 1969; Insurance Counsel Journal, 35:623, Oct. 1968. 6124

Gordon, D. M. "Jurisdictional Fact: An Answer." Law Quarterly Review, 82:515, Oct. 1966. 6125

Hoffman, K. F. "Doctrine of Primary Jurisdiction Misconceived: End to Common Law Environmental Protection." Florida State University Law Review, 2:491, summer 1974. 6126

"Indiana's Need for Legislative Surgery: A Jurisdictional Transplant." Indiana Law Journal, 43:928, summer 1968. 6127

"Jurisdiction--Libel--First Amendment's Role in Determining Place of Trial in Libel Actions." Michigan Law Review, 66:542, Jan. 1968. 6128

"Jurisdiction of the Trial Judge--Wrongful Determination of an Information--Whether Certiorari or Prohibition Should Lie." Criminal Law Quarterly, 15:265, May 1973. 6129

"Jurisdiction Over Federal Enclaves." Baylor Law Review, 26:401, summer 1974. 6130

"Jurisdictional Facts in Enforcement Actions on Cognovit Judgments of Sister States--The Voluntary Waiver." American University Law Review, 22:765, summer 1973. 6131

"Jurisdictions: 'Long-Arm' Expansion." Oklahoma Law Review, 19:443, Nov. 1966. 6132

"Juvenile Court and Direct Appeal from Waiver of Jurisdiction in Ohio." Akron Law Review, 8:499, spring 1975. 6133

Karasik, S. Z. "Jurisdiction of Trial Court After Notice of Appeal." Illinois Bar Journal, 53:30, Sept. 1964. 6134

Lissitzyn, O. J. "In-Feignt Crime and United States Legislation." American Journal of International Law, 67:306, April 1973. 6135

"Long-Arm Jurisdiction in Alimony and Custody Cases." Columbia

Law Review, 73:289, Feb. 1973. 6136

MacDonald, J. A. "Juvenile Court Jurisdiction." Criminal Law Quarterly, 7:426, Feb. 1965. 6137

McDonald, K. "Wyoming Nonresident Motor Statute." Wyoming Law Journal, 18:231, spring 1964. 6138

"Minority Rights and American Indians." North Dakota Law Review, 51:137, fall 1974. 6139

Moreland, R. "Conflict of Laws--A Rationale of Jurisdiction." Kentucky Law Journal, 55:11, fall 1966. 6140

________. "Conflict of Laws--A Rationale of Jurisdiction--Service of Process." Kentucky Law Journal, 56:629, spring 1967-68. 6141

Napley, D. "Jurisdiction." Criminal Law Review, 1966:529, Oct. 1966. 6142

"Nonresidents and Jurisdiction: A Modern Dilemma in Civil and Criminal Procedure." Villanova Law Review, 10:518, spring 1965. 6143

Orland, L. H., and Fishnaller, B. F. "Jurisdiction Salad: Washington Style." Gonzaga Law Review, 9:1, fall 1973. 6144

"Pennsylvania's New Long-Arm Statute: Extended Jurisdiction Over Foreign Corporations." Dickinson Law Review, 79:51, fall 1974. 6145

"Practice of Law by Out-of-State Attorneys." Vanderbilt Law Review, 20:1276, Nov. 1967. 6146

"Preemption As a Preferential Ground: A New Canon of Construction." Stanford Law Review, 12:208, Dec. 1959. Preemption decisions do not uniformly represent sound statutory construction. 6147

"Refusal of State Court to Assume Jurisdiction After Federal Abstention." Southwestern Law Journal, 20:402, June 1960. 6148

"Review of Improper Juvenile Transfers." Virginia Law Review, 60:818, May 1974. 6149

Shaneyfelt, D. L. "War Crimes and the Jurisdiction Maze." The International Lawyer, 4:924, Oct. 1970. 6150

"Single Act Statute for North Dakota." North Dakota Law Review, 43:299, winter 1967. 6151

Spiegal, S. A., and Doolings, J. F., Jr. "Accord and Conflict

Between State and Federal Court Jurisdictions." New York County Bar Bulletin, 27:58, 1969-70. 6152

Stamm, M. J. "Transfer of Jurisdiction in Juvenile Court: An Analysis of the Proceeding, Its Role in the Administration of Justice, and a Proposal for the Reform of Kentucky Law." Kentucky Law Journal, 62:122, 1973-74. 6153

"Sovereign Immunity--May a State Assert in Personam Jurisdiction Over a Sister State Without Its Consent?" Boston University Law Review, 53:736, May 1973. 6154

"Subjection of American Military Personnel to Foreign Criminal Jurisdiction: The Territorial Imperative." Iowa Law Review, 58:532, Feb. 1973. 6155

"Survey of Air Law Applicable When Death Occurs on the High Seas in an Aircraft." Lincoln Law Review, 7:100, Dec. 1971. 6156

Swann, J. B. "Bringing Home the Nonresident Infringer: How Long or Short Should the Jurisdictional Arm Be?" Trademark Republic, 62:267, July, Aug. 1972. 6157

"Territorial Fairness: A Due Process Standard for Quasi in Rem Jurisdiction." University of Miami Law Review, 28:439, winter 1974. 6158

Tiverski, A. D. "Return to Jurisdictional Due Process--The Case for the Vanishing Defendant." Insurance Counsel Journal, 37: 265, April 1970. 6159

"Trial of a United States Soldier by a Foreign Power [Girard v. Wilson, 77 Supreme Court 1409]." Louisiana Law Review, 18: 173, Dec. 1957. 6160

Uhlenhoop, H. "Some Plain Talk about Courts of Special and Limited Jurisdiction." Journal of the American Judicature Society, 49:212, April 1966. 6161

"Validity of United States Magistrates Criminal Jurisdiction." Virginia Law Review, 60:697, April 1974. 6162

"Venue Problems in Wisconsin." Marquette Law Review, 56:87, winter 1973. 6163

"Waiver of Juvenile Jurisdiction and the Hard-Core Youth." North Dakota Law Review, 51:655, spring 1975. 6164

Ward, R., Jr. "Criminal Law and Jurisdiction Over American Servicemen in Japan." American Bar Association Journal, 52: 61, Jan. 1966. Describes the provisions of the Status of Forces Agreement between U.S. and Japan under which American servicemen may be tried in Japanese courts and under Japanese law for certain criminal offenses. Outlines Japanese criminal law and tells of cooperation. 6165

Weissman, D. A. "Georgia Long-Arm Statute: A Significant Advance in the Concept of Personal Jurisdiction." Georgia State Bar Journal, 4:13, Aug. 1967. 6166

E. STATUTE OF LIMITATIONS

"Amended Petitions and the Statute of Limitations in Missouri." University of Missouri at Kansas City Law Review, 38:422, spring 1970. 6167

"Annotated Table of California Statutes of Limitations." Southwestern University Law Review, 6:237, summer 1974. 6168

Bell, I. "Offers in Compromise: How do they affect the Statute of Limitation?" Journal of Taxation, 31:247, Oct. 1969. 6169

"Conflict of Law--Statutes of Limitations--Substantive Foreign Statute Commencing at Time of Discovery Governs." Mississippi Law Journal, 44:276, April 1973. 6170

"Constitutional Law-Retroactive Application of a Statute Removing a Statute of Limitations Bar." Tennessee Law Review, 41:914, summer 1974. 6171

Corley, R. N. "Limitations Act: A Proposed Review." Illinois Bar Journal, 48:838, July 1960. 6172

"Criminal Contempt: A Means to Circumvent the Criminal Statutes of Limitations." University of Miami Law Review, 23:843, summer 1969. 6173

"Criminal Law--Limitation of Actions--Intent to Avoid Justice." (Donnell v. U.S. 229 F. 2d 560)." Minnesota Law Review, 41:352, Feb. 1957. 6174

"Criminal Law: Limitation of Prosecution--Time." Land and Water Law Review, 5:179, 1970. 6175

"Criminal Law--Limitations of Prosecutions--Limitations Applicable [State v. Brown (NJ), 126A 2d 161]." North Dakota Law Review, 33:315, July 1957. 6176

"Criminal Law--Limitations of Prosecutions--Whether Under Timely Indictment for Felony One Convicted or Included Misdemeanor May Assent Limitation Defense Applicable to Misdemeanor Charge, [State v. King, (West Virginia) 84 SE. 2d 313]." Chicago-Kent Law Review, 33:355, Sept. 1955. 6177

"Criminal Law--Statute of Limitations--Absence of Accused from Jurisdiction Tolls Statute Only When Intent to Evade Is Shown (Donnell v. U.S. 299 F 2d 560)." Virginia Law Review, 42:681, June 1956. 6178

"Criminal Procedure--Preaccusation Delay As Violation of Due Process: Absence of Statute of Limitations Is Factor to Be Weighed Against Murder Defendant's Allegations of Actual Prejudice." Washington Law Review, 49:973, May 1974. 6179

Davidson, J. W. "Application of Limitation as to Damages Caused by Public Improvements." Baylor Law Review, 16:32, winter 1964. 6180

"Does War Toll the Statute of Limitations?" Columbia Law Review, 57:1140, Dec. 1957. Soriano v. United States 352 U.S. 270 (1957); rule--war neither tolls the statute of limitations nor creates a legal disability to sue--this should be legally corrected. 6181

"Extradition--Statute of Limitations--Mere Absence Is not Equivalent to Fleeing from Justice Under 18 U.S.C. 3290." Vanderbilt Journal of Transnational Law, 7:503, spring 1974. 6182

"Federal Courts--The 'Erie Doctrine' and Tolling of the State Statute of Limitation." North Carolina Law Review, 47:715, April 1969. 6183

"Forgotten Sponge and the Statute of Limitations." Washburn Law Journal, 1:257, spring 1961. 6184

Glover, F. G. "Limitation of Actions." New Law Journal, 116: 1222, 1242, Aug. 25, Sept. 1, 1966. 6185

Jackson, D. "Legal Effects of the Passing of Time." Melbourne University Law Review, 7:407, April 1970. 6186

"Last Vistage of the Citadel." Hofstra Law Review, 2:721, summer 1974. 6187

"Limitation of Actions--Claims Between Spouses." North Carolina Law Review, 44:197, Dec. 1965. 6188

"Limitation on Actions for Deprivation of Federal Rights." Columbia Law Review, 68:763, April 1968. 6189

"Marriage of Minors and the Running of the Statute of Limitations." Alabama Law Review, 18:121, fall 1965. 6190

"Negotiable Instruments--A Cause of Action on a Cashier's Check Accrues from the Date of Issuance." New Mexico Law Review, 4:253, May 1974. 6191

"Operation of Amendment to Limitation of Action Statute." West Virginia Law Review, 62:360, June 1960. 6192

"Pleading: Substituting a Defendant After the Statute of Limitations Has Run." Oklahoma Law Review, 26:105, February 1973. 6193

Sacks, S. "Statutes of Limitations and the Undercovered Malpractice." Cleveland-Marshall Law Review, 16:65, Jan. 1967. 6194

Solis, C. "Statute of Limitations in Legal Malpractice Cases: The California Supreme Court Establishes New Guidelines." University of San Francisco Law Review, 7:85, Oct. 1972. 6195

"Statute of Limitations--Negligence--Medical--Malpractice Cases--Proposed Legislation." Oregon Law Review, 45:73, Dec. 1965. 6196

"Statute of Limitations: No Longer An Absolute Bar." University of Miami Law Review, 26:844, summer 1974. 6197

"Time Limitations in Criminal Prosecution." Loyola Law Review, 10:97, 1959-1960. 6198

"Tolling the Statute of Limitations When a Case Has Been Previously Dismissed for Lack of Jurisdiction or for Improper Venue." University of Richmond Law Review, 7:319, winter 1972. 6199

"Torts--Statute of Limitations--New Rule for Medical Malpractice Actions." Mercer Law Review, 23:697, spring 1972. 6200

"Trial Practice: Running of the Statute of Limitations: When Demand Is Necessary." Oklahoma Law Review, 17:353, Aug. 1964. 6201

"Twenty-Five Year Statute of Limitations." Baylor Law Review, 10:196, spring 1958. 6202

"Wrongful Death and the Statute of Limitations." Montana Law Review, 34:170, winter 1973. 6203

Wurfel, S. W. "Statute of Limitations in the Conflict of Laws." North Carolina Law Review, 52:489, Feb. 1974. 6204

F. GRAND JURY

"Adminstrative Agency Access to Grand Jury Materials." Columbia Law Review, 75:162, Jan. 1975. 6205

"American Grand Jury: Investigatory and Indictment Powers."

Cleveland State Law Review, 22:136, winter 1973. 6206

Bickner, M. K. "Grand Jury ... A Layman's Assessment." California State Bar Journal, 48:660, Nov.-Dec. 1973. 6207

Boudin, L. B. "Federal Grand Jury." Georgetown Law Journal, 61:1, Oct. 1972. 6208

Braun, R. L. "Grand Jury-Spirit of the Community?" Arizona Law Review, 15, 893, 1973. 6209

"Calandra--The Present Status of the Exclusionary Rule." Capital University Law Review, 4:95, 1975. 6210

Carp, H. A. "Harris County Grand Jury--A Case Study." Houston Law Review, 12:90, Oct. 1974. 6211

"Constitutional Law--Grand Juries--Use of Voice Exemplars in Investigations Upheld." Mercer Law Review, 25:365, winter 1974. 6212

"Constitutional Law--Juror Selection--Equal Protection Denied When Master Grand Jury List Significantly Underrepresent's Defendant's Race." Mississippi Law Journal, 46:539, summer 1975. 6213

"Constitutional Law: The Balancing Procedure Applied in Search and Seizure." University of Missouri-Kansas City Law Review, 43:98, fall 1974. 6214

"Criminal Law--Grand Juries, Exemplars, and Prosecutors." De-Paul Law Review, 22:737, spring 1973. 6215

"Criminal Procedure--Grand Juries--Lack of Miranda Warnings for Virtual Defendant Results in Suppression of Perjurious Testimony." Texas Law Review, 53:156, Dec. 1974. 6216

"Criminal Procedure--Grand Jury--Remedy of Exclusionary Rule Held Inapplicable to Grand Jury Proceedings." Seton Hall Law Review, 5:917, summer 1974. 6217

"Criminal Procedure--The Grand Jury." DePaul Law Review, 22:260, fall 1972. 6218

"Discriminatory Jury Selection: Reversible Error Regardless of Defendant's Own Race." University of Miami Law Review, 27:238, fall-winter 1972. 6219

"Evaluating the Grand Jury's Role in a Dual System of Prosecution: An Iowa Case Study." Iowa Law Review, 57:1354, June 1972. 6220

"Evidence--Grand Jury: Applicability of Exclusionary Rule to Grand

Jury Proceedings." Washburn Law Journal, 14:377, spring 1975. 6221

"Federal Wiretap Law and the Grand Jury." Houston Law Review, 10:1156, July 1973. 6222

"Grand Jury: Bulwark of Prosecutorial Immunity?" Loyola University Law Journal (Chicago), 3:303, summer 1972. 6223

"Grand Jury: Powers, Procedures and Problems." Columbia Journal of Law and Social Problems, 9:681, summer 1973. 6224

"Grand Jury Proceedings: The Prosecutor, The Trial Judge, and Undue Influence." University of Chicago Law Review, 39:761, summer 1972. 6225

"Grand-Jury--Reports Not Amounting to a Presentment." Wayne Law Review, 18:1643, Sept. 1972. 6226

"Grand Jury Secrecy: Should Witnesses Have Access to Their Grand Jury Testimony as a Matter of Right?" UCLA Law Review, 20: 804, April 1973. 6227

"Grand Jury Secrecy: Waiver and the Public Interest." Washington Law Quarterly, 1974:153, 1974. 6228

"Grand Jury Selection: Voter Registration Lists As a Cross Section of the Community." Oregon Law Review, 52:482, summer 1973. 6229

"Grand Jury Subpoena Not a Fourth Amendment Seizure." American Criminal Law Review, 11:1087, summer 1973. 6230

"Immunity and the Grand Jury." Land and Water Law Review, 8: 629, 1973. 6231

Knudsen, W. J., Jr. "Pretrial Disclosure of Federal Grand Jury Testimony." Washington Law Review, 48:423, Feb. 1973. 6232

Kuhns, R. B. "Limiting the Criminal Contempt Power: New Roles for the Prosecutor and the Grand Jury." Michigan Law Review, 73:483, Jan. 1975. 6233

Makowski, R. E. "Effectively Representing a Client Before a Grand Jury." Practical Lawyer, 20:59, Nov. 1974. 6234

Petersen, A. W. "California Grand Jury System: A Review and Suggestions for Reform." Pacific Law Journal, 5:1, Jan. 1974. 6235

"Search and Seizure: Recognizing the Limits of the Exclusionary Rule in a Federal Grand Jury Proceeding." University of

Florida Law Review, 26:624, spring 1974. 6236

"Selected Materials on the Grand Jury." Record of the Association of Bar of the City of New York, 27:628, Nov. 1972. 6237

Shannon, J. P. "Grand Jury: True Tribunal of the People or Administrative Agency of the Prosecutor?" New Mexico Law Review, 2:141, July 1972. 6238

Solowey, F. J. "Grand Jury and Past--Watergate America." Trial, 10:32, Nov., Dec. 1974. 6239

Sperlich, P. W., and Jaspovice, M. "Grand Juries, Grand Jurors and the Constitution." Hastings Constitutional Law Quarterly, 1:63, spring 1974. 6240

"Unexcited View of United States v. Calandra." Chicago-Kent Law Review, 51:212, summer 1974. 6241

"United States v. Dionisio: The Grand Jury and the Fourth Amendment." Columbia Law Review, 73:1145, May 1973. 6242

"Use of Grand Jury Testimony to Impeach Credibility at Trial." Loyola Law Review, 18:468, 1971-72. 6243

G. COMMENCEMENT OF CRIMINAL PROSECUTION

(1) INDICTMENTS AND INFORMATION

Alexander, R. P., and Portman, S. "Grand Jury Indictment Versus Prosecution by Information--An Equal Protection--Due Process Issue." Hastings Law Journal, 25:997, March 1974. 6244

"Criminal Law--Misdemeanor Indictment Cannot Be Constructively Amended." Fordham Law Review, 43:648, March 1975. 6245

"Criminal Law--Sufficiency of Indictments in Statutory Language." North Carolina Law Review, 35:118, Dec. 1956. 6246

"Criminal Law--Uniform Traffic Ticket Held Insufficient As An Information Upon Which a Misdemeanor Conviction May Be Based [People v. Scott (NY) 143 NE. 2d 901]." New York Law Forum, R, 244, April 1958. 6247

"Criminal Procedure--Constitutionality of Short Form Indictment." Louisiana Law Review, 18:734, June 1958. 6248

Gaines, L. P. "Complaints, Information, and Grand Jury Indictments." Chicago Bar Record, 41:456, June 1960. 6249

"Grand Jury Indictment Based on Incompetent Evidence." California Law Review, 43:859, Dec. 1955. United States v. Costello 221 F. 2d 668 (1955); admission of incompetent evidence at the inquest is not a ground for dismissing the indictment. 6250

"Information of Complaint: A Case Under the Dogs Act, 1871." Journal of Criminal Law. (English) 25:151, April-June 1960. 6251

"Initiation of Prosecution by Information--Leave of Court or Preliminary Examination?" Montana Law Review, 25:135, fall 1963. 6252

Johnson, D. D., and Ammer, W. "Waiver of Indictment by Grand Jury." Ohio Bar, 35:1, Jan. 1, 1962. 6253

"Joinder of Substantive Offenses and Perjury in One Indictment." Journal of Criminal Law and Criminology, 66:44, March 1975. 6254

Kaufman, I. R. "Grand Jury: Sword and Shield." Atlantic, 209: 54, April 1962. It is the "citizen's personal entry into government and justice." 6255

"Kentucky Constitutional Limits and Proposed Changes in the Use of the Information." Kentucky Law Journal, 47:51, summer 1959. 6256

"New Waiver in Texas Criminal Procedure." Baylor Law Review, 24:635, fall 1972. 6257

Newman, Donald J. "Pleading Guilty for Considerations: A Study of Bargain Justice." The Journal of Criminal Law, Criminology and Police Science, 46:780, March-April 1956. 6258

Oberer, W. E. "Deadly Weapon Doctrine--Common Law Origin." Howard Law Review, 75:1565, June 1962. 6259

Orfield, L. B. "Indictment and Information in Federal Criminal Procedure." Syracuse Law Review, 13:14, 218, 389, fall 1961--spring 1962. 6260

"Preliminary Hearing Versus the Grand Jury Indictment: Wasteful Nonsense of Criminal Jurisprudence." University of Florida Law Review, 26:825, summer 1974. 6261

Scigliano, R. G. "Grand Jury, the Information, and the Judicial Inquiry." Oregon Law Review, 38:303, June 1959. 6262

"Special Appearance in California." Stanford Law Review, 10:711, July 1958. Analyzes distinctions presently drawn between special and general appearances and examines problems which may require additional legislation. 6263

Watson, K. T. "Information or Complaint." Law Journal, 110:216, April 1; May 6, 1960. 6264

Watt, R. C. "Information or Complaint." Law Journal, 111:70, Feb. 3, 1961. 6265

Wright, G. S. D. "Defective Information Gambit." Criminal Law Quarterly, 1:332, Nov. 1958. 6266

Wright, K. E. "Use of Prerogative Writs in Attacking Inferior Court Rulings on Motions to Quash Defective Informations and Indictments." Criminal Law Quarterly, 16:178, Feb. 1974. 6267

(2) PLEADINGS

"Acquittal Rates and Not Guilty Pleas: What do the Statistics Mean?" Criminal Law Reporter, 1974:401, July 1974. 6268

"Alabama Pleading--Change in Party's Designation by Amendment: Is This an Entire Change of Parties?" Alabama Law Review, 15:67, fall 1962. 6269

Albrethsen, H. "Scope of the Plea of Former Conviction or Acquittal in Idaho." Idaho Law Review, 2:58, fall 1965. 6270

"Amended Complaints: Power of Court to Allow an Amendment Which Defeats Jurisdiction." California Law Review, 43:352, May 1955. In Thomasian v. Superior Court 122 Cal. App. 2d 322; it was decided that the municipal court had the power to allow the amendment which would change jurisdiction to the superior court. The District Court of Appeal held that the power does exist. 6271

"Amendment of Pleadings." Law Times, 227:141, March 13, 1959; Scottish Law Review, 77:21, Feb. 1961. 6272

Arafat, I., and McCahery, K. "Insanity Defense and the Juror." Drake Law Review, 33:538, June 1973. 6273

Bakes, R. E. "Appellate Procedure--An Evolutionary Backwater." Idaho Law Review, 10:117, spring 1974. 6274

Barton, P. S. "Abuse of Process as a Plea in Bar of Trial." Criminal Law Quarterly, 15:437, Aug. 1973. 6275

Bein, R. H. "Implementation of Kellett's Command: Joinder of Misdemeanors and Felonies in Superior Court." San Diego Law Review, 7:1, Jan. 1970. 6276

Bishop, A. N. "Guilty Pleas in Texas." Baylor Law Review, 24:301, summer 1972. 6277

Bishop, H. H. "Present Concepts of Pleadings." Texas Bar Journal, 17:457, Aug. 1954. 6278

Bradley, J. "Pleading the Statute of Limitations in Oklahoma." Oklahoma Bar Association Journal, 28:673, May 25, 1957. 6279

Casey, O. L. "Form and Content of Pleadings." Mississippi Bar Journal, 30:373, Aug. 1959. 6280

Cogan, N. H. "Guilty Pleas: Weak Limbs in the 'Broken Chain'." Criminal Law Bulletin, 10:149, March 1974. 6281

"Competence to Plead Guilty: A New Standard." Duke Law Journal, 1974:149, March 1974. 6282

"Convictions of Unincluded Lesser Offenses: Informal Amendments and Plea Bargains." Hastings Law Journal, 25:1075, March 1974. 6283

Dershowitz, A. "Doing Time; Reducing Sentence by Plea Bargaining." Harper, 248:8, Jan. 1974. 6284

Desiderio, J., Jr., and Dinoso, F. P. "Rules Regarding Demurrer in the Evidence in Civil and Criminal Cases." Philadelphia Law Journal, 25:541, June 1950. 6285

"Entrapment--A Call for the Elimination of the Ninth Circuit Prohibition Against Pleading Inconsistent Defenses." Southwestern University Law Review, 4:121, spring 1972. 6286

Epstein, R. A. "Pleading and Presumptions." University of Chicago Law Review, 40:556, spring 1973. 6287

Erickson, W. H. "Finality of a Plea of Guilty." Notre Dame Lawyer, 48:835, April 1973. 6288

Franck, L. J. "Practice and Procedure in Mississippi: An Ancient Recipe for Modern Reform." Mississippi Law Journal, 43:287, 1972. 6289

Fraser, G. B. "Inconsistent Theories and Facts." Oklahoma Law Review, 25:404, Aug. 1972. 6290

Goodman, M. J. "Amendments of Pleadings--A Reprise." New Law Journal, 120:473, May 21, 1970. 6291

Guiliani, A. "Influence of Rhetoric on the Law of Evidence and Pleadings." Juridical Review, 1962:216, Dec. 1962. 6292

"Guilty Plea in South Dakota." South Dakota Law Review, 15:66, winter, 1970. 6293

Hallworth, G. L. "More Justice to Come? The Use of the Guilty

Plea." America, 122:390, April 11, 1970. 6294

"Improper Choice of Law Affirmed Where Proper Law Is Overlooked at Trial." Stanford Law Review, 14:162, Dec. 1961. Jannenga v. Nationwide Life Ins. Co. 288 F. 2d 169 (D.C. Cir. 1961). Since a federal district court is not bound to apply the proper law on its own initiative, a case will not be remanded unless injustice results from failure to apply the correct law. Reversal for failure to apply the proper law should be governed by a uniform federal rule. 6295

"Inconsistent Defenses." Oklahoma Law Review, 9:204, May 1956. 6296

"Is the Accused Insane? Twelve Layman Shouldn't Decide." Texas Southern University Law Review, 2:195, winter 1973. 6297

"Joinder of Cases of Action, Parties and Defense." Oklahoma Law Review, 3:456, Nov. 1950. 6298

"Joinder of Crimes in the Same Indictment." West Virginia Law Review, 57:196, May 1955. 6299

"Joinder of Parties and Causes--Alleging Case Against Masters and Trespass Against Servant in Same Count. [Sebley v. Odum (Alabama) 58 So. 20 896]." Alabama Law Review, 4:303, spring 1952. 6300

Lewin, N. "Bargaining with Federal Prosecutors: Plea Bargaining." New Republic, 169:12, Oct. 6, 1973. 6301

Lyons, C., Jr. "Proposed Rules of Practice in Alabama." Alabama Lawyer, 33:285, July 1972. 6302

McBride, R. L. "Law and Fact in the Judicial Process." Ohio Opinions, 5:193, March-July 1958. 6303

McDonald, R. W. "Alternative Pleading in the United States." Columbia Law Review, 52:443, April-May 1952. The extent to which the various jurisdictions of the U.S. accord the plaintiff the right to assert his factual contentions in the alternative and the right of the defendant to rely on alternative defenses. Discusses methods of avoiding abuse of an unlimited right to plead alternatively. 6304

McEwen, J. M. "Criminal Pleadings in Florida." University of Florida Law Review, 16:248, fall 1963. 6305

Nichols, L. C. "Accusatory Pleadings Framed in Statutory Language--Requirement of Notice to Defendant." Lincoln Law Review, 7:64, Dec. 1971. 6306

"Not Looking the Complaint in the Face: Judicial Notice of Demurrer." *University of San Francisco Law Review*, 4:433, April 1970. 6307

Owens, C. "Plea Bargaining ... Agreeing ... Recommending?" *Brief Case*, 26:55, Dec. 1967. 6308

"Particulars and Technicalities." *South African Law Journal*, 76:36, February, 1959. 6309

"Personal Jurisdiction in Nebraska: The Need for a Long-Arm Statute." *Nebraska Law Review*, 45:166, Jan. 1966. 6310

"Personal Jurisdiction Over Non-Residents: Some Statutory Developments." *William and Mary Law Review*, 7:146, Jan. 1966. 6311

"Pleading and Demurrer Problems Re-Examined--New Proposals in New York." *Columbia Law Review*, 60:115, Nov. 1960. Proposed revision of the New York Civil Practice Act and Rules of Civil Procedure includes a new general pleading rule in terms of "fair notice" cases, a novel approach to the demurrer problem; evaluated for procedural reform. 6312

"Pleading in Search of Justice." *Indiana Legal Forum*, 2:123, fall 1968. 6313

"Pleading--Joinder of Defendants--Use of and/or to Join Defendants in Joint Contract Action Not Demurrable and Does Not Exonerate All Defendants After Directed Verdict for One." *Alabama Law Review*, 22:223, fall 1969. 6314

"Pleading: Joint Demurrer Rule." *Oklahoma Law Review*, 9:113, Feb. 1966. 6315

"Pleading: Pleading and the Doctrine of Res Ipsa Loquitur." *Oklahoma Law Review*, 26:100, Feb. 1973. 6316

"Pleading Under the Michigan General Court Rules of 1963." *Wayne Law Review*, 8:542, summer 1962. 6317

"Pleadings and Answers." *St. Louis University Law Journal*, 3:419, fall 1955. 6318

"Post Conviction Guilty Plea Withdrawals." *Louisiana Law Review*, 33:439, spring 1973. 6319

"Procedure Demurrer--Necessity of Specificity in Objections [Greenville Cabinet Co. v. Hauff (Tennessee), 263 SW 2d 526]." *Tennessee Law Review*, 23:440, June 1954. 6320

Reid, J. "From Common Sense to Common Law to Charles Doe: The Evolution of Pleading in New Hampshire." *New Hampshire Bar Journal*, 1:27, April 1959. 6321

Reppy, A. "Demurrer--At Common Law, Under Modern Codes, Practice Acts, and Rules of Civil Procedure." New York Law Forum, 3:1, 175, Jan.-April 1957. 6322

"Right to Amend." Scottish Law Review, 67:212, Aug. 1951. 6323

"Right to Change Defense of Claim by Amendments to the Pleadings." Nebraska Law Review, 36:591, June 1957. 6324

Rothblatt, H. B., and Leroy, D. H. "Motion in Liminie in Criminal Trials: A Technique for the Exclusion of Prejudicial Evidence." Kentucky Law Journal, 60:611, spring 1972. 6325

Rubinstein, A. "Bad on Its Face." Public Law, 1964:256, autumn 1964. 6326

Ryall, V. "Information Defective and Bad." Australia Law Journal, 26:360, Nov. 1952. 6327

Salhany, R. E. "Duplicity: Is the Rule Still Necessary?" Criminal Law Quarterly, 6:205, Nov. 1963. 6328

Sarpy, L. "Decisions on Pleading and Practice July 1966 Through June 1967." Loyola Law Review, 14:337, 1967-68. 6329

"Simplified v. Long-form Indictments." Albany Law Review, 20:38, January 1956. 6330

Stern, I. J. "Variance in Medical Proofs--What Constitutes." Pennsylvania Bar Association Quarterly, 21:54, Oct. 1949. 6331

Sugar, M. E. "Duplicitous Allegations in Indictments." West Virginia Law Review, 58:18, December 1955. 6332

Tate, A., Jr. "Amendment of Pleading in Louisiana." Tulane Law Review, 43:211, Feb. 1969. 6333

Tocher, J. P. "Process and Pleadings." Massachussetts Law Quarterly, 48:137, June 1963. 6334

Traser, G. B. "Pleading: Joinder of Claims." Oklahoma Law Review, 15:82, Feb. 1962. 6335

_______. "Pleading: Testing the Petition During Trial." Oklahoma Law Review, 15:85, Feb. 1962. 6336

"Unavoidable Accident, Act of God, Sudden Emergency." Oklahoma Law Review, 9:21, May 1956. 6337

Vickery, A. A. "Providency of Guilty Pleas: Does the Military Really Care?" Military Law Review, 58:209, fall 1972. 6338

"Vitiation of Compulsory Joinder by Rule 42." South Texas Law

Journal, 3:163, winter 1957. 6339

"Waiver of Error in Overruling a Demurrer [Cleary v. Sewell (Oklahoma) 299 P. 2d 524]." Oklahoma Law Review, 10:210, May 1957. 6340

Walker, A. G. "Written Pleadings." Scottish Law Review, 79:161, Sept. 1963. 6341

Weltner, C. L. "Right to Amend--Case of Legislative Liberty Versus Judicial Conservatism." Georgia Bar Journal, 12:127, Nov. 1949. 6342

Williams, G. "Venue and the Ambit of Criminal Law." Law Quarterly Review, 81:395, 518, July-Oct. 1965. 6343

Wood, R. L. "Some Observations on Lesser Included Offenses." Military Law Review, 30:120, Oct. 1965. 6344

Zimroth, P. L. "101,000 Defendants Were Convicted of Misdemeanors Last Year. 98,000 of Them Had Pleaded Guilty to Get Reduced Sentences." New York Times Magazine, May 28, 1972. 6345

H. PRETRIAL PROCEDURES

Adams, J. E. "Pretrial Discovery." Criminal Law Review, 1966: 602, Nov. 1966. 6346

"Administration of Pretrial Release and Detention: A Proposal for Unification." Yale Law Journal, 83:153, Nov. 1973. 6347

Alexander, R. C. "Discussing Medical Issues in Opening Statements for the Defense." Defense Law Journal, 14:633, 1965. 6348

"Amendments to the Federal Rules of Criminal Procedure--Expansion of Discovery." Journal of Criminal Law and Criminology, 66: 23, March 1975. 6349

Arens, R.; Granfield, D.; and Susman, J. "Jurors, Jury Charges and Insanity." Catholic University Law Review, 14:1, Jan. 1965. 6350

"Arraignment, Pre-Trial Motions and Pleas in Virginia." Washington and Lee Law Review, 22:336, fall 1965. 6351

Austin, A. D. "Prejudice and Change of Venue." Dickinson Law Review, 68:401, summer 1964. 6352

"Basic Survey of Work Product in Federal and State Jurisdictions in

Civil and Criminal Proceedings." Tennessee Law Review, 35: 474, spring 1968. 6353

"Bibliography: Criminal Discovery." Tulsa Law Journal, 5:207, May 1968. 6354

Bowmer, J. D.; Jones, L. E., Jr.; and Millen, J. H. "Charge in Criminal Cases." Baylor Law Review, 12:261, summer 1960. 6355

Bruce, J. W. "Pretrial Investigation: Some Practical Considerations." JAG Journal, 26:225, spring 1972. 6356

Carter, R. M. "Diversion of Offenders." Federal Probation, 36: 31, Dec. 1972. 6357

"Change of Venue in Federal Courts: New Restrictions Upon Choice of Transferer Forum." Northwestern University Law Review, 54:489, Sept.-Oct. 1959. 6358

"Civil Rights--Section 1983--Jailer Held Liable for Unlawful Detention Despite Lack of Malice, Improper Motive or Negligence." New York Law Review, 44:1154, Dec. 1969. 6359

Clark, T. C. "Omnibus Hearing in State and Federal Courts." Cornell Law Review, 59:761, June 1974. 6360

Colson, W. R. "Final Argument." Mississippi Law Journal, 36:500, Oct. 1965. 6361

"Comments to the Jury on the Defendant's Failure to Testify." Dickinson Law Review, 64:164, Jan. 1960. 6362

"Commitment of the Mentally Ill in South Carolina." South Carolina Law Quarterly, 5:559, June 1953. 6363

"Competency to Stand Trial--Pretrial Procedures." Southwestern Law Journal, 22:857, Dec. 1968. 6364

Cooney, R. J. "People v. Paul Crump: Closing Argument for the State." Trial Lawyer's Guide, 6:7, Aug. 1962. 6365

Corboy, P. H. "Pattern Jury Instruction--Their Function and Effectiveness." American Bar Association Section of Insurance Negligence and Compensation Law, 1964:119, 1964. 6366

"Criminal Contempt: Federal Court's Power to Dismiss Proceeding Before Trial." Columbia Law Review, 66:182, Jan. 1966. Based on the premise that since a criminal contempt is a "sui generis proceeding" for the protection of judicial integrity, the court has the "power and authority" to dismiss proceedings which they have initiated. 6367

"Criminal Discovery." St. Louis University Law Journal, 10:518, summer 1966. 6368

"Criminal Discovery." Chicago-Kent Law Review, 51:663, 1974. 6369

"Criminal Discovery in Louisiana." Tulane Law Review, 42:620, April 1968. 6370

"Criminal Law: Instructions on Manslaughter: When?" Oklahoma Law Review, 17:327, Aug. 1964. 6371

"Criminal Law: Pre-Trial Discovery--The Right of an Indigent's Counsel to Inspect Police Reports." St. Louis University Law Journal, 14:310, winter 1969. 6372

"Criminal Procedure, Depositions and Change of Venue." Temple Law Quarterly, 36:326, spring 1963. 6373

"Criminal Procedure--Discovery--Criminal Witness Discovery Under Wyoming Rule." Land and Water Law Review, 10:293, 1975. 6374

"Criminal Procedure--Due Process--Defendant's Right to a Lineup As a Means of Discovery." Wayne Law Review, 21:991, March 1975. 6375

"Criminal Procedure--Venue Requirements for the Prosecuting Parish (State v. Bloomenstiel [LA]) 106 S. 2d 288)." Louisiana Law Review, 20:756, June 1960. 6376

Cunningham, T. J. "Should Instructions Go Into the Jury Room?" Journal of the State Bar of California, 33:278, May-June 1958. Discusses present inconsistent practices, recently proposed revisions, arguments in favor of giving written instructions to the jury, and arguments in opposition. 6377

Curran, W. J. "Hospitalization of the Mentally Ill." North Carolina Law Review, 31:274, April 1953. 6378

Dershowitz, A. M. "Origins of Preventive Confinement in Anglo-American Law--Part I: The English Experience." University of Cincinnati Law Review, 43:1, 1974. 6379

________. "Preventive Confinement: A Suggested Framework for Constitutional Analysis." Texas Law Review, 51:1277, Nov. 1973. 6380

"Disclosure of an Informant's Identity-The Substantive and Procedural Balance Tests." Albany Law Review, 39:561, 1975. 6381

"Discovery in Criminal Cases: Denial to Misdemeanants As a Violation of Due Process and Equal Protection." Journal of Criminal Law and Criminology, 65:181, June 1974. 6382

"Discovery of an Attorney's Work Product in Subsequent Litigation." Duke Law Journal, 1974:799, Sept. 1974. 6383

Dunn, V. S. "Venue and Jurisdiction in the Circuit Court." Mississippi Law Journal, 30:352, Aug. 1959. 6384

Duree, J. R. "Defense Counsel and the Pre-Trial Investigation." Air Force JAG Law Review, 9:14, July-August 1967. 6385

English, H. G. "Opening and Closing to a Jury." Practical Lawyer, 9:69, May 1963. Enumerates the essential steps in a logical sequence in the opening and closing statements to a jury. 6386

"Evidence--Improper Argument by Solicitor (Cornett v. State (Georgia) 128 SE. 2d 317)." Georgia Bar Journal, 285:448, May 1963. 6387

"Expanding Defendant's Discovery: The Jencks Act at Pretrial Hearings." Buffalo Law Review, 24:419, winter 1975. 6388

"Failure to Disclose Names and Addresses of Witnesses in Discovery Proceedings." Montana Law Review, 35:144, winter 1974. 6389

"Fair Trial and Free Press: Preliminary Hearing--Gateway to Prejudice." Law and Social Order, 1973. 6390

"Final Argument in Iowa." Drake Law Review, 15:115, May 1966. 6391

"Florida's Unique Dismissal--The Non-Suit." University of Florida Law Review, 13:105, spring 1960. 6392

Frank, J. P. "Pretrial Conferences and Discovery--Disclosure or Surprise?" Insurance Law Journal, 1965:661, Nov. 1965. 6393

Friedman, H. G. "Some Jurisprudential Considerations in Developing an Administrative Law for the Criminal Pre-Trial Process." Journal of Urban Law, 51:433, Feb. 1974. 6394

"Function of the Preliminary Hearing in Federal Pretrial Procedure." Yale Law Journal, 83:771, March 1974. 6395

Galiher, R. W. "Defendant's Opening Statement." Insurance Counsel Journal, 31:478, July 1964. 6396

Gardner, E., and Carlisle, M. "Preliminary Inquiries--The Case for Reform." Criminal Law Review, 1966:490, Sept. 1966. 6397

Gordon, D. M. "Renewal of Motion After Dismissal." University of British Columbia Law Review, 1:659, April 1963. 6398

Hails, F. G. "Summary Hearing in Defendant's Absence." Justice of the Peace, 114:629, Nov. 4, 1950. 6399

"Handbook for Effective Pretrial Procedure." Federal Rules Decisions, 37:255, July 1965. 6400

"Has Anyone Here Seen Brady?: Discovery in Criminal Cases." Criminal Law Bulletin, 9:325, May 1973. 6401

Holladay, D. C. "Pretrial Mental Examinations Under Military Law." Air Force Law Review, 16:14, fall 1974. 6402

Hooper, A. "Discovery in Criminal Cases." Canadian Bar Review, 50:445, Sept. 1972. 6403

"Implementing Brady v. Maryland: An Argument for a Pretrial Open File Policy." University of Cincinnati Law Review, 43:889, 1974. 6404

"Inadequacy of Pre-Trial Discovery in Missouri Criminal Cases." Missouri Law Review, 31:424, summer 1966. 6405

Jenswold, J. F. "Pre-Trial Confluences." Wisconsin Bar Bulletin, 38:35, Oct. 1965. 6406

"Judicial Panel and the Conduct of Multidistrict Litigation." Harvard Law Review, 87:1001, March 1974. 6407

"Juvenile Offender's Procedural Rights in the New York Family Court." St. John's Law Review, 41:386, Jan. 1967. 6408

Kendig, D. A. "Procedures for Management of Non-Routine Cases." Hofstra Law Review, 3:701, summer 1975. 6409

Leibowitz, S. S. "Classic Jury Charge." Trial Lawyer's Quarterly, 2:18, spring 1965. 6410

Levine, M. "Closing Argument." Plaintiffs Advocate, 7:8, Jan. 1963. 6411

________. "Summation--Inflammatory or Proper Argument?" Plaintiff's Advocate, 7:28, July 1963. 6412

"Louisiana and Criminal Discovery." Louisiana Law Review, 35:596, summer 1973. 6413

McBurney, F. W., Jr. "Written Interrogatories: A Pre-Trial Discovery of Wisconsin Needs." Wisconsin Bar Bulletin, 39:30, Oct. 1966. 6414

McDermott, J. T. "Transferee Judge--The Unsung Hero of Multidistrict Litigation." Montana Law Review, 35:15, winter 1974. 6415

McHugh, J. J. "Change of Venue: Its Application in Military Law." JAG Journal, 15:49, April-May 1961. 6416

McInerney, D. "Discovery and Use of Grand Jury Minutes." Antitrust Law Symposium, 1966:91, 1966. 6417

"Manual of Jury Instructions in Federal Criminal Cases." Federal Rules Decisions, 36:457, April 1965. Applicable principles of law, supplemented by comments and citations of recent cases analyzing the rules of law which they embody. 6418

Masington, R. S. "Venue in the Federal Courts--The Problem of the Inconvenient Forum." University of Miami Law Review, 15:237, spring 1961. 6419

Meyer, H. H. "Constitutionality of Pretrial Detention." Georgia Law Journal, 60:1139, 1381, May-June 1972. 6420

Miller, F. W., and Dawson, R. O. "Non-Use of the Preliminary Examination: A Study of Current Practices." Wisconsin Law Review, 1964:252, March 1964. 6421

Moss, E. C. "Criminal Discovery: California's Treatment of Pretrial Notice of Alibi." Southwestern University Law Review, 7:338, summer 1975. 6422

Nakell, B. "Criminal Discovery for the Defense and the Prosecution--The Developing Constitutional Considerations." North Carolina Law Review, 50:437, April 1972. 6423

Napley, D. "The Case for Preliminary Inquiries." Criminal Law Review, 1966:480, Sept. 1966. 6424

"Need for Liberalized Rules of Discovery in Criminal Procedure." Marquette Law Review, 49:736, May 1966. 6425

Neubauer, D. W. "After the Arrest: The Changing Decision in Prairie City." Law and Social Review, 8:495, spring 1974. 6426

"Omnibus Hearing: A Proposal for California Criminal Pretrial Motion Procedure." Pacific Law Journal, 4:861, July 1973. 6427

"Omnibus Proceedings: Classification of Discovery in the Federal Courts and Other Benefits." St. Mary's Law Journal, 6:386, summer 1974. 6428

Orfield, L. B. "Arraignment in Federal Criminal Procedure." Louisiana Law Review, 20:1, Dec. 1959. 6429

Osburn, J. W. "Pretrial Discovery Under the Oregon Criminal Procedure Code." Willamette Law Journal, 10:145, spring 1974. 6430

Parnell, A. W. "Uniform Jury Instructions." Wisconsin Bar Bulletin, 32:58, Aug. 1959. 6431

Petersen, T. K. "Dade County Pretrial Intervention Project: Formalization of the Diversion Function and Its Impact Upon the Criminal Justice System." University of Miami Law Review, 28:86, fall 1973. 6432

Pious, R. M. "Pretrial and Nontrial in the Lower Criminal Courts." Current History, 61:20, June 1971. 6433

Pollack, M. "Pretrial Procedures More Effectively Handled." Federal Rules Decisions, 65:475, April 1975. 6434

Portman, S. "'To Detain or Not to Detain'?--A Review of the Background, Current Proposals and Debate on Preventive Detention." Santa Clara Law, 10:224, spring 1970. 6435

"Preclusion Sanction--A Violation of the Constitutional Right to Present a Defense." Yale Law Journal, 81:1342, June 1972. 6436

"Preliminary Examination Potential." Marquette Law Review, 58: 159, 1975. 6437

"Preliminary Hearings--The Case for Revival." University of Colorado Law Review, 39:580, summer 1967. 6438

"Pretrial Conference Procedures." South Carolina Law Review, 26: 481, Dec. 1974. 6439

"Pretrial Diversion from the Criminal Process." Yale Law Journal, 83:827, March 1974. 6440

"Pretrial Identification Confrontations." Mississippi Law Journal, 45:489, April 1974. 6441

"Pretrial Identification Procedures: The Expanded Duty to Disclose Favorable Evidence." Notre Dame Lawyer, 50:508, Feb. 1975. 6442

"Pretrial Mental Examinations in Maine: Are They Mechanisms for Compelling Self-Incrimination?" Maine Law Review, 18:96, 1966. 6443

Prettyman, E. B. "Jury Instructions--First or Last?" American Bar Association Journal, 46:1066, Oct. 1960. Suggests that instructions to the jury be given at the beginning of a trial; present procedure makes much of the trial mere "mumbo jumbo" since the jurors are not in a position to listen intelligently to matters that they are expected to decide. 6444

"Pugh v. Rainwater (483 F. 2d 778): Spotlight on the Preliminary Hearing." Virginia Law Review, 60:540, March 1974. 6445

"Recommended Procedure in Criminal Pre-Trials." Federal Rules Decisions, 37:97, May 1965. Rules and proceedings for handling of voluminous documentary evidence and the resolution of procedural problems. 6446

Selzer, M. L. "Paranoid Mental Illnesses and the Courts." Michigan State Bar Journal, 45:12, Aug. 1966. 6447

Shapiro, I. "Jury Selection in Criminal Term, Supreme Court." Brooklyn Bar, 15:235, May 1964. 6448

Shayne, N. T. "Attorney's View: Calendar Practice-What a Waste." Hofstra Law Review, 3:723, summer 1975. 6449

Solomon, G. J. "Techniques for Shortening Trials." Federal Rules Decisions, 65:485, April 1975. 6450

"State Statute to Liberalize Criminal Discovery." Harvard Journal on Legislation, 4:105, Dec. 1966. 6451

Stein, J. E. "Your First Criminal Case Appointment." D. C. Bar Journal, 39:56, May-Sept. 1972. 6452

"Territorial Jurisdiction." Mississippi Law Journal, 29:320, May 1958. 6453

Thornton, J. W. "Expanding Videotape Techniques in Pretrial and Trial Advocacy." Forum, 9:105, fall 1973. 6454

Todd, S. M. "Pretrial Conference Is Here to Stay." Journal of the Bar Association of the State of Kansas, 35:97, summer 1966. 6455

Traynor, R. J. "Devils of Due Process in Criminal Detection, Detention, and Trial." Catholic University Law Review, 16:1, Sept. 1966. Major judicial decisions on due process and their far reaching consequences; cases cited are Mapp v. Ohio, Gideon v. Wainwright, Escobedo v. Illinois, Malloy v. Hogan and the McNabb-Mallory Rule. 6456

"Two Dismissal Rule." Wyoming Law Journal, 12:276, spring 1958. 6457

"Untimely Ends in County Courts." Solicitor's Journal, 103:950, Dec. 4, 1959. 6458

"Use and Disclosure of Presentee Reports in the United States." Federal Rules Decisions, 47:225, Oct. 1969. 6459

"Vermont's Experiment in Criminal Discovery." *American Bar Association Journal*, 53:732, Aug. 1972. 6460

Wald, M. S. "May Day Revisited." *Criminal Law Bulletin*, 10:377, June-July-Aug. 1974. 6461

"Want of Prosecution and Iowa Rule 215:1." *Iowa Law Review*, 49: 876, spring 1964. 6462

White, P. S. "Some Approaches to the Instructional Problem." *Nebraska Law Review*, 40:413, April 1961. 6463

Whyte, J. P. "Final Argument: Conduct of Virginia Counsel." *William and Mary Law Review*, 5:1, 1964. 6464

Wiehofen, Herbert. "Improving Legal Procedure for Hospitalizing the Mentally Ill." *Dicta*, 31:81, March 1954. 6465

Wilder, M. S. "Prosecution Discovery and the Privilege Against Self Incrimination." *American Criminal Law Quarterly*, 6:3, fall 1967. 6466

Williams, G. "Venue and the Ambit of Criminal Law." *Law Quarterly Review*, 81:276, April 1965. 6467

Willis, W. "Inroad of Pre-Trial Discovery on Attorney-Client Privilege." *Antitrust Law Symposium*, 1966:109, 1966. 6468

Wilson, P. E. "New Approaches to Pretrial Detention." *Journal of the Bar Association of the State of Kansas*, 39:13, spring 1970. 6469

Woodhouse, J. "Commitment Procedures in Colorado." *Dicta*, 29: 273, Aug. 1952. 6470

Yellowlees, H. "Guilty But Insane." *Journal of Forensic Medicine*, 1:211, April-June 1954. 6471

J. PLEA BARGAINING

Bishop, A. N. "Broken Bargains." *Journal of Urban Law*, 50:231, Nov. 1972. 6472

_______. "Guilty Pleas in the Eastern Midwest." *Ohio Northern Law Review*, 2:258, 1974. 6473

_______. "Waivers in Pleas of Guilty." *Federal Rules Decisions*, 60:513, Jan. 1974. 6474

"Constitutionality of an Equivocal Guilty Plea." *Gonzaga Law Re-*

view, 8:332, spring 1973. 6475

Cooper, H. H. A. "Plea Bargaining: A Comparative Analysis." New York University Journal of International Law and Politics, 5:427, winter 1972. 6476

"Criminal Law--Enforcement of Plea Bargaining Agreements." North Carolina Law Review, 51:602, Jan. 1973. 6477

"Criminal Law--Federal Rules of Criminal Procedure--Discretion of Court to Refuse a Guilty Plea Under Rule 11." Wayne Law Review, 20:1359, Sept. 1974. 6478

"Criminal Law--Plea Bargaining--Full Disclosure of Any Plea-Inducing Promise Should Be Incorporated Into the Record." Hofstra Law Review, 3:819, summer 1975. 6479

"Criminal Law: Plea Negotiations--Legitimizing the Agreement Process." Oklahoma Law Review, 27:487, summer 1974. 6480

Dean, J. M. "Illegitimacy of Plea Bargaining." Federal Probation, 38:18, Sept. 1974. 6481

DonVito, P. A. "Experiment in the Use of Court Statistics." Judicature, 56:56, Aug.-Sept. 1972. 6482

"Effective Assistance of Counsel in Plea Bargaining: What Is the Standard?" Duquesne Law Review, 12:321, winter 1973. 6483

"Elimination of Plea Bargaining in Black Hawk County: A Case Study." Iowa Law Review, 60:1053, April 1975. 6484

Ferguson, G. A. "Role of the Judge in Plea Bargaining." Criminal Law Quarterly, 15:26, Dec. 1972. 6485

Fischer, D. A. "Beyond Santobello--Remedies for Reneged Plea Bargains." University of San Fernando Valley Law Review, 2:121, summer 1973. 6486

Gallagher, K. "Judicial Participation in Plea Bargaining: A Search for New Standards." Howard Civil Rights Law Review, 9:29, Jan. 1974. 6487

Goldstein, J. "For Harold Laswell: Some Reflections on Human Dignity Informed Consent and the Plea Bargain." Yale Law Journal, 84:683, March 1975. 6488

Heberling, J. L. "Judicial Review of the Guilty Plea." Lincoln Law Review, 7:137, June 1972. 6489

"Judicial Discretion to Reject Negotiated Pleas." Georgetown Law Journal, 63:241, Oct. 1974. 6490

Klein, J. F. "Habitual Offender Legislation and the Bargaining Process." Criminal Law Quarterly, 15:417, Aug. 1973. 6491

Mather, L. M. "Some Determinants of the Method of Case Disposition: Decision-Making by Public Defenders in Los Angeles." Law and Society Review, 8:187, winter 1974. 6492

Newman, D. J. "Agnew Plea Bargain." Criminal Law Bulletin, 10:85, Jan.-Feb. 1974. 6493

"Plea Bargain in Historical Perspective." Buffalo Law Review, 23: 499, winter 1974. 6494

"Plea Bargaining Mishaps-The Possibility of Collaterally Attacking the Resultant Plea of Guilty." Journal of Criminal Law and Criminology, 65:170, June 1974. 6495

"Plea Bargaining." American Journal of Criminal Law, 2:187, April 1972. 6496

"Restructuring the Plea Bargain." Yale Law Journal, 82:286, winter 1972. 6497

"Supreme Court's Changed View of the Guilty Plea." Memphis State University Law Review, 4:79, fall 1973. 6498

Thomas, E. S. "Plea Bargaining: The Clash Between Theory and Practice." Loyola Law Review, 20:303, 1973-74. 6499

Wheatley, J. R. "Plea Bargaining--A Case for Its Continuance." Massachusetts Law Quarterly, 59:31, spring 1974. 6500

"Withdrawal of Negotiated Pleas: Quid Pro Quo from Defendants." Southwestern University Law Review, 5:124, spring 1973. 6501

K. TRIAL JURORS

Abrahams, G. "Legal Attitude of Jurors." Solicitor's Journal, 110:799, Oct. 28, 1966. 6502

"After the Verdict: May Counsel Interrogate Jurors?" Catholic University Law Review, 17:465, summer 1968. 6503

Ames, M. L. "Ethics of Post Trial Interviews with Jurors." Brooklyn Barrister, 20:202, May 1969. 6504

Arafat, I., and McCahery, K. "Insanity Defense and the Juror." Drake Law Review, 33:538, June 1973. 6505

"Bias in the Jury Box." Time, 95:61, April 6, 1970. 6506

Broeder, D. W. "Importance of the Scapegoat in Jury Trial Cases: Some Preliminary Reflections." Duquesne University Law Review, 4:513, summer 1966. 6507

"Case for Black Juries." Yale Law Journal, 79:531, Jan. 1970. 6508

"Court Control Over the Voir Dire Examination of Prospective Jurors." DePaul Law Review, 15:107, autumn-winter 1965. 6509

"Criminal Contempt and Trial by Jury." William and Mary Law Review, 8:76, fall 1966. 6510

"Criminal Procedure--The Selection of Tales. Jurors." Loyola Law Review, 16:228, 1969-70. 6511

Duncan, P. C.; Hendrickson, C. W.; and Morrison, D. J. "What Is Your Verdict?--A Model Jury Argument." Federation of Insurance Counsel Quarterly, 16:8, summer 1966. 6512

Egge, E. "Maturity an Asset for Jury Duty." Harvard Years, 12: 43, Jan. 1972. 6513

"End to Peerless Juries." Time, 92:58, Sept. 27, 1968. 6514

Etzioni, A. "Creating an Imbalance." Trial, 10:11, Nov.-Dec. 1974. 6515

"Fair Jury Selection Procedures." Yale Law Journal, 75:322, Dec. 1965. Cites cases and references to show that no Negroes had served on jury venires over a long period. Congressional legislation suggested by some. To avoid Congressional intervention, the Court should require the states to use fair procedures for selecting veniremen. 6516

"Fair Trial v. Free Press: The Psychological Effect of Pretrial Publicity on the Juror's Ability to Be Impartial: A Plea for Reform." Southern California Law Review, 38:672, 1965. Prejudice created by the news media in the mind of a prospective juror is analyzed and a remedy suggested. 6517

Field, L. "Voir Dire Examination--A Neglected Art." University of Missouri at Kansas City Law Review, 33:171, summer 1965. 6518

Galihor, R. W. "Crisis of the Jury System." Insurance Counsel Journal, 31:589, Oct. 1964; New York State Bar Journal, 34: 439, Oct. 1965. 6519

"Hand-Picking Ends; Federal Court Juries." Senior Scholastic, 92: 22, April 11, 1968. 6520

Head, B. T. "Confessions of a Juror." Federal Rules Decisions, 44:330, July 1968. 6521

Henson, H. E., Jr. "Hung Jury: A Court-Martial Dilemma." Military Law Review, 35:39, Jan. 1967. 6522

Hermann, P. J. "Occupations of Jurors As an Influence on Their Verdict." Forum, 5:150, Jan. 1970. 6523

"Impeachment of Jury Verdicts by Jurors: A Proposal." University of Illinois Law Forum, 1969:388, 1969. 6524

"Is the Accused Insane? Twelve Layman Shouldn't Decide." Texas Southern University Law Review, 2:195, winter 1973. 6525

Jones, A. P. "Preemptory Challenges--Should Rule 233 Be Changed?" Texas Law Review, 45:80, Nov. 1966. 6526

"Juries and Jurors--What Evidence Is Admissible in Impeachment of Verdict by Chance." Southern California Law Review, 6:246, March 1933. By general rule, a jury is not allowed to impeach its own verdict (People v. Azoff 105 Cal. 632). However, in the case People v. DeVoe (123 Cal. App. 233), it was held that the court should have permitted an inquiry as to how the jurors arrived at the verdict and that the court should have decided, as a question of law, whether the verdict was arrived at by a lot or chance. 6527

"Juror Misconduct: Availability of a Hearing on Alleged Illegal View." Washington Law Review, 41:346, April 1966. 6528

"Jury: A Reflection of Prejudices of the Community." Hastings Law Journal, 20:1417, May 1969. 6529

"Jury Discretion and the Unitary Trial Procedure in Capital Cases." Arkansas Law Review, 26:33, spring 1972. 6530

"Jury Selection: The Need for Statutory Reform in Minnesota." Minnesota Law Review, 53:977, April 1969. 6531

"Jury Voir Dire: Useless Delay or Valuable Technique." South Dakota Law Review, 11:306, spring 1966. 6532

Kaufman, I. R. "Judges and Jurors: Recent Developments in Selection of Jurors and Fair Trial--Free Press." University of Colorado Law Review, 41:179, May 1969. 6533

Lindquist, C. A. "Analysis of Juror Selection Procedure in the United States." Temple Law Quarterly, 41:32, fall 1967. 6534

Miech, R. J. "Jury Views in Wisconsin Trials." Gavel, 26:10, Dec. 1965. 6535

Moore, H. A. "Redressing the Imbalance." Trial, 10:11, Nov.-Dec. 1974. 6536

Mossman, A. K. "Justice and Numbers." Trial, 10:11, Nov.-Dec. 1974. 6537

Napley, D. "Jury System." New Law Journal, 116:1620, Dec. 8, 1966. 6538

"Pauper--Short Changed at the Jury Box." West Virginia Law Review, 74:392, Sept. 1972. 6539

"Personality Tests for Prospective Jurors." Kentucky Law Journal, 56:832, summer 1967-68. 6540

"Right to Trial by Jury: Is It Necessary?" DePaul Law Review, 15:398, spring-summer 1966. 6541

Rothblatt, H. B. "Techniques for Jury Selection." Criminal Law Bulletin, 2:14, May 1966. 6542

Rothstein, P. F. "Beacon Theatres and the Constitutional Right to Jury Trial." American Bar Association Journal, 51:1145, Dec. 1965. With reference to Supreme Court 1959 decision in Beacon Theatre Inc. v. Westover (359 U.S. 500), discussed the complexities of determining which actions or issues are legal and which are equitable, on which hangs the right to trial by jury. 6543

Saks, M. J. "Ignorance of Science Is No Excuse." Trial, 10:11, Nov.-Dec. 1974. 6544

Sealy, A. P., and Cornish, W. R. "Jurors and Their Verdicts." Modern Law Review, 36:496, Sept. 1973. 6545

Sparling, J. "Women, Pimps, Blacks, Hippies Need Not Apply; Excerpts from Jury Selection in a Criminal Case." Time, 101:67, June 4, 1973. 6546

Sutzinger, E. F. "Jury System--Elimination, Modification or Improvement?" Federation of Insurance Counsel Quarterly, 15:8, summer 1965. 6547

"Swain v. Alabama (85 Supreme Court 824): A Constitutional Blueprint for the Perpetuation of the All-White Jury." Virginia Law Review, 52:1157, Oct. 1966. 6548

Thompson, E. "Jury. Six Will Do." Trial, 10:11, Nov.-Dec. 1974. 6549

"Trial by Jury." New Law Journal, 116:928, June 9, 1966. 6550

"Trial by Jury in Criminal Cases." Columbia Law Review, 69:419, March 1969. 6551

Tucker, S. W. "Racial Discrimination in Jury Selection in Virginia." Virginia Law Review, 52:736, May 1966. 6552

"Twelve Good Persons and True...." Harvard Civil Rights Law Review, 9:561, May 1974. 6553

"Verdicts--Resort to Determination of Chance As Misconduct of the Jury." Southern California Law Review, 8:163, Jan. 1935. The Mirabito v. San Francisco Dairy Company, 88 Cal. Dec. 180 (1934) case held that: the jurors were not induced to assent to the verdict by a resort to the determination of chance within the meaning of Cal. Code Civ. Proc., 657. 6554

Weiner, S. A. "Civil Jury Trial and the Law--Fact Distinction." California Law Review, 54:1867. The categories of "questions of law" and "questions of fact" are closely discussed in this article as they relate to the respective provinces of the judge and the jurors. 6555

Wolf, R. C. "Trial by Jury: A Sociological Analysis." Wisconsin Law Review, 1966:820, summer 1966. 6556

"Women on Juries." Trans-Action, 9:12, Jan. 1972. 6557

Zeisel, H. "Twelve Is Just." Trial, 10:11, Nov.-Dec. 1974. 6558

L. VERDICTS

"Admissibility of Evidence to Impeach Jury Verdicts." University of Miami Law Review, 22:729, spring 1968. 6559

Arnold, M. S. "Law and Fact in the Medieval Jury Trial: Out of Sight, Out of Mind." American Journal of Legal History, 18: 267, Oct. 1974. 6560

Bagalay, J. E., Jr. "Directed Verdicts and the Right to Trials by Jury in Federal Courts." Texas Law Review, 42:1053, Oct. 1964. 6561

Braybrooke, D. "Logical Character of Verdicts: A Case Study." University of Toronto Law Journal, 22:221, autumn 1972. 6562

Brizius, C. O. "Directed Verdicts on Uncontradicted Testimony." Trial Lawyer's Guide, 3:87, Nov. 1959. 6563

Brown, J. R. "Federal Special Verdicts: The Doubt Eliminated." Federal Rules Decision, 44:338, July 1968. 6564

"Brown v. Commonwealth [(KY) 490 S.W. 2d 731]: The Courts Balks on Quotient Verdicts." Kentucky Law Journal, 62:243, 1973-74. 6565

"Compromise Verdicts in Criminal Cases." Nebraska Law Review, 37:802, June 1958. 6566

"Constitutional Law--Johnson v. Louisiana (92 Sup. Ct. 1620): State Criminal Juries Need Not Reach Unanimous Verdicts." DePaul Law Review, 22:634, spring 1973. 6567

"Constitutional Law--The Unanimous Verdict--No Longer a 'Fundamental' Right in State Criminal Trials." Suffolk University Law Review, 7:762, spring 1973. 6568

"Constitutional Renvoi: Unanimous Verdicts in State Criminal Trials." Fordham Law Review, 41:115, Oct. 1972. 6569

"Criminal Law--The Constitutionality of Lesser-Than-Unanimous Criminal Jury Verdicts in State Courts." Wake Forest Law Review, 8:610, Oct. 1972. 6570

"Criminal Law--Jury--Unanimous Jury Verdict Is Not Constitutionally Required in State Criminal Cases." Wisconsin Law Review, 1973:926, 1973. 6571

"Criminal Law: Validity of Inconsistent Verdicts [U.S. v. Maybury, 274 F. 2d 899]." Duke Law Journal, 1961:133, winter 1961. 6572

"Criminal Procedure--Majority Verdicts in Criminal Trials." Tennessee Law Review, 40:91, fall 1972. 6573

"Directing a Verdict for Defendant After Plaintiff's Opening Statement." Iowa Law Review, 44:182, fall 1958. 6574

Finz, L. L. "Does the Trend in Our Substantive Law Dictate an Expanded Use of the Special Verdict?" Albany Law Review, 37:229, 1973. 6575

"Evidence--Sufficiency for Directed Verdicts--Can a Judge Hold a Candle to Twelve Reasonable Men?" DePaul Law Review, 18:322, autumn, 1968. 6576

"Impeachment of Jury Verdicts by Jurors: A Proposal." University of Illinois Law Forum, 1969:388, 1969. 6577

"In the Wake of Apodaca v. Oregon (92 Sup. Ct. 1928): A Case for Retaining Unanimous Jury Verdicts." Valparaiso University Law Review, 7:249, winter 1973. 6578

"Informing the Jury of the Effect of Its Answers to Special Verdict Questions: The Minnesota Experience." Minnesota Law Review, 58:903, April 1974. 6579

"Jury Unanimity: Historical Accident or Safeguard of the Accused?" University of Florida Law Review, 25:388, winter 1973. 6580

McBride, R. L. "Special Verdicts and Findings." Ohio Opinions, 10:373, Dec. 1959-Feb. 1960. 6581

Miller, Robert Wyness. "Notabilia of American Civil Procedure." Harvard Law Review, 50:1017, May 1937. From 1887-1937 important principles were formed which recent "changes" have merely amended or reconstructed. 6582

Moore, S. D. R. "Century Old Problem: Federal or State Law As Determinative of a Directed Verdict in a Federal Court." University of Richmond Law Review, 4:282, spring 1970. 6583

Morano, A. G. "Retreat from Unanimity and Reasonable Doubt in Criminal Cases." University of Toledo Law Review, 1969:337, spring 1969. 6584

"Motion to Set Aside the Verdict: Evidence Deficiencies." William and Mary Law Review, 6:216, April 1965. 6585

"New Trial: Impeachment of Jury's Verdict by Affidavit of Juror: Agreement to Abide by Majority Vote As Determination of Chance." California Law Review, 23:218, Jan. 1935. This concerns the Mirabito v. San Francisco Dairy Co., 88 Cal. Dec. 180 (1934), which held that the jurors were not induced to assert to the verdict by a resort to the determination of chance within the meaning of California Code Civ. Proc., Section 657. 6586

Orfield, L. B. "Verdict in Federal Criminal Cases." Mercer Law Review, 15:378, spring 1964. 6587

Parker, G. E. "Verdicts of Manslaughter--An Addendum." Alberta Law Review, 3:205, 1964. 6588

Pope, J. "New Start on the Special Verdict." Texas Bar Journal, 37:335, April 1974. 6589

"Post-Verdict Motions Under Rule 50: Protecting the Verdict-Winner." Minnesota Law Review, 53:358, Dec. 1968. 6590

"Remitters of Jury Verdicts in Iowa." Iowa Law Review, 48:649, spring 1963. 6591

Scott, I. R. "Criminal Procedure: Inconsistent Verdicts." Solicitor's Journal, 117:103, Feb. 9, 1973. 6592

Sealy, A. P., and W. R. Cornish. "Jurors and Their Verdicts." Modern Law Review, 36:496, Sept. 1973. 6593

Shaffer, T. L. "Appellate Courts and Prejudiced Verdicts." University of Pittsburgh Law Review, 26:1, Oct. 1964. 6594

"Should Jury Verdicts Be Unanimous in Criminal Cases?" Oregon Law Review, 47:417, June 1968. 6595

"Should Reliable Scientific Evidence Be Conclusive and Binding on the Jury?" Chicago-Kent Law Review, 48:39, spring 1971. 6596

Slovenko, R. "Control Over the Jury Verdict in Louisiana Criminal Law." Louisiana Law Review, 20:657, June 1960. 6597

Sue, S., and Smith, R. E. "How Not to Get a Fair Trial." Connecticut Bar Journal, 48:328, Sept. 1974. 6598

"Trial--Post Trial Makers--Judgment on Special Findings of Fact, [Holt v. Bills (Kansas), 366 P. 2d 1009]." Kansas Law Review, 11:293, Dec. 1962. 6599

"Trial Practice: Inconsistent Verdicts: The Power of the Judge to Amend: Master and Tenant." California Law Review, 25:121, Nov. 1936. This concerns the Curtis v. San Pedro Transportation Co., 10 Cal. App. (2d) 547 (1935) decision, which held that the trial judge properly corrected the erroneous verdict, and in entering the joint judgment, gave effect to the jury's intention. 6600

"Unanimous Jury Verdict: Its Valediction in Some Criminal Cases." Texas Tech Law Review, 4:185, fall 1972. 6601

Walker, R. J. "Finality of Jury Verdicts." New Law Journal, 118: 886, Sept. 12, 1968. 6602

Weldman, E. N. "Pfaffenbach's Progeny--A Case for the Directed Verdict." Trial Lawyers Quarterly, 9:11, fall 1973. 6603

Williams, G. "Application for a Directed Verdict." Criminal Law Review, 1965:343, June 1965. 6604

Wilson, D. R. "Motion for New Trial Based on Inadequacy of Damages Awarded." Nebraska Law Review, 39:694, June 1960. 6605

M. SENTENCING

"Aggregation of Sentences: Obtaining Jury Trials for Petty Offenders." Iowa Law Review, 59:614, Feb. 1974. 6606

Allen, F. A. "Legal Values and Correctional Values." University Toronto Law Journal, 18:119, 1968. 6607

"Appellate Review of Sentences: A Survey." St. Louis University Law Journal, 17:221, winter 1972. 6608

"Appellate Review of Sentencing." Louisiana Law Review, 33:559, summer 1973. 6609

Barkin, E. M. "Emergence of Correctional Law and the Awareness of the Rights of the Accused." Nebraska Law Review, 45:669, July 1966. 6610

_______. "Sentencing Problems." Federal Rules Decisions, 39: 523, May 1966. 6611

Blake, L. W. "Case for Retribution." New Law Journal, 123:862, Sept. 20, 1973. 6612

"Bourgeois As Disciplinarian; Judges and Sentences." Nation, 206: 749, June 10, 1968. 6613

Brewster, L. "Appellate Review of Sentences." Federal Rules Decisions, 40:79, July 1966. Why author does not regard appellate review of sentences as an affront to the competence or integrity of the trial judge. Mere reading of a record is not enough. 6614

Bronstein, A. J. "Rules for Playing God." Civil Liberties Review, 1:116, summer 1974. 6615

Burgess, M. "Practical Aspects of Penology." Solicitor's Journal, 109:640, Aug. 13-Sept. 10, 1965. 6616

Carney, F. L. "Indeterminate Sentence at Patuxent." Crime and Delinquency, 20:135, April 1974. 6617

Carpenter, L. A. "Federal Work Release Program." Nebraska Law Review, 45:690, July 1966. 6618

Chase, E. "Schemes and Visions: A Suggested Revision of Juvenile Sentencing." Texas Law Review, 51:673, April 1973. 6619

Chase, J. D. "Citizen Participation: An Experiment in Prison-Community Relations." Federal Probation, 30:18, Dec. 1966. 6620

Closk, J. E. "Texas Prerelease Program." Federal Probation, 30:53, Dec. 1966. 6621

Cohen, F. "Sentencing Probation and the Rehabilitative Ideal...." Texas Law Review, 47:1, Dec. 1968. 6622

"Constitutional Law--Equal Protection--Sex Discrimination in Sentencing Criminal Offenders Is Unconstitutional." North Dakota Law Review, 50:359, winter 1974. 6623

"Constitutional Law--Sentencing --Withholding Good Time Credit from Prisoners Awaiting Appeal." Texas Law Review, 51:348, Jan. 1973. 6624

"Constitutionality of the Imposition of a Jail Sentence by a Lay

Magistrate in South Dakota." South Dakota Law Review, 20:456, spring 1975. 6625

"Creative Punishment: A Study of Effective Sentencing Procedures." Washburn Law Journal, 14:57, winter 1975. 6626

"Credit for Time Served Between Arrest and Sentencing." University of Pennsylvania Law Review, 121:1148, May 1973. 6627

"Criminal Law and Procedure--Federal Appellate Review of Sentences." Suffolk University Law Review, 7:1128, summer 1973. 6628

"Criminal Law--Concurrent Sentencing--Multiple Convictions." Denver Law Journal, 48:591, 1972. 6629

"Criminal Law--Increased Sentences on an Appeal by Right from Inferior Courts." North Carolina Law Review, 51:882, March 1973. 6630

"Criminal Law--Presentence Reports Allegations of Prior Criminal Activity--Factual Determination--Degree and Burden of Proof." Ohio State Law Journal, 3:960, 1972. 6631

"Criminal Law--Sentencing--Denial of Credit for Time Served or Longer Sentence Imposed at Retrial." North Carolina Review, 46:407, Feb. 1968. 6632

"Criminal Law--Severity of Sentence, As Well As Sentencing Procedure, Is Subject to Appellate Review in the Eighth Circuit." Drake Law Review, 23:191, Sept. 1973. 6633

"Criminal Procedure--Probable Cause and Due Process at Sentencing." North Carolina Law Review, 50:925, June 1972. 6634

"Criminal Procedure--Resentencing: The Procedural Due Process Protections Established in North Carolina v. Pearce to Guard Against the Possibility of Vindictiveness When a Judge Imposes a Harsher Sentence Upon Retrial Are to Be Applied Only Prospectively and Are Inapplicable to Those Cases in Which the Jury Performs the Resentencing Function." Brooklyn Law Review, 40:786, winter 1974. 6635

"Criminal Sentencing: An Overview of Procedures and Alternatives." Mississippi Law Journal, 45:782, June 1974. 6636

Cross, R. "Sentencing in a Rational Society." Criminal Law Reporter, 1970:4, 1970. 6637

"Daniels v. United States (U.S. v. Daniels, 446 F. 2d 967): Appellate Review of Criminal Sentencing--Limiting the Scope of the Non-Review Doctrine." University of Pittsburgh Law Review, 33:917, summer 1972. 6638

De Costa, F. A., Jr. "Disparity and Inequality of Criminal Sentences: Constitutional and Legislative Approaches to Appellate Review and Reallocation of the Sentencing Function." _Howard Law Journal_, 14:29, winter 1968. 6639

Dershowitz, A. M. "Indeterminate Confinement: Letting Therapy Fit the Harm." _University of Pennsylvania Law Review_, 123: 297, Dec. 1974. 6640

"Discretion in Felony Sentencing--A Study of Influencing Factors." _Washington Law Review_, 48:857, Aug. 1973. 6641

Dombrass, E. E. "Imprisonment Too Little or Too Much?" _Legal Aid Brief Case_, 24:133, Feb. 1966. 6642

Dubose, E. Z., Jr. "Criminal Sentencing: Point and Counterpoint." _Journal of Criminal Law_, 65:112, March 1974. 6643

Eaton, Joseph W. _Stone Walls Do Not a Prison Make._ Springfield, Ill.: Charles C. Thomas, 1962. 212pp. Discusses planned administrative changes in prisons. Primary emphasis is on the men who are expected to run them--prison officials and their staffs. 6644

Edwards, L. R. "Air Force Clemency and Rehabilitation." _Air Force JAG Law Review_, 8:38, May-June 1966. 6645

"Emergence of Individualized Sentencing." _Temple Law Quarterly_, 45:351, spring 1972. 6646

"Equal Protection Applied to Sentencing." _Iowa Law Review_, 58:596, Feb. 1973. 6647

Fahringer, H. P. "Sentencing--Making the Best of a Bad Situation." _New York State Bar Journal_, 46:279, June 1974. 6648

Farrier, M. D. "Young Adult Offenders: Report of the Advisory Council on the Penal System." _Modern Law Review_, 37:670, Nov. 1974. 6649

Finckenauer, J. O. "Theory and Practice in Sentencing the Political Criminal: A Comment." _Criminal Law Bulletin_, 10:377, Oct. 1974. 6650

Finston, C., and Ragen, Joseph Edward. _Inside the World's Toughest Prison._ Springfield, Ill.: Charles C. Thomas, 1962. 927pp. Ragen, former Warden of Joliet-Stateville Prison, Ill., described incarceration of inmates, guard training, rules, emergency action and Illinois crime trends. 6651

Green, Edward. _Judicial Attitudes in Sentencing._ New York: St. Martin's Press, 1961. 149pp. Study of sentencing practice of the Criminal Court of Philadelphia. After a searching analysis of the criticism of the sentencing practices in criminal courts, Green concludes that to a great extent it is deduced from objections to the system of criminal justice rather than induced from any sound factual basis. 6652

________. "Sentencing Practices of Criminal Court Judges in Philadelphia." American Journal of Correction, 22:32, July-Aug. 1960. 6653

Haddad, J. B. "Parole Term Concept." Illinois Bar Journal, 63: 236, Jan. 1975. 6654

Hamann, C. M. "Confinement and Release of Persons Acquitted by Reason of Insanity." Harvard Journal of Legislation, 4:55, Dec. 1966. 6655

Herlands, W. B. "When and How Should a Sentencing Judge Use Probation?" Federal Rules Decisions, 35:487, Oct. 1964. Probation analyzed as not only an enlightened procedure for the rehabilitation and conservation of human resources but also as an instrument for the effective dispensation of justice to offenders. 6656

Hoover, J. E. "Primacy in Parole and Probation." Kansas Law Review, 13:343, March 1965. 6657

Hughes, S. H. S. "Some Comments on Sentencing." Canadian Bar Journal, 8:221, Aug. 1965. 6658

Hyde, L. M., Jr. "If Prisoners Could Talk to Judges." Judicature, 51:257, Feb. 1968. 6659

"Imprisonment for Nonpayment of Fines and Costs: A New Look at the Law and the Constitution." Vanderbilt Law Review, 22:611, April 1969. 6660

Kaufman, I. R. "Forward: The Sentencing Process and Judicial Inscrutability." St. John's Law Review, 49:215, winter 1975. 6661

Kay, Barbara A., and Vedder, Clyde Bennett. Probation and Parole. Springfield, Ill.: Charles C. Thomas, 1963. 208pp. For practitioners and other students of probation, parole, and corrections. 6662

Knowles, M. F. "Lawlessness in Our Criminal Law: Criminal Sentences and the Need for Appellate Review." Alabama Lawyer, 35:450, Oct. 1974. 6663

Kuh, R. H. "Sentencing: Guidelines for the Manhattan District Attorney's Office." Criminal Bulletin, 11:62, Jan.-Feb. 1975. 6664

Kutak, R. J., and Gottschalk, J. M. "In Search of a Rational Sentence: A Return to the Concept of Appellate Review." *Nebraska Law Review,* 53:463, 1974. 6665

Luger, M., and Lobenthal, J. S., Jr. "Cushioning Future Shock in Corrections." *Federal Probation,* 38:19, June 1974. 6666

McGee, R. A. "New Look at Sentencing." *Federal Probation,* 38: 14, June-Sept. 1974. 6667

MacLeod, A. J. "If a Penologist Was the Sentencing Judge." *Canadian Bar Journal,* 9:24, Feb. 1966. 6668

Mattina, J. S. "Anarchy of Sentencing in the Federal Courts. W. J. Zumwalt; Sentencing: A Judge's Inherent Responsibility." *Judicature,* 57:96, Oct. 1973. 6669

"Modern Trends in Sentencing." *American Bar Association Committee on Criminal Law,* 1962:45, 1962. 6670

Morris, N. "Lessons from the Adult Correctional System of Sweden." *Federal Probation,* 30:3, Dec. 1966. 6671

Morris, N. R. "Research Punishment and Rehabilitation." *Legal Aid Brief Case,* 24:91, Dec. 1965. 6672

"Narrowing the Pearce Doctrine: Increased Sentence on a Trial De Novo." *St. Louis University Law Journal,* 18:426, spring 1974. 6673

Newark, M.; Samuels, A.; and White, S. "Sentencing the Multiple Offender: Concurrent and Consecutive Sentences." *Northern Ireland Legal Quarterly,* 23:133, summer 1972. 6674

Newman, J. O. "Parole Release Decision Making and the Sentencing Process: A Project Forward." *Yale Law Journal,* 84:810, March 1975. 6675

Palmer, L. I. "Model of Criminal Dispositions; An Alternative to Official Discretion in Sentencing." *Georgia Law Journal,* 62:1, Oct. 1973. 6676

Playfair, G. "Why Imprisonment Must Go." *Kentucky Law Journal,* 53:415, spring 1965. 6677

"Present Limitations on Appellate Review of Sentencing--McGee v. U.S. (462 F. 2d 243)." *Iowa Law Review,* 58:469, Dec. 1972. 6678

"Presentence Reports: Utility or Futility?" *Fordham Urban Law Journal,* 2:27, fall 1973. 6679

"Proposed Changes in Presentence Investigation Report Procedures."

Journal of Criminal Law and Criminology, 66:56, March 1975. 6680

"Prosecutor's Role in the Sentencing Process: A National Survey." American Journal of Criminal Law, 1:75, Feb. 1972. 6681

Rubin, S. "Disparity and Equality of Sentencing--A Constitutional Challenge." Federal Rules Decision, 40:55, July 1966. Considers various approaches to solving or ameliorating the problem. Discusses the theme that disparity in sentencing is a violation of Constitutional rights of defendants as well as the facts of disparity. 6682

________. "Due Process of Law in Probation and Parole Revocation Proceedings." Brief Case, 23:219, April 1965. 6683

________. "Probation and Due Process of Law." Crime and Delinquency, 11:30, Jan. 1965. 6684

"Sentence Crediting for the State Criminal Defendant--A Constitutional Requirement." Ohio State Law Journal, 34:586, 1973. 6685

"Sentencing and Parole Eligibility Under Repealed Criminal Statutes." Memphis State University Law Review, 5:235, winter 1975. 6686

"Sentencing Criminals in California." Stanford Law Review, 13:340, Discusses statutory provisions and criticism of the discretionary powers to sentence offenders. 6687

"Sentencing Disparity: Causes and Cures." Journal of Criminal Law, Criminology and Police Science, 60:182, June 1969. 6688

"Sentencing in Cases of Civil Disobedience." Columbia Law Review, 68:1508, Dec. 1968. 6689

"Sentencing in the Criminal District Courts." Houston Law Review, 9:944, May 1972. 6690

"Sentencing on Review; New Limitation on the Sentencing Power of Trial Judges." Time, 98:80, Nov. 8, 1971. 6691

"Sentencing Patterns in the Northern District of Alabama: An Empirical Study." Cumberland-Samford Law Review, 5:88, spring 1974. 6692

"Sentencing: The Good, The Bad and the Enlightened." Kentucky Law Journal, 57:456, 1968-69. 6693

"Sentencing Under the Federal Youth Corrections Act: The Need for an Explicit Finding and a Statement of Reasons." Boston University Law Review, 53:1071, Nov. 1973. 6694

"Separation of Powers--The Suspended Sentence." North Carolina Law Review, 51:184, Nov. 1972. 6695

"Sex and Sentencing." Southwestern Law Journal, 26:890, Dec. 1972. 6696

Signorelli, E. L. "Judicial Analysis and Critique of the New Drug and Sentencing Laws." New York State Bar Journal, 46:9, Jan. 1974. 6697

Singer, R. G. "Sending Men to Prison: Constitutional Aspects of the Burden of Proof and the Doctrine of the Least Drastic Alternative As Applied to Sentencing Determinations." Cornell Law Review, 58:51, Nov. 1972. 6698

Smith, S. "Delinquency and the Panacea of Punishment." Federal Probation, 29:18, Sept. 1965. 6699

"Solution to an Incredible Dilemma: The Original Sentence As a Ceiling." South Dakota Law Review, 13:130, winter 1968. 6700

Specter, A. "Diversion of Persons from the Criminal Process to Treatment Alternative." Pennsylvania Bar Association Quarterly, 44:691, Oct. 1973. 6701

Stacy, D. R. "Constitutional Right to Sentence Credit for Pre-Trial Incarceration." University of Cincinnati Law Review, 41:823, 1972. 6702

Temin, C. E. "Discriminatory Sentencing of Women Offenders: The Argument for ERA in a Nutshell." American Criminal Law Review, 11:355, winter 1973. 6703

Thomas, D. A. "Establishing a Factual Basis for Sentencing." Criminal Law Review, 1970:80, Feb. 1970. 6704

Thompson, R. C. "Sentencing the Dangerous Offender." Federal Probation, 32:3, March 1968. 6705

"Toward a Probable Cause Standard in Sentencing." Maryland Law Review, 34:133, 1974. 6706

"Toward Lawfulness in Sentencing; Thank You, Professor Dworkin." Rutgers Camden Law Journal, 5:80, fall 1973. 6707

"Treger, H. "Meaningful Inquiry into the Life of an Offender." Crime and Delinquency, 11:249, July 1965. 6708

White, S. "Assessing the Severity of Sentence on Appeal." Modern Law Review, 36:382, July 1973. 6709

Wilson, J. Q. "If Every Criminal Knew He Would Be Punished If Caught." New York Times Magazine, p. 9, Jan. 28, 1973. 6710

"Wyatt v. Stickney (344 F. Supp. 387) and the Right to Civilly Committed Mental Patients to Adequate Treatment." Harvard Law Review, 86:1282, May 1973. 6711

Young, S. G. "When Should the Judge State a Minimum Sentence?" Pennsylvania Bar Association Quarterly, 44:551, June 1973. 6712

Youngdahl, L. W. "Developments in the Federal Probation System." Federal Probation, 28:3, Sept. 1964. 6713

N. APPEALS

(1) GENERAL WORKS

"Appeal of Errors in the Absence of Objection--Pennsylvania's 'Fundamental Error' Doctrine." Dickinson Law Review, 73:496, spring 1969. 6714

"Appealable Orders, Prohibition and Mandamus in Minnesota." Minnesota Law Review, 51:115, Nov. 1966. 6715

"Appealing Jury Findings." Houston Law Review, 12:65, Oct. 1974. 6716

"Appellate Delay in Criminal Cases." American Criminal Law Quarterly, 2:150, summer 1964. 6717

"Appellate Review for Juveniles: A Right to a Transcript." Columbia Human Rights Law Review, 4:485, fall 1972. 6718

"Appellate Review of Circumstantial Evidence in Indiana Criminal Cases." Indiana Law Review, 7:883, 1974. 6719

"Appellate Review of Sentences: A Survey." St. Louis University Law Journal, 17:221, winter 1972. 6720

"Appellate Review of Sentences and the Need for a Reviewable Record." Duke Law Journal, 1973:1357, Jan. 1973. 6721

"Appellate Review of Sentencing." Louisiana Law Review, 33:559, summer 1973. 6722

Aspen, M. E. "Representing the Indigent Defendant: New Illinois Appellate Procedure in Criminal Cases?" Illinois Bar Journal, 53:52, Sept. 1964. 6723

"Before Sentence Is Pronounced ... A Guide to Defense Counsel in the Exercise of His Post Conviction Responsibilities." Criminal Law Bulletin, 9:140, March 1973. 6724

Bell, G. B. "Appellate Court Opinions and the Remand Process." <u>Georgia Law Review</u>, 2:256, summer 1968. 6725

_______. "Federal Appellate Courts and the All Writs Acts." <u>Southwestern Law Journal</u>, 23:858, Dec. 1969. 6726

Biddle, M. F. "Brief Look at the Air Force Boards of Review." <u>Air Force JAG Law Review</u>, 8:12, May-June 1966. 6727

Borman, P. D. "Chilled Right to Appeal from a Plea Bargain Conviction: A Due Process Cure." <u>Northwestern University Law Review</u>, 69:663, Nov.-Dec. 1974. 6728

Brown, L. "Handling of Supreme Court Cases--Processing Practice and Procedure." <u>Arkansas Law Review</u>, 22:679, winter 1969. 6729

Calvert, R. W. "Appellate Court Judgments; or, Strange Things Happen on the Way to Judgment." <u>Texas Tech Law Review</u>, 6:915, spring 1975. 6730

Carrington, P. D. "Crowded Dockets and the Courts of Appeals: The Threat to the Function of Review and the National Law." <u>Harvard Law Review</u>, 82:542, Jan. 1969. 6731

_______. "Power of District Judges and the Responsibility of Courts of Appeals." <u>Georgia Law Review</u>, 3:507, spring 1969. 6732

Choper, J. H. "On the Warren Court and Judicial Review." <u>Catholic University Law Review</u>, 17:20, fall 1967. 6733

"Constitutional Law--An Indigent's Right to a Free Trial Transcript." <u>Land and Water Law Review</u>, 7:707, 1972. 6734

"Constitutional Law--The Right to Counsel on Permissive Appellate Review." <u>Wake Forest Law Review</u>, 9:579, Dec. 1973. 6735

"Cost of Appeal." <u>Montana Law Review</u>, 27:49, fall 1965. 6736

"Courtroom Restraint of the Criminal Defendant." <u>Baylor Law Review</u>, 25:147, winter 1973. 6737

"Criminal Law and Procedure--Federal Appellate Review of Sentences." <u>Suffolk University Law Review</u>, 7:1128, summer 1973. 6738

"Criminal Law--Free Transcripts--Indigent Misdemeanants." <u>Gonzaga Law Review</u>, 8:321, spring 1973. 6739

"Criminal Law--The Right of the State to Appeal in Criminal Cases." <u>North Carolina Law Review</u>, 42:887, June 1964. 6740

"Criminal Procedure: No Right to Counsel on Discretionary Appeal." North Carolina Law Review, 35:560, Feb. 1975. 6741

Dean, M. "Criminal Appeal Act--1966." Criminal Law Review, 1966:535, Oct. 1966. 6742

"Discretionary Appointment of Counsel at Post-Conviction Proceedings: An Unconstitutional Barrier to Effective Post-Conviction Relief." Georgia Law Review, 8:434, winter 1974. 6743

"District Court's Trial De Novo on Appeal from the Probate Court." Baylor Law Review, 24:547, fall 1972. 6744

Doherty, J. J. "Few Suggestions for Handling Criminal Appeals." Brief Case, 27:124, Feb. 1969. 6745

Doyle, J. E. "Court's Responsibility to the Inmate Litigant." Judicature, 56:406, May 1973. 6746

"Effects of Immunity Grant on Criminal Appeal, Sentencing, and Parole." Stanford Law Review, 18:709, Feb. 1966. Angelone v. United States, 347 Fed. 486. The precise issue was whether immunity granted after conviction and sentencing but while appeal was pending required the appellate court to reverse the conviction. Decision--Angelone did not deserve to have his conviction reversed on appeal merely because he had been granted immunity while his appeal was pending. The Fifth Amendment did not require it and a broad interpretation of the immunity statutes would be improper due to the particular facts involved. 6747

Feld, B. "What Is the Appellate Record? Appellate Inferences and Judicial Notice." JAG Journal, 20:51, Sept.-Nov. 1965. 6748

"Fresh Evidence in Criminal Appeals." Solicitor's Journal, 110:280, April 15, 1966. 6749

"Frivolous Appeals and the Minimum Standards Project: Solution or Surrender?" University of Miami Law Review, 24:95, fall 1969. 6750

"Government Appeal in Criminal Prosecutions: The 1970 Amendment to 18 U.S.C. 3731." American Criminal Law Review, 12:539, winter 1975. 6751

"Government Appeals of 'Dismissals' in Criminal Cases." Harvard Law Review, 87:1822, June 1974. 6752

Hood, J. T., Jr. "Right of Appeal." Louisiana Law Review, 29:498, April 1966. 6753

Hopkins, J. D. "Winds of Change: New Styles in the Appellate Process." Hofstra Law Review, 3:649, summer 1975. 6754

Hrusko, R. L. "Appellate Review of Sentences." American Criminal Law Quarterly, 8:10, fall 1969. 6755

"Individualized Criminal Justice in the Supreme Court: A Study of Dispositional Decision Making." Harvard Law Review, 81:1260, April 1968. 6756

Joseph, C. C., Jr. "Assignment of Error." Louisiana Law Review, 35:597, spring 1975. 6757

Klein, E. "Reviewing the Evidence on Appeal." Los Angeles Bar Bulletin, 44:159, Feb. 1969. 6758

Komar, B. M. "On the Reform of Appellate Procedures of the United States Supreme Court." Chicago-Kent Law Review, 44:28, spring 1967. 6759

Leflar, R. A. "Appellate Judicial Innovation." Oklahoma Law Review, 27:321, summer 1974. 6760

Meador, D. J. "Appellate Case Managements and Decisional Processes." Virginia Law Review, 61:255, March 1975. 6761

Meyer, K. G., and Yackle, L. W. "Collateral Challenges to Criminal Convictions." Kansas Law Review, 21:259, spring 1973. 6762

O'Connell, K. J. "Streamlining Appellate Procedures." Judicature, 56:234, Jan. 1973. 6763

O'Connor, M. "Evidence Points on Appeal." Texas Bar Journal, 37:839, Sept. 1974. 6764

Palmer, L. I. "Implementing the Obligation of Advocacy in Review of Criminal Prosecutions." Journal of Criminal Law and Criminology, 65:1267, Sept. 1974. 6765

Pope, J. "Argument on Appeal." Practical Lawyer, 14:33, Dec. 1968. 6766

"Post-Conviction Relief After Release from Custody: A Federal Message and A New Mexico Remedy." Natural Resources Journal, 9:85, Jan. 1969. 6767

"Present Limitations on Appellate Review of Sentencing--McGee v. U.S. (462 F. 2d 243)." Iowa Law Review, 58:469, Dec. 1972. 6768

Prettyman, E. B. "Uniform Appellate Rules: A Pending Venture in the Federal Judiciary." American Bar Association Journal, 52:123, Feb. 1966. 6769

Redish, M. H. "Pragmatic Approach to Appealability in the Federal

Courts." Columbia Law Review, 75:89, Jan. 1975. 6770

Sargart, T. "Legal Aid in Criminal Appeals." New Law Journal, 117:1067, Oct. 5, 1967. 6771

Scanlan, A. L. "Effective Appellate Advocacy in the Court of Appeals of Maryland." Maryland Law Review, 29:126, spring 1969. 6772

________. "Trial and Appeal of Constitutional Issues." Catholic Lawyer, 20:386, autumn 1974. 6773

Schwab, H. M., and Geddes, R. D. "Expediting Disposition of Criminal Appeals in Oregon." Oregon Law Review, 51:650, summer 1972. 6774

Shaffer, T. L. "Appellate Courts and Prejudiced Verdicts." University of Pittsburgh Law Review, 26:1, Oct. 1964. 6775

"Should Arizona Have Automatic Appeal in Capital Punishment Cases?" Arizona Law Review, 2:106, fall 1965. 6776

Sokol, R. P. "In Forma Pauperis Appeals: The University of Virginia Experiment with a Neglected Asset." Journal of Legal Education, 18:96, 1965. 6777

"State Appeals in Criminal Cases." Tennessee Law Review, 32:449, spring 1965. 6778

"Statutory Criteria for Review in the Federal Courts: The Proper Indicia of Appealability?" University of Pittsburgh Law Review, 29:365, Dec. 1967. 6779

Wheatley, William G. "Coram Nobis in Oregon and the Need for Modern Post-Conviction Procedure Legislation." Oregon Law Review, 38:158, Feb. 1959. Clarifies the Oregon Law with respect to this extraordinary writ. 6780

Wiever, F. B. "English and American Appeals Compared." American Bar Association Journal, 50:635, July 1964. 6781

(2) CERTIORARI

"California Certiorari: A Misused Writ." Hastings Law Journal, 15:205, Nov. 1963. Demonstrates extension of certiorari beyond the jurisdictional limits set by the statutes (Sec. 1068 Cal. Code of Civil Prac.) when the writ is used to review the decisions of a local board or agency. 6782

Cantrell, B. H. "Review of Administrative Decisions by Writ of Certiorari in Tennessee." Memphis State University Law Review, 4:19, fall 1973. 6783

"Certiorari: Advantage to State in Criminal Cases." Drake Law Review, 17:255, May 1968. 6784

"Certiorari in Arkansas." Arkansas Law Review, 17:163, summer 1963. 6785

"Criminal Law: Certiorari." New Zealand Law Journal, 35:177, July 7, 1959. 6786

Farner, J. A. "Natural Justice and Licensing Applications: Hohfeld and the Writ of Certiorari." New Zealand Universities Law Review, 2:282, April 1967. 6787

Gessman, E. "Much Ado About Certiorari." Georgetown Law Journal, 57:742, summer 1964. 6788

Gordon, D. M. "Challenging Convictions by Habeas Corpus and Certiorari." Criminal Law Quarterly, 2:296, Nov. 1959. 6789

Haines, B. M. "Committals and Certiorari." Criminal Law Quarterly, 8:141, Oct. 1965. 6790

Hanus, J. J. "Certiorari and Policy-Making in English History." American Journal of Legal History, 12:63, April 1968. 6791

________. "Denial of Certiorari and Supreme Court Policy-Making." American University Law Review, 17:41, 1967. 6792

James, D. H. "Certiorari Power of the Florida Supreme Court to Review Decisions of the District Courts of Appeal." University of Miami Law Review, 15:258, spring 1961. 6793

"Jurisdiction of the Trial Judge--Wrongful Determination As to Validity of an Information--Whether Certiorari or Prohibition Should Lie." Criminal Law Quarterly, 15:265, May 1973. 6794

Madden, J. W. "One Supreme Court and the Writ of Certiorari." Hastings Law Journal, 15:153, Nov. 1963. Discussion of the ancient writ of certiorari and how it prevents the Supreme Court from being overwhelmed with judicial business. Details of the certiorari practice in the Supreme Court. 6795

Nettheim, G. "Place of the Declaratory Judgment in Certiorari Territory." Sydney Law Review, 6:184, Oct. 1969. 6796

________. "Privy Council, Natural Justice and Certiorari." Federal Law Review, 2:215, 1966-67. 6797

Prettyman, E. B., Jr. "Opposing Certiorari in the United States Supreme Court." Virginia Law Review, 61:197, Feb. 1975. 6798

Stockmeyer, N. O., Jr. "Rx for the Certiorari Crisis: A More

Professional Staff." American Bar Association Journal, 59:846, Aug. 1973. 6799

Wade, H. W. R. "Future of Certiorari." Cambridge Law Journal, 1958:218, Nov. 1958. 6800

Weintraub, H. "Mandamus and Certiorari in New York from the Revolution to 1880: A Chapter in Legal History." Fordham Law Review, 32:681, May 1964. 6801

(3) PROHIBITION

Boone, W. B. "Prohibition: Use of the Writ of Restraint in California." Hastings Law Journal, 15:161, Nov. 1963. Discussion of the problems and issues common to the writ proceedings, including jurisdiction, discretion, prerogative, adequacy of the legal remedy and the like. Covers: Principles affecting the issuance of prohibition; Use of prohibition before trial; Use of prohibition during trial; Use of prohibition after trial or judgment. 6802

Bosson, R. C., and Sanders, S. K. "Writ of Prohibition in New Mexico." New Mexico Law Review, 5:91, Nov. 1974. 6803

"Evidence--Illegal Search and Seizure--Writ of Prohibition [In re Raymo's Petition (Vermont) 154 A. 2d 48]." Boston University Law Review, 40:304, spring 1960. 6804

"Jurisdiction of the Trial Judge--Wrongful Determination As to Validity of an Information--Whether Certiorari or Prohibition Should Lie." Criminal Law Quarterly, 15:265, May 1973. 6805

Mariash, I. "Use of the Writ of Prohibition to Avoid a Criminal Trial." Criminal Law Review, 6:1, 1959. 6806

Simko, J. S. "Mandamus and the Prohibition in Idaho." Idaho Law Review, 4:5, fall 1967. 6807

"State ex rel City of Huntington v. Lombardo (West Virginia) 143 S.W. 3d. 535." West Virginia Law Review, 68:62, Dec. 1965. 6808

Tonahill, J. H. "Mandamus and Prohibition Against Trial Judges." Texas Bar Journal, 20:626, Nov. 1957. 6809

"Writ of Prohibition in Missouri." Washington University Law Quarterly, 1972:511, summer 1972. 6810

"Writ of Prohibition Issued Discharging Grand Jury Convened to Investigate Criminal Activities of Local Labor Union [In re Petition of Grace (PA) 154 A. 2d 592]." University of Pennsylvania Law Review, 108:449, Jan. 1960. 6811

"Writ of Prohibition--Restraint of a Texas District Court Judge [State v. Judge Cullen W. Briggs (Tex.) 351 SW. 2d 892]." South Texas Law Journal, 6:156, spring 1962. 6812

Yardley, D. C. M. "Grounds for Certiorari and Prohibition." Canadian Bar Journal, 37:294, May 1959. 6813

_______. "Prohibition and Mandamus and the Problem of Locus Standi." Law Quarterly Review, 73:534, Oct. 1957. 6814

(4) MANDAMUS

"Appellate Review 1404 (a) Orders--Misuse of an Extraordinary Writ." John Marshall Journal, 1:297, winter 1968. 6815

"Change of Venue in Criminal Cases: Mandamus to Review a Pretrial Order." Washington and Lee Law Review, 26:89, spring, 1969. 6816

"Constitutional Law--Standing to Sue--Standing in Actions Under the Mandamus and Venue Act Depends on Availability of Remedy." Texas Law Review, 52:1421, Nov. 1974. 6817

"Criminal Law--Mandamus--Lifting of Detainer [Baker v. Marbury (Md) 141 A. 2d 523]." Maryland Law Review, 18:352, fall 1958. 6818

"Degree of Discretionary Authority Possessed by University Officials in Student Disciplinary Matters--The Availability of Mandamus." Southwestern Law Journal, 21:664, fall 1967. 6819

Dumars, C. T., and Browde, M. B. "Mandamus in New Mexico." New Mexico Law Review, 4:155, May 1974. 6820

"Federal Courts--Mandamus--Federal District Court Lacks Jurisdiction to Grant Mandamus Procedures Available Under State Law." Villanova Law Review, 13:225, fall 1967. 6821

"Federal Procedure--Jurisdiction--Jurisdiction of District Courts to Issue Mandamus in Original Proceedings." Wayne Law Review, 14:667, spring 1968. 6822

"Federal Rules of Civil Procedure--Discovery--Denial of Discovery Pretaining to Subject Matter Jurisdiction and Standing--Mandamus As a Means of Review." Boston College Industrial and Commercial Law Review, 14:1116, May 1973. 6823

Jaffe, L. L. "Standing to Secure Judicial Review: Public Actions." Harvard Law Review, 74:1265, May 1961. Problem presented when individuals seek judicial review to vindicate not their personal rights but the public interest. Reviews common law development of "public actions" and analyzes their justification and proper role. Formulates principles for courts in deciding when to accede to an individual plaintiff's demand for judicial intervention. 6824

Lipton, P. P. "Use of Extraordinary Writs in a Criminal Case." Wisconsin Bar Bulletin, 39:23, Dec. 1966. 6825

"Mandamus--An Expended Concept." Washburn Law Journal, 8:71, fall 1968. 6826

"Mandamus Characterization No Longer a Bar to Federal Jurisdiction." Temple Law Quarterly, 41:466, summer 1968. 6827

"Mandamus in Administration Actions: Current Approaches." Duke Law Journal, 1973:207, April 1973. 6828

"Mandamus in Missouri: Old Standards and New Developments." Washington University Law Quarterly, 1972:719, fall 1972. 6829

"Mandamus in the Federal Courts as an Original Action." Dickinson Law Review, 72:468, spring 1968. 6830

"Mandamus May Lie to Compel a Public Official to Enforce a Local Ordinance [Ciminera v. Sahm, 176 NYS 2d 257]." Syracuse Law Review, 10:159, fall 1958. 6831

"Mandamus Proceedings in the Federal Courts of Appeals: A Compromise with Finality." California Law Review, 52:1036, Dec. 1964. Attempts to discover a pattern in the courts of appeals' decisions to review trial court actions through mandamus proceedings to test the trial court's determination of personal jurisdiction. Limited to discussion of civil cases. 6832

Meyer, E. "Peculiarities and Pitfalls of Mandate." Los Angeles Bar Bulletin, 36:223, May 1961. Discussion of the law and procedural steps with which counsel should be familiar when considering whether a proceeding for a writ of mandate can be successfully undertaken. 6833

"State of Texas v. Sewell [Texas 487 SW 2d 716]--Applying the Writ of Mandamus." Baylor Law Review, 25:385, spring 1973. 6834

"Supervisory and Advisory Mandamus Under the All Writs Act." Harvard Law Review, 86:595, Jan. 1973. 6835

"Use of Mandamus to Review Administrative Action in Alabama." Alabama Law Review, 11:289, spring 1959. 6836

Weintraub, H. "Development of Scope of Review in Judicial Review of Administrative Action: Mandamus and Review of Discretion." Fordham Law Review, 33:359, March 1965. 6837

Yardley, D. C. M. "Purpose of Mandamus in English Law." Juridical Review, 1959:1, April 1959. 6838

(5) HABEAS CORPUS

"Allowance of In Forma Pauperis Appeals in §2255 and Habeas Corpus Cases." Federal Rules Decisions, 43:343, March 1968. 6839

Bator, P. M. "Finality in Criminal Law and Federal Habeas Corpus for State Prisoners." Harvard Law Review, 76:441, Jan. 1963. Extensive treatment, both historical and analytical, of the legal doctrines governing federal review of habeas corpus in state criminal convictions. 6840

Bines, H. E. "Remedying Ineffective Representation in Criminal Cases: Departures from Habeas Corpus." Virginia Law Review, 59:927, Sept. 1973. 6841

Carter, J. D. "Use of Federal Habeas Corpus by States' Prisoners." American Criminal Law Quarterly, 4:20, fall 1965; Washington and Lee Law Review, 23:23, spring 1966. 6842

Chisum, D. "In Defense of Modern Federal Habeas Corpus for State Prisoners." DePaul Law Review, 21:682, spring 1972. 6843

"Collateral Estoppel Effect of State Criminal Convictions in Section 1983 Actions." University of Illinois Law Forum, 1975:95, 1975. 6844

"Constitutional Law--Guilty Plea--Federal Habeas Corpus Relief Available When Statute Permits Post Guilty Plea Appellate Review of Constitutional Challenges." Vanderbilt Law Review, 28: 898, May 1975. 6845

"Constitutional Law--Missing Trial Transcript--Constitutional Violation of Duty of Federal Habeas Corpus Proceeding to Create Substitute." University of Toledo Law Review, 4:254, winter 1973. 6846

"Constitutional Law--Requirement of Superintendent's Certificate Prior to Release on Habeas Corpus from Mental Hospital Violates Due Process." Cumberland-Samford Law Review, 3:517, fall 1972. 6847

"Core of Habeas Corpus: A New Definition, a New Test." Capital University Law Review, 3:197, 1974. 6848

"Criminal Procedure--Habeas Corpus--Waiver of Relief Under the West Virginia Post-Conviction Habeas Corpus Act." West Virginia Law Review, 76:242, Feb. 1974. 6849

Crowe, W. L., Sr. "Great Writ: A New Doctrine of Convenient Forum?" Louisiana Bar Journal, 21:263, March 1974. 6850

"Custody Requirement and Territorial Jurisdiction in Federal Habeas Corpus: Ward v. North Carolina (406 F. 2d 352)." University of Pennsylvania Law Review, 118:629, Feb. 1970. 6851

"'Custody' Requirement for Habeas Corpus." Maryland Law Review, 26:79, winter 1966. 6852

"Development in the Law: Federal Habeas Corpus." Harvard Law Review, 83:1038, March 1970. 6853

"Development of the Plenary Bearing Requirement in Federal Habeas Corpus for State Prisoners." Brooklyn Law Review, 34:247, winter 1968. 6854-5

"Discretionary Appointment of Counsel at Post-Conviction Proceedings: An Unconstitutional Barrier to Effective Post-Conviction Relief." Georgia Law Review, 8:434, winter 1974. 6856

Eades, R. W. "Appellate and Post-Conviction Relief in Tennessee." Memphis State University Law Review, 5:1, fall 1974. 6857

"Federal Courts--Habeas Corpus--State Prisoner Attacking Conviction in Another State Which Underlies a Detainer Filed with Confining State Held to Have Present Right to Bring Habeas Corpus in Sentencing State." New York University Review, 44:845, Oct. 1969. 6858

"Federal Habeas Corpus and the State Prisoner." Washburn Law Journal, 8:248, winter 1969. 6859

"Federal Habeas Corpus Confronts the Colorado Courts: Catalyst or Cataclysm?" University of Colorado Law Review, 39:83, fall 1966. 6860

"Federal Habeas Corpus Jurisdiction Over Court-Martial Proceedings." Wayne Law Review, 20:919, March 1974. 6861

"Functional Approach to Habeas Corpus Jurisdiction." Connecticut Law Review, 6:567, spring 1974. 6862

Gallipoli, M. "Federal Habeas Corpus, the Threat and the Challenge." American Criminal Law Quarterly, 4:211, summer 1966. 6863

Grancicci, R. R. "Review of Criminal Convictions by Habeas Corpus in California." Hastings Law Journal, 15:189, Nov. 1963. How habeas corpus has been developed into a remedy which supplements but does not substitute for appellate review. 6864

"Habeas Corpus--An Erosion of Law and Order?" Catholic Lawyer, 14:293, autumn 1968. 6865

"Habeas Corpus and the Military: The Crippled Attack on Court Martials." Kentucky Law Journal, 61:333, 1972-73. 6866

"Habeas Corpus and the State Prisoner." Gonzaga Law Review, 3: 115, spring 1968. 6867

"Habeas Corpus Challenges to Prison Discipline." Fordham Law Review, 43:963, May 1975. 6868

"Habeas Corpus: Fourth Circuit Allows Writ to Issue to State Prisoner Not Yet Serving Sentence Under Attack." Duke Law Journal, 1966:588, spring 1966. 6869

"Habeas Corpus: Jurisdiction of Federal District Courts." Notre Dame Law Review, 47:52, summer 1971. 6870

"Habeas Corpus--Prematurity Rule--State Prisoner Held Entitled to Federal Court Writ to Attach Future Sentence Not Affecting Present Parole Eligibility." New York University Law Review, 43: 588, May 1968. 6871

"Habeas Corpus--Prison Management--Custody and Control of Prisoners--Constitutional Law--Double Jeopardy." Case Western Reserve Law Review, 25:684, spring 1975. 6872

"Habeas Corpus Relief for the Military Prisoner: The Double Standard." Drake Law Review, 21:572, June 1972. 6873

"Habeas Corpus Review." Wisconsin Bar Bulletin, 42:20, Oct. 1969. 6874

"Habeas Corpus--The Fifth Circuit Considers the Effects of Waiver on Habeas Corpus Availability." Creighton Law Review, 8:541, 1974-75. 6875

"Habeas Corpus--The Nature of Restraint in Parole and Probation." Connecticut Bar Journal, 40:473, Sept. 1966. 6876

Hooper, F. A. "Habeas Corpus." Georgia State Bar Journal, 9:29, Aug. 1972. 6877

"In Defense of Modern Federal Habeas Corpus for State Prisoners." D. Chisum, DePaul Law Review, 21:682, spring 1972. 6878

"In Search of the Optimum Writ: A Suggestion for the Improvement of Federal Habeas Corpus." Journal of Public Law, 22:465, 1973. 6879

"Incarcerated for Non-Payment of Fines." Capital University Law Review, 2:177, 1973. 6879a

"Indigents' Rights in Habeas Corpus Appeals and Attorney Compensation." DePaul Law Review, 20:769, spring 1971. 6880

Katz, L. R., and Nelson, G. S. "Need for Clarification in Military Habeas Corpus." Ohio State Law Journal, 27:193, spring 1966. 6881

Kelman, M. "Federal Habeas Corpus As a Source of New Constitutional Requirements for State Criminal Procedure." Ohio State Law Journal, 28:46, winter 1967. 6882

Kiechel, W. "Scope of Collateral Review of Court-Martial Convictions in Federal Courts." JAG Bulletin, 4:3, March-April 1962. 6883

Kinkead, S. C. "Interstate Detainer Warrant Dilemma." Kentucky Bar Journal, 36:26, Oct. 1972. 6884

Koplovitz, J. N. "ABC of Federal Habeas Corpus." Criminal Law Bulletin, 2:15, July-Aug. 1966. 6885

Kutner, L. "Legal Ultimate for the Unity of Mankind." Notre Dame Law, 40:570, Aug. 1965. 6886

________. "World Habeas Corpus: Ombudsman for Mankind." University of Miami Law Review, 24:352, winter 1970. 6887

Lughton, G. N. "Federal Supremacy and Federal Habeas Corpus." St. Louis University Law Journal, 12:74, fall 1967. 6888

Meader, D. J. "Impact of Federal Habeas Corpus on State Trial Procedures." Virginia Law Review, 52:286, March 1966. 6889

Meyer, K. G., and Yackle, L. W. "Collateral Challenges to Criminal Convictions." Kansas Law Review, 21:259, spring 1973. 6890

Miller, P. E. "Right to Counsel in Collateral Proceedings--Habeas Corpus." Howard Law Journal, 15:200, winter 1969. 6891

"Mootness Question in Habeas Corpus Proceedings Where Petitioner Is Released Prior to Final Adjudication." Utah Law Review, 1969:265, Jan. 1969. 6892

Morris, G. H. "Habeas Corpus and the Confinement of the Mentally Disordered in New York: The Right to the Writ." Harvard Journal on Legislation, 6:27, Nov. 1968. 6893

"Multi-Party Federal Habeas Corpus." Harvard Law Review, 81:1482, May 1968. 6894

Murch v. Mottram (93 Sup Ct. 71): Repetitious Habeas Corpus--A

Possible Breakthrough." Utah Law Review, 1973:94, spring 1973. 6895

"Negro Defendants and Southern Lawyers: Review in Federal Habeas Corpus of Systematic Exclusion of Negros from the Juries." Yale Law Journal, 72:559, Jan. 1963. The conditions are blamed on the lawyers themselves, tradition of excluding Negroes from juries and the social environment built on segregation. 6896

"New Barrier to Federal Court Review: The Habeas Corpus Exhaustion Requirement As Applied to Prisoner's Conditions of Confinement." New England Law Review, 9:615, spring 1974. 6897

Oaks, D. H. "Legal History in the High Court--Habeas Corpus." Michigan Law Review, 64:451, Jan. 1966. Townsend v. Sain 372 U.S. 293 (1963); Fay v. Noia 372 U.S. 391 (1963); and Jones v. Cunningham 371 U.S. 236 (1963). 6898

"Original Habeas Corpus Proceedings in the Courts of Civil Appeals." Texas Bar Journal, 33:183, March 1970. 6899

"Prisoner's Rights--Habeas Corpus Petitions of State Prisoners Stating Claims Cognizable Under the Civil Rights Act of 1871 to Be Read by the Federal Courts As Civil Rights Actions Thus Circumventing the Habeas Exhaustion Requirement." Villanova Law Review, 17:980, May 1972. 6900

"Problems of Federal Habeas Corpus Involving State Prisoners." Federal Rule Decisions, 45:45, Oct. 1968. 6901

"Proposed Modification of Federal Habeas Corpus for State Prisoners--Reform or Revocation?" Georgia Law Journal, 61:1221, May 1973. 6902

"Proposed Reformation of Federal Habeas Corpus Procedure: Use of Federal Magistrates." Iowa Law Review, 54:1147, June 1969. 6903

Rafalko, W. A. "Indigent Prisoner's New Hope: The Old Writ of Habeas Corpus and the Right to Counsel." North Dakota Law Review, 42:168, Jan. 1966. 6904

Raper, J. F. "Post Conviction Remedies." Wyoming Law Journal, 19:213, fall 1965. 6905

"Reconsideration of the Scope of Review for Habeas Corpus from Military Courts." Duquesne Law Review, 11:49, fall 1972. 6906

Reeves, A. J. "Louisiana Habeas Corpus Catechism." Louisiana Bar Journal, 22:123, Sept. 1974. 6907-8

Rubenstein, A. "Habeas Corpus As a Means of Review." Modern Law Review, 27:322, May 1964. The constitution adopted by the Confederacy during the Civil War was modeled closely after the U.S. Constitution. The Confederate provision dealing with the suspension of the writ of habeas corpus was taken verbatim, but interpreted differently. Different treatments of that issue which still exist at present are studied. 6909

Santarelli, D. E. "Habeas Corpus: A Debate; Too Much Is Enough." Trial, 9:40, May-June 1973. 6910

Shapiro, R. "Where Have All the Lawyers Gone?" Trial, 9:40, May-June 1973. 6911

Smalls, O. "Habeas Corpus in the District of Columbia." Catholic University Law Review, 24:75, fall 1974. 6912

Smith, F. W., Jr. "Federal Habeas Corpus: State Prisoners and the Concept of Custody." University of Richmond Law Review, 4:1, fall 1969. 6913

"State Criminal Procedure and Federal Habeas Corpus." Harvard Law Review, 80:422, Dec. 1966. Reforms of state procedure needed to provide post-conviction remedies. 6914

Tuttle, E. P. "Reflections on the Law of Habeas Corpus." Journal of Public Law, 22:325, 1973. 6915

Veverka, D. J. "Federal Habeas Corpus." Illinois Bar Journal, 57:634, April 1969. 6916

Weatherly, G. "Federal Habeas Corpus Relief from State Court Convictions." Texas Bar Journal, 31:367, May 1968. 6917

Weick, P. C. "Apportionment of the Judicial Resources in Criminal Cases: Should Habeas Corpus Be Eliminated?" DePaul Law Review, 21:740, spring 1972. 6918

Wilkes, D. E., Jr. "New Role for an Ancient Writ: Post Conviction Habeas Corpus Relief in Georgia." Georgia Law Review, 8:313, winter 1974; 913, fall 1974. 6919

Williamson, R. A. "Federal Habeas Corpus: Limitations on Successive Applications from the Same Prisoner." William and Mary Law Review, 15:265, winter 1973. 6920

Wilson, F. W. "Federal Habeas Corpus and the State Court Criminal Defendant." Vanderbilt Law Review, 19:741, June 1966. 6921

Wulf, M. L. "Limiting Prisoner Access to Habeas Corpus--Assault on the Great Writ." Brooklyn Law Review, 40:253, fall 1973. 6922

Zagaris, B. 'Recent Developments in Prison Litigation: Procedural Issue and Remedies." Santa Clara Lawyer, 14:810, summer 1974. 6923

AUTHOR INDEX